HENRI BE
AND VISUAL
CULTURE

HENRI BERGSON AND VISUAL CULTURE

A Philosophy for a New Aesthetic

Paul Atkinson

BLOOMSBURY ACADEMIC

LONDON • NEW YORK • OXFORD • NEW DELHI • SYDNEY

BLOOMSBURY ACADEMIC
Bloomsbury Publishing Plc
50 Bedford Square, London, WC1B 3DP, UK
1385 Broadway, New York, NY 10018, USA

BLOOMSBURY, BLOOMSBURY ACADEMIC and the Diana logo are trademarks
of Bloomsbury Publishing Plc

First published in Great Britain 2021

Cover design by Charlotte Daniels
Cover image: Light and Colour (Goethe's Theory) by J. M. W. Turner

Bloomsbury Publishing Plc does not have any control over, or responsibility for,
any third-party websites referred to or in this book. All internet addresses given
in this book were correct at the time of going to press. The author and publisher
regret any inconvenience caused if addresses have changed or sites have ceased
to exist, but can accept no responsibility for any such changes.

A catalogue record for this book is available from the British Library.

Library of Congress Cataloging-in-Publication Data
Names: Atkinson, Paul, 1967- author.
Title: Henri Bergson and visual culture: a philosophy for a new aesthetic /
Paul Atkinson.
Description: London; New York: Bloomsbury Academic, 2021. | Includes
bibliographical references and index.
Identifiers: LCCN 2020026657 (print) | LCCN 2020026658 (ebook) |
ISBN 9781350161764 (hardback) | ISBN 9781350161788 (ebook) |
ISBN 9781350161795 (epub)
Subjects: LCSH: Bergson, Henri, 1859-1941–Aesthetics. | Time and art.
Classification: LCC B2430.B43 A885 2021 (print) | LCC B2430.B43 (ebook) |
DDC 194–dc23
LC record available at https://lccn.loc.gov/2020026657
LC ebook record available at https://lccn.loc.gov/2020026658

ISBN: HB: 978-1-3501-6176-4
PB: 978-1-3501-6177-1
ePDF: 978-1-3501-6178-8
eBook: 978-1-3501-6179-5

Typeset by Deanta Global Publishing Services, Chennai, India
Printed and bound in Great Britain

To find out more about our authors and books visit www.bloomsbury.com and
sign up for our newsletters.

To Karen, for giving me the impetus to write and
enduring all that followed

CONTENTS

4 PERCEPTION 185

FIGURES

INTRODUCTION

The philosophy of Henri Bergson was immensely important during the first decades of the twentieth century both in France and internationally due to his theory of *durée* and his critique of the spatialization of time. His work served as an alternative to the increasingly ornate conceptual systems adopted in philosophy and the attempt to understand time without reference to human experience in science. He argued that the various features of lived time (becoming, continuity, differentiation, immanence) are not properly attended to in those theories that seek to represent, measure and externalize time. Bergson privileged lived time invested in the interiority of consciousness, the integrity of life and the continuity of gesture, and even suggested that material movements require some residual form of memory. This critique of spatialization and the complementary promotion of a processual metaphysics does not readily lend itself to the study of the visual arts, where painting, drawing, photography and sculpture hypostatize time in concrete artefacts and represented objects. Can we talk about lived time in objects that retain their material form well past the death of the artist and the ephemerality of spectatorship? Should we talk about works that are inherently spatial through a theory that is founded on the critique of spatialization?[1] Bergson does not offer a clear direction as to how to reimagine the visual arts in terms of time, a problem that becomes more acute due to the fact that his discussions of art often refer to the ineffability of the work and the ipseity of the artist's experience. The fact that there is no extended examination of any of the arts does not preclude a reworking of Bergson's ideas in terms of aesthetics or the philosophy of art, for his works display a richness such that any minor comment on aesthetics or reference to the arts can be traced back to a much more comprehensive metaphysics. This book provides an extensive overview of Bergson's aesthetic ideas and how they are intimately connected with his metaphysics, reviews his many references to art and considers how his ideas can be extended and developed through new examples. These examples do not necessarily illustrate a Bergsonian idea, for they have largely been chosen as a means of rethinking Bergson's claims and examining how they can be modified to better address the variability of aesthetic experience.

The book refers to all of Bergson's major works and outlines many of his key ideas; however, the aim is not to provide an exhaustive account of each book and place it within a chronology, as many excellent works have already undertaken this task. This project does not lend itself to this type of approach because Bergson's references to aesthetics and the role of art are scattered across his oeuvre, and are usually deployed to justify ideas that are not strictly related to art. Some texts only make brief reference to art and aesthetics such as *Duration and Simultaneity* and *The Two Sources of Morality and Religion* and, therefore, in order to maintain a consistency of argument, I do not outline their respective critiques of the theory of simultaneity and moral obligation. Instead, I follow particular ideas in Bergson's philosophy that usually arise in one work – for example, ideas about rhythm, gesture and grace in *Time and Free Will* and the concept of life in *Laughter* and *Creative Mind* – but resonate through many others, including some of Bergson's minor writings. Rather than describing an intention to be comprehensive or exhaustive, the inclusion of these minor texts – short lectures, letters and so on collected in *Mélanges*, *Oeuvres* and *Correspondances* – provide additional context to Bergson's arguments in the major works.

One of the difficulties in writing on Bergson is that his philosophy weaves together empirical statements, derived from either scientific texts or introspection, with examples and ideas expressed metaphorically. However, it is often difficult to even ascribe the term 'metaphor', because the image might express the movement of an idea rather than substituting for an object. For example, in one of the most famous passages in *Creative Evolution* as part of a discussion on the impetus of evolutionary life, Bergson states:

> The animal takes its stand on the plant, man bestrides animality, and the whole of humanity, in space and in time, is one immense army galloping beside and before and behind each of us in an overwhelming charge able to beat down every resistance and clear the most formidable obstacles, perhaps even death.[2]

Here Bergson aims to demonstrate the overwhelming insistence of the movement of life that draws together all species in the metaphor of the galloping army. The image helps indicate the strength of the impulsion driving evolution, but it shifts between the metaphorical and the literal – life is more an internal movement than the conquest of space represented in the galloping army, but surprisingly Bergson does believe that it can perhaps overcome death. The latter can only be known through reference to his theory of pure memory, where the continuity of memory could outlast the body. With a poetic sensibility he addresses topics germane to the philosophy of science, from evolution to the theory of relativity, creating a quite unusual tension between the movement of ideas and the concrete examination of particular phenomena. Henri Gouhier argues in his introduction to *Oeuvres* that Bergson regarded his approach to philosophy as scientific and would not publish or write a philosophical treatise until he had acquired sufficient results or evidence.[3] One of his key proponents, Vladimir Jankélévitch, supports this when he argues that each of Bergson's works operates independently according to its own 'line of facts' (*ligne de faits*), but also notes that these facts do not lead to a philosophical system. With his particular élan, Bergson aims to resolve a problem in each book in a way that resembles a coming together of musical themes rather than a structure based on non-contradiction.[4] In addition to foregrounding the main ideas, writing on Bergson involves carefully attending to these converging and diverging themes that demonstrate an aesthetic approach to the empirical, while always gesturing towards the metaphysical.

Although there are some key ideas that have been present throughout all of his major works, Bergson does create a metaphysical, epistemological or logical system that can be fully separated from the particular fields he investigates. He works through different ideas in each text in order to expand the horizons of the theory of *durée*, rather than carefully systematizing the ideas already developed in his early works. In *Matter and Memory*, Bergson posited an incredibly novel ontology of images that resolved many major philosophical problems in philosophy, including the split between idealism and realism. Despite the depth of the argument and the fact that it appeared quite early in his career in 1896, his subsequent major works – *Laughter* and *Creative Evolution* – do not begin by re-establishing the theory of images and then applying it to a new context. One of the reasons why Bergson does not return to the ontology is that he rejects philosophical systems and does not seek to develop philosophy as an end in itself. In most cases, he seeks to rephrase problems in other fields of research. Unquestionably there is a distinctively Bergsonian philosophy based on *durée*, but it is often revealed through the process of rephrasing and developing questions that run like a thread through the various texts. Gabriel Marcel argues that anyone who attempts to derive a system from Bergson's philosophy would actually negate the philosopher's approach, and with regard to his own preliminary investigation into Bergsonism and music, states that to properly undertake the task would involve analysing music in a similar manner to how Bergson analysed both experimental psychology and biology.[5] This presents a number of difficulties when addressing his work in terms of a particular field of philosophy, in this case aesthetics and the philosophy of art, because there is no singular text that brings together his thoughts on the field. A theory of aesthetics can only be gleaned through his various comments on the relationship between art, life and intuition, but also through his many claims about the relationship between perception and time.

In some ways this makes it difficult to write a book on Bergson's aesthetics, because any attempt to parse the ideas or to directly apply them could also serve to degrade them. Bergsonism is essentially a temporal philosophy that does not seek rigid definitions or to propose a definitive reading of a work. The approach taken in this book is to look to develop new arguments that align with Bergson's philosophy and yet extend it in directions that the philosopher might not have considered. In a temporal philosophy based on concrete time, novelty and an unforeseeable future, we should always remain open to the emergence of new ideas while accepting the general direction of Bergson's thought. Vladimir Jankélévitch speaking on the anniversary of Bergson's death remarked that it was important to reflect on Bergson's legacy, but this should not be a simple act of commemoration or historical exegesis, but 'rethinking Bergson as Bergson wanted to be rethought'.[6] In this book on Bergson's aesthetics and ideas on the philosophy of art, this involves working back to find the initial inclination of an idea, and then exploring how it can diverge when presented with new questions. Many of the questions come from various studies in the philosophy of art or on particular artists that were not written in response to Bergsonism, but nevertheless raise some questions about the temporality of the visual arts in both reception and production. Most of the visual art examples were produced in Bergson's lifetime, with some artists arguing that they were inspired by the philosopher, but there are also a few contemporary works that were chosen due to the novelty of their approach to time.

The book is set out in four chapters each of which addresses a theme and context underpinning Bergson's writings on aesthetics, creativity and art. They follow the line of an idea across a number of works, and make suggestions about how they relate to particular examples of visual art. Due to the complexity and subtlety of these ideas, each of the chapters addresses several different themes that often diverge from the broader idea. The first chapter, 'Durée', places Bergson's thought within the European fin de siècle and explains how his philosophy challenged entrenched scientific and philosophical ideas, as well as opening up a space for an experiential understanding of time. It addresses two of his main ideas, *durée* and intuition, both of which were prominent in his references to art, and traces how their popularity led to the adoption or rejection of Bergsonism by a number of avant-garde movements. The second chapter, 'Gesture', explores in detail the continuity of the corporeal gesture and how it operates on the threshold between the body and consciousness, and dematerializes in the movement of aesthetic sympathy and grace. The chapter outlines the early arguments in *Time and Free Will* on the relationship between the deep feelings and duration, and how aesthetic reception is moderated by the body and its rhythms. The third chapter, 'Life', examines how the continuous gesture is rethought in terms of the movement of life, both the individual life of the comic in *Laughter* and a much more expansive evolutionary conception of life in *Creative Evolution*. Life can be used as a principle for evaluating works in the opposition between the living and the mechanical, but Bergson also asks us to think of artworks as only moments in enduring processes of differentiation. The fourth chapter, 'Perception', outlines Bergson's theory of utilitarian perception, which he argues prevents a proper aesthetic engagement with time as duration. Aesthetics is here distinguished in terms of how it lifts the veil of ordinary perception to reveal a processual ontology, in which the real presents itself in the variability of appearance. Our perception contracts processual differences into a macroscopic world of solid bodies and fixed qualia, and the role of a truly Bergsonian aesthetics is to reverse the process.

The Bergsonian aesthetics developed in this book is a reimagining of Bergson's philosophy that demonstrates how his processual theories can be relevant to the visual arts. It is not strictly an application of his philosophy to art, but, rather, a process by which his philosophy develops new aspects through engaging with particular artworks, ideas and theories. *Durée* can always be invoked as a counterpoint to the abstraction and spatialization of time, but is at its most relevant when it confronts the particular questions inherent to a field of study, as Bergson so ably demonstrates in his own work.

1 DURÉE

Henri Bergson was one of the most celebrated philosophers of the fin de siècle. His belief in time as *durée* transformed intellectual life in France and across the continent, where he inspired artists and writers, as well as philosophers and social theorists. There is no single explanation for this success, but it is notable that Bergson presented a philosophy that heralded life and critiqued the increasing systemization of thought in the sciences. He rejected determinism in his first published work by accentuating the time of human consciousness, and this initial idea later evolved into a broad theory of creative endeavour. Despite this interest in creativity and life, Bergson did not write extensively on art or aesthetics. There is no explicit theory of aesthetics in his work, nor does he examine the practices of particular artists, or, indeed, musicians, even though there are many references to the value of art and music in his work. The closest Bergson comes to the direct investigation of art is his book *Laughter* (1900), in which he develops a theory of humour that includes a brief analysis of the difference between comedy and tragedy. In fact, Bergson is less interested in the links between humour and artistic genres, and more interested in the way in which humour arises out of the juxtaposition of the mechanical and the living. Bergson's philosophy is nevertheless amenable to discussion in terms of aesthetic theory, and in many respects, his focus on the haecceity of time lends itself to an aesthetic approach. He was able to inspire artists because his reimagining of time and movement could not be reduced to scientific conceptualization or philosophical systemization, as well as reasserted the value of human creativity. Moreover, he wanted the readers of his philosophy to be attentive to the variability of the real in intuition, that is, he wanted readers to develop an aesthetic and metaphysical sensibility rather than a conceptual understanding. In order to draw out this aesthetic sensibility, this opening chapter will examine Bergson's most celebrated idea of time as *durée*, explaining its importance in turn-of-the-century thought and indicating how *durée* along with intuition remains central to a Bergsonian aesthetics.

The poetics of philosophical argument

Bergson's ideas continue to be invoked in contemporary debates in philosophy, and have been applied in the humanities to the examination of literature and the arts. While his ideas remain potent, it is important to recognize that they were shaped in response to a particular social and intellectual milieu in which scientific ideas were increasingly adopted in philosophy, social sciences and the humanities. Bergson was a philosopher who straddled two centuries; he was born in 1859 and died in 1941, and his most celebrated and influential works appeared between 1889 and 1911. Philosophically he was grounded in nineteenth-century metaphysics, in the tradition of spiritualist philosophers such as Maine de Biran and Félix Ravaisson, and this informed some of his early teaching, while also being interested in the empiricism of Charles Darwin and Herbert Spencer.[1] At first glance, these approaches seem to be incompatible; however, spiritualism can be associated with empiricism insofar as mind, perception and consciousness can be taken as the object of empirical observation. It is an empiricism of the particular, which differs quite significantly from scientific empiricism with its aim of deriving general principles through induction. French spiritualism, or voluntarism, is linked to religious humanism, but one of the features that probably attracted Bergson was the specific interest in the 'spontaneity of the human will', a quality that cannot be explained using scientific causality.[2] This is evinced throughout Bergson's oeuvre, particularly in his critique of theories of determinism, and his belief in the *ipseity* or selfhood of human consciousness, including the independence of artistic creation. This interest in both the sciences and a philosophy thoroughly grounded in the humanities can be traced back to Bergson's early philosophical training. At school, he was lauded for his mathematical ability and was encouraged to pursue his studies in mathematics, and it is notable that his first publication was a solution to a mathematical problem.[3] Although Bergson is noted for his critique of some of the fundamental principles of the sciences, he maintained an interest in the sciences throughout his oeuvre. He directly discussed principles of evolutionary theory, psychological theories of memory, and even the Lorentzian calculations underpinning the special theory of relativity. He did not reject science outright, but argued that it presented only a partial view of the real due to its overemphasis on material explanation. He maintained that there were other, more direct, ways of apprehending the real in philosophy, and even in the arts.

At the end of the nineteenth century Bergson was well known in French philosophical circles following the publication of his critique of associationism, *Matter and Memory* in 1896. This eventually led to a teaching role at the Collège de France, where his lectures became so popular that the lecture room could not house all the interested parties and measures had to be implemented to restrict audience numbers. Due to the fuss, Bergson reduced the number of lectures he presented, and gradually came to devote all his time to his written work.[4] One of the reasons for the popularity of his work was the fact that he carefully critiqued the specific claims of scientific disciplines as well as the broader assumptions of scientism on their own ground, rather than retreating to a humanist or spiritualist position. This critique was well received by those among the intellectual community in France who wanted to refute determinism, and Bergson was consequently known as the 'liberator'. 'Thanks to Bergson it was possible for modern intellectuals to reaffirm the reality of the human spirit without ignoring the major achievements of natural science and without reverting to the traditional doctrines of the church.'[5] During this time, scientific humanism, manifest as mechanism and determinism, dominated the intellectual culture of France and was entrenched in the curriculum at the Sorbonne University, which led to the disillusionment of many of its students.[6] In this context, Bergson's lectures at the Collège de France provided inspiration for many young intellectuals dissatisfied with the positivist principles of 'Comte, Taine, and Renan'.[7] The Collège de France was a very different institution to the Sorbonne, and this was typified in Bergson's lectures which inadvertently attracted the disillusioned students, many of whom would themselves become prominent intellectuals, including Henri Focillon and Jacques Maritain.[8] Albeit unwillingly, Bergson provides an early example of the celebrity philosopher who was able to significantly affect cultural debate, and much of the success of his ideas can be attributed to his development of a viable alternative to the cultural dominant of scientism.

Bergson's popularity grew with the publication of his 1903 essay, 'Introduction to Metaphysics', and reached its apex in the period following the publication of *Creative Evolution* in 1907. With this work, Bergson achieved worldwide fame, such that he 'became the most popular philosopher of his day', which led to keen critical interest in his work in the period before the beginning of the First World War.[9] One of the reasons for the success of *Creative Evolution* was its capacity to generate interest in a philosophy of direct experience in which even the study of biology was not overdetermined by the systematic operation of reason:

> However much he denied it later, Bergson called his generation to turn away from the restrictions of a logical thought which could only distort truth and to give themselves instead to an immediate, intuitive grasp of truth in a world that had to be felt and experienced to be really known. *Creative Evolution* inspired his readers with an appreciation of the tremendous importance of this life – a cosmos which was free and changing and which creatively transcended everything.[10]

The introduction of terms such as intuition in the 'Introduction to Metaphysics' and *élan vital* (vital impetus) in *Creative Evolution* also contributed to the popularity of Bergson's philosophy. This terminology brought with it an alternative mode of thinking that was thoroughly grounded in a dynamic notion of life realized in change rather than taxonomy. The problem with these terms is that they can easily be misused, for intuition has a popular meaning outside of philosophy, and life is a term that is very malleable and can be used to justify even conflicting theoretical positions. Bertrand Russell asserted that Bergson's popularity was a direct result of scepticism before the First World War and that many people found in the irrational and romantic aspects of *Creative Evolution* an expression of their own desire for change.[11] Likewise, critics of the very popular 'Introduction to Metaphysics' claimed that its critique of scientific positivism extended to all forms of rationalism and that Bergson was an irrationalist who undermined the ideals of the Enlightenment.[12]

Irrespective of the veracity of such claims, many found in Bergson's philosophy what they sought rather than what he said. Some Bergsonians believed that Bergson had thoroughly rejected scientific method and that the real could be readily accessed through a semi-mystical intuition. In the 'Introduction to Metaphysics', Bergson certainly makes a clear distinction between the immediacy of intuition and the relativity of the intellect with regard to the apprehension of the real, but his nuanced use of the term intuition was overlooked by many of his followers. Although characterized as a form of direct apprehension, intuition brought together a number of ideas associated with his philosophy of time including its endurance and differentiation. Bergson also had some misgivings about the popularity of the critique of science in the 'Introduction to Metaphysics', for in a footnote accompanying the reproduction of the work in the collection, *Creative Mind* (1934), he noted that he had developed a much more detailed and precise understanding of science since writing the essay.[13] Bergson's long-time friend, Jacques Chevalier argues that many of the misreadings of Bergson's philosophy are the result of his followers taking extreme positions and creating fixed oppositions, when, in fact, Bergson usually takes the middle ground.[14] For example, even in the work that most clearly contrasts science and metaphysics, the 'Introduction to Metaphysics', Bergson acknowledges that many scientific developments are dependent on intuition, including the reimagining of physical movement in the infinitesimal calculus.[15] Such subtleties were often lost in popular debate and when Bergson's philosophy was used to support a political or social agenda.

Bergsonian intuition lost much of its specificity in its application by many of the Bergsonians writing in the first couple of decades of the twentieth century, who were more interested in what intuition was not – mechanistic, rational, determinist – rather than how it reveals the object in its haecceity. This is not surprising because in most of Bergson's writings there is an emphasis on critique, particularly of the bias towards spatialization implicit in philosophical and scientific thinking. As he was operating in an intellectual milieu in which scientific and pseudo-scientific ideas were reaching ever further into the analysis of human experience, particularly in psychology, Bergson had to develop a critique to clear the ground for his new approach to philosophy. He had to expose the limits of the technical language and epistemological models that dominated contemporary thought. Bergson acknowledges this emphasis on critique, stating in a discussion with Chevalier that it is, in many respects, the most accurate and precise feature of his work, for many of his other ideas were subject to constant change and revision.[16] In many respects, this is a necessary feature of his philosophy, for the theory of *durée* and intuition are inextricably implicated in becoming such that they must be rethought and reconsidered in relation to a specific object or philosophical question. *Durée* cannot be posited as an object nor can intuition be posited as a method with fixed and durable contours.

The enduring criticism that intuition was vague and irrational was one of the factors that led to the eventual waning in popularity of Bergsonism after the First World War, in addition to the fact that many younger philosophers felt that it did not properly address the problems of history raised by the war.[17] This is probably why Gilles Deleuze in his book *Bergsonism* – a book that many years after its release was instrumental in reviving interest in Bergson's work – was keen to state from the outset that intuition is a method that is 'as precise in *its* field, as capable of being prolonged and transmitted as science itself is'.[18] However, in order for it to maintain this precision, it should not be simply conceived as the apprehension of lived time, where it would be subject to the vagaries of temporal change, but must also be seen as a means of rethinking the real, by restating problems with regard to time and by properly recognizing 'differences in kind'.[19] Bergson spoke of intuition's capacity to reveal the immediacy of lived time, which was a key argument in the 'Introduction to Metaphysics', but Deleuze argues that intuition is something that is found in the way that Bergson approaches problems. It is not so much immediacy, nor the givenness of intuition that is most important in Bergson's work, but, rather, the way that he finds solutions to philosophical problems by rethinking the very ground on which they are posed. Bergson recognizes this in his 1911 lecture on 'Philosophical intuition' – yet another correction to the popular 'Introduction' – where he argues that intuition forces reason to turn back to the self, that is 'draw closer to life', in the reformulation of arguments.[20] This principle is evident throughout his oeuvre. Even before he had begun to use the term intuition, Bergson applies such a method in *Time and Free Will* to the debate about the nature of free will. Rather than reinvesting in existing distinctions, such as the notion of a will freed from constraint, he states that the accrual of experience in lived time is what actually individualizes and differentiates each action. In free action, the particularity of the past comes to bear on the present and guide the action and not the discontinuity of events as part of a causal sequence as imagined in determinism. In intuition, the direct apprehension of time in lived experience initiates the fundamental rethinking of a problem rather than substituting for this rethinking.

Bergson's popularity was attributable not only to the themes of his lectures and writing but also to the beauty of their delivery. Gabriel Marcel comments on the assuredness and 'felicity' of Bergson's lectures for the Collège de France, in which his speech gave the impression that he was captivated by a continual process of discovery.[21] Even the sound of the speech was worthy of mention, with Marcel stating that it was 'permeated by the pleasant tremor that vibrates in the voice of an explorer when he tries to evoke the ineffable peace of some inviolate shore or perhaps a sojourn in the midst of a fabulous tribe'.[22] This account of Bergson's graceful delivery of philosophical argument can be linked to the importance he attributes to movement in communication, where the listener must learn to fall in step with the speaker, in order to identify with the movement of the argument as much as with its referent. Bergson argued in an early lecture that intellectual engagement requires politeness, by which he meant a subtleness of thought that seeks to engage calmly and respectfully with others. To explain this intellectual politeness, he claimed that many ancient Greek scholars arrived at an idea through the gentle process of dialogue and reflection in the form of a 'promenade', which he argued can be contrasted with contemporary theoretical discussion where ideas are placed in opposition and separated from our appetites and desires.[23] This courteous approach to debate belies Bergson's significant role in transforming theoretical debate in early-twentieth-century France, but indicates his belief that language is underpinned by movement; for Marcel it is the 'pleasant tremor' whereas for Bergson it is the promenade. For an audience member to understand the speaker's argument, they must join with the speaker in the same movement or take the same promenade. According to Chevalier, in 1926 Bergson complained that he was beginning to have problems with his movement and claimed that this also affected his thought. Bergson was someone who liked to move around while thinking and while teaching, and he did not like the way that the École normale and the Collège de France limited his movement.[24] It is not clear what restrictions were placed on lecturers at these institutions, but Bergson's belief that thought is constituted first as a movement is repeated in a number of his works. There is a rhythm to thought and to language that gives it a unity that cannot be found in individual statements, and effectively the rhythm precedes the specific articulation of the idea.

This attentiveness to the variability of language in philosophy, often akin to poetry, seems contrary to Bergson's strong interest in scientific concepts and empiricism, in which concepts supplant the aesthetic qualities of language. The expressive range of Bergson's writing probably contributed to the appeal of his work, but it was also subject to much criticism. Bertrand Russell accused his French counterpart of being an 'anti-intellectual' and an 'irrationalist', citing his poetic style as evidence and claiming in *A History of Western Philosophy* that the 'large part of Bergson's philosophy, probably the part to which most of its popularity is due, does not depend on argument, and cannot be upset by argument. His imaginative picture of the world, regarded as a poetic effort, is in the main not capable of either proof or disproof'.[25] Russell states that an argument that is largely dependent on 'similes' and 'analogies' cannot be refuted any more than a work by Shakespeare can be considered incorrect.[26] This criticism is valid if one believes that the role of philosophy is to strip language of its expressive functions to retain only a logical substratum such that it resembles mathematics and its relationship to the physical world. For Bergson, however, science, philosophy and poetry are not incompatible; a belief that somewhat derives from his training in the classics. Early in his career Bergson wrote a commentary on Lucretius's poem *De Rerum Natura* (*On the nature of things*), and the aspect of this work that he most heralded was the poet's capacity to expound the physical laws of atomism in a way that remained thoroughly poetic and vital. Lucretius was able to see 'the double aspect of things', both the beauty of their living form and the geometrical beauty of the laws underpinning physical movement.[27] The language of philosophy should retain this 'double aspect' of attending to the living particularity of the real as well as expounding its general principles. The poet has the ability to bring to life the forms of the natural world, even when the theory deals with a subject as inanimate as atomism, as long as the writing coincides with the very things it describes. The problem with many philosophical arguments is that they are more attentive to the clarity of the system than to the world they purport to explain.

The quality of his writing probably contributed to Bergson winning the Nobel Prize for Literature in 1927. After reading Bergson's *Creative Evolution*, the American psychologist William James wrote a letter to Bergson[28] praising his achievement, not only for the quality of the ideas but for its style, arguing that, in contrast with transcendental philosophy which is 'written in a language so obscure, so cruel and so inaccessible', Bergson's writing has a 'beauty of form that renders it classic'. James recalls the pleasure of reading *Creative Evolution*, which he compares to his reading of Gustave Flaubert's *Madame Bovary*, and states that the experience was one of flow, in which there is little to prevent the passage of an idea. This might be regarded by Russell as a form of false reasoning that seduces due to its 'poetic effort', but for Bergson flow is as integral to his philosophy as the movement of thought and ideas. How is it possible to render the living movement of an idea except in a form that recreates that movement?

Bergson's style is accessible when compared to some of the more technical philosophical writing in the nineteenth and early twentieth century, for he wrote without introducing many neologisms or large swathes of interlocking premises. This stylistic accessibility, however, often masks a complexity in argument. In a letter to his Polish translator, F. Znianiecki, Bergson states that despite the apparent simplicity of translating *Creative Evolution*, a number of translators found the task difficult and had resorted to employing a range of experts from various disciplines, including literature and biology. Indeed, completion of the German translation in 1911 was delayed due to problems addressing the range of disciplines and, most importantly, the philosophical argument that depended on 'images' rather than abstract 'concepts'. Bergson argues that these images exceed (*dépasser*) the concepts, and their importance is further summarized in the final line: 'the image here is not an ornament, but the sole means of expression adapting to thought.'[29] Bergson refers here to his belief that philosophical argument is founded in the continuity of thought and a particular 'concrete intuition', which the reader must try to discern and which the writing must attempt to convey. The problem is that this concrete intuition cannot be directly communicated in the text due to the constraints of language, nor can it be communicated by the creation of a series of new concepts, which will only fragment and dissemble it. The intuition can only be conveyed by something that approximates its nature and movement, which Bergson argues takes place through intermediary images.[30] John Mullarkey importantly points out that the Bergsonian image is not like most philosophical concepts because it is necessarily 'vague' and 'incomplete', and comes to invoke directly the real only through the coming together or integration of multiple images in intuition. Conversely, the intuition reveals the real in its ipseity but can only communicate this 'indirectly' to others through incomplete images.[31] These images, often in the form of metaphors in Bergson's writing, guide the reader to the intuition by emulating its movement and recovering its impetus. This language appears at first to be simple because it uses words that are common, but it is, in fact, much more complex than technical language because it must carry with it the complex multiplicity of thought in movement.

The distinctiveness of Bergson's writing and language was also acknowledged by the poet and philosopher Paul Valéry in a memorial speech delivered on 9 January 1941 on behalf of the French Academy. Valéry spoke of the significance of Bergson's philosophy in a period in which Kantian philosophy dominated French thought, of Bergson's unwillingness to submit to this philosophical milieu and of his efforts to revitalize metaphysics by returning to the very conditions of what it means to think.[32] Rather than creating a new system of thought, Bergson developed new ways of thinking through philosophical problems as a way of revitalizing philosophy. Valéry argues that one of Bergson's greatest contributions to philosophy was the development of an alternative language to the sciences and systematic philosophy, which brought together poetry with the rigour of the exact sciences in order to reveal the orientation of a philosopher's thought.[33] Valéry's description of Bergson's thought and writing resembles Bergson's own claims about the value of Lucretius's work, which is revealed in the double aspect of poetry and scientific argument. Again the emphasis on precision is important because it counters the common critique of vagueness and irrationality. Unlike a philosophical system based on analytical logic, the precision cannot be found in the multiplication of non-contradictory statements and the exclusion of a middle term, because such precision does not properly acknowledge the object. Bergson seeks, rather, the precision of the poet and the fidelity with which they recreate or emulate a sentiment or feeling. Valéry argues that in this combination of poetry and rigorous philosophical thinking, there is a Frenchness to Bergson's thought and language that can be compared to Claude Debussy's musical style.[34] The comparison is apt, for over and above the complexity of his harmony, Debussy's Impressionist approach to music often engages with natural events, such as the movement of the sea or reflections in water, in a way that reproduces and rearticulates the movement and flow – although Jankélévitch would argue that his philosophy is closer to Ravel than Debussy.[35] Like music, Bergson's language demonstrates an attentiveness to the sensual conditions of movement in a way that cannot be invoked in formal academic or scientific language.

The theory of *durée*

Bergson usually invokes the value of a truly dynamic and sensual language as part of a broader critique of the limits of scientific reasoning and language, which eschews those aspects of sensual experience that do not readily conform to the requirements of measurement. Bergson argues that philosophy need not remain in the shadow of science, where its role is limited to reflecting upon science's advances, for it can directly apprehend the real, including the particularity of sensual experience and the aesthetic differences that characterize it. Bergson chose to rethink the role of philosophy in a period in which the explanatory capacity of science had significantly expanded due to the increasing precision with which measurement supplanted direct human observation, in addition to breakthroughs in the language of mathematics. For Deleuze, Bergson's philosophy raises the question, 'Why is there still philosophy, why is science not enough?' (*pourquoi il y a encore de la philosophie, en quoi la science ne suffit pas?*),[36] to which there are two possible responses: philosophy should either reflect science's epistemology or it could indicate the limits of science by attending to the 'thing in itself' (*chose en elle même*).[37] Bergson adopts the latter approach, in part through an analysis of the empirical observations of a number of disciplines, including physics, psychology and biology, but, most importantly, by rephrasing the claims of both science and philosophy in terms of time. He argues that science always seeks to correlate time with space and extension because the latter are directly measurable, which could include any linear or numerical representation of time from the movement of a hand on an analogue clock to its placement as a variable in a mathematical equation. Regardless of the precision of these representations of time, the more they rely on spatial reasoning, the less they are capable of understanding time, which can only be retrieved in direct experience and disciplines that attend on this experience, most importantly metaphysics and the arts.

Bergson argues that the value of a philosopher's work should be judged by the degree to which the key ideas can lead to the rethinking of existing categories and that 'any philosopher worthy of the name has never said more than a single thing'.[38] For Bergson this 'single thing' is the proposition that time is only conceivable as *durée*, a term that can be roughly translated into English as duration. The emphasis is on how time endures over a concrete period, which serves as a direct criticism of theories of time that refer to instants or, if we are to think spatially, models that refer to points of time. Algot Ruhe and Nancy Margaret Paul state that Bergson formulated the theory of *durée*, his response to the philosophy of the Eleatics, while taking a walk during his tenure at Clermont-Ferrand.[39] This anecdote seems appropriate, for what better way to reject temporal atomism than by the concrete act of walking, with its own definite time and distinctive rhythm. Indeed, thought, like time, is not something that the mind can grasp in an instant, for it has a rhythmic pattern that can only gestate and form over a definite period. In Bergson's philosophy, the very idea of *durée* always carries with it the time of its imagining, the rhythmic quality of the walk, in addition to the time to which it refers.

This theory of time, first expounded in Bergson's published thesis *Time and Free Will*, is usually aligned with the temporal experience of consciousness, which is continuous and irreversible, and involves the interpenetration of the past within the present, as well as the projection of the present towards the future. Abstract notions of time are only ever secondary to conscious or lived experience, which is why Bergson criticized psychological attempts to measure conscious experience using temporal measures. In *Time and Free Will*, *durée* began as an examination of the interiority of experience according to Bergson's spiritualist method, but over the course of his oeuvre came to encompass all aspects of temporality, from the movement of life to the time inherent in matter. One of the most direct statements on the nature of *durée* came in his critique of Einstein's special theory of relativity, *Duration and Simultaneity*, which appeared late in his career:

> There is no doubt but that for us time is at first identical with the continuity of our inner life. What is this continuity? That of a flow or passage, but a self-sufficient flow or passage, the flow not implying a thing that flows, and the passing not presupposing states through which we pass; the *thing* and the *state* are only artificially taken snapshots of the transition; and this transition, all that is naturally experienced, is duration itself.[40]

The metaphor of flow somewhat suits the depiction of *durée*, because it provides an image of time that is directional and undergoing constant change, and it is for this reason that it has often been used since the pre-Socratics to describe time. Unlike the continuous movement of the hand of a clock, where time is registered by the external relationship between the hand and the marks on the clock face, flow cannot be described in terms of a single point or the space between points. Due to its emphasis on the physicality of change, flow can refer to the feeling of time from within consciousness, whereas the hand of the clock is always externally articulated in space. However, the problem with using the term 'flow' is that we can also think of objects caught in the flow, such as a boat floating down a river, or the rate of flow of a river measured against the embankment. This is why Bergson has to qualify the description, by arguing that we should not seek to anchor flow spatially through positing an external frame of reference, for time is characterized by its immanence. Indeed, the difficulty for Bergson is to try and describe *durée* without recourse to substantives, and this is why there are few extended descriptions of this key idea in his work. He has to approach *durée* obliquely through a range of metaphors that are capable of invoking the experience, without fully reducing it to a spatial measure or set of axioms, for *durée*, like flow, always exceeds the present or any non-temporal description of it. There is an enduring and concrete time to flow that cannot be supplanted by representation.

Durée always refers to the lived continuity of time, which is exemplified in conscious experience, where the past is always implied in the present, in every feeling, desire, intention or inclination. We feel time as an impetus in which the past pushes towards the future, that is, a form of psychic orientation in which the present cannot be isolated. Our consciousness cannot be laid out as a collection of discrete events on a timeline, because past events, and our memories of those events, continue to affect the present in shaping the subject's orientation, decision-making and action. Even the simplest aspects of perception require some notion of duration, for all sensual data must be revealed over a definite duration. It is impossible to hear a sound in the space of an instant, because sound is inherently temporal even when considering its materiality, which is manifest as vibration. Even sight, which is often discussed in terms of the presentness of the spatial world that appears to the viewer in an instant, is also underpinned by the temporality of the vibrations of light. Moreover, to perceive or make sense of this sensual data requires the integration of past knowledge with present perception. We do not see light vibrations and then retroactively interpret them as a colour; rather, we have a predisposition to colour that shapes the vibration in the time it is perceived. The past is always working on the present, and the present is always gesturing towards the future. This complex interplay of temporal periods in perception is what comprises *durée*, but both the French expression and its English equivalent can be a little misleading, because they can also be used to describe certain measures of time. In response to the question of what the duration of a journey or an event is, it is easy to respond with a simple quantity such as three minutes or two hours. However, such a quantity does not have the inherent movement of flow or consciousness, because it merely describes the space between two limits. F. C. T. Moore argues that the translation of *durée* as duration omits one of the other senses of the word as '*the fact or property of going through time*' or continuance and, consequently, he argues that the English expression 'durance' is more suitable.[41] Here the emphasis shifts from the description of a temporal expanse to the movement inherent in time and what it means to endure, for the continuity of time is actually felt as a continuance that is irreducible to an external and measurable representation. A person always endures in time even if there is no notable activity during a particular period, in which case time still makes itself felt in the concrete process of waiting. In some respects, Bergson elevates the process of waiting to the level of ontology, for irrespective of any causal structure, all events must have some definite period of time in which to occur – we cannot circumvent the process of waiting.

In relation to consciousness, the notion of endurance can be understood through memory. The present endures because it carries the past with it. When we recognize an object, we do so because the past guides our current perception to seek out certain features in the environment. When we experience an emotion, it is not as a mere quantity but, rather, as a disposition towards present thoughts and actions, and as such it is always underpinned by the persistence of memory. This endurance is readily understandable in relation to conscious experience, but Bergson in *Duration and Simultaneity* argues that *durée* is not limited to consciousness, because all events require something that holds the past to the present, otherwise all movement would be nothing more than a collection of discrete instants, with no principle describing their coherence. For want of another term to describe this coherence, Bergson uses the term memory to describe the endurance of material qualities as much as lived conscious experience:

> It is memory, but not personal memory, external to what it retains, distinct from a past whose preservation it assures; it is a memory within change itself, a memory that prolongs the before into the after, keeping them from being mere snapshots appearing and disappearing in a present ceaselessly reborn. A melody to which we listen with our eyes closed, heeding it alone, comes close to coinciding with this time which is the very fluidity of our inner life; but it still has too many

qualities, too much definition, and we must first efface the difference among the sounds, then do away with the distinctive features of the sound itself, retaining of it only the continuation of what precedes into what follows and the uninterrupted transition, multiplicity without divisibility and succession without separation, in order finally to rediscover basic time. Such is immediately perceived duration, without which we would have no idea of time.[42]

Bergson readily oscillates between the description of the continuity of inner life and material continuity. The example of a melody is central to this oscillation because a melody cannot be imagined except over a definite duration and it is impossible to invert a melody without creating a new melody, for each sound is always understood in terms of the sounds that came before it, and to speed up or slow down the melody also changes the way we hear it. It is also essential that it endures, because the form of the melody requires that the listener remembers each note as they encounter the next, for the melody emerges out of the relationship between notes. However, Bergson only allows the example to extend so far, because in positing the idea of individual notes, it is possible to imagine a sequence rather than a succession, which is defined by division, the steps of time, rather than the inherence of one moment within the next. The notes might be written on the page as separate units, but the written form is quite different from what we hear. French philosopher and musicologist Vladimir Jankélévitch in his major work on Bergson states that the melody is always latent as a sonic form in the present moment of each note and that when a scholar reads the notes on a page they have an existing understanding of the whole.[43] Their imagination is invested in the continuity of sound even if the score refers mainly to divisions. To truly think duration is to imagine the melody as a continuity without divisions in which one moment adheres to, or, indeed, melts into, the next.

In order to discuss time, it is necessary to refer to actual events and experiences, but for Bergson, it is important that time is not mistaken as a backdrop for such events. When Bergson refers to 'uninterrupted transition' and 'succession without separation', he wants to demonstrate that *durée* is essentially change without reference to specific units of change. It is not about changing into something or changing out of something else, it is about change itself which may momentarily appear to be invested in particular forms. Deleuze states that *durée* is characterized by the Aristotelian notion of *altération*, or the immanent variability of a substance, and this can be distinguished from Plato's *altérité*, where difference is reduced to the external properties of contradiction and opposition.[44] In short, '*durée* is that which differs or which changes in nature, quality, heterogeneity, that which differs from itself. The being of a grain of sugar will be defined by a *durée*, by a certain way of enduring, by a certain relaxing or tension of *durée*'.[45] *Durée* is defined by its endurance but also its heterogeneity, insofar as it must differ from itself, which is readily revealed in introspection where the enduring whole of consciousness nevertheless varies with each successive moment. Nothing can halt this condition of alteration, as long as we remain immanent to consciousness, and it is only when consciousness is examined externally that it is devolved into parts (memories, percepts, etc.). This theme has been taken up by a range of philosophers, most notably Heidegger and the existentialists, but Bergson was the first philosopher to place the notion of enduring lived time, unencumbered by any spatial measure, at the centre of his philosophy.

Between metaphysics and aesthetics

The theory of *durée* seems far removed from any aesthetic argument or the philosophy of the arts because it is derived through introspection, or a form of attention in which the conscious mind turns away from the world. In emphasizing continuous and continual alteration, we imagine *durée* as something unaffected and unencumbered by representation or any principle or practice associated with it. It is not apparent how the visual arts, which are often underpinned by representation, mimesis and the application of spatial principles such as linear perspective, can be supported by a philosophy that depends so much on the erasure of spatial categories and attention to stable objects. However, Bergson is always keen to foreground the link between the arts and philosophy, principally metaphysics, as a form of engagement with the real. A. E. Pilkington argues that Bergson produced only one work that addresses art directly, the short book on the nature of the comic *Laughter*, but points out that Bergson displays an interest in aesthetics across much of his work:[46]

Although explicit references to art are not numerous, and he left no fully worked out aesthetic, there is in his thought an important aesthetic dimension. The reason for this is that the sort of vision of reality which Bergson maintained that the philosopher ought to cultivate, is precisely the vision with which the artist is by nature endowed.[47]

Bergson states that art is valuable inasmuch as it cultivates a form of aesthetic attention for both the artist and the spectator that is akin to philosophical intuition. What distinguishes the artist is their capacity to see the 'inner life of things', and the artist's work should be valued in the degree to which it fulfils 'the loftiest ambition of art, which here consists in revealing to us nature'.[48] The artist serves as a guide, who through their capacity to see nature as temporal becoming creates works that give the viewer the opportunity to re-engage through intuition with *durée*.

Art is coincident with philosophy's empirical orientation, albeit a form of transcendental empiricism, in which the artist engages with the sensual becoming of the real as *durée*. The philosopher begins with introspection and the lived time of consciousness from which they arrive at an understanding of the becoming of all things. Due to the fact that the empirical object is always underpinned by *durée*, Bergson's empiricism is grounded in the relationship between the perceiver and the natural world. This is quite different from scientific methods or a systematic philosophy, which seeks to derive principles that stand outside the particular experience of the observer. In some respects it is about the artist's or philosopher's individual vision, but in a way that allows general principles to be drawn from empirical observation. In a letter to the philosopher William Boyce Gibson in 1911, Bergson argues that philosophy should align itself with art rather than science, because art offers a deepening of perception:

> The object of philosophy, such as I understand it, is simply to permit us to see everything and to see it more and more profoundly, as a landscape painter shows us how better to see the landscape. That is why, if we accept intuition, there can be no question of it creating new concepts, unless they are 'mobile concepts' destined to guide other men through this same intuition or put them on the path.[49]

It is notable that Bergson uses the example of landscape painting to describe this process because it is a form of painting that is linked to an empirical object, and notably he also directly acknowledges two of the leading landscape painters of the nineteenth century Corot and Turner in *The Creative Mind*. Artistic or philosophical intuition is always grounded in empiricism, for it is about seeing a particular landscape, a particular state of consciousness or a particular set of conditions, but in doing so, it also gestures towards a notion of time in which the object must differ from itself. It is impossible to posit clearly defined principles that endure, such as a definition of matter or fixed statements on the nature of resemblance in painting, due to this continual alteration, but it is possible to intuit a particular tendency or direction in the real. This is why Bergson refers to 'mobile concepts' that have the capacity to vary with the object and provide a means by which the observers can align themselves with it.[50] It is not strictly a matter of actual movement, Bergson would not privilege the works of, say, Alexander Calder over Auguste Rodin, or the performing arts over painting, but the implication is that the world is processual and that our aesthetic attention must vary to accommodate this condition of variability. The viewer and the painter share an intuition and an orientation towards the physical world.

From this perspective, the arts derive their value from the artist's capacity to disclose the real, and it is through this intuition that they have an affinity with philosophy. Bergson does not provide an extended account of the precise nature of this relationship; however, his interview with Georges Aimel in 1910 provides some additional detail on his views about art. In response to a question about the relationship between his work and contemporary art, Bergson confirms his view that the arts are founded on intuition like philosophy and that 'philosophy is a genre and the different arts are its species' (*la philosophie est un genre dont les différents arts sont les espèces*).[51] The use of an organic metaphor, which is common in Bergson's work, asserts again the primacy of philosophy, because it is the discipline that most definitely follows intuition in its search for the truth of reality as *durée*, whereas the arts are distinguished in their affiliation as particular species of intuition, each with its own object. As part of this discussion, Bergson makes an unusually direct reference to specific art movements and practices, including the literary Symbolists and his appreciation of the theatrical work of Maurice Maeterlinck. He is quick to point out that he was not aware of the Symbolists while writing *Time and Free Will* in 1889,[52] which is typical of Bergson, who was always keen to prevent any misreading of his work through reference to other philosophies or bodies of thought, but also in accordance with his own belief in the emergence of new philosophical ideas. He does not explain what is distinctive about

Symbolism, and the preference could be simply personal, as he also mentions Honoré Balzac and William Shakespeare in the interview. What he does praise is the creative richness of their personalities which he argues must be comprised of a myriad of embryonic ideas or 'virtualités' due to the diversity of their characters.[53] In this case, the focus is not on intuition as a form of revelation of *durée*, but rather on the generative capacities of art as a process of continuous alteration, in which characters emerge over the course of writing the work. It is about art as immanence and creation and, and to refer back to the claim that the arts are a species of philosophy, the relationship is one of continual differentiation – the arts emerge like characters through the intuition of the real. In the Aimel interview, Bergson also mentions the importance of music and states that he has an instinctual preference for the work of Debussy because his music, along with that of his followers, is readily linked to the theory of *durée*. Bergson made particular note of 'the continuous melody that accompanies and expresses the unique and uninterrupted current of dramatic emotion' (*la mélodie continue qui accompagne et exprime le courant unique et ininterrompu de l'émotion dramatique*).[54] Here music is commended for the sinuosity and continuity of its themes, which works horizontally in the endurance of a melody, but also vertically, in the fact that it draws upon the depth of experience of the listener. In this short interview, Bergson addresses three key themes that reveal the basis of his aesthetics: art's alignment with philosophy in its attention to haecceity of the real; the creativity of art as a temporal process whereby virtualities become actual; and finally, art as a continuity of feeling and expression.

In all of Bergson's works, there is a mixing together of different types of thinking, creativity and action on the basis that they are close to or expressive of *durée*. In *Matter and Memory*, thought is the basic impetus of *durée*, insofar as it is 'striving to transcend the conditions of useful action and to come back to itself as to a pure creative energy'.[55] In *Time and Free Will*, it is about the freedom of each act judged in terms of the extent to which it draws upon the specificity of an individual's past. In *Creative Evolution*, it is the creativity and ramification of life as it engages with matter. There are many examples, but in each case the value of the activity is determined by the degree to which it articulates the variability of *durée* and resists the deployment of static concepts. However, in placing these ideas together, there is a loss of disciplinary difference. Is the pure creative energy discussed in *Matter and Memory* the same as the creative energy invested in making artworks or driving evolution? Is the freedom of the artist identical with the freedom of the philosopher, who both draw upon intuition and the continuity of their past? These questions cannot be decided because Bergson rarely seeks to separate the disciplines, for his interest is in providing an alternative to the main currents of science and philosophy leading up to the early twentieth century rather than developing a set of enduring epistemological claims.

These ideas are necessarily mixed in his work because all derive from his theory of time as *durée*, and, therefore, at some point all will merge into *durée*'s unifying whole. For example, intuition apprehends time as alteration but this apprehension is not given from outside of time as an atemporal conceptualization, for this would undermine the very premise of *durée*. Intuition has to be grounded in an individual's particular time of experience and this means that it is underpinned by a continuity of feeling. Likewise, this continuity of feeling provides empirical evidence of time as *durée*, as it is only through understanding the time of consciousness that one can investigate other times, and the impetus that drives artistic creation and the shift from the virtual to the actual. This latter point is raised in Bergson's last major work, *The Two Sources of Morality and Religion* (1932), where he discusses the importance of the emotions in the context of artistic creation. As Bergson is often dualist in his approach, separating the positive term associated with *durée* from the negative term associated with a spatial conceptualization of time, so too he argues that emotions are of two main types. There are unique emotions, which are fully embedded in the ipseity and time of the individual, and represented emotions that are not specific to any individual and can be readily named – such as generalizable differences between anger, shame, fear and so on. The unique emotion is the ground upon which new ideas are formed and a source of creative energy, curiosity and intellectual engagement.[56]

> It is the emotion above all which vivifies, or rather vitalizes, the intellectual elements with which it is destined to unite, constantly collecting everything that can be worked in with them and finally compelling the enunciation of the problem to expand into its solution. And what about literature and art? A work of genius is in most cases the outcome of an emotion, unique of its kind, which seemed to baffle expression, and yet which *had* to express itself.[57]

The unique emotion cannot be clearly defined through an external frame of reference because it varies with each moment, and this variation is, in itself, a form of creation. Of course, Bergson privileges this type of emotion because it reveals its own temporality, and must be correlated with the positive aspects of artistic creation. However, the emotion underpinning the creative process could be seen as just a fact of *durée* – all states must by necessity undergo qualitative change – and this is indicated by the claim that the emotion '*had* to express itself'. So is the emotion part of a creative process willed by the artist or the author, or is it just a by-product of temporal change? For Bergson, it has to be both, for the durational change immanent to the emotion also describes the intentionality of the philosopher looking to solve a problem or the artist creating a work. The artist or the thinker is driven by the unifying and creative action of the emotion, but their wilfulness and determination is also expressive of a complex emotion that continually alters. In *durée*, the emotion, the creative urge or the individual's will cannot be clearly separated, for they are different facets of the same impulse.

In maintaining a strong line between emotion, genius and the absolute ipseity of creative expression, Bergson is in some respects a romantic thinker, and again this attests to the fact that his thought is grounded in the nineteenth century, while also ushering in philosophical and artistic Modernism. Where he differs is in his metaphysical justification for the creative activity, his constant reference to philosophical intuition as the principal means of revealing the real and the important role of *durée* as the principle of creative differentiation. In *Laughter*, Bergson refers again to the creative richness of Shakespeare and the quasi-biological process through which each character is engendered by the personality of the author. It is notable that he does not mention one of most acknowledged features of Shakespeare's work, the inventiveness of his language, despite the fact that this argument appears in a work that examines the structure of the comic, including comic language. What drives the creation of the work of art, and he here refers specifically to poetry and drama, is the playing out of an artist's inner struggle, which becomes manifest in the differentiation of characters:[58]

> To retrace one's steps, and follow to the end the faintly distinguishable directions, appears to be the essential element in poetic imagination. Of course, Shakespeare was neither Macbeth, nor Hamlet, nor Othello; still, he *might have been* these several characters if the circumstances of the case on the one hand, and the consent of his will on the other, had caused to break out into explosive action what was nothing more

than an inner prompting. We are strangely mistaken as to the part played by poetic imagination, if we think it pieces together its heroes out of fragments filched from right and left, as though it were patching together a harlequin's motley. Nothing living would result from that. Life cannot be recomposed; it can only be looked at and reproduced. Poetic imagination is but a fuller view of reality. If the characters created by a poet give us the impression of life, it is only because they are the poet himself, – a multiplication or division of the poet, – the poet plumbing the depths of his own nature in so powerful an effort of inner observation that he lays hold of the potential in the real, and takes up what nature has left as a mere outline or sketch in his soul in order to make of it a finished work of art.[59]

In this characterization of artistic activity, everything is linked back to *durée* and intuition, which is as much a reflective practice, where the poet delves back into the ipseity of their inner life to allow an initial creative urge to 'break out into explosive action', as it is the production of novelty. Artistic activity must be understood through the continuity of time, in which novelty is dependent on the actualization of inner virtual tendencies in the completed form of the external work. The past of the artist always coexists with the present of the work. The 'heroes' are not external constructions based in the manipulation of language, because this would mean they have lost their connection to the writer or artist's *durée*, and without the continuity of time they would appear artificial.

Bergson does not discuss this idea in reference to particular literary genres except for his contrast between the comic and dramatic in *Laughter*, but Shiv Kumar argues that *le roman fleuve* or stream of consciousness novel has many affinities with Bergson's theory of intuition because it aims to recreate the character from within.[60] In doing so, it differs from the traditional novel because a series of 'nascent states' appear within a character's consciousness that jostle with and impinge upon the character's primary impressions and experiences. Rather than the mere description of a singular experience, each act is underpinned by the interpenetration of a range of experiences and states.[61] This idea of emergent and virtual experiences is what Bergson attributes to the author, but in the stream of consciousness novel this shifts to the character because their identity has to be described through the temporal conditions of consciousness. The creativity of the author is redoubled in the consciousness of the character, in an ongoing process of differentiation and integration. The fact that

Bergson does not directly examine the stream of consciousness novel does not matter, for what is important is that intuition when applied to any situation will reveal emergent processes, or nascent states, virtually integrated into a durational whole. The role of intuition in art or literary criticism is always to resituate any phenomenon, object or event in terms of the emergence of *durée*.

One of the problems with developing an aesthetic theory out of Bergson's claim that philosophy and the arts are both founded in intuition is that the arts are valued only in the degree to which they manifest a philosophical truth. There is only a vague indication of how the arts would operate independently, or what constitutes the particularity of those intuitions favoured or fostered by the arts. Furthermore, it is not demonstrated why art should seek to reveal *durée*, it is just assumed that this is a function of good art, which is always concerned with the real rather than the conditions of its manufacture or creation. This approach has some value as part of a broad aesthetic theory but it is not readily applied to aesthetic judgement within the philosophy of art. Ruth Lorand states that Bergson only mentions art at its most exemplary, that is, in reference to the great works that reveal the truth about *durée*, but also argues that great works cannot be praised unless one can also discuss lesser works that do not possess these exemplary qualities: 'A theory that recognizes only ideal instances is not very useful, especially when it is meant to be relevant to real experience and deal with real objects, not with ideal entities.'[62] In referring to the ideal role of art, Bergson does not have to evaluate the specific features of a work, the practices specific to a medium, or even a particular group of works, because it is largely justified through *durée*. Furthermore, the theory of *durée* should resist any attempt to posit clearly defined and enduring principles. In the exemplary work, art is coincident with philosophy, but it raises the question of what constitutes a derogation of this intuition – at what point does art bar access to the real? The same question can be asked in relation to specific art movements. Should nineteenth-century Realism be preferred to Classicism, because the latter is overly formal in its organization and because the rigidity of form undermines the intuition of time as *durée*? With reference to the difference between mediums, does sculpture have a stronger link to *durée* because the figure is most often presented without the static, structural delimitation of the frame? Bergson never engages with such questions, which is to some degree understandable because he was not specifically interested in aesthetic judgement, but, rather, in co-opting art into his theory of *durée*.

In contrast with Lorand, the conservative critic T. E. Hulme argues that in many ways the lack of a general theory of art and a detailed study of art practice is actually why Bergson's philosophy is best suited to understanding aesthetic experience. He states that the problem with art theory is that it cannot readily posit general concepts that have any degree of consistency and cogency, and it is an area that is overly variegated and subject to change.[63] Hulme does not provide details on why theories of art are lacking rigour, but it is probably due in part to changes in taste, and the fact that art is practised over such a wide range of mediums with different conditions of reception and aesthetic judgement. He argues that what Bergson has revealed instead of an art theory is a detailed metaphysics, or 'account of reality', that provides the basis for any investigation of the arts. This is particularly manifest in Bergson's examination of 'aesthetic emotion' in which, through his 'acute analysis of certain mental processes he has enabled us to state more definitely and with less distortion the qualities which we feel in art.'[64] Bergson's account of aesthetic emotion is largely provided in the books *Laughter* and *Time and Free Will*, and despite Hulme's claim that we 'can state more definitely' the qualities that are felt in response to art, it is not a categorization of emotion, but, rather, an account of how emotion exceeds the very bounds of categorization. Moreover, it is not sufficiently extrapolated to properly address the differences between the arts, because as a theory of *durée*, it always extends beyond any material iteration. However, Bergson does provide the basis for a full rethinking of aesthetic emotion in terms of the duration of qualitative variation and, in this, his work has more value than many others that make overly prescriptive claims about the constitution of feeling.

Another way of considering the relationship between philosophy and art is to consider them as different stages in an intuitive and processual engagement with the real. Rather than stating that art and philosophy have the same intuition, it might be better to place them in a differential but complementary relationship, which supports Bergson's statement that the arts are a species of philosophy, or are at least imbued with a philosophical disposition. Arthur Szathmary argues that Bergson should have placed 'aesthetics as a prelude to metaphysics', for aesthetics concerns itself with a primary attention to the real that can be expanded and developed in philosophy. In aesthetic perception artists would derive the 'first abstractions' that are inextricably tied to the reality of duration, whereas philosophy should seek to transform these first abstractions into 'secondary abstractions' that better correlate with general principles.[65] Philosophy should never be separated from the aesthetic intuitions, as they provide the ground, albeit a variable one, for philosophical reasoning: 'In order to attain its full articulation philosophy must go beyond aesthetics; but without aesthetics as its fundamental point of departure it would be valueless and without content – "a form enclosing a vacuum".'[66] Grounding Bergson's philosophy in aesthetics is a reasonable proposition for, as we have already noted, Bergson's writing displays an aesthetic sensibility, and he often foregrounds the importance of the image in its capacity to carry a philosophical idea. The problem, however, rests in using the term 'abstraction' to describe an aesthetic practice, for it assumes that the role of art is to provide concepts that can then be developed into principles. This notion of an abstraction is not something that can be readily incorporated into Bergsonism due to Bergson's rejection of any type of knowledge built on an edifice of immutable principles. In line with Bergson's own statements, it might be more appropriate to talk about images, mobile concepts or even primary sketches as a means of linking philosophy and art. A sketch differs from a representation because it describes a particular way of seeing through the object rather than substituting for it, that is, it is a map of a certain type of perceptual engagement. The sketch is more mobile than the representation due to the implied movement of the line that follows the contours of the real, and the fact that it presents itself as unfinished.

Bergson gestures towards such an approach in a letter to Harald Höffding, who had written an extended critique of Bergson's philosophy.[67] Bergson commended Höffding for the diligence and impartiality of his approach, but was keen to correct some of the claims, in particular the conflation of the relationship between art and philosophy. He accepts the argument that both begin with a founding intuition of life, but states that philosophy progresses much further than art because it incorporates both intelligence and intuition as it comes to terms with the broader issues of matter and mind. Artistic intuition, in its interrogation of the 'vital', is restricted to concrete intuitions or impressions of life that appear as a scattering (*éparpillement*) of images, whereas philosophy is able to draw these images together in order to disclose the movement underpinning them.[68] Philosophy does not create secondary abstractions that are added to the concrete primary abstractions, but, rather, seeks out those generative concepts that provide their motivation and impetus, such as the *élan vital*. The mobility of the philosophical concept is incipient in the artistic image, and the role of the intelligence, and the philosophical language that comes with it, is to give greater breadth to its intuition of *durée*. One could imagine the *éparpillement* of images as philosophical sketches, or preliminary intuitions, manifest in works by a single artist or even the broader process of inquiry invested in each medium. The various artistic practices could be judged in terms of how they reveal a particular line of philosophical inquiry through aesthetic intuition. For example, drawing could trace the movement in the line itself, which does not simply represent an object, but reveals the virtuality of artistic gesture. In photography, it could be derived from the difference in the duration of film exposure to the duration of the human gaze.[69] In cinema, it might be the indication of a particular duration of viewing that exceeds the depiction of objects. In each case it is about the role of aesthetic intuition in providing the primary image of time that can then be reworked through philosophical investigation.

The types of aesthetic intuition are manifold but always depend on relinquishing structures of representation and accentuating those aspects of the medium that reveal the fluidity and continuity of time as *durée*. This type of task is more readily undertaken in mediums that present actual images of time, such as cinema and the performing arts, rather than the visual arts, in which time has to be extracted from the relative fixity of the work. Andrey Tarkovsky argues that cinema is similar in many respects to music in the sense that it deals directly with time as a substance, although it always remains linked to a 'factual' material world and its temporality. Rendering time visible is not only a matter of depicting the movement of physical bodies but also demonstrating that all objects, even those that appear immobile, are actually embedded 'within the actual course of time'.[70] The true mark of the cinematic is that every frame, even when it does not depict movement at all and regardless of its place within a montage sequence, still presents an image of time due to the endurance of the image.[71] From this perspective, each shot could reveal different aspects of *durée* depending on the type of shot, from images of moving water to long takes of immobile bodies. These concrete, aesthetic intuitions could furnish philosophy with a set of images that could be developed into full principles: the water images could lead to a theory of time as turbulence, whereas the images of still objects could be developed into a theory of waiting based on shot duration.[72] What is important in each case is that aesthetic difference – the difference in the sensual properties of the object – becomes a figure by which to generate philosophical ideas. Bergson does not adopt this approach in his own works because he usually begins with a rebuttal of a philosophical or scientific idea, such that references to a particular image or aesthetic intuition are usually used to support the existing critique rather than to generate it.

Another way of thinking of the relationship between art and philosophy from a Bergsonian perspective is proposed by Gilles Deleuze in his cinema books, where he begins with Bergson's processual ontology and uses it to generate formal and qualitative differences immanent to cinema. In *Matter and Memory*, Bergson argues that all matter and consciousness are comprised of images and that perception is just a means of converting material images into action. In placing images at the centre of the ontology, he resolves some of the key problems in philosophy that are associated with the differences between body and mind, as well as perception and matter. Deleuze argues that these images are properly called movement-images because they are identical with '*flowing-matter*' joining together within a 'plane of immanence' and that cinema, due to its capacity to generate and combine images, is a microcosm of this plane.[73] Movement-images are constantly changing 'lines or figures of light' and because they comprise matter, as well as perception and consciousness, everything is light itself, which also entails that '[t]hings are luminous by themselves without anything illuminating them: all consciousness *is* something'.[74] This processual ontology of light and image, in which there are neither solid bodies nor fixed viewpoints, becomes the basis for a conceptualization of cinema. Firstly, Deleuze completely bypasses the role played by an individual consciousness and intuition in forming a bridge between *durée* and physical action, for it is cinema itself that constitutes the ontology of images. This serves to downgrade the importance of the filmmaker and spectator as the key drivers in a theory of art.[75] Secondly, he creates categories of images based on Bergson's argument that perception passes through the body and, in doing so, is transformed into action. This basic schema can be divided into three main stages, the image as perception, the image reflected in the body, and the image as action, which he appropriately names, respectively, the perception-image, the affection-image and action-image.[76] Deleuze argues that there are many other types of images that describe different relationships with the temporal whole, such as memory and time images, all of which can be used to rethink cinema as a processual whole. The shot is no longer a simple container for action, or a frame for the mise en scène but, rather, the extension of particular types of movement that are associated with corporeal, perspectival and even affective changes. It is a novel reworking of Bergson's philosophy that could be adapted for each of the arts, but it relinquishes the grounding of *durée* in the consciously perceiving body, whereby the individual apperception of *durée* in introspection also reveals universal *durée*. It also differs from Bergson's notion of the image, which is something less formed, and, indeed, more incipient, than any individual cinematic shot or frame.

In the study of digital art, Mark Hansen celebrates many aspects of Deleuze's rereading of Bergson's theory of the image, although he notes that in proposing a cinematic ontology, Deleuze does not fully attend to the corporeality of the sensorimotor body inherent in the original theory.[77] In addition to the body's role in selecting images, Hansen foregrounds the affective and corporeal complexity of the body as an image that mediates between perception and action, and how this complexity is increasingly brought into play in response to digital art:

> Active affection or affectivity is precisely what differentiates today's sensorimotor body from the one Deleuze hastily dismisses: as a capacity to experience its own intensity, its own margin of indeterminacy, affectivity comprises a power of the body that cannot be assimilated to the habit-driven, associational logic governing perception.[78]

Bergson's theory of image is ideally suited to understanding new media art because it describes the virtual action of framing through a body that is not fixed to a concrete perspectival position.[79] Hansen argues that digital artworks such as Robert Lazzarini's *skulls* (2000), in which anamorphic digital images of skulls are fabricated in bone and mounted on a gallery wall, draw upon the tension implicit to a body that constantly redirects perception into action. Because the distended forms do not allow the viewer to adopt a position that will reconstitute typical three-dimensional perspective, the body refracts and creates new haptic and affective spaces underpinning vision.[80] The body's capacity to filter and select creates the spatial world, rather than spatiality serving as the condition for understanding the body. The transmutation of space through the body allows for a greater degree of indeterminacy and foregrounds the affective qualities in any conceptualization of space. Hansen argues that

Bergson's theory can be further expanded to consider digital images in which 'the body now operates by filtering *information* directly and, through this process, *creating* images' rather than selecting pre-existing images.[81] Hansen rightly points out the value of certain aspects of Bergson's philosophy in rethinking new media, and the ontology of images is certainly one of Bergson's most remarkable ideas. However, the problem with adapting particular aspects of Bergson's philosophy to a new theory of art is that they are not easily supported by the theory of *durée*. De Mille and Mullarkey argue that too often Bergson's name has been associated with Deleuzian concepts without sufficient attention given to how they are placed within Bergson's overall philosophy.[82] In many respects, Hansen operates within the shadow of Deleuze rather than in the immanence, ipseity and uncertainty of Bergsonian *durée*. For Bergson, the founding role of *durée* must precede any discussion of material and spatial derivatives from the body through to the image. The body may, indeed, filter information but it can only do so because time endures in all its qualitative variability, and it is this qualitative variability that is always foregrounded in any reference to aisthesis or aesthetic engagement.

There is a difference between positing an aesthetic ontology as a provocation for philosophical speculation and actually developing a Bergsonian aesthetic theory that is integrated with a philosophy of art and art practice. The latter requires a return to conditions of spectatorship and artistic production not necessarily supported by the intuition of *durée* as an exemplary state. For what is an examination of art or the sensual aspects of perception without clear reference to forms, patterns and styles? Dresden explains that one of the reasons why Bergson did not write on art directly is that he overly emphasized the ineffability of *durée* and art's role in revealing it.[83] How is it possible to understand the specific practices and forms of art by always referring to a founding condition that must in principle remain elusive? It is notable that Bergson does not discuss specific artistic practices and the role of expression, which are fundamental to understanding aesthetics from the point of view of the artist, nor does he discuss the structural features of a work or medium and how they affect reception.[84] With reference to poetry, Dresden states that Bergson effectively asks the reader to forget the materiality of language by imagining that they are directly incorporated into the interiority of *durée*.[85] Disregarding the formal properties of the artworks is also a feature of Bergson's discussion of music, the medium that he regards as most closely linked to *durée*, which must have structure in order to develop melodies and themes.[86] In all the arts, there are structures of repetition and principles of organization that give form to the sensual and render it coherent, which does not mean that each work is reducible to these forms and patterns. In music, these principles could include harmony and rhythm; in literature, syntax, rhyme, assonance; and in the visual arts, colour balance, planar division and the Gestalt law of *Prägnaz*. It is difficult to disregard such principles by referring only to the ontological status of the work, or to an untethered and ineffable *durée*.

The problem in describing the structural form of artistic works stems from Bergson's rejection of spatial markers in the description of time, movement or change, in addition to his critique of representation. Maurice Merleau-Ponty states that Bergson, in his rejection of space as an abstraction, does not provide another means of anchoring movement in a meaningful way and that he could have retained a notion of spatiality if he considered it as 'primordial' rather than abstract.[87] Bergson does refer to a notion of space that is thoroughly linked to time, extensity, which will be discussed in Chapter 4, but Merleau-Ponty is nevertheless correct in arguing that there needs to be something to anchor time and movement, especially when considering the relationship between spectatorship and spatial form. This is particularly important in the visual arts due to the predominance of perduring material objects that retain spatial divisions well beyond the specific time of spectatorship. There has to be some means of accounting for this relative spatial stability, while also attending to the *durée* underpinning the experiences and feelings of the spectator, or, indeed, the lived time of the artist in the act of producing the work.

This requirement that art must have some formal stability, is also raised by Susanne Langer in *Feeling and Form*, in her appraisal of the value of Bergson's philosophy in the study of the arts. Although Bergson does not produce a theory of art, his philosophy has quite rightly had a very significant influence on the arts, due to its focus on the contours of the real and the qualitative variations in the 'passage' of time.[88] However, Langer states that one of the key problems with Bergson's work is that he did not develop figures or concepts to describe the variations in lived time and that if he had done so, he could have produced a 'universal art theory'. His complete aversion to philosophical conceptualization had rendered this impossible, for 'in his horror of a pernicious abstraction, he fled to a realm of no abstraction at all, and having wounded his spirit on the tools of physical science he threw away tools altogether'.[89] Langer imagines that a

Bergsonian universal art theory would be derived from the study of music, because it is the art form that is most closely aligned with lived time and presents qualitative variation in a form that does not require the mediation of physical events, discursive concepts or measurement. 'Bergson's dream (one dares not say "concept" in connection with his thought) of *la durée réelle* brings his metaphysics very close to the musical realm – in fact, to the very brink of a philosophy of art.'[90] This dream was not realized because Bergson focused too much on the continuity of time and not sufficiently on the form of lived time in all its qualitative and dynamic variety.[91] Like Bergson, Langer accepts that lived time is 'actual' – not a mere epiphenomenon or by-product of subjective experience – and that it is organized around the rhythms of everyday life, which music has the capacity to extract and express.[92] What Langer outlines here is a positive account of Bergsonism that extends beyond the critique of spatial concepts into an aesthetic theory in which qualitative variation and temporal rhythms are given greater specificity. It becomes a qualitative study of the variability of temporal figures and rhythms, in the same way that musical forms are variable in lived experience, and it is these flexible figures – indeed, mobile concepts – that could be translated across the arts.

Bergson did not adopt such an approach in part because the theory of *durée* does not allow for abstractions, but also due to his emphasis on direct access to the real provided by aesthetic intuition. Langer states that Bergson overly focused on the 'the actual existence of the object to be depicted' as something disclosed to the artist, rather than on how form and appearance are constituted in art.[93] For Langer, when the artist addresses an object, they do not see the thing in itself, but, rather, the 'semblance, the look of it, and the emotional import of its form' with regard to the medium in which they work.[94] Semblance refers to those qualities of an object that are not restricted to any one of the senses, that relate specifically to our engagement with them outside of their 'practical' function. It is the 'otherness' that separates the object from its function, when appearance is unhinged from the materiality of the object.[95] In the visual arts, this semblance is enacted in a virtual pictorial space, which, despite the fact that it could be derived from the real, has a range of affordances that are specific to the spatial construction of the picture plane.[96] It is the semblance of the object, as a qualitative form, that can be rearticulated within the specific constraints of the medium, which from a Bergsonian position could all be articulated temporally. Visual perspective could be regarded as the semblance of actual space, that is, a virtual space that continually expands and contracts between near and far in the lived time of spectatorship. The processual reworking of spatial principles in terms of the movement of semblance would not supplant the intuition of *durée*, but would certainly produce mobile concepts that are much more amenable to a processual philosophy.

The artist is looking to reveal something about the sensible world, because the work is constructed in order to be perceived and, therefore, communicates something about the real to the spectator. The aesthetician Étienne Souriau states that the philosophy of art should examine the work under the conditions in which it appears.[97] Like Langer, he states that the artist is not directly working with sensation or the subjective state of an audience member, but, rather, with the sensible qualities (*qualités sensibles*) that are manifest in the work, which are not mere psychological properties due to their dependence on the particular medium in which the artist is working.[98] For example, Georges-Pierre Seurat does not directly paint what he sees and, instead, engages with formal aspects of the visible world, such as light, tone and form within the particular realm of possibility of a pointillist way of seeing – a form of visibility comprised of dots of four colours. These phenomenal qualities are not entirely in the visible world or the work, for the dots relate to each other in the virtual space of spectatorship. Langer takes this argument further in her theory of semblance, stating that it is important not to restrict it to spatial parameters, for the artist is also able to extract semblances of time, or the virtual contours of experience that are felt as '*tensions* – physical, emotional, or intellectual'.[99] Tension is a felt quantity that invokes the relationships immanent to a range of movements that alter over time, and cannot be reduced to mere quantity. A movement is something that can be transferred from one body or work to another while maintaining its integrity. Although Bergson does not develop an aesthetics of movement or a theory of semblance or sensible quality, he does examine the transcorporeal aspects of gracefulness in *Time and Free Will*; however, in accentuating the movement, he also strongly diminishes the materiality of the medium.

Bergson's influence on the avant-garde

Although Bergson did not develop a full aesthetic theory nor write an extended work on the philosophy of art, he nevertheless influenced a number of avant-garde artists in the early part of the twentieth century. He was the source of inspiration for many writers and artists even though Bergson himself judged this popularity to be often misplaced and without sufficient consideration of his actual philosophy.[100] Moreover, there is very little indication that Bergson took an interest in modern art even though his daughter, Jeanne, was an artist. While sitting for his portrait with the painter Jacques Émile Blanche, Bergson asked Blanche about Cubism because the Cubists were at the time seeking some type of theoretical foundation for their ideas on the fourth dimension, but the interest was only passing. Despite Blanche's willingness to pursue the topic, Bergson soon turned his attention to Mona Lisa's smile and the work of Leonardo and Raphael.[101] The avant-garde's relationship to Bergsonism was predominantly unidirectional and could be compared to the relationship between Sigmund Freud and the Surrealists, where the attraction to the philosophy is not necessarily based on a close reading of the work but rather on the capacity of the work to offer a new way of thinking about, or seeing, the world. Langer argues that Bergson's philosophy was inspirational because it extended the boundaries of philosophy in a way that could be readily embraced by the arts, in particular, in the rejection of discourse as a means of accessing the real. By contrast, Croce and Santayana wrote directly on art, but their work remained of interest only to philosophers and was not a stimulus for artistic activity.[102] For a philosophy to provide the necessary momentum for artistic activity, it does not have to be strictly about art but it has to be presented in such a way that the ideas can find their way into art. Paul Crowther argues that this is realizable with Bergsonism due to the explicit connection Bergson establishes between philosophy and art, and also the implicit suggestion that 'some form of rigorous artistic expression should supersede traditional forms of philosophizing.'[103] In seeking to overhaul metaphysics such that it attends directly to the movement, feeling and impulsion of lived time, it is not surprising that Bergson's philosophy was popular among the avant-garde in Europe, who were also looking for ideas that could aid them in their desire to make a break from an entrenched bourgeois world view.

Because Bergsonism was very popular in the first decade of the twentieth century, many artists would have been aware of it and felt some compulsion to read and respond to its claims even if they did not have a detailed knowledge of the philosophical context in which it was written. The most notable and sustained response came from the Italian Futurists, who saw in Bergson's theories of time, movement and intuition a means of advancing their own artistic aim of developing a true aesthetics of speed and dynamism. The importance of Bergsonism to the Futurist agenda is clearly established. Bergson's writings were well known in Italy at the *fin de siècle* because they were translated in a number of Italian journals. One of these translators, Giovanni Papini, was also an art critic who had contact with the 'Milanese Futurists', as did another Bergson-inspired art critic Ardengo Soffici.[104] There was significant philosophical debate in Italy after Bergson presented his talk on *L'Intuition philosophique* in April 1911 at the Bologna Congress in a period when the Futurists were at their most productive, as well as in the lead up to the Congress when a collection of Bergson's writings on philosophical intuition was published in Italian.[105] The popularity and accessibility of Bergson's philosophy and the fact that it strongly challenged dominant metaphysical ideas, made it well suited to an avant-garde looking for new sources of inspiration.

The Futurist painters were fascinated by what it means to invoke movement in the visual arts, which was prompted to some degree by the technological reconfiguration of social life in the late nineteenth and early twentieth centuries, including the rise of industrialism and the increase in the speed of transportation. They have often been cited for their celebration of the automobile and war, as well as being the avant-garde movement that most clearly welcomed the machine age. Soffici argues that this subject brought with it new forms of plastic expression that are 'more vibrant, more fragmentary, more abrupt, more chaotic and more nervous' than the traditional subject of the nude, still life and landscape.[106] In this respect, the Futurists seem to have little in common with Bergson, who was keen to critique any degradation of *durée*, life and art by mechanical and fragmentary practices, even going as far as to reject cinema and photography in their attempts to record movement. Moreover, Bergson's sensibility, which was to some degree grounded in nineteenth-century traditions, and his place within the French cultural establishment do not align in any obvious way with the celebration of technologically driven social upheaval. At the beginning of the First World War, Bergson even criticized Germany's martialism derived from a Prussian sensibility, which overemphasized industrialism and materialism instead of giving proper attention to life[107] – a criticism that could quite easily be levelled at the Futurists. However, Bergsonism could also appeal to radicals, most notably George Sorel and his particular brand of syndicalism, because they found in his work a philosophical justification for social change and transformation. Indeed, it was through Sorel's notion of intuitive and creative class struggle, which also inspired the Italian nationalists, that the Futurists indirectly adopted many of Bergson's ideas.[108] In the Sorelian conception of an anti-rational proletarian struggle, the nationalism of Marinetti and Boccioni and the early anarchist and syndicalist leanings of Carlo Carrà and Luigi Russolo could converge, which is made manifest in their paintings in the use of 'force lines' and other dynamic visual tropes to represent crowd struggles.[109] Undoubtedly Bergsonism demonstrates a malleability and breadth that allows it to be co-opted by a range of different social and political groups depending on whether Bergson's theory of time is regarded as a response to technological and scientific change, or a means of explaining social change.

Bergson's philosophy offers many ways to reconsider artistic practice in terms of figures of movement, the persistence of time and the intuition of the real, and can therefore be readily adapted to different political and artistic agendas. Many of the Futurists responded directly to Bergson's temporal philosophy in their art. After reading Bergson's 'Introduction to Metaphysics', Gino Severini painted *Travel Memories*, where he combines and intermingles a series of his own memories into a single image of his home town.[110] Severini may have been inspired by one of the key images in 'Introduction to Metaphysics', where Bergson posits a difference between representing the town externally through a collection of discrete images and encountering the same town through the aleatory act of walking.[111] The example provides the basis for an explanation of intuition, where encountering the town intuitively from within is distinguished from an analytical account, which asymptotically attempts to come to terms with the real by increasing the number of viewpoints. Severini highlights the importance of intuition in his discussion of the painting; however, he also claims that he was most interested in how memories form part of a simultaneity of feeling in time, and where plastic and dynamic qualities exceed spatial organization.[112] Brian Petrie argues that the work of Severini and Luigi Russolo, a futurist painter who was strongly interested in the relationship between music and movement in the visual arts, adopted a 'relatively crude psychologism' when it came to responding to Bergson's philosophy, by mapping psychic states onto a visual space rather than truly engaging with the metaphysical ideas.[113] Petrie's criticism is to some degree valid, although it raises the question about what it means to render *durée* visible in an artwork: Should it be the subject of the work, as in Severini's depiction of the interpolation of memory in *Travel Memories*, or should it only be divulged indirectly in the artist's general vision or style?

The psychological interpretations of Severini and Russolo can be contrasted with the art and writings of Umberto Boccioni, a key theoretical protagonist among the Futurists, who fully understood not only the philosophical implications of the endurance of memory but also the value of Bergson's ontology of images in bringing into question the very status of matter.[114] Umberto Boccioni makes reference in his writings to the indivisibility of experience and the impossibility of fully dividing the material world into independent bodies, and demonstrates he had read and annotated *Matter and Memory* by directly citing it in his manifesto, 'The Plastic Foundations of Futurist Sculpture and Painting'.[115] In this article, Boccioni finds in Bergson's philosophy a type of 'physical transcendentalism' in which there are no discrete objects or an intervening 'empty-space', but, rather, a processual whole in which matter reveals itself in the interpenetration of 'intensities'. In this ontology, most readily exhibited as physical vibration, the artist should not try to depict objects and their capacity to move but, instead, try to reveal the movements that traverse matter.[116] Although the Futurists were inspired by the speed and movement of transportation and industrialization in the modern city, for Boccioni the proper subject is the quality and 'feeling' of this movement.[117] He advocates a concrete notion of feeling that is fully invested in matter and can be distinguished from the Italian tradition in sculpture in which feeling and movement are 'diaphanous' or 'sentimental'.[118] Boccioni draws upon a range of Bergsonian ideas, including the processual ontology of *Matter and Memory* and the notion of immeasurable intensities and emotions in *Time and Free Will*, but he is much more focused on the material and plastic implications of these ideas than Bergson. There is also a difference in sentiment because Boccioni strongly engages with an external visible world in which the speed and intensity of material bodies are foregrounded, which differs from Bergson's accounts of grace and other forms of aesthetic feeling that gently give way to the rhythms of consciousness.

To some degree these differences can be attributed to misreadings of Bergson's work, but they also derive from thinking about similar questions in different mediums and with regard to different subjects. Boccioni had to consider the value of a processual ontology underpinned by *durée* in relation to the material conditions of sculpture and painting, as well as a visual environment of the modern city characterized by an increase in the intensity of mobility. Boccioni could accept that the conscious internal experience of motion is absolute, he was also more ready to examine the value of relative motion between moving bodies, despite the fact that it involves an external viewpoint.[119] Relative motion refers to the relative speeds and movements of physical bodies and how they are manifest to a spectator, which is something that Bergson does not really discuss except as part of a critique of the spatialization of time. Boccioni is confronted with the practical problem of how to depict moving objects in a way that properly indicates that they are not at rest, and this involves thinking about the nature of relative movement. In the 1914 manifesto 'Absolute Motion + Relative Motion = Dynamism', he argues that relative motion describes a quality of speed that is irreducible to the displacement of the object in space and that when combined with absolute motion gives rise to a true dynamism.[120] This conjunction of relative and absolute motion can be examined through the mobile living body, in which there is both an internal feeling of continuous change and an external form of visible animated movement. Notably, much of Boccioni's experimentation was undertaken in sculpture, where the internal impetus of the moving body has to be made visible to a spectator, which requires some indication of relative movement.

In Boccioni's most famous sculpture, *Unique Forms of Continuity in Space* (1913), the solid bronze figure pushes forward, demonstrated by the fixity of the gaze, the slightly tilted head, and the length of the stride with its strong diagonal lines extending up through a leaning torso (see Figure 1.1). The forceful indication of direction also invokes the intense internal feeling of human effort required to propel the body, which can be contrasted with *Development of a Bottle in Space* (1912), where movement coalesces around a central and vertical figure of a bottle. In addition to the implication of forward movement, the body is distended by an implied internal force, expanding out through the musculature into the surrounding space. Forward orientation and effort are central to the work, but speed is also a factor that can be considered outside of internal motivation. When we see a car or train rushing forward there is an indication of the intensity of speed even without the invocation of the internal power that drives it, human or machine. The faster a body moves, the more it exceeds the capacity of perception to render it fully intelligible, with clear outlines and simple location. It is not a body that can be visually contained, for in its movement it is always outstripping our capacity to appraise it as a whole and, therefore, can appear as a

FIGURE 1.1 Umberto Boccioni. *Unique Forms of Continuity in Space* (1913).

body stretching out into space. In *Unique Forms of Continuity in Space*, the expansion of the body has a dual purpose in joining the absolute motion of effort with the relative perception of a body at speed, which is central to Boccioni's Futurist dynamism. Stephen Kern states that there was a progression from Boccioni's early *Synthesis of Human Dynamism* through *Speeding Muscles*, to *Unique Forms of Continuity in Space* in which the body lost many of its distinguishing features as the depiction of movement became increasingly streamlined.[121] Streamlining may be Boccioni's solution to representing speed at the very point when it overcomes the physicality of the body, despite the fact that the sculpture is cast in bronze that carries with it a visual weight that undermines the usual association of speed with ephemerality.[122] By contrast, Bergson never properly engages with speed as a quality in its own right because he usually works centrifugally from the interiority of conscious experience, or the impetus of life, to a spatial manifestation, rather than centripetally from perceptual experience to the immanence of time. However, he does indicate the limitations of perception in addressing the movements of vibrations that exceed certain thresholds of perception – a theme that will be examined in more detail in Chapter 4. Boccioni's work demonstrates that an artist's engagement with the visual conditions of movement could also lead to the depiction of movement in a way that confirms Bergson's theory of *durée*, a process that is somewhat necessary if Bergsonism is to realize itself as an aesthetic theory.

The Futurists clearly demonstrated in their manifestos and the pictorial examination of time and movement an interest in Bergson's philosophy, but it had a much less obvious role of shaping other art movements. It would be easy to presume that Cubism, which investigated spatial perspective by breaking objects down into planes and facets, would not readily lend itself to a philosophy of time and a theory of intuition that emphasizes the dynamic interpenetration of qualitative differences. However, according to Mark Antliff, the Puteaux Cubists, principally Albert Gleizes and Jean Metzinger, considered Cubism to have a temporal dimension whereby, over time, the spectator resolves the pictorial planes into a visual unity.[123] Unlike the recognition of everyday objects, the Cubist pictorial object does not immediately appear and depends on the viewer to unite the parts over a more protracted period. Due to this emphasis on temporal unity, the Puteaux Cubists sought Bergson's approval, but the philosopher did not support their appropriation of his ideas because he thought that they deployed a theoretical method rather than artistic intuition in the creation of their works.[124] The incompatibility of aesthetic intuition with intellectual or material methods cannot be easily resolved, because intuition involves the primary apprehension of *durée*, whereas a spatial method requires a secondary process in which the object of the aesthetic vision is decomposed into parts, each of which is only a partial view of the whole. The same criticism could be levelled at the Impressionists and Futurists, who used divisionist techniques, whereby brushstrokes and colours are separated in the production of the work, but are nevertheless resolved in the act of viewing. The use of such methods imposes a theoretical and temporal gap between the primary unity of vision and the finished work, which is somewhat of a problem for Bergsonism, because the painter cannot simply depict what they see in order to reproduce the temporal quality and feeling implicit in their aesthetic vision for a spectator.[125] The painter cannot paint *durée*, the medium does not allow this, but they can create a semblance of the movement inherent in the visible world via these visual methods.

Analytical Cubism is strongly driven by a reconsideration of the relationship between perceptual surfaces and objects in the form of slight variations in perspective, which differs from many forms of representational art, in particular Renaissance perspective, which adopt a singular fixed point of view. Antliff argues that Gleizes and Metzinger criticized the theory of perspective, which in its adoption of perspectival lines divested painting of the time immanent to visual perception and that, instead, vision should be regarded as a movement underpinned by a 'synaesthetic fusion of sensations'.[126] According to this critique, the theory of pictorial perspective is a scientific method that orders the visual field according to principles unaligned with aesthetic intuition and the lived experience of the artist. Instead, the Puteaux Cubists sought a form of perspective that is thoroughly inflected with the artist's vision and personality, as well as invested with felt quality.[127] In addition to surrounding and delimiting objects, space is revealed corporeally and dynamically through the motor and perceptual functions, and because the body joins consciousness to the world, also entails 'the interrelation of consciousness and feeling'.[128] Metzinger and Gleizes state in *Du 'cubisme'* (*On 'Cubism'*) that, despite the analysis of planes, Cubism is not primarily interested in a conceptualization of space but, instead, addresses how tactile and motor sensations traverse and unify space in a manner that involves the engagement of the whole subject, as well as how 'our whole personality which, in contracting or expanding, transforms the plane of the painting' (*notre personnalité entière qui, se contractant ou se dilatant, transforme le plan du tableau*).[129] In order to further demonstrate Cubism's relationship to temporal philosophy, there are also remarks on the depth of *durée* and the rhythm implicit in the visual arts.[130] Although there are no direct references to Bergsonism in *Du 'cubisme'*, Antliff argues that these ideas are remarkably similar to many of Bergson's, in particular the importance accorded to the engagement of the whole personality in truly creative and free acts in *Time and Free Will*,[131] an idea that is also discussed in *Matter and Memory*, as well as the fusion of material and visual differences in perception.

The Cubism of Braque and Picasso was not initiated or provoked by Bergsonian ideas, nor was the main impetus of this artistic movement Bergsonian, and therefore it is likely that the Puteaux Cubists introduced their philosophical explanation retroactively in order to provide a broader psychological context for the works. It is noteworthy that the Puteaux Cubists primarily focus on the reception of the work and not the specific production practices, and, in doing so, foreground the aesthetic vision realized in the finished work and not the primary conception. In the initial aesthetic vision, the artist might approach the object through an analytic method, accepting that at some point the painting will constitute a unity for the spectator, whereby all the painterly gestures will be integrated into the single expanse of the picture plane. Antliff notes that the approach outlined in *Du 'cubisme'* establishes a principle of simultaneity in which the object is understood temporally as a sequence of views and this can be distinguished from a Kantian simultaneity in which the multiple views are a function of the analytical understanding of the object.[132] This process is teleological, for the temporal, spectatorial unity retroactively explains all aspects of the image, including the method of analytical division. For Gleizes and Metzinger, the Cubist separation of planes is necessarily temporal because it serves as a condition for the spectator's unifying vision, which actively generates form as well as a certain level of dynamism and depth.[133] The movement inherent in spectatorship draws together the parts of the whole in a way that retains movement as a subsistent tension between the planes and facets. As long as there is qualitative variation in this movement towards unity, the work can be discussed in terms of Bergsonian *durée*, regardless of whether there was an attempt to engage with the ideas initially.

Timothy Mitchell argues that Hermetic Cubism, a Cubist phase that appeared briefly in the years 1910–12, could be aligned with

Bergson's process ontology due to its accentuation of the continuity and interconnection of the whole visual field.[134] During this period, Picasso and Braque were beginning to experiment with the relationship between figure and ground. A key feature was to bring the ground forward to accord it equal status with the figure, and therefore diminish the role that empty space plays in articulating the figure.[135] Mitchell elevates this painterly principle of creating unity through the contraction of depth to the level of a metaphysic, and he states in relation to Picasso's *Accordionist* and Braque's *Man with a Guitar* that

> [t]here is no sense of solid form distinguished from its surroundings; it is replaced by a shifting ambience in which the distinctions between space and matter are no longer visible. The uniformity of brush stroke and surface texture unite the entire canvas. A strong sense of a common substance, now fluid, now solid, comprises the whole. It is as if, to paraphrase Bergson, the individuality of the body had been reabsorbed in the universal interaction, which is without doubt reality itself.[136]

The argument that Hermetic Cubism is underpinned by a Bergsonian ontology has some credence, but the problem is determining whether or not the unity of the picture plane – something that is a key feature of Modernist painting leading into abstraction – can be readily reconciled with *durée*. Picasso and Braque were predominantly interested in spatial unity during this period, in which case the fluid temporal unity might actually be an unintended effect rather than the expression of a founding aesthetic intuition. Indeed, Norman Bryson argues that Cubism was interested in still life because it was the genre that provided the most 'legible anchor-points' to facilitate the recognition of objects. The ontological experiments with fragmented viewpoints are possible only because the images are grounded in easily recognizable objects, indicated by such elements as the fragment of written text on the outline of a bottle neck.[137] The tension between the still life and the multiplicity of viewpoints creates dynamic effects but this is quite different from Futurism, which tried to come to terms with dynamism itself. It is worthwhile, in this context, distinguishing between a founding dynamism and the dynamism of spectatorship, which are linked but not necessarily identical.

The popularity of Bergsonism in the early part of the twentieth century meant that it could not easily be ignored, especially by artists working as part of an avant-garde and looking to find a place in a milieu of rapidly changing ideas. This does not mean that Bergsonism was readily adopted by all groups, for to argue against Bergson is also a means of establishing a theoretical and artistic identity. This was most evident in the British avant-garde movement, Vorticism, particularly in the claims of its central figure, Wyndham Lewis, who spent time in Paris between 1902 and 1908 and praised Bergson's proficiency as a speaker after seeing him lecture. It is even suggested that before the magazine *Blast* was established and the movement developed the name Vorticism, that Lewis's paintings were underpinned by Bergsonian ideas due to their emphasis on 'energy, matter, and creation'.[138] Lewis did not acknowledge his debt and later denounced Bergsonism despite admitting its crucial role in the development of literary and artistic Modernism, which Mary Ann Gillies attributes to Lewis's wish to distinguish himself from 'mainstream Modernism'[139] – in effect he was rejecting a mainstream that was itself rejecting other traditions – as well as his desire not to appear to be influenced by other thinkers.[140] Bergsonism was popular in part because it offered a nominalist critique of scientific discourse and created a space in which freedom, creativity and spiritualism could flourish, but this popularity also meant that within particular intellectual and artistic circles, it could be associated with the mainstream.

The name Vorticism was first used by Ezra Pound in an interview to describe the group's work in terms of the vortex – the stable but most intensely energetic point in the middle of a cyclone. This notion of a vortex bore a relationship to some of the works, in particular those by Lewis, in which geometric patterns coalesce around a receding negative central space. Nevertheless, it is an odd term to use for an art movement that is geometrical in orientation, with clear rigid lines and angular forms. Gillies states that this guiding image of the vortex, in which the artist was placed at the centre of a greater flux of movement, was further proof of Bergsonian influence,[141] but if this is the case, it is not a straightforward positive influence. In the declamatory paper, 'Our Vortex', Lewis notes the temporal aspects of the artistic vortex, but states that it is thoroughly grounded in a present that is divided from the past and future, for the processual aspects of time are lesser features of life and not of value to art.[142] In this focus on the present and the point of stability, the image of the vortex appears to be a denial of Bergson's *durée*, which is grounded in the interpenetration of the past, present and future. However, it is a denial that nevertheless invokes the very thing it seeks to reject, similar to

Freud's analysand who asserts 'It is *not* my mother', in which the stronger the denial, the greater the proof of influence.[143]

This denunciation of Bergsonism could also be linked to the Vorticists' ambition to distinguish themselves from the Futurists, who were another early influence on the group. Before the group had properly formed under the banner of Vorticism, they were often mistaken for Futurists by a British public, who were acquainted with the Italian artists following a series of Futurist exhibitions in London.[144] When it came to distancing themselves from the Futurists, one of the main criticisms was the Futurist accentuation of dynamic moment and the acceptance of a Bergsonian notion of time.[145] So despite the image of the vortex, which could easily be associated with the movement, emotion and even the *Sturm und Drang* of Romanticism, Lewis states that the 'apprehension of reality is best accomplished by the intellect, working from outside on a field of static matter', and argues that painting with its emphasis on sight is the highest of the arts and that music is much lower due to its attachment to the emotions.[146] This opposition to Romantic sentiment in art was derived in some part from the work of Wilhelm Worringer, who argued that art must transcend life and remain 'sharply defined and wedded to the line',[147] but Lewis nevertheless invokes Bergson's distinction between intellect and intuition. In adopting the intellect as the principal means of accessing the real, Lewis inverts Bergson's dichotomy and implicitly rejects intuition, a form of apprehension that is often discussed using examples of music and emotion.

In the journal *Blast*, Lewis wrote a series of invectives against the conflation of life and art, arguing that life is not an appropriate subject for art, nor should it be used to evaluate works, because it lacks specificity and effectively substitutes for a proper discussion of art itself. He lists Bergson as one of a number of thinkers who falsely rely on the notion of life to discuss art and associates this attention to life with Modernist movements such as Impressionism, and even goes so far as to argue that Bergson is a 'philosopher of Impressionism'.[148] The link between Bergson and Impressionism is not properly established and could simply be based on conflating two sets of ideas that Lewis had chosen to reject, but it is noteworthy that Bergsonian ideas were also used by the Futurists and Puteaux Cubists as a means of distancing themselves from Impressionism. Gleizes and Metzinger argue that Impressionism is a 'superficial realism' (*réalisme superficiel*) that engages only with what appears on the retina, and consequently fails to address the spirit of the work and the proper formation of appearances.[149] Despite the fact that many of these founding statements are coherent only in their opposition, the criticism that life is too readily used in the analysis and evaluation of art is legitimate, especially when the actual physical attributes of art are ignored. This is certainly a limitation of a number of Bergson's aesthetic claims, particularly in *Laughter*, where the value of art is directly related to its alignment with life, but where the attributes of life are to some degree malleable. On the whole, in the Vorticist's determination to break with tradition, there is no proper engagement with Bergsonism, which is largely deployed as a shibboleth in internecine avant-garde politics.

Bergson's influence on the avant-garde extended across Europe, with each movement extracting those aspects of his philosophy that served their particular agenda for social or aesthetic change. According to Hilary Fink, the Russian Modernists were particularly interested in the neo-Romantic qualities of intuition and *durée*, for it presented an alternative to rationalism in the form of a 'more pragmatic philosophy of life [. . .] compatible with the modernist revolt in Russia, Europe, and America against the often dehumanizing philosophical conventions of nineteenth-century scientific determinism'.[150] This was quite a contrast to the Vorticists and Futurists, who did not regard determinism or scientism as something that they needed to reject, for they retained a strong interest in and support for technological change. For Russian Modernism part of the appeal of Bergsonism was due to its radically new 'secular' vision of 'art and life',[151] rather than a conservative appeal to tradition. A distinctive feature of Bergson's method is the willingness to address the expansion of scientific thought on its own ground, and to invoke notions of creativity without recourse to transcendentalism.

The influence of Bergsonism on Russian Modernism was most marked in the field of 'Symbolist aesthetics', in which there was not only a rejection of 'nineteenth-century mechanism' and rationalism but also a rejuvenation of the notion of an inviolable 'interior life'.[152] The Symbolists argued that through the use of symbols, art could penetrate into the interior of things and access the absolute,[153] an argument that calls forth intuition and the value of concrete images in providing an indirect means of engaging with the real. This focus on the creativity of the inner life motivated a number of artists, including the Futurist composer and artist, Mikhail Matiushin, who used Bergsonism to argue that the Italian Futurists overly focus on external rather than internal movement.[154] This is certainly true, as the Italian Futurists sought to address relative motion and speed in their works and therefore they could not fully accede to a notion of *durée* in which the very vehicles of movement disappear. The debt to Bergson was not always acknowledged or made explicit. Fink argues that Kasimir Malevich's writings often mirrored Bergsonian ideas despite the fact that there is no direct reference to the philosopher, and his paintings sought to represent movement as a 'dynamic essence' in contrast to the much more static work of the Cubists.[155] It may have also inspired some of the ideas in Wassily Kandinsky's *Concerning the Spiritual in Art*, in particular when he talks about the importance of the 'vital impetus', in which the artist as part of a spiritual avant-garde is guided by 'feeling' as they strive towards the 'immaterial'. This can be contrasted with most forms of philosophy and science, which look back and cling to what is already known.[156] This interest in a vital spiritualism was also adopted by artists outside of Russia, including the Czech painter František Kupka whose paintings sought to link the creative act with the continuity and movement of spirit, life and the cosmos.[157] What Bergsonism offered for many of these artists was a way a thinking about change and creativity that is strongly grounded in a theory of life and evolution, and, yet, still allows room for spiritualism, which notably Bergson also directly addresses late in his career in *The Two Sources of Morality and Religion*. Bergson's philosophy always gestures beyond its own epistemological limits due to its celebration of time as change, an openness to the future that would have attracted many in the avant-garde.

Conclusion

The readiness of the avant-garde to deploy Bergson's ideas was in large part due to the popularity of Bergsonism, for it is difficult to ignore a theory that is regularly discussed and debated in intellectual and artistic circles. In many cases, the reading of the work is superficial and not entirely germane to the uses to which it is put, but what these examples demonstrate is the adaptability and breadth of the ideas. Although there is no readily applicable aesthetic, Bergson's openness to matters of creativity and life, as well as the aesthetic sensibility in his writing, would have been appealing to many artists. Bergson is attentive to aesthetic differences despite his enduring interest in the sciences, which is manifest in his use of concrete images and mobile concepts, and his insistence that metaphysics must attend to the haecceity of things. The fact that the Futurists were able to draw out of the description of force lines in *Matter and Memory* a concrete image of dynamic movement is testament to Bergson's unusual ability to combine scientific ideas with a poetic metaphysics. In all his major works, there are key guiding images that give form to time and movement, and create a bridge between philosophy and art. These images cannot be drawn together as unchanging parts in a system, nor can they be aggregated to comprise an aesthetics, for they work, instead, as creative concepts that push the philosophy into new fields, and inspire artists and philosophers to do likewise. Not only does the philosophy appeal to artists for its creativity and aesthetic vision but, importantly for the avant-garde, it also proposes a break with the past. Each artistic movement chooses to eschew a different past, ranging from the torpor of bourgeois life to the rigidity of scientism, which can be supported by a Bergsonian idea from the notion of enduring change, the creative division implied in life, to the image of an immanent time that overflows matter. Another reason why Bergson's ideas are so adaptable is that they appear at first to be very general, and this is also why they are often misunderstood. The most obvious example is the populist assumption that intuition is something immediate and untutored, whereas for Bergson it also involves the ability to think within the endurance of things and thus resist the normal inclinations of our perception. Even the notion of the *élan vital* can often be confused with the free and conscious creative act, when, in fact, it is also grounded in material becoming. To some degree these problems are due to the peculiarity of Bergson's method, in which he seeks broad metaphysical principles that can integrate smaller concepts in movement rather than conceptual generalities that strip the idea of any particularity. His philosophy cannot be applied capriciously, because it demands that every idea still remains attached to the real in its becoming. There is always an attention to the sensuality of things as revealed in enduring perception, and this is why Bergsonism always borders on aesthetics. The role of the philosopher and, indeed, artist is to recover the initial impetus of these ideas and images, and then reimagine their reworking in new sensual contexts.

2 GESTURE

Aesthetic experience in Bergson's work is associated with the temporality of mind and spirit, and can be contrasted with science, which is materially orientated and characterized by extension, measurement and the clear division between objects. This distinction operates throughout Bergson's oeuvre, although it becomes much more nuanced in later works when both art and science are repositioned to accommodate the theory of intuition, and his pluralistic, processual ontology is sufficiently expanded to incorporate matter. In *Time and Free Will*, aesthetic responses to art are examined in relation to *durée*, where the deepest aesthetic feelings are most fully integrated into the time of consciousness. Bergson examines how movement in art, particularly the performing arts, is valued aesthetically in terms of the degree to which it can overcome the perceived materiality of bodies. Unfortunately, these discussions are not explicitly framed in terms of aesthetic theory or the analysis of specific artworks, for they are largely deployed to articulate a metaphysics of qualitative difference and to critique the quantification of time. The discussion of aesthetics and movement also reveals some of Bergson's early influences, including the philosopher Herbert Spencer, whose writings on the material conditions of aesthetic feeling provide a platform for understanding how the movement of bodies is itself a form of feeling that can provoke the movement of consciousness. One of the most significant aspects of Bergson's discussion of movement and dematerialization in the arts is his emphasis on the body and gesture, in particular the graceful gesture, and how this can be associated with particular contours of feeling and the removal of the impression of effort. Bergson is often criticized (see Merleau-Ponty and Dufrenne) for his overemphasis on the intuition of duration to the exclusion of all spatial and material properties, but this early discussion of intervening corporeal states gives some indication of how duration can be revealed through the body in the performing arts, and how this corporeality underpins the creative gesture in the visual arts, in particular, the line in drawing and the brushstroke in painting.

Introspection, corporeality and the aesthetic feelings

Bergson does not provide many explicit statements on the aesthetic properties of individual art forms, for art is usually a vehicle for the examination of duration and the ontology of creativity. However, in his early works *Time and Free Will* and *Laughter*, he directly engages with aesthetic theories concerning the nature of drama and comedy, the sensuality of movement in dance and music and the constitution of aesthetic feeling. In *Time and Free Will*, in the lead up to Bergson's first extended discussion of *durée*, aesthetic feelings provide evidence of the ipseity of conscious experience and, because they are not susceptible to physical or quantitative explanation, also serve as a prelude to Bergson's critique of determinism. Alongside the explication of the conscious depth of feeling, Bergson also highlights the continuity and fluidity of aesthetic movement, in particular graceful movement, in his discussion of dance and the visual arts. Gracefulness describes the quality of those movements that follow a gentle rhythm, and because there are no abrupt changes, the spectator can follow the movement with a reasonably clear expectation of future states. In general, the aesthetic feelings have the capacity to implicate consciousness in a movement that extends beyond the present material conditions of the artwork or performance. They gesture towards the future in a way that other feelings, such as pain, cannot. The aesthetic feelings are also the highest example of intensive states, or those conscious states that can only be revealed through introspection because they are so thoroughly integrated into the temporality of consciousness. They do not have properly external properties and are, therefore, resistant to scientific measurement and evaluation or any attempt to fully compartmentalize them.

Time and Free will does not set out to define aesthetic feelings because these form part of a broader argument about the irreconcilability of intensity and extensity. The book addresses the theory of art from within a polemic against scientism and positivism, an approach that came to distinguish Bergson in French intellectual circles. At that time sociology was becoming increasingly popular within French universities as a science of society. Bergson was writing at the same time as the sociologist Emile Durkheim, although each represented different elements of the French educational system; Durkheim with his strong faith in reason and scientific method was very critical of the philosophy of Bergson whom he regarded as representing the 'dilettantism' of much of French thought.[1] The criticism was unjustified, for Bergson always engaged with the sciences and had an ongoing interest in scientific theories, and what he generally spoke out against was the excesses of scientism, which usually placed him on one side of a broader cultural debate. In this context, *Time and Free Will* was an important text because it appeared in the latter part of the nineteenth century when scientific models were being applied to all aspects of social life. Hippolyte Taine, for example, adapted models from physics, biology and chemistry to describe a range of cultural phenomena including art. In *Philosophie de l'Art* he compared culture to different species of plants and argued that cultural changes could be gauged by measuring such general quotients as physical temperature.[2] The great advances in physical science, and the success of physical models, meant that it was increasingly common to adopt such ideas in psychology, humanities and the arts. *Time and Free Will* directly responded to this state of affairs and one of its advantages, despite the many accusations of irrationalism levelled at Bergson, was its questioning of positivism and other scientistic approaches, without recourse to theism or mysticism. Central to the book is a critique of psychological positivism manifest in 'psychophysics', the 'associationist doctrine' and the 'materialist position',[3] which was certainly an appropriate object for critique for the young Bergson because psychology was an incipient field that was only just beginning to be scientifically codified, and its object of study, the mind, was still something that philosophy could lay claim to.

The basis for Bergson's critique is much more clearly stated in the French title of the work and the subtitle of the English translation: *An Essay on the Immediate Data of Consciousness*. The English title, *Time and Free Will*, emphasizes the radical critique of determinism expounded in the final section, whereas the original French title foregrounds the philosophical method, in which the contents of consciousness are revealed through introspection prior to, and beyond any, transcription into scientific and philosophical discourse. The importance of introspection as a method is made clear in the 1915 review of French philosophy by Bergson, in which he hails Maine de Biran as the greatest French metaphysician since

Descartes and Malebranche, and predicts that he will have an increasingly important place in French thought in the early twentieth century.[4] Introspection is able to unveil truths about human experience, such as the experience of effort, which cannot be translated into other modes of knowing, as well as being able to apprehend metaphysical truths by fully investigating the particularity of consciousness.[5] Bergson describes Biran's method as one in which 'he conceived the idea of a metaphysics rising ever higher, towards the universal spirit, as consciousness descends to the depths of internal life' (*il a conçu l'idée d'une métaphysique qui s'élèverait de plus en plus haut, vers l'esprit en général, à mesure que la conscience descendrait plus bas, dans les profondeurs de la vie intérieure*).[6] By dwelling in the interiority of consciousness, the philosopher develops an understanding of the complex relationship between perception and apperception, which in turn discloses the particular orientation of the mind. The method is empirical insofar as it attends to the specific contents of consciousness, but also transcends the immediacy of consciousness to describe processes and states that are immanent to consciousness in general – in other words, a type of transcendental empiricism.

For Maine de Biran, this introspective and subjective method begins with sensations and experiences that are peculiar to the interior life of the individual and can be contrasted with the objective method which always links such experiences to exterior facts and in doing so renders the subject passive.[7] This introspective method does not produce a foundational argument or a clearly delineated statement on the conditions of experience; instead, it traces the argument back to its origin and discloses the direction of experience and thought as akin to a curved line.[8] The philosopher must descend into consciousness through introspection in order to arrive at a metaphysical idea, usually as a particular tendency in thought. To some degree, this approach resembles Bergson's method in *Time and Free Will* where an introspective examination of qualitative differences in conscious experience, from pain to the aesthetic feelings, leads to the theory in which free will is an inclination or tendency, although Bergson does not interrogate personal experiences in the way that Biran does. For example, Bergson argues that the emotions are directional, with joy characterized by an orientation towards the future and sadness by an orientation towards the past.[9] Orientation refers to a general directedness in feeling derived from the qualitative variation of psychic states rather than a spatial direction or even a phenomenological intention. Unlike Kantian idealism, Bergson does not begin with a set of categories that serve as conditions for experience, because experience always retains its specificity and the further we descend into consciousness, the more difficult it is to separate psychic states or find external mechanisms to represent them. The qualities revealed through introspection are felt conditions, or felt movements, that are unrepresentable but, nevertheless, condition the way we engage with the world.

Bergson questions the assumption that the psychic states that comprise consciousness are comparable to those physical objects analysed using scientific methods. *Time and Free Will* begins with a critique of psychological accounts of intensive states where any variation of feeling is represented and codified as a change in magnitude. Bergson acknowledges that emotions, efforts and sensations are commonly described as being stronger or weaker, or more or less intense, and because these psychic states appear to admit of degrees it is assumed that they are analogous to external magnitudes.[10] This principle appears to also obtain to aesthetic feelings where, in popular criticism, great works are often celebrated for their capacity to evoke strong emotions. When there are clear differences between more or less, there is always the potential for actual measurement. The difficulty, however, is devising a method to measure experiences that are truly intensive, such as aesthetic feelings that are not directly visible, or only become visible through communication and representation. Psychophysics came up with a solution in the latter part of the nineteenth century in Gustav Fechner's theory of minimum differences, which formalized the relationship between internal and external magnitudes by associating changes in a psychic state with quantitative changes in a stimulus. If the intensity of the stimulus increases or decreases, it can be claimed by analogy that the sensation also increases or decreases in response to such a stimulus.[11] Researchers could increase the intensity of a painful stimulus (light, temperature, etc.) and correlate this with the subject's account of the intensity of their experience, and through the multiplication of the experiments, researchers should be able to calibrate the changes in conscious experience, a method that is still central to experimental psychology today.

Bergson does not reject the results of these experiments but rephrases the problem by inquiring if these variations in the intensity of psychic experience, despite their correlation with a stimulus, are actually changes in magnitude.[12] The measurements are not necessarily wrong, for they do measure something, but the measured phenomenon is not necessarily representative of the introspectively articulated experience.

This leads Bergson to question what a magnitude is, which is not a matter of providing a technical definition, for magnitude should be revealed through introspection, that is, through foregrounding images that reveal a particular mental or empirical tendency:

> If we now ask ourselves in what does this idea consist, our consciousness still offers us the image of a container and a contained. We picture to ourselves, for example, a greater intensity of effort as a greater length of thread rolled up, or as a spring which, in unwinding, will occupy a greater space.[13]

Introspection provides the appropriate image upon which the definition is founded, in this case, the relationship between container and contained as a foundation for understanding the more or the less. The spring might have tension or force, and the spool might have movement, but the difference is always articulated at some point as a greater or lesser extension in space. Space is the founding image by which differences in magnitudes can be readily observed and compared, and as such is particularly suited to the analysis of physical behaviour. In physics, space underpins kinematics, where the magnitudes of acceleration and speed are described in terms of changes in position, and thermodynamics, where temperature and pressure derive from the movement of molecules in a contained space or volume. For Bergson, in its most abstract form space is a conceptually neutral ground, an empty grid that allows for the external comparison without necessarily revealing any internal change in the objects under comparison. To analyse intensive states in terms of magnitude, he places them within a universal, abstract space that also effaces the haecceity of conscious experience.

This discussion of magnitude might appear to be a digression from an analysis of Bergson's aesthetic arguments; however, it is necessary because it invokes the key image of homogeneous space, which serves as the ground for all discussions of externality. To arrive at a metaphysics, or, indeed, an aesthetics, Bergson usually proceeds through a critique of external representation, for it is only by stripping away the deceptive figure of space that it is possible to recover the heterogeneity of time. Homogeneous space is a conceptual other against which Bergson is able to articulate his metaphysics of art, time, life and movement. In *Time and Free Will*, magnitude operates as the vehicle for Bergson's arguments on duration and conscious experience, which is why he does not overly engage with the epistemology of measurement. Intensive magnitudes, as internal states, are resistant to conceptualization in terms of the relationship between container and contained, and by extension homogeneous space. Bergson argues that the word intensity is used too broadly in psychological literature to describe modulations in a range of feelings, including effort, pain and the aesthetic feelings. To better understand what is actually under analysis, Bergson separates those sensations that have a direct external cause from those that are 'self-sufficient', which he refers to as the 'deep-seated feelings'.[14] Feelings such as pain are much closer to the physical surface of the body and its organs, especially in the form of a localized sensation, which has a reasonably determinate spatial boundary. By contrast, the deep-seated feelings are so fully embedded within consciousness that any external expression fundamentally changes them. Furthermore, the deep-seated feelings do not resemble their cause, for a wide range of events could lead to, for example, the blossoming of passion, joy and sorrow.[15] Likewise in the aesthetic feelings, a particular artwork could invoke a whole range of feelings that do not exactly resemble the aesthetic object.[16] We might feel that we experience more or less joy, more or less sadness – physiological accounts might attribute such feelings to changes in endorphin levels or other related bodily chemicals – but for Bergson the impression of an increase or decrease in these 'deep-seated' feelings is the result of a variation of a 'quality or shade which spreads over a more or less considerable mass of psychic states'.[17] The idea of more or less here is not like the image of the spring or spool because there is no continuous measure of variation or an isolatable general quality that can be quantified. Every variation in feeling brings with it a qualitative change that cannot be properly apprehended through the aggregation of intensity.

This emphasis on the interconnectedness of conscious states is valuable as a critique of scientific accounts of feeling and emotion, but it does not readily present itself as a means for understanding either art objects or aesthetic feelings. One cannot talk simply of aesthetic feelings that reside deep in consciousness, for there must also be some explanation of the sensory relationship with the artwork, as well as the work's material qualities. Bergson indirectly addresses this issue through an examination of the link between corporeal feeling and the aesthetic emotions, and in doing so somewhat pre-empts recent affect theory with its emphasis on the contours of feeling rather than readily isolatable emotions. This connection is not overly surprising because in *Time and Free Will*

Bergson draws openly on William James's theory of the emotions, which is an antecedent to recent affect theory. James and Bergson became friends over the course of their careers, reading and commenting on each other's work. After reading Bergson's *Creative Evolution*, James wrote a letter celebrating their shared approach to philosophy in the battle against intellectualism and their wish to place life and the continuity of movement at the centre of any method.[18] Bergson's response confirms this common effort, remarking that James's pragmatism is a philosophy of the future, which, through its development of flexible ideas, is much better suited to the description of the real than intellectual or rationalist methods.[19] The other important early influence on Bergson was Herbert Spencer whom Bergson directly references in his examination of aesthetic feeling. In *Time and Free Will*, Bergson's debt to James and Spencer is most evident in the discussion of how the body is aligned with the qualitative variability of emotional states. Bergson acknowledges the liminality of the body as a sensorial surface that is outwardly receptive to the variability of perceptual experience but also inwardly connected to the deeper feelings, including the aesthetic feelings. The body is spatially extended, it can be tracked in terms of movement in space, and yet is directly connected to consciousness in a way that cannot be fully accounted for in terms of magnitude. Throughout Bergson's work, the body serves as a threshold between two movements: a centripetal movement towards the deep feelings that are qualitatively and temporally interconnected, and the centrifugal movement in which internal movement extends outward and exhausts itself in the solidity and fixity of matter.

In *Time and Free Will*, Bergson addresses the body's liminality by giving particular attention to muscular activity and the feelings associated with muscular effort, which he also links to the 'deeper' feeling of emotion. To support his argument, he refers to James's articles 'The Feeling of Effort' (1880) and 'What is an emotion?' (1884), both of which were later collected in his *Principles of Psychology* (1891).[20] In the latter work, James argues that bodily changes and movements always accompany emotion and the aim of psychology should be to understand the principles that generate them.[21] He makes a bold claim that bodily indications of emotion are not ancillary to a cognitive state, providing some kind of support for a pre-existing mental condition, for '*bodily changes follow directly the perception of the exciting fact, and that our feeling of the same changes as they occur IS the emotion*'.[22] James does not posit a psychic intermediary, an internal conscious articulation of the emotion that is subsequently expressed, because the bodily response can be said to be directly triggered by a stimulus. The feeling of fear, for example, involves a set of bodily movements – increased heart rate, the tensing of muscles and so on – that are caused by a threatening object without mental deliberation. Furthermore, James argues that without this corporeality, there would be no true feeling of emotion, only a cognitive state that is 'pale, colorless, destitute of emotional warmth' – in other words, there would be the idea of emotion rather than the feeling of emotion.[23] Bergson accepts that psychic states such as anger and love are directly linked to the movement of the body, but he also adapts this argument to address his initial problem: How do we come to describe these states in terms of changes in intensity?[24] Why do we not simply refer to specific corporeal changes – for example, the widening of the eyes in fear or the relaxing of the muscles in love – rather than to an overall change in intensity? Bergson proffers two main reasons for this: when we look to understand emotion, we apply a coordinating idea that groups together the various feelings into a single emotion and then correlate the effort associated with the corporeal changes with the feeling of intensity.[25] This is an important shift because the body provides a means by which intensity in the form of effort can be mapped onto the qualitative variability of emotion. Bergson is often criticized for his unrelenting nominalism, but even in this early work, he recognizes a series of processes that are necessary for the transformation of the emotion from one state to another, and from the specific conditions of feeling to a form that can be both represented and measured. For James the body provides the very condition for what it means to feel an emotion, but for Bergson it also explains why we attribute intensity to what is essentially a qualitative experience.

The feeling of effort is foregrounded in much of Bergson's work because it operates on the threshold between the interiority of consciousness and the exteriority of visible movement. It can be used to explain the feeling of intensity, for the force needed to perform an external action can be correlated with changes in the internal feeling of effort, a kinaesthetic change, peculiar to living organisms, that accompanies any movement. Effort attests to the reality of lived movement, unlike the external description of movement in terms of a trajectory, where a moving object might appear at rest depending on the frame of reference. In *Matter and Memory*, Bergson illustrates this by referring to Henry More's quip that the expression of feeling 'flushed' is a good indicator of being in motion regardless of any noticeable change in position.[26] This interest in effort as a philosophical principle shows his debt to philosophers such as Spencer, Maine de Biran and Berkeley. Biran was particularly important due to his deployment of such concepts as *motilité*, which Jonathon Crary describes as 'willed effort against felt resistance'.[27] This willed effort distinguishes the interiority of movement from any scientific characterization of it. Even visual perception, which was often described in terms of the external properties of the image or the direct passage of knowledge through the senses, was for Biran 'inseparable from the muscular movements of the eye and the physical effort involved in focusing on an object or in simply holding one's eyelids open'.[28] The feeling associated with a body's movement is at the centre of sensual activity, as well as philosophical investigation and introspection.

In addition to foregrounding the interiority of movement, effort is a feeling that endures throughout an activity or movement and thus proves the deep connection between the past and the present. In the article 'Intellectual Effort', which appeared in the *Revue Philosophique* in 1902, Bergson explains why we experience effort in intellectual activities, even though these activities do not necessarily involve actual physical effort. He argues that effort is required to transform the general form of an idea, what he refers to as a 'dynamic scheme', into a concrete image. The process is felt as tension, insofar as the general movement of the dynamic scheme must shift and reform to accommodate the concrete images – the process of searching for something new is conducted against the resistance of the old. Importantly for Bergson, this is also a reason to dismiss mechanical and associationist accounts of thought, which assume that ideas are simply joined or connected based on principles of resemblance or logic. Why would we feel mental strain or effort, if the mental acts are merely the recombination or substitution of parts?[29] The movement of thought always extends through the particular products of thought – discrete ideas, concepts and so on – and thinking involves habits and practices that endure, like physical movements. For this reason, Bergson uses the example of learning to dance to illustrate intellectual effort, where the individual might have a clear visual image of what they should do, seeing another person perform the dance, but this visual image does not directly translate into movement. Rather, the body must gradually accommodate the visual image of the dance into an existing motor scheme, in which the body's 'kinaesthetic images' provide a general contour through which to learn the precise movements.[30] This movement and impetus of thought is continuous and interconnected and can, therefore, be aligned with corporeal movement and, in this context, deriving a new idea involves a change in direction. To change, deter or differ a direction, and initiate an expected movement involves effort.

In *Time and Free Will*, this emphasis on the continuity of effort provides the foundation for a critique of the psychophysical and materialist belief that quantitative variation underpins qualitative difference. Bergson also foregrounds effort because, unlike the 'deep feelings', it appears ostensibly to be an example of an intensive magnitude where the internal feeling of effort can be correlated with an external force. In the localized application of effort, the greater the force used, the greater the expenditure of energy and the greater the feeling of intensity.[31] However, Bergson questions this purely quantitative characterization of effort by arguing that it is underpinned by a range of qualitative changes. Drawing again on the work of William James, Bergson argues that the increase in the feeling of effort is actually an indication of the degree to which the whole of the body is involved in the effort. As the 'intensity' increases, the individual feels the muscles working harder but also experiences a change in corporeal tension as ever more muscles are implicated in the effort.[32] For example, when increasing the force of a clenched fist:

> You will have the impression of a sensation of effort entirely localized in your hand and running up a scale of magnitudes. In reality, what you experience in your hand remains the same, but the sensation which was at first localized there has affected your arm and ascended to the shoulder; finally, the other arm stiffens, both legs do the same, the respiration is checked; it is the whole body which is at work.[33]

The addition of muscles, from the shoulder through to the legs, describes an increase in number, and in this regard can be understood quantitatively. But it is also a qualitative movement because the different parts of the body bring with them different sensations – the feeling of a shoulder moving is different from the squeezing of the fingers. Bergson argues that this change in the overall qualitative contour of effort, as increasing numbers of muscles are deployed, is posited in psychology as a change in intensity due to the conventions of language, in which words nominate a single quality that varies by degree. Language simplifies corporeal feeling by failing to recognize the complex braiding of different muscular sensations, which can be compared to the qualitative shading of an emotion in consciousness.[34] Although the application of the muscles is understood in psychology and physiology in terms of the capacity to apply force, what Bergson is interested in is a broader aesthetic approach to the body in which qualitative differences comprise the immanence of feeling. Recovering the exact conditions of feeling in introspection is an aesthetic act whereby we notice slight qualitative variations and how they play out across the interior surface of the body.

Bergson's early discussions of time, movement and the body show some debt to Herbert Spencer. Bergson was always interested in arguments derived from the sciences – his first published article was actually a solution to a mathematical problem – and was attracted to philosophers, such as Spencer, who adapted physical and dynamic principles to explain psychological ideas. However, his interests were always quite diverse, and while writing *Time and Free Will*, Bergson was also teaching at Clermont-Ferrand, where his lectures focused on the spiritualist tradition. Although there was no immediate revelation during this period, he was beginning to develop a new direction in his thought through his critique of Spencer's work.[35] In the article, 'The Possible and the Real', Bergson states that he came to a new concrete theory of time after recognizing Spencer's failure to adequately account for time in his evolutionary theorizing.[36] Like James, Spencer directly linked emotion to corporeality in his influential 'The Origin and Function of Music' (1857), which served as a foundation for a theory of aesthetic value, although with one key difference: for Spencer bodily disposition responds to a feeling rather than constituting it. He proposes that 'a highly agreeable taste is followed by a smacking of the lips' and that the response to pain produces a plethora of movements which are directly related to intensity:[37]

A sudden twinge produces a convulsive start of the whole body. A pain less violent, but continuous, is accompanied by a knitting of the brows, a setting of the teeth, or biting of the lip, and a contraction of the features generally. Under a persistent pain of a severer kind other muscular actions are added: the body is swayed to and fro; the hands clench anything they can lay hold of; and should the agony rise still higher, the sufferer rolls about on the floor almost convulsed.[38]

This corporeal responsiveness is not limited to pain, for even with pleasurable feelings, the intensity and range of movement increases as a person shifts from smiling to laughing.[39] From these examples, Spencer derives a general principle in which greater intensity of feeling is correlated with greater movement, which he argues is probably a reflex response.[40] This argument in many ways resembles Bergson's discussion of the role of the body in response to pain; the difference, however, is that Spencer accepts that intensity is directly related to movement, whereas Bergson would argue that the sufferer feels a 'sensation of increase' rather than an 'increase of sensation'.[41] The difference is important: for Bergson, the corporeal response cannot be separated from consciousness, as it is just another facet of a continually varying field of qualitative difference.

Spencer extends this analysis of the corporeal foundation of pain and emotion to the analysis of the intensity of feeling in music, in particular singing, which is contingent on muscular action and the degree of 'force' deployed in the execution of a movement. As the muscles contract with differing degrees of intensity and force, affecting both the pitch and volume of a sound, the aesthetic feelings vary.[42] Effort does not follow a linear scale from lowest to highest, because the most comfortable singing position is in the mid-range, and comfortableness is associated with emotions such as calmness. To significantly raise or lower the pitch involves effort, and a consequent decrease in comfort and the intensification of certain types of feeling.[43] Although Spencer examines key points in the production of sound, all vocal expression requires some effort such that the tessitura of sound is bound to the tessitura of effort. In *Time and Free Will*, Bergson's arguments on the constitution of feeling are quite similar to Spencer's, in particular when he states that many psychological states are accompanied by muscular changes, such as the furrowing of the brows in concentration and attention.[44] Likewise, in the reception and appreciation of music, the impression of intensity in pitch and volume has a corporeal correlate. The introspective method requires an understanding not just of the physical amplitude or wavelength of a note but also of the feelings associated with vocal production, including the effort of stretching the muscles of the vocal chords and the silent rearticulation of sounds while hearing.[45] With regard to pitch, the qualitative differentiation between higher and lower notes relates to how sound is distributed across the body with the higher notes resonating in the skull, using a greater array of muscles, whereas the lower notes resonate in the thorax with less effort. This resonance might not actually occur when hearing a sound but it nevertheless operates as a kinaesthetic background to pitch organized around a vertical scale.[46] This correlation of effort and the qualitative differences in feeling is a feature of both Spencer's and Bergson's accounts of tension in music, but Bergson takes the argument one step further by questioning why we do not sufficiently acknowledge the role of the body when discussing aesthetic experience, and concludes that it is because spatial representation too readily substitutes for the corporeal expression of feeling. Pitch might be felt differentially across the body but the spatial distinction between high and low supplants a proper understanding of corporeal and kinaesthetic differences.

Bergson critiques the distancing role of metaphor, which draws the subject away from their internal experience to an external surrogate, which will eventually usurp the feeling by incorporating it into a general category. Although he would not accept the kinaesthetic explanation for musical feeling, musicologist and key exponent of Bergson's philosophy Vladimir Jankélévitch agrees that spatialization – most evident in the score with its arrangement of lines on a two-dimensional page and the assumption that melody is horizontal in form and harmony vertical – has diminished attention to the particularity of musical becoming.[47] He claims that musical discourse is so thoroughly infused with spatial metaphors, or 'optical idols', that it 'would need a second Bergson to root out the mirages of spatialization that are scattered throughout musical aesthetics'.[48] For Bergson, these metaphors prevent an introspective return to the particularity of lived experience because they extract qualities that can then be described in terms of quantitative differences – higher and lower, faster and slower, darker and lighter. However, Bergson never fully explores the range of corporeal metaphors that mediate the static spatial description of intensive magnitudes and lived corporeal experience. The philosopher Mark Johnson argues that we learn about the movement of a musical work through its alignment with the movement of our own body, as the tension and relaxation of pitch, volume and rhythm: 'if the music builds to a climax of high drama and tension, the engaged listener experiences (in their own feeling body-mind) that dramatic tension.'[49] Many of the metaphors used to describe the experience of sound and movement are linked to the body and locomotion, including 'speed up, walk, float, stumble',[50] or how the music directly affects our own movement in phrases such as 'carry you along, transport you, give you a lift'.[51] They attest to the continuity of musical experience and not just to those qualities that can be represented spatially through the score or in the description of musical parts, such as notes and chords. In the analysis of art, the metaphors that draw upon the lived experience of movement are much more compatible with the theory of durée than those that posit discrete qualities that only change in intensity.

Aesthetics, movement and decorporealization

Bergson does not provide a full account of corporeal experience, which is something that was central to phenomenology after Merleau-Ponty, because his aim was always to reveal the haecceity of time by removing any traces of space. In *Time and Free Will*, corporeality subtends lived experience but in itself does not provide an account of the deep emotions associated with aesthetics, for this can only occur by extracting from the body movements that are not overly encumbered by physicality. The felt interior of the body is different to its physical exterior and is much more strongly associated with the aesthetic feelings. Bergson characterizes this relationship in terms of a centripetal movement towards the 'deep-seated feelings' of conscious experience and the centrifugal movement outwards to objects extended in space. The greater the push to the surface, the more a feeling is understood as a collection of parts – the division of individual muscles, cutaneous sensation and so on – but in the drive from the surface to the centre of consciousness, the whole of consciousness is more fully implicated in the particular feeling. The physically articulated exterior of the body dissolves the more it is integrated and implicated in the extentionless *durée* of consciousness.[52] For Bergson, art should invoke the deeper feelings and is therefore aligned with the centrifugal movement from the periphery of sensation towards the centre of consciousness, which raises the question as to how these deep-seated feelings are actually conveyed in artistic practice. How can art, which is mostly manifest in the form of physical artefacts or images, be allied with the depths of consciousness with its interpenetrating psychic states and lack of physical boundaries? Bergson does not raise this particular question in *Time and Free Will*, for the aim of the work is to critique the spatialization of psychic states and time, but nevertheless this centripetal movement of greater interpenetration underpins Bergson's later arguments about how art reveals *durée*.

It is notable that Bergson chooses dance as the principal example in his explanation of aesthetic feeling because, as one of the performance arts, it addresses actual movement rather than the implied movement of the plastic arts, and is often allied with music, which he repeatedly uses to illustrate his theory of *durée*. Dance can also be described both kinaesthetically and optically: a limb does not simply move; it requires the dancer's effort, which links the visual plane to the continuity of effort and consciousness. Outside of the functional role it plays in Bergson's philosophy, this focus on dance, effort and movement should also be considered in terms of the growing interest in the physiology of movement during the latter part of the nineteenth century. Francis Sparshott argues that during this period ballet did not have the prominence it has today and that for French ballet audiences there was a general interest in gymnastics and the physiology of movement,[53] which was associated with a wider preoccupation with 'the establishment and describing of the true facts of animal locomotion in general and human locomotion in particular'.[54] Philosophical texts also discussed the relationship between efficiency and gracefulness in animal and human movement, which was a key focus of Paul Souriau's *L'esthétique du mouvement* published in 1889, the same year as Bergson's *Time and Free Will*. Further precedents can be found in the work of Francis Hutcheson in 1725, who in turn influenced Kant and the aesthetic writings of Herbert Spencer,[55] who, as we have already seen, directly influenced Bergson.

In *Time and Free Will*, the analysis of the aesthetic feeling of grace is combined with a discussion of effort in a way that can be clearly traced to the work of Spencer. Bergson accentuates the value of internal feeling but Spencer restricts his focus to the physical conditions of gracefulness, arguing that graceful movements do not appear to require significant effort and involve a greater 'economy of force'. This applies to all types of movements, from the gracefulness of animals and humans to inanimate objects that mimic these organic movements,[56] for example, the curved branch of a willow might be regarded as graceful because it can be compared to the curved arc of a limb.[57] Graceful movements give the impression of a body without tension, with greater emphasis on the relaxing of muscles in performance than their contraction. Spencer states that in walking, the style should be 'moderate in velocity, perfectly rhythmical, unaccompanied by violent swinging of the arms, and giving us the impression that there is no conscious exertion, while there is no force thrown away'.[58] This economy of effort is also a feature of balanced movements, for example, in walking the movement of an arm should counterbalance the movement of a leg.[59] Similarly, a curve is more graceful than a jagged movement because the latter requires abrupt changes in the direction in which a force is applied,[60] which in dance takes the form of a 'natural' flow that follows a clear and predictable path.[61] Souriau adopts a similar position in the *Aesthetics of Movement* when he states that pleasure is associated with the relaxation of effort, and pain with increased effort and the feeling of tension. The sensation of effort has, fundamentally, a 'disagreeable character', and becomes more disagreeable with attempts to sustain the effort, which is manifest in everything from the loss of breath and the expansion of the capillaries to the visible symptoms of redness and perspiration.[62] In these nineteenth-century accounts, physiology underpins aesthetics – with an emphasis on lived movement rather than cognitive judgement – in terms of the way the body is mapped onto the formal properties of the work.

Bergson also analyses the aesthetic feelings through the physiology of movement and the effortlessness of grace, but foregrounds the time and rhythm of movement and the spectator's sense of its future direction – something that is only suggested in Spencer in the notion of 'natural' movement. Indeed, Bergson criticizes Spencer for limiting his argument to the effects of effort, which he argues are not sufficient to describe the complexity of aesthetic feeling.[63] For Bergson, a movement is graceful due to its continuity, a thread linking the past, present and future, that can be compared to the continuity of our inner life. We find pleasure in the gracefulness of a dance performance because fluidity provides the viewer with an understanding of the general line of movement and rhythm, which can be contrasted with the disconnectedness of a 'jerky' movement that 'is self-sufficient and does not announce those which are to follow'.[64]

> If curves are more graceful than broken lines, the reason is that, while a curved line changes its direction at every moment, every new direction is indicated in the preceding one. Thus the perception of ease in motion passes over into the pleasure of mastering the flow of time and of holding the future in the present.[65]

This corresponds to early-twentieth-century studies of the affective qualities of lines, which demonstrated that jagged lines are associated with intense, often negative, feelings in contrast to the more relaxed feelings of curved or smooth lines.[66] Unlike these early psychological studies, Bergson provides a temporal explanation, in which the pleasure of mastery is grounded in the spectator's intentionality and the fact that they are able to follow and preempt the dancer's movement as an imaginary line animated by a definite rhythm.[67] The feeling of control is realized in the presentiment of the future as a rhythmic unfolding. The spectator sees a dancer's limb moving but also the general continuity of its movement in an extended present. By contrast,

Spencer limits his analysis to the corporeality of the body and the degree to which effort is distributed equally through the movement. Effort is still a factor in understanding the affective quality of the dancer's movement, but it is now a temporal contour that virtually subtends the visual articulation of the movement.

The alignment of the movement of the dancer with the intentionality of the spectator not only is cross-sensual or multimodal but provides a principle by which feeling can be transmitted between bodies. Movement coordinates the different senses and the very conditions of feeling that underpin aesthetic value, and Bergson argues that this process begins with the spectator corporeally mimicking and completing the movements of the dance performance, which eventually develops into a physical sympathy derived from rhythm that takes 'complete possession of our thought and will'.[68] Interestingly, despite Bergson's criticism that Spencer overly focused on effort in aesthetic feeling, Spencer proposed a similar idea in arguing that the emotions are transmitted between bodies through muscular mimicry:

> The same faculty which makes us shudder on seeing another in danger – which sometimes causes motions of our own limbs on seeing another struggle or fall, gives us a vague participation in all the muscular sensations which those around us are experiencing.[69]

In this example, the body responds reflexively, similar to the way that we automatically begin to yawn when witnessing another person yawning, whereas for Bergson, mimicry is the basis for a much more complex empathetic process that still involves intention. Grounding intersubjective feeling in corporeal mimicry was a key part of aesthetics in the nineteenth century, in particular in Robert Vischer's notion of *Einfühlung*, translated into English as empathy, which explains how the viewer enters the space and inner form of an object, and was later used to explain how mental movements are provoked by seeing corporeal movements.[70] *Einfühlung* is a general receptiveness to the movement of bodies, most clearly evinced in natural objects that reproduce movements and feelings within the spectator's body,[71] and was extended by the critic John Martin to describe how viewers respond with 'kinaesthetic empathy', a form of 'inner mimicry', to the movement of dancers on stage.[72] In empathy, the physicality of movement is only a vehicle for a much more profound aesthetic feeling in which the mind is moved as much as the body.

In *Time and Free Will*, an underlying principle of aesthetic feeling is to make someone receptive to a particular aesthetic idea by the 'process of our art' rather than to represent what is already beautiful in nature, which is achieved by suspending or limiting the resistance of 'personality', a process that Bergson likens to hypnosis.[73] It is a matter of turning attention away from a personality invested in the practicality of everyday life, and finding a movement that is more fully integrated with our deeper feelings of consciousness. For Bergson, the emphasis is on rhythm, which not only describes a non-physical movement but also opens the listener or spectator to a level of feeling that extends beyond the immediacy of the sensation:

> Thus, in music, the rhythm and measure suspend the normal flow of our sensations and ideas by causing our attention to swing to and fro between fixed points, and they take hold of us with such force that even the faintest imitation of a groan will suffice to fill us with the utmost sadness. If musical sounds affect us more powerfully than the sounds of nature, the reason is that nature confines itself to *expressing* feelings, whereas music *suggests* them to us.[74]

The formal rhythmic structure of a music, or, indeed, any temporally structured art form, creates the conditions for feeling in which the representation of a particular emotion is embedded. While inhabiting the rhythm, aesthetic feeling can overcome the physical and optical boundaries that define the performance, which explains how the external articulation of movement can lead to an internal invocation of rhythm, and from there the higher values often associated with art.

This discussion of musical feeling is not part of an extended analysis of music or dance, nor does it contribute to a theory of musical emotion that compares with Bergson's analysis of laughter and the comic. However, rather than considering such analyses as merely incidental, they could also be regarded as refrains that repeat across Bergson's work to provide a speculative foundation for some of his main aesthetic ideas. Musical feeling as a form of immersive movement appears again later in *The Two Sources of Morality and Religion*, as a way of introducing a type of morality based on common feeling or shared emotion:

> Let the music express joy or grief, pity or love, every moment we are what it expresses. Not only ourselves, but many others, nay, all the others, too. When music weeps, all humanity, all nature, weeps with it.

In point of fact it does not introduce these feelings into us; it introduces us into them, as passers-by are forced into a street dance. Thus do pioneers in morality proceed. Life holds for them unsuspected tones of feeling like those of some new symphony, and they draw us after them into this music that we may express it in action.[75]

Musical emotion here is rhythmic orientation that can incorporate others into its movement which, like every true moral disposition, creates a unique feeling that resists any form of generalization.[76] The artist's experience furnishes the emotion, thus preserving its particularity, into which the sensations are incorporated like notes into a musical whole. Musical emotions may have common themes, but they are nevertheless motivated by distinct timbres and harmonics.[77] Bergson returns to the idea that music suggests certain movements and feelings, which again indicates that movement is itself the very condition for feeling, and the role of art is to provoke and initiate such movements.

This shift from effort to the movement of effort over time is also an aesthetic shift in which the quality of the movement is partially separated from the figure that bears it. It is not a matter of the dancer experiencing a particular affective state that is communicated to the spectator, but an affective quality that operates through the dancer and is re-enacted in the spectator's body. This argument in *Time and Free Will* preempts the way in which Susanne Langer applies her theory of semblance to dance, in which form and movement create a 'virtual image' that exceeds the particular physical attributes of the dancer and the location in which the performance takes place.[78] The physical qualities of the dance disappear as the focus shifts to the virtual features of the movement, such as rhythmic alterations of the 'dynamic image'.[79]

> The stuff of the dance, the apparition itself, consists of such non-physical forces, drawing and driving, holding and shaping its life. The actual, physical forces that underlie it disappear. As soon as the beholder sees gymnastics and arrangements, the work of art breaks, the creation fails.[80]

The dance does not 'express' the feelings of the dancer, the bodily manifestation of a particular mood or state; rather, it creates a semblance of a more expansive feeling that is commensurate with the life of the artist.[81] There are certainly physical forces in any dance, such as the tension in the body when holding a position or enacting a lift or jump, but they are only components of a broader contour of feeling, and it is only the latter, with its particular tensions and alterations in rhythm, that can truly engage the spectator. Because feeling courses through the performance and underpins the overall form of the work, Langer states that language is insufficient in accounting for aesthetic value: '[t]he important fact is that what language does not readily do – present the nature and patterns of sensitive and emotional life – is done by works of art. Such works are expressive forms, and what they express is the nature of human feeling.'[82] This expressive movement remains concrete, insofar as it is lived feeling that concords with the impetus of life, while also extending beyond the physical as a virtual movement.

This simple line of movement is, for Bergson, a concrete abstraction that is invested in a particular material occurrence, kinaesthetic or optical, and yet exceeds the moment in which it appears due to the continued reference to a virtual past and an openness to a future yet to come. In some respects, it is a more expansive specious present. Brian Massumi in *Semblance and Event* adapts Susanne Langer's term semblance, as well as Deleuze's concept of the virtual, in order to describe how we engage with an event in terms of its potentiality. The act of seeing discloses a visual whole but also a general line of becoming, where what does not appear, the past and future, is as important as what does appear, the concrete sensual surfaces of perception. For Massumi, the temporality of lived abstraction or semblance always incorporates the non-sensual into the sensual in the movement joining the past to the future.[83] Appearance describes a condition of being felt as an 'arc' of abstraction that may be realized or provoked by a single sense, such as vision, but can extend through the act of seeing to include the other senses.[84] In a processual reversal of materialist theories, Massumi argues that semblance describes the contour of the reality of becoming and that '[t]he being of an object is an abstraction from its becoming.'[85] Bergson arrived at a similar argument in his later works, in particular his characterization of materiality and life as tendencies of which discrete bodies, living or non-living, are just expressions. In *Time and Free Will*, the argument is still in its early stages and restricted to the discussion of the incorporeality of grace, which is a figure that is not contained by the body, the spectator's vision of the body's movement, or even by a particular sense. In seeing the direction and curve of movement, the spectator also engages kinaesthetically with the movement and the intensiveness of effort.

Another way of addressing the relationship between feeling, effort and expressivity is to imagine it as a liminal state between the interiority of consciousness and the objectivity of a thoroughly measurable external world. The musicologist Victor Zuckerkandl argues that music serves as an objective proof of *durée* and, as such, can be used to counter those criticisms proposing that *durée* should be restricted to psychological experience. Moreover, he argues that time has a reality in music that is comparable to its function in biological processes.[86] Music is often discussed in terms of the opposition between internal and external states, whereby the physicality of the tone is contrasted with the feelings it invokes, but such a division does not sufficiently attend to the 'dynamic qualities' of music, which can be expressed in terms of variations in tension, and the play of non-physical forces.[87] Zuckerkandl states that in music we hear notes in terms of their attraction to other notes, in particular in terms of the dynamic values of the scale. Music relies on the movement towards certain key notes, such as the tonic and dominant, and the movement away from other notes, and for this reason dynamism cannot be situated *in* the tone as a purely physical property.[88] Unlike words, in which meaning can be circumscribed by signification, the tone does not have a specific meaning but, rather, 'indicates' the direction between tones, in a continual process of gesturing beyond itself.[89] The dual meaning of the French word *sens*, as both direction and meaning, better describes the dynamic forces that operate through music. Zuckerkandl states that these dynamic properties are always manifest in a particular material medium but nevertheless transcend that medium: '[w]hen meaning sounds in a musical tone, a nonphysical force intangibly radiates from its physical conveyor.'[90] When considered in relation to aesthetic feeling, the physical tone serves to first 'trigger' the dynamic set of forces operating through the tone, and the emotional response is an 'after effect' carried by these forces – a theory of forces that Zuckerkandl argues could be applied to all art.[91] To return to Bergson's examination of aesthetic emotion, the reason why he argues that music or dance suggests a feeling rather than expressing or denoting that feeling can in part be understood through this notion of dynamic forces. It is only after succumbing to the particular movement of a work, and its play of non-physical forces, that the emotion can be invoked. The spectator or listener has to inhabit the direction of the movement before they can feel it, and through this process of inhabitation, the surface phenomena mapped out in a physical space transform into the intensities of lived experience.

Although the emphasis is largely on the performing arts, Bergson argues that corporeal movement and rhythm also underpin the aesthetic feelings in painting and architecture. The balance and rhythmic harmony of the whole work in painting and the repetition of features in architecture are the means by which feeling and sympathy are communicated to an observer.[92] Instead of foregrounding the static aspects of spatial proportion, rhythm directly enjoins the formal properties of the artwork with the rhythm of life and the deeper aesthetic feelings of the spectator. Interestingly, Bergson characterizes this engagement as 'physical contagion',[93] which has to be qualified because it implies a purely physical action outside of the spectator's control, when in fact Bergson argues that the aesthetic feelings are 'suggested and not *caused*' by the rhythmic distribution of the spectator's attention in contemplating the artwork.[94] This is important because *Time and Free Will* critiques determinism, and therefore the artwork should not determine an aesthetic feeling in the same way that a stimulus invokes a response. Despite a lack of specificity, contagion is a suggested movement found in the work itself that provokes the spectator to act, which over a definite duration fosters the aesthetic feeling. In questioning the direct causal relationship in aesthetic feeling, Bergson further critiques the psychophysical models that seek to reduce the complexity of feeling to the augmentation or diminution of simple qualities.

This notion of a virtual rhythmic movement certainly reappears as a theme across Bergson's oeuvre. In 1917, when he had already acquired international fame, Bergson wrote the preface to a book by Viviani, a figure who played a part in encouraging the United States to enter the First World War. In this patriotic text, Bergson celebrates the rousing speeches of Viviani, who was able to incite positive feelings in an audience even when they had little or no knowledge of the French language. What the audience members were drawn to, argues Bergson, was the rhythmic and emotional import of the orator's gestures; they could enter into Viviani's beliefs and feelings by 'adopting the rhythm of the emotion, falling into step with the thought' (*adoptaient le rythme de l'émotion, emboîtaient le pas à la pensée*).[95] Rather than serving as a poor substitute for a semantically rich language, the dynamic and sensual form of the speech functions as the very condition of meaning, as well as the vehicle by which the intention of the speaker is carried.[96] Rhythm is something that is clearly articulated on the surface in the continuity of movement of gestures and vocalization, and is also coincident with the lived time and aesthetic feelings immanent just below the surface. The greater the implication and interpenetration of psychological states, the greater the meaning that can be communicated. This rhythm can never be fully abstracted from any of its instantiations – the speaker's continuity of thought or the sound of the speech – for it draws them together in a common lived time underscored by shared feeling.

A number of Bergson's aesthetic arguments are linked to this notion of rhythmic sympathy, in which engaging aesthetically extends beyond the artwork through rhythm to its creator, and this becomes a principle for all communication. In an address presented to his students at the lycée Clermont-Ferrand around the same time that *Time and Free Will* was published, Bergson uses aesthetic examples to explain the characteristics of politeness as a form of sympathy. Politeness does not entail conforming to particular codes of behaviour – in the same way that morality cannot be found in the adherence to rules – but, rather, in adopting 'la politesse de l'esprit' that is expressed as a general openness and sympathy to the lives and ideas of others.[97] Like art in *Time and Free Will*, this sympathy requires graceful movements without any jolts, bumps or shocks.[98] The latter are associated with weight and materiality, but grace and materiality must transcend any material support by engaging with the movement of the thoughts of others, in particular, in developing a

> sympathy for the lightness of the artist, the idea that we strip away our heaviness and our materiality. Enveloped in the rhythm of the dance, we adopt the subtlety of its movement without taking on the effort, and in this way we find again the exquisite sensation of those dreams where our body seems to have cast off its weight, its resistance and its material form.[99]

Both artist and spectator resonate with a common movement and the more the rhythm is foregrounded the less the artwork, as in dance, is encumbered by the resistance and weight of matter. The aim of politeness is to engage with another through shedding the weight of habitual gestures, cumbersome language and obsequiousness, and likewise great art should engage the spectator in its immanent movement without the encumbrance of the body and its physicality. In both cases, the aim is to realize a direct relationship through sympathetic harmony to the interior movement of another (artist or interlocutor), and this can only be achieved by going beyond the superficial and material aspects of appearance, as well as physical effort. Bergson was certainly interested in effort as a philosophical concept, due to his allegiance to both Spencer and Maine de Biran, but not as the absolute foundation for aesthetic feeling or *durée*. Effort as the inner surface of corporeal movement operates as a transitory stage between the materiality of things and the interiority of time.

Bergson argues that aesthetics should attend to the qualitative transformation of movement from 'facility' or 'ease', in which movement follows a clear and understandable pattern, to the aesthetic qualities of 'sympathy' or 'higher grace'.[100] In this case, the adjective higher does not refer to transcendence, which is somewhat rarefied and extracted from experience, but, rather, with a deeper or more profound fluidity of movement elicited through sympathy. In highlighting this qualitative movement, Bergson downplays the cognizable and quantifiable sensation in favour of 'degrees of depth or elevation' that reveal the complex interplay of emotional differences in the artist's experience.[101] The quality of the aesthetic experience is dependent on the degree to which it penetrates below the level of the personality, undifferentiated sensation or the body such that it implicates the whole of consciousness. Truly great art invokes feelings whose subtlety derives from the integration of qualitatively different states in the ipseity of the artist's experience, which Bergson argues differs from those arts that are preoccupied with sensation and intensity: 'If the art which gives only sensation is an inferior art, the reason is that analysis often fails to discover in a sensation anything beyond the sensation itself'.[102] These inferior arts should be criticized for their incapacity to truly invoke the complexity of aesthetic experience and because they are so facilely analysed using scientific or positivist methods. The sensation resides in the surface of the body as something that is closely related to the object that provokes it, which itself can be readily analysed in terms of its properties. However, there is no means of passing from the isolated property and corresponding sensation to the sympathetic engagement with the artist and their work.

The difficulty in positing a direct sympathetic understanding of the aesthetic import of an artist's experience is the fact that the spectator must pass through the surface qualities of an artwork or performance – those aspects of the work that are more easily characterized in terms of their capacity to invoke sensation. These surface properties are, as material or conceptual facts, temporally and spatially separated from the artist's experience in producing the work and the viewer's experience in its reception. Bergson argues that it is only through moving figures that the various surface properties can be reintegrated in order to reveal the emotional complexity of the artist's experience.[103] The artist must incorporate those movements that are most aligned with his or her experience:

> This he will bring about by choosing, among the outward signs of his emotions, those which our body is likely to imitate mechanically, though slightly, as soon as it perceives them, so as to transport us all at once into the indefinite psychological state which called them forth. Thus will be broken down the barrier interposed by time and space between his consciousness and ours: and the richer in ideas and the more pregnant with sensations and emotions is the feeling within whose limits the artist has brought us, the deeper and higher shall we find the beauty thus expressed.[104]

The process can be characterized as one of expansion and contraction, where the feelings of the artist are contracted into the artwork and its various material properties, and expand out again in the reception of the work. The process of imitation on the surface level of the body is important because it re-establishes the continuity of experience through rhythm and movement, but it also presumes that a psychological state is the main condition for generating the work and not the artist's engagement with the medium or material. In his article on intellectual effort, Bergson argues that all works begin with an 'incorporeal' scheme that must acquire concrete images in order to become manifest. The novelist requires characters, the painter colours, the musician notes, in order to transform a schematic sense of the whole into the complete work.[105] The scheme also draws together the artist's thoughts, feelings and memories into its 'elastic and mobile' form[106] – a flexibility that also facilitates the integration of these feelings and ideas into the work. The imitation of the material movement of the work by the spectator, listener or reader is a means of discovering the schema of creation and the various feelings that are attendant on it.

This notion of a scheme demonstrates Bergson's interest in movement's immateriality, which is only partially tied to the material work or its images. Indeed, these images are valued in their capacity to suggest movement, particularly in the continuity of grace and rhythmic repetition, for movement is something that always extends beyond any material support and the categorical fixity of space. For Bergson, rhythm is a formal property of the artwork that has the capacity to engage the spectator's body and to act as a point of transition between physically extended forms and the intensive deep feelings. He does not apply these ideas to a specific artwork as this does not really further the philosophical aims of *Time and Free Will*, which is primarily concerned with developing the theory of *durée*. However, his explanation of the transition from materiality, via corporeality, to temporal immateriality in movement can be used to reconsider a range of works, specifically those with definite rhythmic patterns. For example, the liminal function of rhythm can be used to reappraise Henri Matisse's *Dance (II)* (*La Danse*) (1909–10), a large oil painting displayed in St Petersburg's Hermitage museum. Mark Antliff argues that Matisse experimented with colour and rhythm in the early part of the twentieth century, which could have been informed by Bergson's philosophy, as the artist possessed a number of Bergson's works, mentions *durée* in 'Notes of a Painter', and maintained a friendship with the Bergsonian Matthew Stewart Prichard during this period.[107] It is not difficult to find rhythm in *Dance (II)*, as it depicts five dancers performing a circle dance, who are presumably moving to the rhythm of the music played by the singers and musicians in the accompanying panel, *Music* (*La Musique*) (1910). Matisse's paintings were described as '*panneaux décoratifs*' when exhibited at the 1910 Salon d'Automne, a nomination that does not sit easily with the way the themes are depicted. Alastair Wright highlights the distinctiveness of Matisse's works by comparing them to Maurice Denis's decorative panels in the same salon and which also depicted a circle dance and explored the theme of music, although in a classical style foregrounding the harmony and gentleness of movement.[108] Denis's panels are Apollonian in character, which can be contrasted with Matisse's strong emphasis on both the primitive and Dionysian which may not have pleased the early critics: 'In Matisse's paintings, the classical origin became the site not of a comforting myth of pre-cultural activity but of a tense standoff between Apollo and Dionysos, between violins and pan-pipes – between, in short, civilization and barbarism.'[109] The Dionsysian most readily appears in the centrifugal energy, particularly in *Dance*, that expands towards the edges of the works, and is amplified by the absence of the typical decorative edges found in many decorative panels.[110] Outside of Dionysian excess, the works invoke the primitiveness of early cave painting due to the lack of a definite perspective that results in the figures appearing to 'float' in the picture frame.[111] Without the constraints of perspective, *La Danse* more readily transitions from the painterly depiction of space, in which each figure is individuated against a clearly distinguishable ground and situated in perspectival depth, to a formal and qualitatively variable rhythm extracted from the implied movement of individual bodies. From Bergson's perspective, this transition from corporeal individuation to formal movement should mimic the viewer's own reception of the work and the invocation of the deep aesthetic feelings.

Dance (II) has a rhythmic quality that is most strikingly produced by the use of bold colours, which is also a feature of *Music*. The dancers or musicians are painted in a terracotta red which projects them forward against the cooler colours of the background (the blue of the sky) and the middle ground (the green of the earth). Albert Kostenevich claims that Matisse used saturated colours to create natural absolutes (the blue of the sky, the vermillion of the bodies and the green of the trees) that, in turn, establish a cosmic unity between the realms of heaven and earth.[112] The simple colour separations of the pictorial ground qualitatively vary but do not have definite spatial markers that refer to a particular place. The lack of detail directs attention to the abstract quality of movement invested in colour rather than to figures moving across a definite terrain, and in this sense can be contrasted with other depictions of circle dances, such as Nicolas Poussin's *A Dance to the Music of Time* (1634–6) in which, despite the mythical theme, the figures are clearly moving within a three-dimensional space. Matisse's use of clearly demarcated colours flattens the picture plane and strips the dancers of their individuality, transforming them into beats operating across the blue and green expanses. Without the encumbrance of detail, the spectator can quickly shift their gaze from each foregrounded figure to the next, traversing the work without necessarily referring to the scene of the painting.[113]

The endlessly deferred gaze creates a rhythm in which the colour of the foregrounded figures oscillates with the ground. Due to the consistency of its hue, the paint is somewhat abstracted from the body, creating relationships and movements between figures, for example, the fact that the hands of the two figures in the left foreground do not quite touch does not signal disconnection as they are held together by the simple interpolation of the terracotta red of another dancer's leg. The colours create their own rhythm that is not reducible to the figures or the space that subtends them. The space around the bodies expands and contracts depending on how the bodies are positioned and their size. The wide space in the bottom left between the two figures, in which one dancer seeks to grasp the hand of another, can be contrasted with the enclosed space of the two figures in the top left, whose heads appear to point towards each other. Furthermore, the tension between the colours creates qualitative movements that operate within the painting but always gesture beyond it. Foster et al. state that the size of the work and its large swathes of colour contribute to the oscillatory movement of the spectator's gaze, which is unable to hold onto each figure because the colour directs attention to the other figures.[114] The eye cannot rest due to the sheer size of the work and the irreconcilability of the colours: 'Figure and ground constantly annul each other in a crescendo of energies – that is, the very opposition upon which human perception is based is deliberately destabilised – and our vision ends up blurred, blinded by excess.'[115] For Matisse, it is not the individual figures who express feeling and movement but the whole of the work.[116] For Eric Alliez, colour in Matisse's painting has movement and direction that is not contained by surfaces and develops a tension across the picture plane through the deployment of contrasting *sensational blocks of forces*.[117] Matisse sought to undermine static form, in which the pictorial elements are finite and contained, in preference for living form, which is always in movement and cannot be attributed a stable identity based on the represented object.[118] Antliff argues that in Matisse's painting the interplay of colour changes the nature of space, which is understood through its extensity rather than Euclidean dimensions. Even quantitative variations in the volume of space contribute to its expressive or even musical quality, which is clearly indicated in the title of works such as *Harmony in Red* (1908).[119] Due to its relative independence of painting from the demands of depiction, this alternation and movement of colour cultivates the types of intensities that Bergson regarded as integral to consciousness and aesthetic experience.

In addition to the variations in colour, the lines outlining each of the bodies acquire rhythmic independence due to their weight and formal repetition. The linking of the arms moves up and down in a series of arcs or waves as the eye scans across the work from left to right and then from right to left. In a circle dance, which does not have a definite end point, the curved lines endlessly rise and fall. The curved line is graceful because it follows a definite path that aligns with the direction of the bodies in which the ease of movement ensures continuity. The left leg of the dancer in the middle of the painting is drawn with a line that curves up through the torso and arm to almost touch the hand of the next dancer, who is articulated by a smooth line curving from the foot to the crux of the left arm. The difference between the sections of the body is less important than the formal continuity of the line and the continuity between the dancers, creating an arabesque rhythm in which the body disappears. The joined hands mark the end of each curve but also operate as a formal syntax, or a beat that shifts as the viewer glances from one figure to the next. The intensity of the movement, as well as its direction, is demonstrated by the curve of the bodies, arching both outwards and inwards at different points in the circle. The colours and curved lines combine to create movements that stand outside the details of the location and the individuality of the dancers, and acquire momentum as the viewer shifts their gaze between figures, which further dematerializes the painting. The bodies are simply a means of instantiating the rhythm, but it is the rhythm itself which is the source of the deeper feelings. One could imagine the dancers as mere moments within an overarching qualitative rhythm rather than vehicles for movement, or the instigators of a represented movement. In addition to the viewer's engagement with the formal qualities of the work, the dematerialization of the line is also indicative of Matisse's method, in which he removed details in order to develop or recover the simplicity of the line and its capacity to carry the emotion and thought of the artist.[120] Simplicity results from a mental and material process of extracting pictorial qualities over a long duration rather than from representing the immediacy of an impression, for the latter is too encumbered by the weight of its optical specificity. The works might be inspired by an impression – La Danse was inspired by a performance at Le Moulin de la Gallette – but simplicity can only be derived through a much longer process of reimagining and condensation.[121] The dematerialization of the pictorial form requires the condensation of a series of impressions into a rhythm that nevertheless maintains the trace of past forms in a way analogous to the contraction of the past into the simplicity of Bergsonian intuition.

The dematerialization of the body should not be discussed only in terms of the rhythms of formal contrasts and continuities, for there has to be sufficient speed for the bodies to disappear into the movement. This disappearance or dematerialization is more likely to occur with faster rhythms, for the slower the movement, the more the viewer can attend to the specificity of individual forms. Certainly, there is a difference in the presentation of speed when watching dancers in actual movement and attending to the implied movement of a painting. Matisse attempts to increase the acceleration of the movement by expanding and contracting the volume and extension of the dancers, for example, in using oblique angles (most notable in the central foregrounded figure), foreshortening (the right arm of the right-hand figure) and maximum extension (the two left-hand figures in the foreground). In creating strong contrasts between contraction and expansion, the 1910 *La Danse* can be placed between *Le Bonheur de vivre* (1905–6), where half the figures dancing in a circle are mostly upright, and the much later *The Dance* (1932–3) at the Barnes Foundation in which the figures occupy intensely contracted positions emphasized by the curve of the tympana, and are even juxtaposed across the vertical axis in extreme positions of high and low to further increase the tension. This tension in the figures contributes to the movement of the viewer's gaze which traverses the figures across the horizontal or within the closed circuit of the circle dance. In *La Danse*, the dancers appear to accelerate and decelerate as the spectator's eye repeats the movement around the circle in a clockwise direction, creating the variability of *durée* and interpolating lived time into the flat expanses of the picture plane. The work acquires a musical quality in the degree to which space defers to movement and the oscillation between contraction and expansion.

One way of describing Bergson's examination of the aesthetic feelings in *Time and Free Will* is to argue that they operate across two axes: the continuity of rhythm, movement and gesture, and the centripetal movement from materiality to immateriality, the extended to the unextended, and the measurable to the intensive. The continuity of movement is implicit in three components of aesthetic feeling (ease, certainty and control), each of which contributes to the audience's sympathy with the performance. Ease describes the effortless, graceful flow of a movement, whereas certainty and control refer to an understanding of its direction and rhythmic form. Bergson does not examine the formal characteristics of such movements for he is more concerned with the centripetal movement by which the reception of the artwork passes from a visual and material instantiation of graceful movement, through effort and bodily feeling, to the interiority of consciousness as a form of moral sympathy. George Mourélos argues that Bergson's method is largely underpinned by two movements, the movement towards the exterior of things, which eventually leads to scientific analysis, and the synthetic movement inwards, which integrates all the levels of consciousness.[122] In most cases, Bergson attends to the former as part of a larger interrogation of the sciences, whereas the synthetic movement is only really discussed in relation to aesthetics in *Time and Free Will*. In the later works, Bergson does not outline how the materiality of work gives way to the immateriality of feeling in aesthetics and metaphysics because the analysis is largely recast in terms of intuition, in which *durée* is directly apprehended. This also means that there is less attention to the role of the body in mediating different levels of aesthetic experience when intuition is invoked. It is also possible to see the influence of Félix Ravaisson here, who stated that habit is the basis for the transformation of particular practices into dispositions. With regard to the higher feelings, habit describes the process by which the effort associated with a difficult task can gradually become easier, and eventually manifests as a pleasure. Morals and virtues, which are first learnt with difficulty, become '*seconde nature*' through repetition.[123] The repetition of habit can be compared to the rhythmic principles in art which inculcate a disposition in the viewer and, in doing so, align the viewer's movements as well as feelings with that of the artist. Of course, this operates over a much shorter period and does not develop into a true habit, but the principle of decorporealization underpins both.

The value of Bergson's argument for the study of the arts depends on the degree to which the material properties of the artwork are still foregrounded in the centripetal movement towards aesthetic and moral sympathy. In always gesturing beyond the material or corporeal to the qualitative interpenetration of the artist's or audience's experience, Bergson does not sufficiently address the specific conditions of perception and how they inform the articulation of aesthetic feeling. In addition to judging the particular instantiation of a work, one would also have to judge the role of the medium in the communication and coordination of aesthetic feeling, and it could be assumed that some mediums are better suited to the transmission of feeling than others. Would literature, in its retention of the voice of a narrator – to put aside the intentional fallacy for a moment – be more suited to the presentation of an artist's experience than sculpture, with its hard and resistant surfaces that do not necessarily show the hand of the artist? Should music be privileged because sound and rhythm can invoke movement without the mediation of representation or a spatially defined object?

Like Bergson, the philosopher John Dewey states that it is important to examine the processual aspects of feeling in all forms of human endeavour, from aesthetics to epistemology, but notes that each of the senses has its own particular way of coordinating feeling.[124] He argues that there is an inverse relationship between feeling and knowledge, in which sight and hearing possess the least emotion because they are most clearly associated with objects of knowledge: 'in general it may be said that the more value a sensation has for knowledge, the less it has for feeling *directly*. Thus sensations of sight seem to possess, as mere sensation, the least degree of emotional quality.'[125] Sight has a distancing effect that prevents the spectator from being fully immersed in the feeling. The more the spectator attends to the complexity of the visual object, the less they can become part of the immediacy of sensation, and this is why sight 'is pre-eminently fitted for becoming the vehicle of higher enjoyments and sufferings.'[126] There are some problems with Dewey's position, especially in his arguing that hearing also has a distancing effect when music is as much felt in the body as vibration and rhythm as it is at a distance in the sound source. In general, Dewey contrasts the higher aesthetic feelings with the immediacy of physical sensation, such as pleasure and pain, which accords with Bergson's argument that art should not overly emphasize sensation. However, Dewey also argues that the aesthetic and higher feelings are also dependent on the complexity of the object, a complexity that prevents any collapse into mere sensation. The sensual object that continues to provoke interest, which for Dewey would more likely be a visual object, will also engage the higher feelings. For Bergson, the capacity for the artwork to generate movement is more important than its sensual complexity, because movement will engage the body and, in turn, engage the deep-seated feelings. The problem for any analysis of the art object is determining which movements are more likely to engage the aesthetic feelings, for even the most banal works might create definite rhythms that draw the viewer or listener beyond the materiality of the present. In emphasizing the value of grace, those rhythms that gently rock or lull the attention would be privileged over those that engage, disturb or even confound the audience.

The notion that art should provide a means of returning its audience to the interiority of feeling does not fully attend to the temporal structure of the work. With regard to music, the phenomenologist Mikel Dufrenne criticizes Bergson's argument that a listener should allow themselves to be 'lulled' by melody and thus give themselves up to unstructured duration. The rhythm of music and its schemata of succession actually prevents the act of listening from losing its connection to the material and collapsing into duration.[127] Through listening to a musical work, rhythm does not yield to the aesthetic feelings but remains invested in the body and senses as a schema: 'Schematizing is an art deeply hidden within the human body. Thus rhythmic schemata are necessary for the apprehension of the work. They need not be explicitly indicated, as in a musical analysis. They need only be felt.'[128] The rhythmic schemata are a means of aligning the listener's body with the work, and providing a structure through which the listener can imagine the music's organization.[129] They give form to duration both in the composition of the work and in listening to it. It is about imagining duration through a set of contours and accents that depend on, but are not reducible to, a notion of space or its numerical equivalent.[130] 'In recognizing themes and in imitating them, as in counting rhythm and sensing harmony, it is the body which orders duration and unites with it.'[131] Bergson's description of grace in terms of ease, certainty and control corresponds with the rhythmic schemata, for it requires a sense of order and repetition but the centripetal movement towards the centre of consciousness also involves eschewing the weight of the body to arrive at an understanding of the psychological state that generated it. The sensual movement in which the body aligns with the rhythmic properties of the work must recede, but this does not entirely make sense because the artwork continues to make itself felt – the viewer remains standing before the painting, the plot of the play continues to unfold and so on. In relation to music, variations in rhythm, melody and harmony continue to the end of the work, which means that there is time in which the corporeal succeeds to the incorporeal.

The problem with the concept of depth is that it does not necessarily operate within the time of the performance, for it gestures towards a realm of meaning, or even feeling, that stands before or adjacent to the work. When Bergson refers to the consciousness of the artist as the direct experience of *durée*, Dufrenne interprets it as something that stands outside the particular rhythmic form of the work – as an invocation of time that has eschewed its sensual particularity. The time of creation, replete with the many decisions made by the artist, can also be regarded as outside the time of the artwork or performance. Jankélévitch argues that when it comes to music, the idea of recovering the depth of the artist's experience is not easily justified, for the infinity of 'nuances' immanent to creation cannot be recovered in the act of listening or performing. The more the philosopher or performer tries to reimagine the very nature of the production of the work, the more they realize that there is an 'infinitude' of 'bifurcations' that can never be truly retrieved.[132] He also questions the application of the term depth to music because it assumes an external motive that can explain the whole, whereas, as a purely phenomenal event, music is superficial.[133] Another way of thinking about the notion of depth is in terms of the act of deliberation and contemplation. Jankélévitch states that depth could be considered the time it takes to ponder, unravel or recognize the complex threads of the music – a temporal process that runs 'perpendicular to the time of the performance'.[134] The time of contemplation is not necessarily commensurate with the time of listening in music, for while contemplating the listener cannot necessarily attend to the sensuous becoming of the music. Jankélévitch acknowledges this when he argues that if a mind could ponder the various aspects of musical form in the time of performance, then such deliberation would no longer constitute depth, it would be part of the surface form of the music.[135] In invoking the depth of aesthetic feeling, Bergson does not properly distinguish between the arts, and it is a notion that seems better suited to the visual rather than the performing arts. In the visual arts, aesthetic engagement with a work could proceed by a gradual process of decorporealization, in which form gives way to rhythm and finally to a form of sympathy, because the work does not physically change in the time of viewing.

Depth could also be considered as something that remains immanent to the work rather than a movement that passes perpendicularly through the body of the spectator or listener and away from the work. Adopting a Bergsonian perspective, Jankélévitch argues that we can still talk about depth in terms of the infinite number of virtual movements implicated in a work and, with reference to music, he refers to how the 'whole melody slumbers, enfolded, in each harmony'.[136] In his book on Bergson, Jankélévitch states that *durée* can also be likened to a melodic theme that integrates the sounds and virtual movements into a musical whole, where, in the time of listening, the music diverges and converges both virtually and actually.[137] The interpenetration of sounds in *durée* is what constitutes the feeling of a work, and to explain this Jankélévitch argues that each composer can be distinguished by their particular relationship to a musical key, which acquires an authorial inflection such that it seamlessly infuses the whole of a work or works.[138] Bergson somewhat acknowledges this when he talks in *Laughter* about how an artwork initiates a mood or emotion – 'And thus they impel us to set in motion, in the depths of our being, some secret chord that was only waiting to thrill',[139] but again it is not clear if this feeling is coincident with the work or simply a means of invoking a complex multiplicity of feelings latent in consciousness. For Jankélévitch, it is not so much a matter of the listener developing a sympathetic understanding with the artist or the psychological state that generated the work, but, rather, of engaging with the duration and feeling of the work in which the composer's influence is virtually enfolded. In this conception of depth, the aesthetic feelings remain attendant on the performance and its duration, where rhythm is thoroughly implicated with the melody and harmony, and where the listener comes to an awareness of *durée* without needing to be lulled by the rhythm.

Another criticism is that the gestures, movements and rhythms in art do not necessarily refer back to a particular artist, and cannot be recovered in the act of viewing a work or listening to a performance. Susanne Langer criticizes Bergson for assuming that the artist 'shows us the unique character of such completely individual objects or persons',[140] and argues, with reference to modern dance and Mary Wigman in particular, that there is sometimes confusion between the representation of emotion and the actual felt emotions of the dancer. The dancer does not directly convey their own feelings to an audience, as they could not possibly live through the feelings they portray, which might range from joy to terror and madness. What they do, instead, is create the semblance of emotion through the balancing of affective tensions and the 'illusion of emotions and wills in conflict'. The emotions are always virtual, schemas or symbols rather than actual experiences that can be referred back to the individual.[141] The dancer certainly feels something to support the emotional contours and tensions visible in the dance movements; however, this is not the same as expressing feelings.[142] Semblance is to some degree a generality or abstraction, but one that requires physical instantiation in the lived time of the audience's engagement with the work and its formal properties. From Bergson's perspective, one could argue that it is the choreographer rather than the dancer who provides the emotional provenance for the work, as they are directly responsible for the creation of the whole work and could live through the feelings that, in turn, give rise to the work of art. However, any such argument also leads to its own impasses, for most dance works also comprise music, and should one argue that it is the lived experience of the composer or the choreographer that comes to the fore? Can we argue that Vaslav Nijinsky's and Claude Debussy's *Prélude à l'après-midi d'un faune* originates from a common centre even though the music was written before the choreography and the composer did not like Nijinsky's interpretation? Or, indeed, should we return to the original poem by Stéphane Mallarmé, and its own particular configuration of feeling?

Alternatively, art could be discussed in terms of different levels of sympathetic engagement where those mediums that align most closely with the movement of the body, that have gestures that can be directly mimicked, will be accorded greater value over those that require a process of working through or interpretation to arrive at the artist's gesture, movement and feeling. The reason Bergson does not address such questions in this early work is that his argument is overly invested in the distinction between depth and surface, where aesthetic feelings are only invoked to describe some of the features of the qualitative and unmeasurable depth of *durée*. It is accepted that true aesthetic feeling is found in the very interior of consciousness, where all spatial distinctions have given way to qualitative ones and that this is the same for both the artist and for the public who view an artist's work or attend a performance. The greatest works are consequently those that present the fewest barriers to the sympathetic connection between artist and public – those works that do not linger in sensation and allow thought to pass most directly through the body. The problem with Bergson's argument is not only in ascribing this notion of sympathy to art but also in passing too quickly between the various layers of consciousness in order to arrive at sympathetic understanding. Formal properties are only invoked insofar as they present a stage through which movement is invoked and the weight of the body is elided.

Following the line between touch and vision

In Bergson's analysis of the aesthetic feelings in *Time and Free Will*, the emphasis on harmony and grace somewhat limits a proper analysis of the materiality of the artistic gesture. In foregrounding the ease and lightness of movement, there is little scope for the discussion of the corporeality of the artistic work and the viewer's response to it. In this account of grace, aesthetic pleasure derives from the audience's control of the future direction of the movement which, at its incorporeal limit, is a repetitive and hypnotic rhythm that invokes feelings in the depth of consciousness. Although rhythm can move the body over an extended duration, a repetitive rhythm is predictable and can therefore be contrasted with directional or even aleatory movement that is always unmaking itself in the very moment it appears. In general, Bergson emphasizes the unforeseeability and novelty of time which is at odds with grace in which movement and the line are projected into a knowable future. The unity of the work is given greater value – through notions of grace, harmony and balance – than the disruptive movement of an individual line. The focus on grace can, in part, be attributed to Bergson's own aesthetic sensibilities as he did not demonstrate a strong interest in modern art and many of his preferences were founded in the nineteenth century. The reference to harmony and even a rhythmic and sympathetic harmony between artist and viewer precludes the Modernist aim of defamiliarization or its emphasis on the plasticity of the work.

Bergson's brief discussions of the value of art are also shaped by his intellectual interests and the work of other philosophers from the nineteenth century, including Félix Ravaisson, a philosopher whose writings on art drew much inspiration from Leonardo da Vinci. In 'The Life and Work of Ravaisson' (1904), Bergson referred directly to Ravaisson's examination of drawing and the importance of the line in understanding the living centre of a work:

> There is, in Leonardo da Vinci's *Treatise in Painting*, a page that Ravaisson loved to quote. It is the one where the author says that the living being is characterized by the undulous or serpentine line, that each being has its own way of undulating, and that the object of art is to render this undulation distinctive. 'The secret of the art of drawing is to discover in each object the particular way in which a certain flexuous line which is, so to speak, its generating axis, is directed through its whole extent, like one main wave which spreads out in little surface waves'. It is possible, moreover, that this line is not any of the visible lines of the figure. It is not in one place any more than in another, but it gives the key to the whole.[143]

The reference to the 'undulous or serpentine line', which provides the means of accessing the living movement of the body, follows a similar line of reasoning to the discussion of grace in *Time and Free Will*. Da Vinci refers specifically to a quality of the living body, but Ravaisson shifts the focus to an incorporeal resonance of the work as a whole, which in Bergson's account of grace is a movement that is carried from the creator of the work to the viewer in the recreation of the feeling. Bergson accentuates the generative principle, as a 'virtual centre' that organizes the whole of the painting, and indicates the painter's expression that can be, to some degree, recovered by the spectator.[144] Although there is an emphasis on the line in this description, it is subsumed in the work as an organizational principle that generates the whole, and as such, it is better understood through vision and notions of harmony and balance than it is in the physical gesture of making marks in painting or drawing.

Bergson's placement of the whole, albeit a whole that generates novelty, in the mind of the artist before the act of producing the work – the work is a reflection of these aesthetic feelings – is largely borrowed from Ravaisson. In his key work on drawing, *L'Enseignement du Dessin dans les Lycées* (1854), Ravaisson argues that the artist must enter into things and seek the spirit (*esprit*) which animates them through the proper representation of their gestures and movements. In addition to the representation of living bodies, this spirit is found in the composition of the work and distribution of parts within a whole, where a great work can be judged by its harmony of spirit.[145] Consequently, it is the sense of sight that best discloses the spirit of a visual work (drawing, painting or sculpture) despite the emphasis on the sensual line, for senses such as touch are hampered by the successive presentation of sensual data. Through sight, harmony and proportion are revealed all at once, and therefore serve as a guide for the drawer.[146] The sensual line is contained by the artist's vision and an intellectual conception of the whole before the first mark is made. There is certainly no great difficulty in emphasizing sight and the visual whole in the description of the visual arts, for most artists start with a compositional idea and make sketches of a work before developing the final work. The difficulty from a Bergsonian perspective is reconciling the sensuousness of the artistic gesture, the directedness of bodily movement, and the unforeseeability of *durée* with a notion of a harmonious visual whole, even if it is imagined through a generative principle.

Unless the actual generative movement describes the material genesis of the work, the sinuous line could be reduced to a trace that invokes a rhythm without the muscular or kinaesthetic feeling involved in the production of the work – visual rhythm supplants tactile expression. When Bergson refers to oscillation or hypnotic rhythm it is within the confines of a pre-existing spatial frame, in which the line loses its materiality and its directionality. Bergson presents an aesthetic theory that is determined more by the finished artwork than the process of producing that work. In overemphasizing moral and aesthetic sympathy as a centripetal movement from matter to the depths of feeling, Bergson has not attended sufficiently to the lateral movement of the body and gesture in a process of becoming, or even the slowness of artistic production and reception. In *Laughter*, this centripetal movement is characterized in terms of disinterestedness, in which the artist or audience member recovers the real as the movement of life in perception, such as the sounding of a chord or the collective pleasure of a dance. It is about overcoming the externality and materiality of perception in order to sympathetically engage with life's 'immateriality'[147] – which will be discussed further in Chapter 4 in terms of utility and the logic of solid bodies. In combining disinterestedness with immateriality, the generative capacity of the gesture linked to the intentionality of the artist is missing. Bergson moves too quickly to the deep feelings rather than focusing on what it means to make a mark on the canvas and to actually generate the rhythm of the work.

Art does not simply recreate the sensibility of the artist, for this would ignore the differences between mediums and practices of production; indeed, the act of producing the work drives the aesthetic process of reimagining the medium. Jean-François Lyotard in 'The Pictorial Event Today' states that the proper subject of painting is the painterly gesture, which extends beyond the pictorial object to question the very limits of painting. Over the course of the history of painting, visual speculation and investigation are driven by the concrete fact of painting, which took the form of a reinstitution of the painterly gesture in the form of a 'pictorial spasm' for the avant-garde.[148] The spasm prevents painting from being reduced to the representation of intelligible objects, for example, Picasso's Cubist figures always reside on the threshold of intelligibility with the painterly marks resisting any reduction to the status of objects.[149] Moreover, the variability of the colour in the Cubist facets also prevents a purely geometrical reading of the work. Lyotard states that the emphasis on the unpredictability of gesture also rejects a bourgeois sensibility that dominated painting since the seventeenth century, in which painting is celebrated for its intelligibility and the degree to which it can be subject to reason.[150] By contrast, he argues that painting should foreground the visual (*visual*) over the visible in order to counter this emphasis on order and intelligibility.[151] Bergson also seeks from art something beyond intelligibility in the invocation of aesthetic feeling as a deep-seated qualitative movement. However, this movement is valued inasmuch as it is coincident with the immateriality of consciousness and therefore does not cleave sufficiently to the sensuousness of the visual. Of course, Bergson developed most of these ideas looking back to the nineteenth century and earlier rather than in concert with the burgeoning avant-garde.

In order to recover some notion of materiality, Bergson's preliminary discussion of the role of effort in mediating the material and immaterial could be reworked to include the physicality and directionality of movement, as well as the specific duration of an artistic gesture. It is a matter of slowing down rhythmic sympathy by noting the different levels of time that are manifest in a work of art and the viewer's response to it. The time of the line is different from the time of the kinaesthetic feeling that accompanies it. The feeling of lightness and grace might be understood as optical qualities that are attendant on the physical surface of the work over and above the compositional whole. Rather than something to be overcome through repetition, the materiality of the artwork could provide the resistance that allows for a particular line or a particular shape to be produced in a definite duration, and prepare the way for a discussion of the different ways that the levels of materiality and immateriality operate in the reception of the work. It is about how the structure of the work suggests an interpenetration of psychic states. Bergson dismisses sensation and effort because they are located closer to the surface of the body and, by consequence, closer to those intensive qualities isolated and measured by the psychophysicists. However, Bergson's own claim that the overall qualitative surface of the musculature alters as the effort increases, or is perceived to increase, provides a better foundation for the understanding of interpenetrative or connected movement in art than does the concept of grace. It is probably neglected because Bergson focuses on the centripetal movement away from spatialized matter, but it could be reinvigorated through according greater attention to the centrifugal movement from depth to surface, or by considering how the intensity of aesthetic feeling responds to different levels of materiality and opticality in the visual arts. This could involve examining how intensive states are expressed as lateral continuous movements in a visual artwork, which involves beginning with the underside or inner skin of movement and then working out towards the material traces of a gesture.

Bergson discusses the immanence and interiority of physical movement in a number of his works, usually as the basis for his critique of spatialization and of time and movement, but also to resolve philosophical problems, such as Zeno's paradoxes. In the paradox of Achilles and the tortoise, Achilles gives the tortoise a head start in a race in which he is clearly the faster competitor. However, Achilles cannot catch up with the tortoise for he has to reach the tortoise's previous position before he can overtake, which Zeno argues he is unable to do. 'By the time that Achilles has reached the place from which the tortoise started, the latter has again advanced to another point; and when Achilles reaches that point, then the tortoise will have advanced still another distance, even if very short'.[152] The distance is never covered because there are an infinite number of points between Achilles and the tortoise, which translates into an infinite distance.[153] Bergson argues that this paradox conflates the real movement of the runner's steps with the points that are said to correspond to those steps and that if we put to one side the spatial image of the trajectory, Achilles can overtake the tortoise due to the indivisibility of his internal and external movements: 'It is either an indivisible bound (which may occupy, nevertheless, a very long duration) or a series of indivisible bounds.'[154] Achilles overtakes the tortoise in indivisible strides that cannot be divided like the line because they are 'articulated inwardly', that is, they remain continuous with Achilles's internal state.[155] Internal qualitative indivisibility is the very condition of Achilles's movement, for he is not forced to move from outside like a marionette nor does he occupy a particular position. This particular condition of continuity also differs from the spectator who is carried along by the grace of a dancer's movement and rhythm, hypnotically forgetting their own corporeality. The inward articulation of feeling remains strongly linked to Achilles's desire to move, felt as an internal impulsion, and also the feeling of internal effort. The problem with Bergson's account of the sinuous line in Ravaisson's philosophy is that he does not talk about the inwardly articulated relationship between willed movement, direction and effort which is as relevant to drawing a line as it is to running, and, instead, rushes to the virtual centre of the image and a generalized rhythm.

Bergson wants to return aesthetics to the depth of feeling of an artist or spectator, and for this it is important to imagine oneself within the lived time of the artwork's production, that is, within the becoming of the work. This involves a partial rejection of the role of the line in describing the boundary of objects, and a greater emphasis on what it means to move within the time of a line. Paul Valéry talks about his own experience of copying images through the medium of drawing in his short article 'Seeing and Copying' and argues: 'There is a tremendous difference between seeing a thing without a pencil in your hand and seeing it while *drawing* it.'[156] One of the distinctive features of drawing is that it is a 'willed' movement and this differentiates it from seeing, where compositional elements such as harmony are foregrounded.[157] The act of drawing requires muscular action and the ability to resist those movements that are 'naturally' inclined in the hand and this can be contrasted with the much more aleatory movements of the eye: 'To free the hand *in the visual sense* is to take away its liberty *in the muscular sense*; particularly it has to be trained to draw in any direction against its instinct.'[158] This implies that the person looking at an artwork 'while drawing it' sees the work according to two movements operating in different durations: the duration of moving the pencil across the page, including the muscular control that is required to sustain this, and the duration of the eye's movement, which is able to traverse the whole of the line at a glance. This durational difference is a function of the different times of attention: the slow conscious time of willing and traversing versus the faster speed of immediate attention, or what draws the eye to the work.

Valéry's example raises the question as to what degree the tension of a willed movement underscores the durational continuity in all aesthetic experience. In considering the time of a work, should each individual movement (a drawn line or brushstroke) be considered independently of the formal optical whole of the work? Should aesthetic feeling be considered, first, effortful, willed movement? One way to address such questions is to return to the notion of schemas of movement that, necessarily, assume corporeal continuity. The relationship between schemas and feeling in art has found new expression in the field of 'neuroesthetics', where it is argued that the viewer responds to the artwork through neurologically duplicating its movements – which is similar in some respects to Spencer's and Bergson's claims about mimicry. David Freedberg and Vittorio Gallese state that the motor cortex may respond directly to a represented movement or emotion, thus empathetically reproducing the emotion, as well as other physical features such as instability, exertion or imbalance in a work of art. In each case 'beholders might find themselves automatically simulating the emotional expression, the movement or even the implied movement within the representation'.[159] This is not limited to represented feelings, for Freedberg and Gallese argue that non-representational works, such as those of Fontana and Pollock, might reveal the artist's material gestures which can also invoke 'empathetic movement'.[160] The viewer might empathize with the hand cutting the canvas in Fontana's works or the hand distributing the streaks of paint in Pollock's. This neuroesthetic approach differs from earlier theories of empathy because the transfer of feeling does not require conscious or semi-conscious mimicry of the movement, for the movement is transmitted directly to the motor cortex. The authors refer to the discovery of mirror neurons that describe the 'Activation of the same brain region during first- and third-person experience of actions' and these neurons, found in animals and humans, are the oldest structures underpinning empathy and other forms of emotion.[161] This work in neuroesthetics presents another way of considering how material gestures can be mimicked or reproduced without necessarily being interpreted through vision. From a Bergsonian perspective, the internal, virtual movements of the deep feelings could be expressed centrifugally in material gestures. Centripetally, regardless of how far we descend into the qualitative multiplicity of consciousness, a trace of the felt movement remains bringing with it the qualities of directionality and musculature tension.

This difference between a slow willed movement, felt as tension in the body, and the apprehension of the optical whole as noted in the work of Ravaisson, can be theorized in terms of the difference between touch and vision. Kinaesthetic feelings are much more strongly associated with touch than sight, because the former requires the conscious engagement of muscles in an activity, whereas eye movements operate at such a pace that they are usually not felt or consciously motivated.[162] Drew Leder argues that one of the features of vision is its ecstatic engagement with the sensible world, where the eye as a felt corporeal object disappears in the degree to which the world is revealed.[163] The eyes cannot be seen in the act of seeing, except, of course, in the odd cases of looking into a mirror, and this principle applies to most of the senses, in a phenomenological condition that Husserl refers to as the null-point of perception. This argument also applies to touch – using the example of Merleau-Ponty's two hands touching, Leder argues that there is no point, regardless of how the relationship is configured, in which the hand can both touch and be touched.[164] However, it should be noted with regard to the arguments of Maine de Biran, Bergson and Spencer that the body is still present in terms of an internal feeling of effort, which may not be manifest in the tips of a finger, but is still felt kinaesthetically in willed movement. Touch opens the body to the world by providing a continuous surface in movement, subtended by the continuity of kinaesthetic feeling.

Bergson provides many references to touch and sensation that could complement the analysis of aesthetic sympathy and the movement between different levels of feeling in the body and consciousness. Furthermore, they could aid us in better understanding the many dimensions of artistic gesture that remain undeveloped insofar as they are constrained to the critique of spatialization. For example, in *Duration and Simultaneity*, Bergson compares the felt movement of touch to the visual apprehension of motion:

> If I draw my finger across a sheet of paper without looking at it, the motion I perform is, perceived from within, a continuity of consciousness, something of my own flow, in a word, duration. If I now open my eyes, I see that my finger is tracing on the sheet of paper a line that is preserved, where all is juxtaposition and no longer succession; this is the unfolded, which is the record of the result of motion, and which will be its symbol as well. Now, this line is divisible, measurable. In dividing and measuring it, I can then say, if it suits me, that I am dividing and measuring the duration of the motion that is tracing it out.[165]

Bergson uses this example to explain why the awareness of time as *durée* differs from the concept of time as extension in order to rethink the principle of simultaneity in physics. The example is also worth noting because it demonstrates the importance of the body as 'perceived from within' when attending to perceptible differences – which is here precipitated by the introspective method of closing one's eyes. With vision occluded, we are able to feel the qualitative variation of sensation in the tip of the finger which is closely associated with the interior surface of the body and also the continuity of the body's movement. Leder may refer to the absence of the ecstatic body in perception, whereas what Bergson recognizes in touch is the continuous variation of sensation without reference to externality or spatial displacement. This qualitative continuity is analogous to the conscious experience of duration. Why is this continuity present in touch rather than vision? One of the main reasons is that the slow movements of touch are closely associated with willed movements and invoke both effort and intention; moreover, the felt sensation in a finger is always on the threshold of the touching (acting upon the world) and touched (the continual variation in tactile feeling).

In relation to Bergson's aesthetics, should we emphasize continuity of bodily sensation in touch, which is closely aligned with intention and effort, or the apprehension of the whole which is revealed in sight? The former must retain something of the directionality of movement, because tactile sensation requires the motivation of the external surfaces of the body, whereas sight predominantly operates at a distance from the body. Hearing also attends to objects at a distance, the sources of sound, but is more easily introjected into the body and, therefore, better approximates the interior experience of *durée*. Most of Bergson's examples in *Time and Free Will* are derived from sight – the rhythm of an image, the movement of a dancer's body – and sight, because it operates at a distance, requires a principle by which the external movement can breach the surface of the body and motivate the various psychological states in the depth of aesthetic feeling. However, the whole matter looks a little different if aesthetic engagement begins with the continuity of the artist's experience, which appears first as orientational or directional movement rather than rhythmic sympathy. It is about the desire to produce an artwork and the specific time it takes to produce it, which is more easily imagined through touch because it foregrounds the continuity of contact with the work. The continuity of effort was certainly central to Biran's philosophy but it was also evident a generation later in the work of Jean-Marie Guyau. Guyau argued that the concept of time is derived from primitive corporeal movement that is primarily understood in terms of the unity of effort, which becomes intention as the organism develops an awareness of what it is doing.[166] In animals this intention is grounded in appetition, where the animal moves to fulfil the intention or satisfy the appetite, which is felt as muscular efforts that can be divided into a series of steps. It is only after the fact that these efforts and movements are correlated with a line, which in its traversal becomes the abstract figure of time.[167] Guyau sees time as derived from space, for desire and intention are linked to the capacity to move towards an object, which differs from Bergson's aim of removing the spatial object in the centripetal push towards the deep feelings. However, the idea of beginning with the continuity of movement corresponds with Bergson's solution to Zeno's paradoxes because the intention to move precedes the description of the trajectory. It is also relevant to a philosophy of art in which the process of production is derived from a unity of action, comprised of singular gestures which, over the course of production, take a concrete spatial form. When the spectator recovers the movement of a visual artwork – specifically painting, sculpture and drawing – it will include these gestural intentions in addition to the overall rhythmic property of the work.

Another way of phrasing this is to argue that centripetal integration of psychic states in aesthetic experience must intersect with the centrifugal concentration of these states in the artistic gesture. Bergson must work out from the centre of unextended and intensive qualitative multiplicity through to the various levels of corporeal and material continuity. If rhythm, movement and the sinuous line are the aesthetic ground for sensual engagement with the artwork and somehow lead the viewer back to the temporal centre of the artist's sensibility, then it is important to begin with the movement that underpins this sensibility and which finds concrete expression in the artwork. The artistic gesture should comprise corporeal, intentional, directional and affective aspects which can never be truly parsed. In the example of the finger moving across the paper, Bergson focuses on the qualitative variation manifest in the fingertip, but he should also discuss the direction, incipient movement and willingness to move across the paper that underpin the sensation. The artistic gesture can be understood as a process in which the qualitative variability of experience finds a tendency to move that is eventually manifest in the materiality of the work. Maxine Sheets-Johnstone in her work on the phenomenology of movement argues that before we consider any type of movement in space, we should examine the body's inclination to move and the variation in qualitative feeling that is attendant upon it. She is critical of phenomenology's overemphasis on visual perception as the means of understanding corporeal movement and proposes that we should, instead, consider the condition of 'animatedness'.[168] At the centre of such movement is a basic willingness to move, the 'I can' of living in the world and coming into being through movement that pre-exists any reflection on the social purpose or form of movement.[169] Sheets-Johnstone argues that this primary 'kinaesthetic consciousness' is the very basis for our understanding of time as flow or flux because kinaesthetic movement cannot be easily broken down into parts without changing the nature of the movement.[170] The kinaesthetic feelings are not readily associated with objects unlike the other senses, in which qualia such as sounds, tastes, textures and images can be partially separated and sequenced in terms of the past, present and future. Kinaesthesia is suffused throughout the body without any clear spatial divisions, and because it is always present, albeit changing in quality, Sheets-Johnstone states that its temporal quality can better be described as a 'kinetic lingering aura'.[171] Sheets-Johnstone's account of kinaesthetic feeling combines willed movement, as a basic willingness to move, with the sensual continuity of time that is central to Bergson's *durée*. Feeling in the body is something that stretches across the past into the future through expectation and the endurance of feeling, and can be understood in itself without reference to actual movements in space.

When Bergson refers to the need to recover *durée*, he talks about returning to the interiority of experience by stripping away the various artefacts of spatial description, from words through to the atemporal and measurable trajectory. Sheets-Johnstone provides similar advice with regard to kinaesthetic feeling, stating that by removing the purpose of movement, we can focus on its qualitative unfolding as the very condition for the perception of time.[172] She suggests a phenomenological reduction in which the researcher conducts bodily exercises with the eyes closed and repeats the exercises until an understanding of the 'invariant' phenomenal properties is gained.[173] This phenomenal introspection reveals four main aspects:

> In a very general sense, the felt tensional quality has to do with our sense of effort; the linear quality with both the felt linear contour of our moving body and the linear paths we sense ourselves describing in the process of moving; the amplitudinal quality with both the

felt expansiveness or contractiveness of our moving body and the spatial extensiveness or constrictedness of our movement; the felt projectional quality with the way in which we release force or energy.[174]

Sheets-Johnstone argues that all these qualities are integrated into kinaesthetic feeling. The linear and amplitudinal aspects concern the body's process of reaching out into space, whereas the tensional and projectional do not require reference to the actual change in a body's position and therefore are temporal in form. These temporal aspects reveal the intensity of an action and its expenditure through movement and, insofar as they are projected forward, have protentive and retentive qualities that do not require an optical representation.[175] These kinaesthetic aspects have an internal (non-optical) expression but also create linear designs in the world that can be considered to be expansive or contracted depending on how the energy is directed.[176] From the perspective of Bergson's philosophy, the kinaesthetic feelings have the qualitative interpenetration and variability that distinguishes his *durée*, but even in the depth of feeling they retain much more of the qualities of willed movement, expressed as effort, tension and intensity. As such, kinaesthesia provides a better bridge between the depth of feeling and the surface properties of sensation than does the notion of rhythmic sympathy or the effortlessness of grace.

The diffusion of kinaesthetic feeling through a work derives from the artist, with each brushstroke or strike of the chisel indicating a type of labour invested in the body, and can be used to think about how feeling conditions the internal organization of the work. In other words, the sinuous line could derive its unity from a muscular tension – from Bergson's perspective, the distribution of tension throughout the qualitatively varying surface of the musculature – that is immanent to the body, rather than the dissolution of tension in grace. This tension can be most readily evinced in dance, in particular, Modernist dance in which the body reveals itself as a source of feeling outside of any narrative ascription. Louis Horst, a prominent dance teacher and theorist in the first half of the twentieth century, argues that what distinguishes modern dance is its ability to convey 'intimacy' through the body's physicality and musculature: 'This is not at all the ballet dancer's awareness of line, of speed or balance, and dramatic portrayal of a role. It is, rather, an inner sensitivity to every one of the body's parts, to the power of its whole, and to the space in which it carves designs.'[177] The modern dancer does not seek to hide bodily tension as in Romantic ballet, but, rather, aims to communicate kinaesthetic feeling by highlighting the 'tension of relaxation', as well as 'contraction and release'.[178] Kinaesthetic feelings assure the continuity of aesthetic movement by bringing together the intensive variations in the musculature which Bergson argues is also the qualitative basis for the understanding of effort. It is possible that Bergson would have attributed greater value to the physicality of the artwork, in this case the corporeal effort implicit in dance, if he was more open or exposed to a Modernist aesthetic.

Brian Massumi takes this argument one step further when he looks at the work of the contemporary dancer and choreographer Merce Cunningham, who also accentuates the physicality of the body, which is achieved by disrupting those gestures that provide any reference to a narrative or the dancer's ability to express an inner feeling. Disrupting a gesture prevents the spectator from finding a principle of intelligibility in the movement and, by doing so, reveals 'pure movement'.[179] 'The focus on pure movement brings dance integrally back to the "kinesthetic sense", as taken up in vision: specifically at the vanishing point where proprioception enters into a zone of indistinction with thought.'[180] In contemporary dance, the gesture remains in 'perpetual nascency', thus revealing time as continuous qualitative change without a clear sense of futurity. Stripped of a point of termination for an action, the gesture appears as pure variation or the capacity of the body to differ from itself.[181] Now there is no reason to argue that all dance, or indeed all art, should seek to reveal pure movement through such truncated gestures, but this argument links Bergson's arguments about the continuity of inner feeling with the deep feelings. The inner feeling that attests to Achilles's movement in Bergson's solution to Zeno's paradoxes does not have to be felt as completed steps, which is somewhat of an external characterization of the inner feeling. Instead, the variable continuity of feeling, particularly as kinaesthetic feeling, persists throughout the movement irrespective of any narrative description. Bergson's argument differs from Cunningham's invocation of pure movement insofar as he has the tendency to refer to a path already covered, or a movement unfolded. The path of graceful movement allows us to gain control of the movement through rhythm, the speech of Viviani allows the spectator to forget about the movement of his mouth and lips, and the stride of Achilles indicates its own completion in the overtaking of the tortoise. In each case, movement is described in terms of legible continuity, in which the listener or spectator can somewhat imagine the future course of an action. This contrasts with Massumi's pure movement in which change is in a perpetual state of beginning, which better accords with Bergson's argument that *durée* is novel. What this suggests is that art can direct its audience to different aspects of *durée* (novelty, continuity, tension, etc.) depending on its material or, indeed, immaterial features.

This emphasis on tension, intensity and the internality of kinaesthetic feeling can be transferred from dance to painting through the artistic gesture. When Bergson rejects the artwork that focuses on sensation, he treats sensation as something that is separated from the continuity of movement and the complex conditions of qualitative variation. However, sensation could serve as the virtual centre of an artist's action if it is grounded in kinaesthesia and a nascent pure movement that integrates body and mind. Rather than talking about the compositional rhythms of the finished work, it would describe a type of intensive movement that is tied to the time of the production of the work, a true sinuous line, through which the other aspects of painting and feeling are brought together. How is this actually manifest in the visual arts? At one level of organization, represented figures indicate a type of nascent movement by the very fact that they are analogous to living beings and their willed movement. Every gesture, expression and stance indicates a capacity for movement in which we experience the various qualities associated with 'animatedness'. We see bodies through our own capacity to move or reanimate the movements and feelings of others in rhythmic sympathy. In terms of the representation of dance in the visual arts, this could refer to a smooth, continuous or graceful line, or even the expressive line, all of which reveal an arc of movement, which is certainly a key feature of many of Matisse's works. The gesture is not limited to corporeal empathy, for it also describes the continuity and distribution of tension in a work that is held together by kinaesthetic, tactile and visual principles of organization. These formal tensions restrict and imply movement in a way that can be compared to the musculature, which expands outwards in the expression of a movement and also pulls the body back to a virtual centre. As kinaesthetic feeling is continuous throughout the body, it holds together all the individual tensions that are spatially distributed across the body's surface. Moreover, kinaesthetic feeling underlies the production of each of the artist's marks. To make a mark is to move this body, but as the body is a continuous whole, just like Achilles's steps, each mark attests to its continuity, in which case the continuity of artistic production aligns with the formal and rhythmic continuity of the whole.

The depiction of dance in terms of tension is most evident in the sculptural work of the Vorticist, Henri Gaudier-Brzeska, who was acquainted with Bergson's philosophy and had read *Creative Evolution*.[182] Gaudier-Brzeska was attracted to the more radical side of Bergson's philosophy, particularly his nominalism and vitalism, which was supported by another Vorticist, the poet Ezra Pound, who stated that sculpture should place greater emphasis on 'emotional force'.[183] In Gaudier-Brzeska's *Red Stone Dancer* (c. 1913), the movement of dance is not evoked through the graceful line except for the curve of the dancer's right arm drawn behind the head and the left shoulder, nor are there clear lines describing completed movements (see Figure 2.1). Dance is often represented by limbs extending away from the body that give the impression of a body lightly moving through space, whereas in *Red Stone Dancer*, the body is enfolded back in on itself in a state of perpetual tension. All the joints are bent at right angles to the point where the muscles display their greatest exertion. One of the arms is bent back

FIGURE 2.1 Henri Gaudier-Brzeska. *Red Stone Dancer* (c. 1913).

around the head in a contortionist's posture and the hips operate against the torso and legs in an extreme form of *contrapposto* stance, albeit one that is accentuated by the bend in the legs. Even the knees are separated to describe a torsional movement working against the fixed position of the feet and hips. Every limb appears at an oblique angle from the body. Rudolf Arnheim argues that the most common means of representing tension in the visual arts is obliquity, because the oblique line draws the eye away from the fixed or normal position and can also indicate a movement back towards a state of rest.[184] It also depends on the type of figure that is represented, for a human figure with arms raised in a Y shape would have greater tension than a tree describing a similar position.[185] The fact that the oblique lines are associated with the human body draws the eye towards the centre of the work, the dancer's torso and an indivisible but infinitely variable, kinaesthetic feeling in which each of the limbs is implicated.

The viewer is asked to attend to the points of stretching and pulling of the body in a work that is also contained by the thickness and heaviness of the block forms carved in stone. The body moves centrifugally by rotating around an axis with each elbow describing points like hands on a clock, and also centripetally due to a tension in the material that draws any outward movement back to the centre. It is not a representation of dance in the sense of an unfolding of movement in space, where the movement is judged in terms of its linear breadth, but rather a torsional movement that returns dance to the physicality of the body. Mark Antliff argues that spiral movements stretch the boundaries of the body by highlighting the expansion of the muscles in movement. He refers specifically to Boccioni's *Unique Forms of Continuity in Space* in suggesting that these movements indicate as much the 'creative will' of the figure as the physical performance of an action.[186] In some respects, the creative will is not easily attributed to a sculptural figure, which is a fictional construct that cannot really have its own creative will. Indeed, the artist's creative will might be better understood through the process of manufacture, and Antliff notes that Gaudier-Brzeska advocated 'direct carving' because the marks of the tools are visible, as are the sculptor's individual actions.[187] Whether or not it can be attributed to the will, the body has an animating centre that becomes visible through its material and corporeal form, creating tensions that draw upon the viewer's understanding of their own corporeality. Seeing the centre of the work through a play of forces reflects back to the viewer their own kinaesthetic experience and, by extension, the continuity and variability of the deeper aesthetic feelings. Unlike rhythmic sympathy, the interiority of the figure is manifest as a general bodily feeling that is contingent on the physicality and materiality of the artwork.

Kinaesthesia can operate at another level of organization outside of the representation of a body in the completed work that refers directly to the specific time of making art. If Bergson wants to refer to the artist's lived time in the work, he must first consider the very movements that produce the work and the vestiges of effort that linger in each mark. In contrast to an optical vision of the whole that stands outside the body, the spectator could develop some sympathy for the artist in terms of a corporeal movement that operates in a time analogous to that felt by the spectator. When invoking the deep feelings, there is no need to eschew the body because the kinaesthetic core of artistic practice is itself a demonstration of the qualitative multiplicity of *durée* combined with the directedness of a body acting in the world. Valéry's pencil tip encompasses the will to mark the surface of the paper and the muscular arc of the body with its attendant feelings, feelings that both propel and hold the movement – the longer the movement, the greater the tension implicit within the stroke. Different kinaesthetic feelings are invoked at each movement of the drawn line depending on where the hand is placed relative to the surface: there are broad arcs that require the movement of the whole arm and others that operate within the restricted movement of the wrist.

These corporeal differences are further differentiated depending on the speed of the drawn gestures, for each speed has a different *durée*, as well as different affective and kinaesthetic qualities. Outside of any conceptualization of the whole, each line brings with it qualitative variation, something that can often be forgotten with many paintings seeking to mask the gestural marks, including the indication of speed, in order to emphasize the representational function. It is only in the twentieth century that works began to consistently explore the speed of the artist's gesture. With regard to gestural speed in Abstract Expressionism, Stanley Hayter argues that the perception of movement depends on the thickness and form of the line:

the form of the drops progressing from circular, at slow speed, to elongated and linear, with increasing speed, amplifies the sense of increasing velocity along the trace. Where the projection is made upward with a rotary movement of the hand, it can be seen that the trace will have a parabolic form. The speed will increase along the direction of movement as it is registered on the canvas, although if we follow the parabolic path of any one, its speed is decreasing.[188]

Due to the strong relationship between the painterly gesture and the lived movement in Abstract Expression, Hayter argues that the paintings should be displayed in a position similar to that in which they were painted.[189] The viewer needs to be aligned with the artist's movement in order to facilitate sympathy with the speed of the work, and by extension its duration. To return to Matisse's *Dance (II)*, one of the key aspects is the length of the brush strokes outlining the bodies, for in the long arc the rhythm of the artist's gestures amplifies the speed of the body in movement. The viewer inhabits the time of the line with its particular speed, and this contributes to the feeling of movement in the painting as whole without being fully reducible to it.

Corporeal rhythm is much more tangible in those types of contemporary painting that emphasize the gestural freedom of the artist, such as Abstract Expressionism, rather than the modelling of a subject. In Cy Twombly's *Bacchus* series (2005) at the Tate Modern, the large size of the canvases that extend beyond four by three metres accentuates the kinaesthetic properties of the brushstrokes for both artist and spectator. In these works, the curved red brushstrokes, the colour of blood and wine, fill the canvas with a frenzied movement indicated by the errant drips of paint and the diffusion of colour, all of which clearly contribute to the bacchanalian theme. The expansive movements required great effort from Twombly over a very short period, which differs from many of his earlier works that were reworked over a long period in the studio.[190] The unbroken arcs of the brushstrokes, which maintain their tension over a short duration, also attest to the singularity of each gesture in the same way that Achilles's steps inhere over a single duration stretching from the past into an indeterminate future. The amplitude of this movement-tension is augmented by the sheer size of the works, all of which operate outside the gestural breadth of the artist's body – indeed, the work was painted 'with a brush affixed to the end of a pole'.[191] When the spectator stands before the work, the brushstrokes refer back to the physical continuity of the artist's body, in the same way that a dancer's body supports the arc and continuity of a single movement. The traces carry with them the implied weight of the brush, the tension of the stretch and the striving to reach the edges of the canvas, all of which invoke a duration that subtends the body.

Indeed, there is a visual difference between the bottom and top halves of the works that relates to the anisotropy of corporeal movement. The top sections are lighter because the brushstrokes lose their thickness the further they are away from the body's centre, whereas the brushstrokes in the bottom half are thicker and denser because they are closer to the body – each painting brings together a range of corporeal tensions. Although each work has a specific rhythm, which can be addressed as a whole, the continuously varying brushstrokes exceed the spectator's own dimensions and invoke a duration based on the kinaesthetic feeling of stretching away from the body's virtual centre. In these works, rhythm must be understood through the various kinaesthetic feelings that accompany the body unlike in Bergson's argument that rhythm must eschew the body in order to reveal the *durée* of the inner states. It is the inner surface of the body, as well as the intensive variation in kinaesthetic feeling, that brings forth the qualitative multiplicity of the deep feelings and the interconnection of psychic states.

Material gestures and the resistance of matter

The kinaesthetic centre of movement is another way of considering the centrifugal path from artist to work, or, indeed, the centripetal movement from spectator to artist, without requiring any reference to the quality of gracefulness. The variation of form remains continuous with the life of the artist – through imagining the body and the lived time of artistic production – without being reducible to it. Another aspect of this centrifugal movement is the role of materiality in delimiting movement and fashioning the artist's relationship to the work. The art critic and historian Henri Focillon sketches out his ideas about the role of materiality in *The Life of Forms in Art*, written in 1934 when Bergsonism still overshadowed French intellectual life, although without the same fervour as in the first decade of the twentieth century. Focillon took an interest in Bergson's work, and even attended the philosopher's lectures at the Collège de France.[192] Although he does not nominate himself as a Bergsonian, he demonstrates an interest in how the variability of time and becoming affects the genealogy of stylistic development and is also critical of Hippolyte Taine for his focus on the external and measurable.[193]

In *Life of Forms*, Focillon examines the continuity of becoming in artistic practice and even acknowledges the notion of the spirit of a work but, unlike Bergson, states that it must be realized through material expression.[194] Form and matter are always combined in a process of mutual affectation in which the artistic materials impose themselves on the way the art object is modelled.[195] The tools of inscription have their own specific modes of expression and technical limits, and should form the basis for any study of formal development: 'That which acts is in its turn acted upon. To understand these actions and reactions, let us abandon the isolated consideration of form, matter, tool and hand, and instead take up our position on the exact, geometric meeting place of their activity.'[196] The material does not merely adopt the form sought by the artist – a material to be worked upon and made subject to the will of the artist – because the principles of formal expression inhere within it, and, therefore, it is more accurate to state that the material 'suggests' the forms that appear.[197] The material itself also suggests particular speeds of inscription or manufacture: the resistance of copper in etching differs from the canvas in oil painting, the malleability of plaster in making a mould differs from the hardness of marble or stone. This is reminiscent of Bergson's argument that art suggests a movement or feeling to an audience rather than directly causing a particular emotion, which, in this case, cannot be fully separated from the resistance and speed immanent to a material. Artistic engagement involves a particular duration, one shaped by the material affordances and the implicit resistances to willed movement and the other by the engagement of the mind and the body in the formal rhythm of the work. In working the two arguments together, we should ask: To what degree does the material suggestion also take part in the spectator's experience, and is there an implicit understanding of the material affordances in reanimating the artist's gesture as well as the affective contours of the work?

Focillon also invokes the sense of touch in a way that has more direct relevance to artistic practice than Bergson's use of it to illustrate the internal continuity of movement. Focillon argues that touch provides the means to create emergent qualities not found in the original state of a material, which are also present to the spectator in their engagement with the work.[198] For Focillon, the activity of the hand should be visible as it works upon matter and, consequently, artistic creativity is diminished in those works in which the artist allocates aspects of production to others. Consequently, he focuses on the plastic arts and is more critical of photography and other works produced without individual touch, because their surfaces lack the life that an artist's hand would bring to them.[199] From a Bergsonian perspective, touch should be foregrounded because it constitutes a sensual condition in which the body of the artist is coincident with the work, and thus could provide an indexical link to the ipseity of the artist's experience. Focillon states that the thoughts and pictorial reasoning of the artist should not be considered abstract when embodied in particular materials that afford direct contact:

> In the mind, it is already touch, incision, facet, line, already something molded or painted, already a grouping of masses in definite materials. It is not, it cannot be, abstract. As such, it would be nothing. It calls importunately for the tactile and the visual. Even as the musician hears, in his own ears, the design of this music not in numerical relationships, but in timbres, instruments and whole orchestras, so likewise the painter sees, in his own eyes, not the abstraction of his painting, but the tones, the modeling and the touch. The hand that is in his mind is at work. It creates the concrete within the abstract, and weight within the imponderable.[200]

This processual analysis of artistic practice is missing from Bergson's discussion of aesthetics, but should nevertheless complement the notion of a Bergsonian schema, because the material gestures are just another way of bringing together concrete images that, in turn, could suggest feelings. The artist's thoughts are closer to schemas the more fully they are invested in touch as a concrete process of working through rather than projecting a fixed image or representation into the space of the work. The intensity of thought as the continual manifestation of *durée* remains connected to this material engagement regardless of the level of abstraction, for the movement endures in the resistance of the material. In the work of Anselm Kiefer, despite the iconoclasm and political critique, it is hard to imagine the works as a projection of an abstract thought or movement, because the formal structure is often overwhelmed by the baseness of the materials. The materials seem to resist the operation of the hand from the muddy brown thickness of paint in his early works, to the solidity and heaviness of lead, sand, dirt and so on. Dirt and sand retain their grittiness even when moulded by the artist and although lead can be bent to give the impression of folds of paper, it is hard to imagine the hand moving quickly through the leaves of a leaden book or tearing them like sheets of paper.

What is most useful about Focillon's emphasis on the primacy of touch in coming to terms with the material world, ontogenetically and phylogenetically, is how it contrasts with vision and its organization of space. Even geometrical forms and numbers are primarily revealed through the manual activity of finger counting and the drawing of straight lines,[201] which Bergson also acknowledges in his discussion of extensity. Focillon talks about how the hands are the principal means of exploration and experimentation in childhood which eventually serves as the basis for the artistic material experimentation:

> The artist prolongs the child's curiosity far beyond the limits of childhood. He touches, he feels, he reckons weight, he measures space, he molds the fluidity of atmosphere to prefigure form in it, he caresses the skin of all things. With the language of Touch he composes the language of Sight – a 'warm' tone, a 'cool' tone, a 'heavy' tone, a 'hollow' tone, a 'hard' line, a 'soft' line.[202]

Touch is a means of corporeal thinking that remains in contact with the continuity of consciousness and the materiality of the art object. From this perspective, Bergson and Ravaisson's reference to the sinuous line need not be grounded in spatial harmony, for it could be considered in terms of the time of production operating from within the work, or a means of feeling one's way through the work. It is a matter of understanding the work through its physical resistances and material modes of endurance.

This approach focuses more on the juncture between the body and the materiality of artistic practice than Bergson's argument about aesthetic feeling and sympathy, but it actually indicates a direction that is nascent in Bergson's philosophy. It concerns a tendency that operates in line with the movement of the body, with reverberations in the interiority of consciousness, in which matter is shaped by the modulation of feeling rather than atemporal spatial reasoning. In his late collection of essays, *The Creative Mind*, Bergson makes some suggestions about scientific practice that align with Focillon's argument about the primacy of the hand. In the second introduction Bergson rethinks the relationship between science and metaphysics, arguing that he does not reject scientific approaches or overly relativize them, as many of his detractors claimed – provoked partly by the success of 'The Introduction to Metaphysics' and its criticism of science's perspectivalism. In the introduction to *Creative Mind*, Bergson states that science education should teach the student how to experiment and invent rather than presenting the student with an existing body of knowledge, or ready-made ideas that are already ossified in language.[203] He argues that science thinks through matter and students should foster an interest in the object itself, which entails physical experimentation and re-establishing the relationship between making (*Homo faber*) and intelligence (*Homo sapiens*): 'Let us apply to a real master, that he may perfect the touch to the point of making it a sense of touch (*d'en faire un tact*): the intelligence will go from the hand to the head.'[204] The hand is the very basis for understanding the object through touch, or what could be regarded as a sensitivity to the qualitative particularity of the object. The properly engaged scientist will retain a lived connection with the hand as a sensual object and instrument of investigation, and this will remain immanent to science as it seeks to systematize its objects of knowledge through measurement and classification.

Bergson introduces this argument through reference to science, but the same underlying principles are deployed in his discussion of literature and philosophy. In literature, sound is the sensual basis for speech that must be recovered if the reader is to properly align with the author's thought. The reader 'must fall into step (*emboîtant*) with him [the author] by adopting his gestures, his attitudes, his gait, by which I mean learning to read the text aloud with the proper intonation and inflection'.[205] In adopting the position of the speaker, the body is returned to literature as something that remains continuous with the enunciation, or remains in contact with the text. In philosophy, the aim is less on the technical meaning of each word than on seeking 'to get back the movement and rhythm of the composition, to live again creative evolution by being one with it in sympathy'.[206] It is a matter of occupying the same sensual and, indeed, corporeal attitude of the author and this involves following their steps, which is itself a form of touch. It is about retracing and recreating the line of the author's movements in order to recreate the qualitative variation of feeling immanent to the text. Bergson still highlights the importance of sympathy but there is greater emphasis on its sensuality and corporeality than in *Time and Free Will*. There is no need to go beyond the material through a concept such as grace or harmony, because the material support is always required to give form to the movement.

Conclusion

In *Time and Free Will*, Bergson speculates on how art can gesture towards the depth of aesthetic experience by invoking movement in the body and transforming the extensive into the qualitative multiplicity of *durée*. From the perspective of a Bergsonian metaphysics, the argument is valuable in describing how rhythm is central to a notion of lived time, but from the perspective of the philosophy of art, there remains the question of what happens to the physical and formal features of the artwork in this centripetal movement. What tactile, material and physical traces of the aesthetic experience endure in this invocation of aesthetic feeling? One of the criticisms of this vertical integration of psychic states is that *durée* loses its articulation, directionality and orientation, which are much more obviously features of directed corporeal action. The value attributed to graceful movement seems to confirm this. Although the gesture is accorded aesthetic merit in the degree to which it aligns with the fluidity of consciousness and confirms the continuity of time, Bergson emphasizes the predictable and repetitive rhythm that draws the spectator away from the conditions of their own material action. Now, of course, Bergson always seeks to maintain an openness to the future in *durée*, but by not attending to the temporal specificity of artistic production in the analysis of aesthetic feeling, he does not fully acknowledge the material openness in producing a work. When he argues that the sensibility or feeling of the artist is reanimated by the reception of the work, Bergson is referring to something like a creative germ that does not require reference to the enduring nature of production, for the latter requires a time in which each line has a specific duration and images are constantly reworked. Indeed, these images of production can be considered in terms of their specificity, just like moments within an ever burgeoning pure memory, each marked by the particularity of time in the moment of production. This can be compared to criticisms of the use of intuition to describe a direct apprehension of lived time as a whole in which the past, the present and the future are combined, which tends to efface the series of sensual movements, each with its own futurity, that interpenetrate to create this whole. This difference is clearly theorized in the visual arts, where the time of production is much slower than the time of apprehension, which leads us to question whether the sympathetic engagement with the artist is also an engagement with this slow process of making. This slowness can be better imagined through the body and the effort that subtends each artistic gesture, which is discoverable in the work as a mark or trace. Effort and the corresponding kinaesthetic feelings provide a sensual foundation for the work that are not reducible to extension. Bergson recognizes this in his discussion of philosophers such as Maine de Biran and Spencer, as well as in the description of Achilles's strides, but tends to neglect this corporeal continuity once the difference between extension and *durée* is established. A reappraisal of Bergson's arguments through the senses of kinaesthesia and touch could provide a means to reinvigorate his philosophy in the visual arts by highlighting the corporeal contact between the artist, the work and the spectator. On the inner surface of the body, these feelings would gesture towards the extensionless interpenetration of psychic states but on the outer surface would invoke the material thinking of the artist as engaging with a medium.

3 LIFE

The difference between living and non-living processes is central to Bergson's philosophy. Although not a dominant feature of *Matter and Memory* and *Time and Free Will*, this ontological distinction is relevant to many of the discussions of consciousness, memory and human freedom, as well as the critique of mechanism. In the early part of the twentieth century as his philosophy grew in popularity, Bergson referred more explicitly to life in a number of his essays and, most importantly, in the books *Laughter* and *Creative Evolution*. In these works, the concept of life progressed from a means of distinguishing between lived time and clock time to a fully developed theory of creation and change. After these books, Bergson's references to art began to place greater emphasis on the creative action and vision of the artist rather than on the reception and transmission of aesthetic feelings. In many respects Bergson's comments on art are aligned with nineteenth-century romanticism and the notion that artistic creation derives directly from authorial sensibility, and many of his references are to the peculiarity of artistic genius and the singularity of the artist's vision. However, where Bergson differs from many earlier philosophers and art theorists is that his conception of creative authorship is supported by a complex and extended rereading of evolutionary theory in terms of a vital impetus. Creativity is as much a part of general organic development as it is an effect of human activity, and understanding life in any context involves following the general lines of its movement back to the fundamental processes of material differentiation. It refers not only to an energy or force in nature but also to the continuity of the past within the present and the individuation of actions within the broader process of evolutionary complexification. In many respects, Bergson's use of the term 'life' is too broad, especially when placed in stark opposition to (non-living) matter, for it operates as an umbrella term for a whole suite of practices from the maintenance of genetic character beyond the lifespan of an individual to the capacity to act freely in spite of the acquisition of habits. Life incorporates too many different processes in Bergson's philosophy to be given a precise form, which, in many respects, is what Bergson requires from any of his major concepts – they must be able to extend across different fields and integrate ostensibly incompatible ideas. The concept of life acquires specificity in his work only when tethered to particular discussions of evolutionary development as well as the relationship between the comic and habit in *Laughter*. Although Bergson focuses on general tendencies in organic development and life, his ideas can be adapted to suit the demands of aesthetics and the philosophy of art, especially when the different aspects of life are clearly differentiated.

Life and the extension of consciousness

Understanding any of Bergson's main ideas always entails a return to *durée* and in this section, I will examine in greater detail the notion of durational continuity before addressing his arguments on life, time, creativity and evolution. This is important because Bergson often talks about creativity in terms of the free act that is drawn from the continuity of lived experience, and also as a creative tendency that constantly divides within evolution. Properly appraising the theory of creative evolution involves understanding how the artist and artwork are placed in relation to these different aspects of life and movement. Bergson's exploration of life's creativity is grounded in the theory of *durée*, principally with regard to the absolute continuity of time and the endurance of the past. Life is not a quality or power that can be extracted from the organism or merely added to matter to animate it, for it coincides with the entire lifespan of an organism drawing together memory, perception and action into a single unbroken movement. The emphasis on continuity could be interpreted in terms of the weight of the past which, in the form of instinctual, habitual or even genetic dispositions, could predetermine individual action. However, Bergson inverts this relationship and argues, instead, that continuity is the condition for freedom, for the more each action is informed by the particularity of an individual's past, the less it is subject to mechanistic principles or laws, which largely operate at the level of efficient causality in a truncated present. This argument informs Bergson's distinction between the comic and the tragic in *Laughter* and also provides the basis for arguing that evolution is inherently creative. The description of the continuity of life resembles in many respects the discussion of *durée* in *Time and Free Will*, but life offers much greater flexibility because it does not have to be tied to consciousness and the diffuse particularity of the deep feelings. Life opens up into the world through the actions of the living from the primitive movement of single-celled organisms to the spontaneous and free actions of an artist. Life also leaves traces in the world: visible contours of lived action that attest to duration's creative impetus and can be contrasted with other non-living material actions. In the context of aesthetic judgement, life becomes the means of evaluating art, for art that cleaves to the movement of life is also able to reveal *durée*.

Bergson's theory of *durée* requires the endurance of time in which it is impossible to impose a strict division between the past and the present, or between the present and the future. In arguing that time always involves the retention of the past within the present, duration could be imagined as a fibrous bundle in which different temporal periods are converging on the present while gesturing towards an unspecified future. Bergson argues that time cannot be understood outside of its capacity to endure, which applies to everything from feelings and perceptions to the maintenance of corporeal form in biological organisms and systems. The previous chapter suggests that the spatial conception of a line should not be rejected outright despite Bergson's rejection of the trajectory to describe time, as it depends on whether this line faces out to homogeneous space or internally to *durée*, consciousness and the body. In *Matter and Memory*, Bergson argues that the aim of philosophy is to find the 'internal lines of the structure of things', which involves a mental effort by which we seek to reimagine the curve of 'human experience'. Bergson compares such a task to the mathematical process of integration by which a curve is generated through integrating all the partial, differential movements.[1] In philosophy, this integration is performed by shifting perspective from the 'duration *wherein we see ourselves acting*', an external representation of our own movement, to a 'duration *wherein we act*',[2] the internal inherence of movement as a qualitative change manifest in the indivisibility of intention. Our action is characterized by continuity, unity and variability in which all is integrated into the qualitative multiplicity of lived experience, which can be distinguished from the scientific characterization of movement in terms of spatial extension. This externalization of time affords greater importance to the positions of a moving body than the quality of a moving body because such positions provide a framework for quantification. Even when scientific theories refer to internal properties such as force, inertia or momentum, they are still represented spatially through the concept of greater and lesser. Consequently, Bergson rejects the use of the line to represent time, for although it appears to be continuous its quantitative continuum can be divided ad infinitum.

To understand *durée* requires thinking in terms of mobile images, which in the context of life are most readily imagined in the growth or movement of an organism, both of which express types of physical action in the world. However, Bergson is also keen to indicate that *durée* involves a particular time that is inherent to the process, and we must see growth as linked to the overall temporality of the system in which the organism is embedded. This is best exemplified in one of Bergson's most famous mobile images in *Creative Evolution*, in which *durée* is invoked by imagining the time it takes sugar to dissolve in a glass of water. Bergson states that there are two ways to conceive of this time of dissolution. The path taken by science is plotting the time it takes the sugar to dissolve against a clock, in which case two points are posited and time is the rate of change between the addition of the sugar and its disappearance. In this model, the various states of the sugar can be imagined as static images, each referring to a particular distribution of the sugar crystals within the water molecules. In this corpuscular interpretation of matter 'the future forms of the system are theoretically visible in the present configuration,'[3] because these states are little more than the reorganization of the parts in space. Time in such a system is restricted to the plotting of change rather than the expression of internally driven qualitative change. Bergson argues that this correlation of material organization against clock intervals does not say much about time, or the fact that the dissolving of the sugar must take place over a definite duration. Time must endure, which means that it can be conceived as a type of resistance to immediate change that involves waiting as much as alteration. When the sugar dissolves, it is embedded in a whole system of temporal differences including the definite experience of the observer waiting:

> If I want to mix a glass of sugar and water, I must, willy-nilly, wait until the sugar melts. This little fact is big with meaning. For here

the time I have to wait is not that mathematical time which would apply equally well to the entire history of the material world, even if that history were spread out instantaneously in space. It coincides with my impatience, that is to say, with a certain portion of my own duration, which I cannot protract or contract as I like. It is no longer something *thought*, it is something *lived*. It is no longer a relation, it is an absolute.[4]

Waiting is not an epiphenomenon of consciousness, something that can be dismissed as peculiar to the observer's psychological state, because time is a concrete feature of any system, including the process of observation. The concrete lived time of the observer is commensurate and continuous with the sugar dissolving and any change in the physical system, for example increasing the heat of the water such that the sugar dissolves more quickly, will also lead to a change in the observer's experience. The observer may feel fascination, boredom or frustration depending on what they expect of the system and their temporal history. The time of waiting is absolute in the sense that the specific feeling cannot be separated from all the psychological and physical processes that combine within a concrete time – there is no measure that stands outside these processes. Moreover, waiting cannot be broken into units of waiting because the feeling is continuous with the individual's past and continually varies in the present as the observer responds to the dissolving sugar.

This example is used by Bergson to demonstrate the concreteness of time, but it also demonstrates another principle central to Bergsonism: any lived event, including all creative acts, cannot be understood in isolation or through the separation of causes and effects. In applying a principle of continuity in *Creative Evolution*, Bergson expands the notion of *durée* to cover all living and physical systems. These systems are open to a qualitative variety of forces manifest in the universe as a whole, even though many of these forces and effects are 'negligible' and therefore disregarded in the study of general forces by science.[5] Any notion of time, irrespective of how it manifests in the universe should be characterized in terms of its capacity to endure, but this involves understanding how each event, and each movement, is always affected by the whole. We tend to forget the interpenetration of physical and non-physical forces in the universe because our perception focuses on particular fields of inquiry that often correspond to isolatable material bodies or processes.[6] Michael Polanyi argues that the problem with reductive physical theories is that they suppose that the system as a whole can be understood through an extrapolation of the laws that apply to its smallest particles, where, in fact, there are boundary conditions that organize and order the lower level processes.[7] Science often imposes container-contained conditions on processes under investigation in which the 'boundary condition is always extraneous to the process which it delimits'.[8] To reuse Bergson's example, the glass would not affect the dissolution of the sugar in the water. However, Polanyi states that living systems do not operate through simple container-contained relationships because each boundary refers to the levels above and below it. The living organism must be seen as a hierarchy of processes with the higher levels imposing restraints or boundary conditions on the lower levels. Evolution is itself the development of the higher processes of life that are built on more primitive forms: physical processes are contained within vegetative processes, which are, in turn, bounded by patterns of growth, and in animal species, instinctive actions form a lower level than the capacity to choose freely.[9] Bergson also recognizes different levels in his philosophy; however, the focus is on how *durée* provides the basis for integration. He usually proceeds from the whole to the parts, in this case, the higher example of the conscious, human process of waiting, integrates the lower level of the sugar dissolving. *Durée* is pervasive as the continuum in which all actions can take place, but manifests differently at each of the levels. When considering creativity, each gesture, thought or act integrates an unlimited number of processes which operate on a hierarchy of levels but also extend through the lived history of the individual and beyond.

Durée provides the means of drawing together a range of processes operating at different levels that are all grounded in the endurance of the present. When it comes to the relatively high level of conscious human perception and apperception, William James argues that the most limited conception of this continuity is the minimum endurance of the present such that we are aware of it (the 'specious present'), which he argues is the condition for all experience.[10] The specious present is experienced in very short durations, no longer than a few seconds, in which the past and present are not distinguishable, and it is only over longer periods that we can look back on our temporal experience in order to separate events and represent them.[11] Edmund Husserl makes a similar claim concerning temporal continuity and the integration of present and past in his *On the Phenomenology of the Consciousness of Internal Time*, although he places greater emphasis on the role of memory than James. He isolates two main types of memory: 'primary memory' or the 'comet's tail' of perception, manifest either as retention or as protention, and 'secondary memory' that serves as the basis for recollection. Primary memory remains continuous with the present, and to explain this Husserl, like Bergson, argues that hearing a melody cannot be understood in terms of the present alone, for it requires a coming together of the 'just past' and the immediate future.[12] Hearing the melody entails '[p]rimary memory of the tones that, as it were, I have just heard and expectation (protention) of the tones that are yet to come [which] fuse with the apprehension of the tone that is now appearing and that, as it were, I am now hearing'.[13] Primary memory is the present's 'temporal fringe' that shapes perception by drawing sense data towards a coherent centre.[14] In both James and Husserl's accounts, perception requires the endurance of time in the integration of the immediate past with the present, as well as the preparation for an imminent future.

Bergson presents similar arguments on the endurance of the present throughout his *oeuvre*, but unlike Husserl and James, he extends the basic principle of temporal continuity well beyond the integration of sense data in the contracted present of perception. As with the example of sugar dissolving, the continuity of memory provides a means of extending temporal reasoning beyond what Husserl refers to as primary and secondary memory. David Carr argues that despite the value of Bergson's critique of temporal atomism, his philosophy does not sufficiently attend to the protention–retention structure as outlined by Husserl, which is organized around actions and perceptions that naturally circumscribe particular durations within becoming.[15] For example, the present might be organized around hearing a tone or completing a movement such as grasping an object, and in recollection, these circumscribed temporal periods are remembered and not the limitless continuity of becoming. The critique holds if the understanding of *durée* is limited to the normative bounds of human perception, but Bergson develops an ontology of perception that coincides with *durée*. Keith Ansell-Pearson states that one of the most important aspects of Bergsonism is to resituate philosophy in perception, not to propose new concepts on how we perceive, but to extend the present well beyond what we experience in order to encompass the much longer duration of processes such as evolution.[16] Bergson certainly addresses human perception and memory but always looks to extend the principles, by following the curve of experience beyond what is humanly conceivable to integrate even non-human processes. When he addresses human memory, he notes differences in kind but always with the aim of reintegrating them into the greater continuum of *durée*. Despite distinguishing between habit memory and recollection in *Matter and Memory*, he argues that both are functions of the degree of tension in our consciousness and as such operate on the same temporal plane. Human memory is suspended between two poles, that of habit, which is more prevalent in the lower animals, and a much more expansive notion of memory, pure memory, that is best exemplified in human reverie or dreaming.[17] For Bergson, it is important to maintain continuity between types of memory and time across all species – to always reintegrate differences in kind into *durée* – although this will appear to lead to some loss of specificity in the description of various fields including creative action and the arts.

In the lecture 'The Soul and the Body', Bergson argues that the continuity of the now can expand to draw together the whole of an individual's past. To explain this, he uses the mobile image of an utterance, arguing that the spoken word must endure over a definite period of time and that this shorter duration must be continuous with the longer duration of the sentence. Like the note in a melody, when uttering each word the speaker must remember what has been said and what will be said, if not they would have lost the 'thread' of speech. The sentence might vary in length but in each case the whole is immanent in the single word.[18] Bergson takes this argument beyond the bounds of human conversation when he speculates on how the awareness of the whole of the sentence could extend beyond the current discourse if the mind has sufficient durational amplitude to retain earlier discourses in the act of speaking.

> Push the argument to its limit, suppose that my speech had been lasting for years, since the first awakening of my consciousness, that it had been carried on in one single sentence, and that my consciousness were sufficiently detached from the future, disinterested enough in action, to be able to employ itself entirely in embracing the total meaning of the sentence; then I should no more seek the explanation of the integral preservation of this entire past than I seek the explanation of the preservation of the three first syllables of 'conversation' when I pronounce the last syllable.[19]

Bergson argues that one of the reasons that we are not able to maintain a broader focus on the past is that our attention is always directed towards the completion of a future action rather than on reflection and contemplation. We are not sufficiently disinterested to allow the broad continuity of *durée* to reveal itself: we operate as actors rather than dreamers. What Bergson is keen to point out is that although our body operates within a very limited temporal period that allows it to directly engage with its material environment, consciousness is able to extend itself over a much longer durations.[20] Again Bergson follows an introspective line of reasoning, in which he speculates beyond the curve of present experience and practical activity, where an expanded consciousness can bring a type of disinterested experience to bear on particular fields of activity including metaphysics and creative practice. It is only by drawing together the awareness of one's life beyond the specious present, through a form of intuition that stretches over longer durations, that the artist is able to fully give sway to their creativity.

To understand the relationship between the extension of the present and the conduct of creative practice, it is necessary to return to *Time and Free Will* and Bergson's critique of both determinist and libertarian accounts of free will. In determinism, any action can be explained through antecedent causes, which, even if not readily visible, might eventually be discovered through the rigorous analysis of events at both a microphysical and a macroscopic level. Bergson's critique requires the separation of the human mind and even the soul from purely material forces, efficient causality and the pressure of an already determined past. However, in accentuating the role of the mind, Bergson does not turn to a 'radically libertarian' approach in which the individual occupies a present free from constraint and where the free will is 'absolute'; instead, he emphasizes the continued effect of the past in providing the impetus for a truly free act.[21] Bergson's argument proceeds, as it does in most of his writing, by isolating what is common to the opposing theories, even the most extreme positions, and using this commonality to stage his own argument. Leszek Kolakowski refers to this method as '*recoupage*' in which Bergson finds the points in which opposing theories overlap and rethinks how they have 'phrased the question.'[22] In this case both libertarianism and determinism pose the question of free will without reference to concrete time and the continuity of experience. The libertarian assumes that the exercise of the will is a matter of choosing between clearly defined options, choices that stand before the subject and are outside of the flow of time. Determinism also describes causality in terms of discrete events through assigning a set of antecedent acts and conditions to each of these choices.[23] In both these cases, cause and effect are separated, either in the subject initiating an action or in a series of antecedent events determining the action of the subject. Bergson argues that our way of thinking about free will changes if we consider action and choice to operate within the continuity of consciousness and the intermingling of psychic states. In this approach, the past must always exert some form of influence on the present such that it is impossible to posit a definite point at which a decision is made. Choice is dependent on the immanent variation of the feelings, thoughts, memories and actions of the person as a whole.[24] One can still talk of the will but not as a separate faculty. The will is an inclination in a particular direction that eventually leads to a choice, and which underpins any rational or determined action.[25] The life of a person is the accretion of their lived experiences through which the whole self 'lives and develops by means of its very hesitations, until the free action drops from it like an over-ripe fruit'.[26] This biological metaphor highlights the importance of maturity rather than youthful spontaneity in the constitution of the free act. Hesitation refers back to Bergson's main thesis that any action must be understood in terms of the endurance of time and the particular internal rhythms that come to comprise the individual.

This argument has parallels with Bergson's discussion of the 'deep feelings' except that there is a shift in direction. The centripetal movement in which the deepening of understanding proceeds from the surface of perception to the depth of consciousness is displaced by a horizontal movement in which the complexity of lived time accrues over the life of an individual. In this conception, freedom is linked as much to feeling as it is to action, for what is important is the qualitative variability of the present and the degree to which it is contingent on actions stretching over from the past. The actions that are most free are those in which the whole of the past is continuous with the present. Bergson states that 'even sudden passion, would no longer bear the stamp of fatality if the whole history of the person were reflected in it'.[27] This also applies to artistic creation, where the truly free action is one that involves the 'whole personality',[28] which also serves as an evaluative principle, for great art is distinguished by its capacity to channel the whole of the artist's personality into the creative act.

This notion of a truly free action, discussed in *Time and Free Will* in terms of individual memory and consciousness, also applies more broadly to life which is also distinguished by its retention of the past. Bergson argues that we always differ from ourselves at each moment irrespective of the development of habits, because our memories accrue without loss. Again a principle of continuity is central to this argument, for at what point can the past truly be separated from the present? The past is continuous with the present in perception and as it accrues the organic unity of the individual changes to accommodate it. Although this accrual is a necessary aspect of lived time, Bergson argues in *Creative Evolution* that it still requires the individual's active engagement with their own past in way that can be compared to artistic creation.[29] The finished portrait produced by an artist is by necessity novel because it is the latest iteration of a continuous process of working through, in which each of the past iterations remains present. Likewise, each new psychological state is the culmination of a life and, therefore, contingent on the subsistence of previous psychological states in consciousness:

> Even so with regard to the moments of our life, of which we are the artisans. Each of them is a kind of creation. And just as the talent of the painter is formed or deformed – in any case, is modified – under the very influence of the works he produces, so each of our states, at the very moment of its issue, modifies our personality, being indeed the new form that we are just assuming.[30]

Like the psychological state, the final form of a work cannot be truly foreseen because it is contingent on the time of its creation and the ceaseless variation in the artist's life.[31] The work is not a plan put into action, driven by a final or formal cause; rather, it is the extension of becoming in which the past continues to grow. The problem here is that Bergson does not make a strong distinction between forms of creation that consciously engage the will and tend towards a definite end, even if the exact properties of the final form are unknown, and novelty as a necessary effect of the accumulation of the past. Life, consciousness, freedom and art are all joined in Bergson's philosophy insofar as all participate in the constant variability and irreversibility of time formed under the burgeoning pressure of the past on the present.

The apprehension of life and art's unforeseeability

Bergson does not provide an account of how creative freedom is actually manifest in a work of art. He highlights the ipseity of novelty rather than principles of fabrication: variations on a theme, the application of formal processes or responses to a model. Although an analysis of the actual manifestation of creativity is not undertaken by Bergson, he nevertheless regularly posits artistic creativity as the exemplar of a particular type of action in which the past remains continuous with the present. Rather than stating what the artist does, he refers, instead, to those practices that do not properly constitute artistic practice in order to contrast life with the non-living. In *Creative Evolution* Bergson states that both finalism and mechanism have failed in their explanation of complex evolutionary change because they focus on material change in the development of complex forms such as the eye, rather than on the principle that drives the transformation. He argues that this evolutionary change can be compared to the role of an artist's intuition in the production of a painting, for both should be understood in terms of an immanent movement, intuition or vital impetus, rather than a finished form:

> An artist of genius has painted a figure on his canvas. We can imitate his picture with many-colored squares of mosaic. And we shall reproduce the curves and shades of the model so much the better as our squares are smaller, more numerous and more varied in tone. But an infinity of elements infinitely small, presenting an infinity of shades, would be necessary to obtain the exact equivalent of the figure that the artist has conceived as a simple thing, which he has wished to transport as a whole to the canvas, and which is the more complete the more it strikes us as the projection of an indivisible intuition. […] It is the picture, *i.e.* the simple act, projected on the canvas, which, by the mere fact of entering into our perception, is *de*composed before our eyes into thousands and thousands of little squares which present, as *re*composed, a wonderful arrangement.[32]

Using this example and the method of recoupage, Bergson rejects the theories of finalism and mechanism. The problem with finalism is that it posits a plan, or final cause, that drives the evolution of the eye, while the problem with mechanism is that it focuses only on the tiles, or parts of the eye, that come together to form the whole. In both theories, the complexity of the eye is derived from an external process of linking together parts to create an 'assemblage', when, in fact, creation depends on a unified single movement that divides and complexifies.[33] Again Bergson places emphasis on the internal movement that unifies the whole in its simplicity, in this case the artist's intuition and evolutionary creativity.

As discussed earlier, intuition can take a variety of forms: immediate knowledge of a present event, a type of knowledge that follows the line of the real, and even reflective knowledge that reintegrates the past in the present. In all cases, intuition provides absolute knowledge because it is coincident with the interpenetration of processual states in a qualitative multiplicity and the continuity between past and present. This can only be imagined from within the movement, for any external perspective would require a break in continuity and a mode of understanding in which falsely separated objects are compared to each other. In the 'Introduction to Metaphysics', intuition is described as absolute because there is no perspectival variation when the object is apprehended from within, which can be contrasted with the relative knowledge of other disciplines that utilize general symbols to describe the real.[34] The absolute knowledge of intuition is characterized as a form of sympathy with the becoming of an object and this is why it is more readily associated with life than with matter. By contrast, analysis describes a process of breaking down the object into parts, which due to their separation from the whole cannot be living, and then attempting to reconstruct the movement from these parts. Regardless of how many parts are posited or how ornate the philosophical method, it is impossible through analysis to reconstitute the simplicity of the movement or object under investigation.[35] Intuition as sympathy can be applied to the study of literature, which Bergson argues involves readers aligning themselves with the main character such that '[t]he actions, gestures and words would then appear to flow naturally, as though from their source'.[36] In this case, the simplicity of the author's intuition is displaced onto the character. Although any literary work is composed of discrete parts (letters, words, sentences), the character describes an underlying continuity that, once established, should integrate all new words and events into its movement. Of course, this precludes any form of experimental literature or metafiction in which the reader is asked to attend more to the text than to the living movement of a character.

The arts are not only celebrated for their capacity to actualie what is revealed by intuition in the work but also valued for their proximity to life. In *Creative Evolution*, Bergson gives much greater specificity to intuition by placing it within an evolutionary epistemology, arguing that it is part of a broader tendency characterized by knowledge drawn from a direct sympathy with life. This can be contrasted with the tendency to analyse, manage and control matter that underpins the development of the intellect: an approach to nature that somewhat resembles Heidegger's notion of enframing, in which nature is understood in terms of a 'calculable coherence of forces'.[37] In order to understand the sympathy underscoring intuition, it is important to trace this tendency back to a biological notion of understanding in instinct. Bergson uses the word instinct in a way that is radically different from its general application in biology, for although instinct is innate it does not describe a mechanical or automatic response to an event or object. Instead, it refers to an approach in which one organism understands another through sympathy, which is at once an awareness of the natural organization of another living organism as well as a general sympathy with all living processes.[38] This innate understanding of the living Bergson compares with Plato's notion of the good dialectician in the *Thaedrus*, who is similar to a 'skilful cook who carves the animal without breaking its bones, by following the articulations marked out by nature'.[39] The feeling of direct sympathy with the natural articulations and rhythms of the natural world can be contrasted with the intellect, which only seeks the quickest and most efficient means of dividing the animal into portions.[40] In human evolution, this sensitivity to natural form that is immanent to all living organisms has been somewhat supplanted by the intellect with its analytic, symbolic and prefabricated response to nature.

Instinct is the basis for a general evolutionary tendency in which understanding is coincident with the internal organization and movement of nature. In this evolutionary account, intuition is an advanced stage of the instinctual tendency in which self-awareness accompanies the sympathetic and direct apprehension of the living: '[I]t is to the very inwardness of life that *intuition* leads us – by intuition I mean instinct that has become disinterested, self-conscious, capable of reflecting on its object and of enlarging it indefinitely.'[41] For Bergson, intuition is a type of reflection in which the object is not located in the past but, rather, brought into the present through the enlargement of perception, and in this sense it has an aesthetic function:

> That an effort of this kind is not impossible, is proved by the existence in man of an aesthetic faculty along with normal perception. Our eye perceives the features of the living being, merely as assembled, not as mutually organized. The intention of life, the simple movement that runs through the lines, that binds them together and gives

them significance, escapes it. This intention is just what the artist tries to regain, in placing himself back within the object by a kind of sympathy, in breaking down, by an effort of intuition, the barrier that space puts up between him and his model. It is true that this aesthetic intuition, like external perception, only attains the individual. But we can conceive an inquiry turned in the same direction as art, which would take life *in general* for its object, just as physical science, in following to the end the direction pointed out by external perception, prolongs the individual facts into general laws.[42]

The existence of the model could pose a problem for a Bergsonian aesthetics because it is external to the creative impetus. However, the artist sees the world through within *durée* and is therefore able to enter into the *durée* of other things including the model. Merleau-Ponty states that one of the distinguishing features of Bergson's philosophy is a type of knowledge in which '[t]he relation of the philosopher to being is not the frontal relation of the spectator to the spectacle; it is a kind of complicity, an oblique and clandestine relationship'.[43] The artist, like the philosopher, also approaches the object obliquely by aligning themselves with the life of the model rather than seeking to reproduce mere external appearances. The difference between art and philosophy is that aesthetic intuition is much more invested in the particular – something it shares with instinct – while gesturing towards a metaphysical breadth and intuitive generality found only in philosophy.

This account of the relationship between instinct and intuition demonstrates how Bergson distinguishes between epistemological attitudes, including in art and philosophy, while maintaining a foundational temporal continuity. Other philosophies adopting a vitalist or natural philosophy approach also have to address the idea of an awareness that distinguishes itself from nature and yet remains immanent to it. Friedrich Schelling argues that philosophy is derived from nature but nevertheless requires a primal separation in which the philosopher is able to reflect on how they differ from nature: 'He who first attended to the fact that he could distinguish himself from external things, and therewith his ideas from the objects, and conversely, the latter from the former, was the first philosopher.'[44] Schelling argues that this separation and reflection expresses a form of freedom from nature, but notes that with this separation also comes the desire to reunite: 'It proceeds from the original divorce to unite once more, through freedom, what was originally and *necessarily* united in the human mind, i.e., forever to cancel out that separation.'[45] Bergson follows a similar line of reasoning in arguing that both freedom and philosophy arise out of nature or life itself. Freedom in many respects coincides with creative life as a differential push in which an individual's whole past is implied in action. Philosophy is a reflection on the generality of life as movement in the form of a tendency that becomes aware of the past. Unlike Schelling, however, Bergson does not emphasize any primal separation because all reflection on life is also an expression of life; it is part of the same movement and therefore there is no need to explain any desire to return to nature.

Embedding an artist's intuition in creative evolution, or, indeed, any general notion of life, does pose some difficulties because life and art are comprised of a variety of types of movement, some of which involve reflection and many that do not. Reference to life in art can take many forms from the examination of vital forces to the development of formal principles based on natural processes. Life could be regarded as a liberating force that attests to the capacity of the human to exceed material limits, but could also be seen to restrain creativity, especially when it is associated with the repetition of natural laws. Étienne Souriau argues that human art and the processes of creation can be analysed in relation to various principles of change, both organic and inorganic, from laws describing the movement of matter to the immanent shifts in phylogeny and ontogeny. However, he argues that there are significant differences between human creativity and natural processes. Evolution might produce new species and other creative acts but this is always conducted in a context of actions that are subject to habit,[46] whereas human action is free to create new forms in art within being thoroughly subject to the natural laws of matter and life.[47] For Souriau, this liberation from the restraints of biological and physical forces characterizes human creativity, whereas for Bergson, these biological processes are embedded within the creative act as part of an overall impetus to create – habit and creativity are contracted into a single tendency.

The main problem with the process of integration is that it can obscure some of the fundamental differences between human intuition and creation, and broader biological and evolutionary tendencies. For example, the artist will have some conception of the final form of a work in a way that evolution does not, for the latter is for Bergson largely driven by impetus. The past might push the artist to create the work, as all living beings are somewhat motivated by the *élan vital*, but intuition provides an awareness of what the artist is about to produce in the form of a virtual image. This is not simply a difference between conscious and non-conscious processes, for we must also address the duration of creative processes and intuition. Intuition could operate in a quite different time frame to the time it takes to produce the work; the intuition grasps the whole in a single movement, whereas making the work is iterative and potentially works over a long duration. The artist often makes many sketches and attempts, each of which brings its own intuition, which can be distinguished from the intuition revealed to an audience in the final work. The same logic could also apply to evolution, where the overall movement of evolution can be contrasted with the iterative processes of reproduction and the many dead ends – species die out, some do not change over long durations and so on. There might be a general push, but this push does not necessarily unify the whole of evolution in a single movement.

Indeed, the problem of applying a principle of continuity is again one of boundary conditions; what is continuous at one level might not be continuous at another. When talking about life and its many actions, these boundary conditions should be imagined temporally as well as spatially. C. H. Waddington argues that one of the features of biology when contrasted with the other sciences is the requirement that it should address multiple time frames all of which are operating at the same time:

> Not only must we study the hour-to-hour or minute-to-minute operations of living things as going concerns, but we cannot leave out of account the slower processes, occurring in period of time comparable to a lifetime, by which the egg develops into the grown-up adult, and finally towards senescence and death. On a longer time scale again, there are phenomena which must be measured in terms of a small number of lifetimes; they are the processes of heredity, by which characteristics of organisms are passed on from parent to offspring. Finally, on the time-scale of many hundreds of generations, there are the slow processes of evolution, by which the character of the individuals in a given population gradually changes, and the population may become split up into two or more different species.[48]

In Waddington's account, each time scale requires a different approach to the conception of life. The gradual slow processes of evolutionary change operate quite differently from the homeostatic operations of a living organism. Bergson does refer to time scales in his work, usually in the context of intuition and in the enlargement of perception from the apprehension of the present moment to the revelation of broad living tendencies. He also notes that in the stabilization of the phenomenal world in perception, different types of movement are revealed, of which he names three: 'qualitative' movement describing the transition from one quality to another; 'evolutionary' movement describing changes in the form of organisms and their development; and 'extensive' movements that are limited to the traversal of space.[49] The processes of a plant growing from a seed, an insect coming into being or a colour changing are quite different, and they must not lose their distinctiveness when integrated into a 'colourless' image of Becoming in general – Becoming should always be conceived as a multiplicity of becomings.[50] Although Bergson notes these differences, how they interrelate within a specific event or definite duration is never properly discussed. That is because he is more interested in foregrounding the principle of temporal unity within each of these becomings rather than in analysing the cross-section of qualitative differences as they appear within a particular perceptual or natural process.

The specific intuition of time should indicate the irreconcilability of different times as much as their integration within specific contexts – for example, how does the evolutionary continuity and novelty appear to someone within a time scale required for the appreciation of a work of art? I will discuss temporal differences in more detail in the next chapter, but at this stage I will focus on how differences between time scales as well as their unity can inform both a theory of life and aesthetics. For example, the composer Olivier Messiaen states that rhythm in music can be informed by the examination of different rhythms in nature, and refers to the mineral, vegetal and animal kingdoms, each of which operates according to its own rhythm, from the gradual formation of mineralogical features to the locomotion and gestures of animals.[51] In the mineral kingdom, rhythms can be derived from the shape of mountains, snow drifts, stalactites and stalagmites, in which the gradual accretion of minerals leads to the formation of patterns.[52] In a Bergsonian evolutionary context, these different levels would be integrated into living tendencies, but from the point of view of aesthetics, the temporal differences may be more important, in particular, how each discloses itself within the particular time of human perception. The pattern of the stalagmites is not revealed through the viewer inhabiting their internal rhythm, but because they appear over a peculiarly non-human period that operates much more slowly than human perception. For Messiaen, it is the difference between mineral and human time that reveals a particular rhythm and form that can be translated into music, rather than the lived time of the stalagmite. If we return to the comparison of evolution and the arts, these temporal differences are also apparent in how we might conceive of futurity. When considering an artist's brushstroke on a canvas, the immediate future of the brushstroke can be somewhat apprehended in the first traces of the stroke – the future is a protention of the action. However, can the same principle be applied to the longer duration of evolution, such that new species would reveal themselves at the outer fringe of an evolutionary arc? The longer the duration contracted into intuition, the further into the future the arc of the present should extend. It is not certain if Bergson would accept this argument, because it would contravene the principle of novelty and unforeseeability – we cannot imagine a species before it has arrived – but this demonstrates a significant difference between short duration movements that protend into an immediate future, and the long duration tendencies.

Bergson's examination of grace and sympathetic movement in *Time and Free Will* examines the immediate future of action and perception, whereas his theory of life addresses creative action over the long durations of evolution and the life of an organism. The artist's work is appraised in the degree to which it expresses the whole personality of the artist and reveals the novelty of an open, living system. Bergson argues in 'The Possible and the Real', an article that was published late in his career, that we can only predict the future in a closed system where all the parts are visible and change is reduced to mapping the rearrangement of the parts.[53] We might imagine that Bergson is thinking here of a thermodynamic or mechanical system in which the parts are discrete and changes can be readily plotted. By contrast, artistic practice and any form of life are open systems in which it is impossible to separate a single state from the general succession of duration. An artwork cannot be predicted because the life of the artist is thoroughly interconnected with the world in which they work. Bergson states that it is impossible to foresee Shakespeare's *Hamlet* without occupying the perceptual, intentional and experiential world of the author. In other words, to become a figure who 'finds himself thinking all that Shakespeare will think, feeling all he will feel, knowing all he will know, perceiving therefore all he will perceive, and consequently occupying the same point in space and time, having the same body and the same soul:

it is Shakespeare himself'.[54] The individual biography of Shakespeare is the condition of the creation of Hamlet but only in terms of its openness to all other movements in the universe at the time of writing *Hamlet* – Shakespeare is as much a monadic as an authorial subject. We cannot truly occupy the position of Shakespeare as a creative force in the same way that we can mimic the movements of a dancer or engage with the rhythm of a painting, due to the particularity of the temporal context in which he writes and the extended duration over which the works appear.

This reference to an open system, in which the operations of any number of living or material events affect the creative process, addresses some of the critiques of the insularity of many of Bergson's aesthetic ideas. For example, Dresden argues that Bergson's invocation of the simplicity of the artistic gesture does not sufficiently explain creativity, because any artistic gesture must be considered in the context of what it responds to and what it opposes.[55] In an open system, the individual serves as an impetus for creation within the context of a universe renewing itself, and Bergson notes in 'The Possible and the Real' that although we might all be 'artisans of our life', the artist is always confronted by matter which resists this self-realization:[56]

> On the other hand, the sculptor must be familiar with the technique of his art and know everything that can be learned about it: this technique deals especially with what his work has in common with other works; it is governed by the demands of the material upon which he operates and which is imposed upon him as upon all artists; it concerns in art what is repetition or fabrication, and has nothing to do with creation itself. On it is concentrated the attention of the artist, what I should call his intellectuality.[57]

The relationship between materiality and creation is not really developed by Bergson and, in many respects, marks a departure from his insistence that art must invoke the immaterial, or reveal *durée* by overcoming the solidity of matter. The argument is facilitated by Bergson's separation of instinct-intuition from the intellect in *Creative Evolution*, for it allows him to retain the distinctiveness of life as a creative impulse – 'nothing to do with creation itself' – while relegating all aspects of repetition and materiality in creative practice to the intellect.

Deleuze argues that this type of reasoning requires the untangling of composites to create 'pure state[s]': one describing a push towards spatialization and the other the production of differences in kind.[58] The *élan vital* or vital impetus and *durée* are realized in the tendency towards differences in kind while material division, repetition, spatial organization and conceptualization are realized in the tendency towards spatialization. This marks an advance from Bergson's earlier arguments, in which differences in kind are distinguished by interiority and differences in degree by exteriority, for it describes two different means of generating difference and also the means to reconnect them: 'Differences in degree are the lowest degree of Difference; differences in kind (*nature*) are the highest nature of Difference'.[59] If we follow the movement of life back far enough, instinct and intelligence, matter and life, all share a common root from which they are differentiated.[60] In this argument, the 'reflexive dualism' in which impure composites are separated is resituated in a 'genetic dualism', in which difference is ceaselessly generated.[61] Life acts within matter rather than in opposition to matter, even though for the sake of argument, it is necessary to clearly separate the two.

In other works, the creativity immanent to the continuity of life and duration is described in terms of the development of a creative or epistemological tendency as well as the movement from interiority to exteriority. In 'The Soul and the Body', Bergson describes thought as 'a continual and continuous change of inward direction, incessantly tending to translate itself by changes of outward direction, I mean by actions and gestures capable of outlining in space and of expressing metaphorically, as it were, the comings and goings of the mind'.[62] While exercising its own freedom, thought acquires material expression by extending itself through speech centrifugally from consciousness into the world, with a musical rhythm maintaining the connection between word and thought.[63] In this case, each of the two tendencies carries the trace of the other in rhythm, which provides a stronger foundation for discussing the relationship between artistic creativity and material form, but it is not so easily integrated into Bergson's argument that creativity refers to a type of freedom in which the whole of the past is contracted into the present articulation. Certainly there is a centrifugal movement, but in what way is this past made visible and does it appear as an accompanying rhythm akin to thought becoming speech? The difference between the two hinges on differences in duration. Thought operates in a similar time to speech, whereas the whole of the past develops over a duration completely different from any form of creative articulation. The past must be transformed in this centrifugal movement for, to use Bergson's example, the audience member attending a production of *Hamlet* could not inhabit the concrete duration in which Shakespeare writes the work or find themselves within the particularity and breadth of the author's past, except in the way that each contributes to the depiction of Hamlet's thoughts and indecisiveness. The issues are even more complex for the examination of visual art because rhythmic forms are spatial and do not resemble the duration of a recent thought, never mind the contraction of a personality.

The problem is not only one of finding an appropriate model for each artistic medium but also one of understanding which aspects of durational continuity are most readily accessible in the reception of a work. Of course, it will differ across the visual arts but there nevertheless should be some principle that underpins the shift from the continuity of personality, time and tendency to the continuity of the work. It concerns the connection between the duration of enunciation, the time it takes to produce the work, and the duration of reception. Bergson does not make a definite statement on this relationship because he emphasizes the capacity of intuition to grasp the whole in artistic vision, in which case the vision exists prior to the time of production. In accentuating the reality and unity of intuition and creativity, it is difficult to imagine to what degree this will change when confronted with the materiality of the work, or to rephrase the problem, when life as a tendency intersects with the intellect as a tendency. This problem is not specific to Bergson's work but presents itself in any approach that emphasizes artistic vision, perception and sensibility over artistic practice and describes how an artist sees the world rather than how they produce a work.

In relation to painting, Norman Bryson refers to this as the 'natural attitude', an expression borrowed from Husserl, in which the work is judged in terms of the artist's capacity to convey the real and remain true to their 'Founding Perception'.[64] In the natural attitude, it is presumed that the painter directly translates to the canvas the reality of the perceptual field as revealed to them, or the optical reality of their imagination. In either case, the vision precedes the work and the work is only valued in the degree to which it can carry this vision, and formal aspects of painting, such as style, are regarded as impediments to its transmission.[65] This natural attitude is primarily invested in the discourse of realism and the belief that painting can convey a truth that stands outside of particular historical conditions in its search for the essential copy. Bryson argues that those approaches that are based on the Founding Perception seek to diminish or efface those deictic, gestural marks that are associated with the act of painting and also with the time of painting. They are more likely to operate within an aorist or preterite tense, in which the past of the Founding Perception is represented generally with little reference to the time of enunciation.[66] Because the Founding Perception is sequestered in the time of the artist's vision, it cannot really be recovered by the viewer in the time of viewing:

> In the Founding Perception, the gaze of the painter arrests the flux of phenomena, contemplates the visual field from the vantage-point outside the mobility of duration, in an eternal moment of disclosed presence; while in the moment of viewing, the viewing subject unites his gaze with the Founding Perception, in a perfect recreation of that first epiphany. Elimination of the diachronic movement of deixis creates, or at least seeks, a synchronic instant of viewing that will eclipse the body, and the glance, in an infinitely extended Gaze of the image as pure idea: the image as *eidolon*.[67]

According to the natural attitude that has played a key role in the Western tradition, art should enable the viewer to occupy the viewpoint of the artist. The problem in occupying this viewpoint is that the particular time of the 'gaze' effaces the body of the artist as well as the time involved in making the image.

Bryson argues that with regard to the techniques used, the time associated with the Founding Perception is quite different from the time associated with the material process of making a work. Oil paint is favoured because the image can be revealed without necessarily showing the artist's brushstrokes. Bryson refers to it as an 'erasive medium' that effectively erases the surface marks of the work in deference to the object that lies behind it, which is achieved by reworking the same marks over a number of days such that the initial brushstrokes disappear.[68] This allows the painter to focus on the Founding Perception that pre-exists the work and which guides each stroke according to the compositional whole.[69] In this approach, the duration of the perceptual whole, and, indeed, the duration of intuition, is realized before the first brushstroke is applied. This can be contrasted with works highlighting the movement of the brushstrokes and which also entreat the viewer to recreate these movements in reception – the viewer imbues these marks with movement as the eye glances across the surface of the work.[70] Such works give the painting a concrete duration because we can imagine the speed with which they are painted, which, in turn, invokes the body of the artist, as was discussed in relation to the paintings of Cy Twombly in the previous chapter. This re-establishes a temporal continuity with the time of painting rather than an aorist past, or any other act of perception that stands outside the work and cannot be located in a definite place or time.

Bergson certainly does not argue for a notion of an indefinite past realized in a singular vision. However, the separation of the material time of the work and the time of intuition in his brief reference to sculpture raises some crucial questions about how the lived time of the artist should be considered or imagined in the time of viewing a work. If the emphasis is on intuition, then we should consider whether there is a difference between a founding intuition and one that is continuous with the duration of the work. In the example of the mosaic, Bergson argues that 'intuitive vision' is something that 'he has wished to transport as a whole to the canvas, and which is the more complete the more it strikes us as the projection of an indivisible intuition,'[71] and as such pre-exists the material form of the work as a founding intuition, and the same applies to the notion of the living movement of a character in a novel. In this approach the artistic vision is fully contingent on the duration of the Founding Perception, in which the artist's personality is contracted into the creative gesture that can be distinguished from the time involved in the fabrication of a work. By contrast, in Bergson's account of creative evolution, creation is co-extensive, or co-durational, with the material form – it does not stand before the work in the concrete perception or intuition of a creator.

Painting poses a number of problems for understanding how the artist's intuition can be revealed or, indeed, expressed through the material due to the multiple levels at which the work operates. Intuition intersects with a range of other acts including corporeal gestures, material movements, and even the viewing position of the artist relative to the canvas, in order to create multiple durations, each of which could contract the painter's past in a different way. The simplicity of the authorial act of creation can be contrasted with the simplicity of the painterly gesture, as Bryson notes, or even with the simplicity of the whole as appraised by the viewer as they stand before the work. This complexity is evident as soon as we address the specific events, times and movements immanent to a work, which extend from the historical time of reception and production, through rhythmic and formal structures, to the time of what is represented.[72]

To better understand the role that intuition could play in a work, it is necessary to remove some of the complexity by considering paintings in which the Founding Perception appears to be manifest in the way the work is painted rather than in a narrative subject. It is also critical that the duration of the work, in both its material expression and representation, operates in a time that is close to the one experienced by the viewer. In light of this, I have chosen to briefly discuss some of the 'zip' paintings of the contemporary American painter Barnett Newman, who sought to create works that operate in a contracted present in which the duration of the artist's vision is inherent in the painted form and coincides with the duration of viewing.

There is much in Newman's approach that opens itself to Bergsonism. Newman rejects painterly systems and methods – which is central to his critique of Mondrian – and he argues that each work should be distinguished by the particularity of the event it embodies.[73] He also argues that his works directly connect the viewer both physically and metaphysically to the painter: 'One thing that I am involved in about painting is that the painting should give man a sense of place: that he knows he's there, so he's aware of himself. In that sense he relates to me when I made the painting because in that sense I was there.'[74] Although he refers to physical place, Newman invokes a type of lived experience, which can become manifest only in the space and time of standing before the work. The relationship extends beyond apperception and the grounding of being to include the direct communication of feeling. In his article 'The Sublime is Now', Newman argues that the new wave of American artists, owing to the fact that they have been liberated from European aesthetics, offer a fresh perspective on art in which the artist's feeling is directly manifest in the work: 'The image we produce is the self-evident one of revelation, real and concrete, that can be understood by anyone who will look at it without the nostalgic glasses of history.'[75] Like Newman, Bergson attributes a directness and self-evidence to art and metaphysics in intuition, which finds some expression in diffuse but interconnected lived feelings. In *Time and Free Will*, the artist's deep feelings are retrieved or echoed by the viewer upon viewing the work, which is facilitated by the work's plastic rhythm.

The idea that art evinces revelation, metaphysically or mystically, coincides in many respects with Bergson's philosophy, but Newman's painting extends well beyond what Bergson could have imagined in the early part of the twentieth century or, indeed, to follow Bergson's own reasoning, beyond what anyone could have imagined without occupying the life of the artist. Newman's zip paintings usually combine large colour fields with vertical figures (zips) that divide the canvas without external reference, except tangentially in the titles. At first viewing, they could easily be grouped with Minimalist and Conceptual Art with its emphasis on concrete simplicity, but Newman notes that his works can be better understood through a notion of life. He points out that he does not want to make art objects that end up dehumanizing art, and highlights, instead, the life and time of painterly enunciation, where the painter is the subject and the painting the verb.[76] Life is invested in the work in the vertical figures, which are referred to as zips, rather than lines or stripes, to foreground a type of movement that both divides and unifies the canvas in gestures of creation.[77] Newman states that *Onement I* (1948), in which a cadmium red zip bisects the neutral brown of the canvas, was a turning point because he found himself as a producer in the living movement in the work, in an invocation of life that does not require reference to nature or 'biomorphic' forms (see Figure 3.1).[78] Rosenberg states that the zip paintings might be abstractions, but they are 'innocent' abstractions in which the viewer looks anew at the world.[79] In this notion of life, each time the viewer addresses the zips, articulated in a vibrant continuous present, they are also connected to the living movement of the artist.

Lyotard states that Newman examines the question of time in the 'picture itself' through the presentness of painting as an act, or the sense that painting becomes an event.[80] Drawing upon the biblical story of the annunciation, he argues that a 'painting by Newman is an Angel. It announces nothing; it is in itself the annunciation'.[81] The works concern themselves with events, moments of creation and beginnings without reference to an agent of the action or any form of narration: 'The flash (like the instant) is always there, and never there. The world never stops beginning. For Newman, creation is not an act performed by someone; it is what happens (this) in the midst of the indeterminate'.[82] Lyotard argues that all of the key works that deploy the zip, concern ontological immediacy which 'announces itself in the imperative'.[83] This imperative is a feature of the series *The Stations of the Cross* (1958–66), in which Newman argues that he was trying to create the immediacy of Jesus's plea to God, in which the 'visual impact had to be total, immediate – at once'.[84] The fourteen paintings that make up the series are all abstract in the sense that not one refers to actual events in the Passion, and the life of the works is largely manifest in the vertical zips that divide

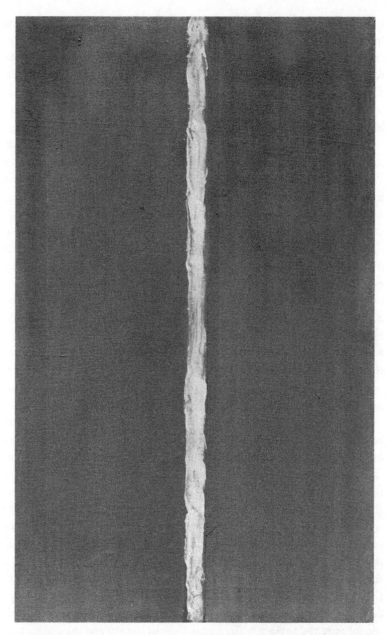

FIGURE 3.1 Barnett Newman. *Onement I* (1948). © 2020 The Barnett Newman Foundation / Artists Rights Society (ARS), New York / Copyright Agency, Sydney.

the canvases. The presentness of the zip's movement is most evident in the *First Station* (1958), where the clean line of the right-hand zip, created using masking tape, can be contrasted with the movement of the rough black brushstrokes that surround it. In this oscillation between the figure created by the tape and the indeterminate brushstrokes, the work embodies a living present in which the viewer is brought into the interiority of the enunciation.

Newman's zip paintings offer a means of thinking about Bergsonian intuition and creativity that does not require reference to a Founding Perception that stands before or outside of the work. Life is manifest in the painting's plasticity through the constant renewal of a wordless utterance, whose movement carries feeling rather than a referent. Despite the unification of artist, viewer and work in the open present of *durée*, we still must be cautious in advocating for a Bergsonian intuition in painting. Intuition proposes the concrescence of the past into an expanded present in which the simplicity of expression is accompanied by a metaphysical awareness; however, the duration immanent to the act of painting undermines the notion of the unity of an aesthetic vision. In Newman's *Onement I*, the zip might simultaneously divide and join the canvas into the singularity of the creative utterance, but there remains a tension between different material durations. The zip, which was created by painting over a strip of masking tape, appears to move at a speed that is much greater than that of the brown background because we can actually see the movement of the brushstroke. By contrast, the brown ground appears lifeless because the brushstrokes are disguised by the evenness of the colour and its application. In an interview with Lane Slate, Newman states that in preparation for a painting, he first creates an 'inert' surface by repeatedly stretching and shrinking the canvas, arguing that the work should acquire life only through the artist's actions[85] – in this case, painting the zips. There are consequently two durations operative in the work, which are unified in the spectatorial oscillation between the colour field and the zip in the finished work. However, with regard to the production of the work, there remains a distinction between two durations, for the ground could be prepared even before Newman has an idea of how he will reconfigure the surface.[86] The future time of the zip and the unification of the work as a temporal whole are unforeseeable in the early stages of the production of the painting, and a trace of this unforeseeability is always retained by the ground. This can be contrasted to the time implicit in an individual brushstroke in which future and past are contracted into a single movement.

In reception, the zip paintings can invoke different times or speeds. How the viewer responds to these durational differences can disrupt as much as encourage temporal continuity. In the notion of the Founding Perception, it is the gaze that unifies the different aspects of the artist's world into a single phenomenal whole, and it is through the gaze that this unity is recovered. Conversely, the viewer might approach the work more obliquely or quickly, depending on certain features of the work – the inability to maintain the gaze when confronted with the large fields of colour, or the eye rapidly following the movement of the brushstrokes in the zips. When glancing at a painting, the eye only lightly touches its surface at speed, creating a different notion of unity from that fostered by the gaze. Edward Casey argues that the glance draws upon the depth of Bergsonian *durée* in which the individual's whole past is contracted into each movement.[87] However, the glance extends the individual's past into the present in a different way from the gaze due to its celerity and suddenness, for it is attuned to the novelty of the future, expecting something to happen before it has happened, and being open to the unforeseeable:[88] 'As in other contexts, it is here a vanguard act, situated at the forward edge of the present, attempting to discern in advance what might happen.'[89] Although the glance can be understood from a Bergsonian perspective, Casey notes that it also undermines the continuity that Bergson attributes to duration, for, insofar as it remains continually 'restless', the 'glance lacerates duration.'[90] As such the glance plays a distinctive role in realizing the variability of becoming, noting variations in the phenomenal world and changes in speed and duration of the perceiving subject.[91] The glance is the spectatorial equivalent of Merce Cunningham's nascent movements in dance, which Massumi argues reveal becoming through the disruption of flow. The types of attention fostered by the material form of the work affects how we should think about the intuition of *durée*, and even the very idea that there is direct connection between painter and viewer. The multiplicity of times engendered by the oscillation between the gaze and the glance can be certainly accommodated in the theory of *durée* but they do not necessarily support the notion of a single aesthetic intuition.

The question we must ask is: At what point in the production of a work does the unifying simplicity of the intuition come into play, such that the work operates into a single, albeit qualitatively differentiated, time? In his short commentary on his series *The Stations of the Cross*, Newman states that his understanding of the value of the works – or the moment when he came to an intuitive understanding of the temporal whole – only occurred post facto. He explains that, when he began his work on the series in 1958, it was unwittingly, for it was only after painting the fourth image that he came to the realization that the works gave an abstract rendering of Jesus's cry, and from that point he began to think of them in terms of the Stations of the Cross.[92] The ideas arose through working with the canvas: 'It is as I work that the work itself begins to have an effect on me. Just as I affect the canvas, so does the canvas affect me.'[93] Moreover, the logic of the series did not fully determine how he would work, for each work was painted individually while working on other paintings over an eight-year period: 'When there was a spontaneous, inevitable urge to do them is when I did them.'[94] Newman makes similar claims with regard to a number of other works, stating that when painting the large black canvas *Euclidean Abyss* (1946–7), at a certain point he decided to experiment with a yellow edge, which curtailed the movement of the eye towards the edge of the canvas. This was not planned and it was only after a year that he understood it was part of a process of invoking life without representing natural forms.[95] In general, Newman states that each painting should embody a distinctive feeling that is only properly distinguished after contemplating the work for a sufficient period of time. It is after the creative material development has ended that the work can be truly evaluated.[96] In this account, there are two quite distinct times, the material spontaneity that creates unforeseeable artistic and aesthetic events and the long duration of retrospective understanding and evaluation that attests to the ipseity of the work and unifies all the parts in a single duration, and the question is whether Bergsonian intuition can accommodate both.

This is the central problem of this chapter: Should the material operation of life in art be subsumed fully into the duration of aesthetic intuition, or should it be addressed through the material production of novelty. The two, of course, are linked, but intuition assumes a contraction of the past and immediate future into a living present, whereas material novelty always sits at the fringe of the present as something that is gestured towards but nevertheless unforeseeable. In experimenting with the material form of the work, the artist is an open system in which each new iteration is drawn into a continually expanding past, ensuring its novelty, and providing the basis for aesthetic intuition. This is a little different from the notion of a Founding Perception which is realized as a unifying image before the material instantiation. Bergson's description of aesthetic intuition sometimes resembles the Founding Perception, especially when he argues that the artist's vision is carried to the work, whereas at other times, it appears to be something that is fully coincident with the production – something that guides each of the artist's gestures. If material change is foregrounded, as in the description of Newman's working process, then intuition plays a different role in retrospectively differentiating and unifying the aesthetic whole – what Deleuze would refer to as the 'discovery of genuine differences in kind'.[97] The artist's actions might be guided by the weight of their past experience, a thoroughly forward impetus, but the apprehension of the unity of such actions could be retrospective, a folding back upon an enduring past.

Life: Materiality and flexibility

One of the problems with Bergson's conflation of life, time, consciousness and art in the artistic vision is that he does not adequately account for the transformation of each of these states into material practices and behaviours. The argument is not easily adapted to a philosophy of art because it is impossible to assess the degree to which the life of an artist, invested in the work as a whole or the material gesture, is actually disclosed in the freedom of a creative act. In what way is the free, creative richness of artistic life available to the spectator except through those traces left upon the page or canvas; marks that are already mediated by the material constraints of fabrication. There might be some value in arguing that a painting requires the whole of a life to produce it, or that our conscious states are an enduring melange of memory, action and life, but this should be distinguished from how the personality of the artist is made visible to others through the work. This making visible operates in a time frame that is never entirely coincident with the duration of an artist's consciousness.

Bergson examined the externalization of personality and consciousness in relation to life and biology rather than in his discussions of art. Indeed, we require some notion of life's external manifestation in everyday judgements about what is living and what is not, based on assumptions about qualities common to all living organisms. Unlike the ipseity of conscious states that provide the basis for sympathetic engagement, life's features are visible in plants and animals irrespective of their capacity for conscious experience, as well as human beings. In *Creative Evolution*, Bergson addresses how the contraction of the whole past is manifest, somewhat externally, as character, whose characteristics can be transmitted from one generation to the next, which is a 'condensation of the history that we have lived from our birth – nay, even before our birth, since we bring with us prenatal dispositions'.[98] The whole of the past is manifest as the 'original bent of our soul' and 'felt in the form of a tendency, although a small part of it only is known in the form of an idea'.[99] This evolutionary argument exceeds even Lamarck's claims about the acquisition of characteristics in arguing that the individual life of an organism forms part of a continuous living impetus passed through the germ cells. Irrespective of the degree to which such claims are at odds with contemporary genetics, Bergson presents here another argument as to how the interiority of personality can be externalized and made visible, as idea and character. In this context, character is a disposition that is revealed in movement rather than a static set of attributes. Translated to an artistic context, the work should encapsulate the personality, character or 'bent of the soul' that is fashioned by the whole of the past, but also a broader evolutionary impetus.

The transmutation of the past into disposition, character and movement provides life with a sufficient level of generality that can be used to judge the freedom of an action, and the freedom immanent to artistic creation. In his essay 'Life and Consciousness', Bergson argues that life is characterized by an organism's control over its own movements, free action and spontaneous movement. It is 'co-extensive' with consciousness because both voluntary movement and consciousness involve the anticipation of the future through the retention of the past.[100] 'We lean on the past, we bend forward on the future: leaning and bending forward is the characteristic attitude of a conscious being' in which case consciousness functions as a 'hyphen' between the past and the future.[101] The greater the involvement of the past, and the more complex the organism, the more flexibly life and consciousness can respond to their environment, which can be contrasted with the inflexibility and predictability of matter, with its fixed laws, such as inertia, geometry and efficient causality.[102] The opposition between matter and life appears through Bergson's oeuvre but one should not assume that it is absolute, for, as with the division between interiority and exteriority in *Time and Free Will*, it admits of degrees. The amount of freedom that life exercises in the material work varies significantly, and matter fluctuates in its resistance to the action of living organisms. This variability means that the relationship between matter and life can be used to evaluate freedom, art and creation, not so much by reference to the whole of the past, but in the degree to which life appears spontaneous and resists the inertia of matter. This freedom should be manifest in the work in the flexibility of a gesture or movement unlike the artistic vision which is sequestered in a time that stands prior to the work.

A feature of Bergson's aesthetic ideas is that an aesthetic object should disclose the internal impetus of life. On one end of the scale is a work that is fully commensurate with the haecceity of life, with the continual iteration of mnemonic differences, of which the most obvious example is Marcel Proust's *À la Recherche du Temps Perdu*. Notably, Bergson congratulated Proust, who was his wife's cousin, on the work and his subsequent success, in particular Proust's capacity to invoke the interior life: 'Rarely has introspection been pushed so far. It is a direct and continuous vision of internal reality' (*Rarement l'introspection a été poussée aussi loin. C'est une vision directe et continue de la réalité intérieure*).[103] Bergson proposed his own example indicative of Proustian memory in his much earlier publication, *Time and Free Will*, describing how the scent of a rose is a means through which the 'confused recollections of childhood come back to my memory'. The scent acquires value due to the accumulation of a qualitative multiplicity of individual memories, like a schema, rather than due to its objective form.[104] This introspective revelation of the interior life can be placed on one end of the scale and on the other is non-life and purely mechanical movement. Between these two extremes are forms of behaviour in which the particularity of experience is transformed into physical processes from the gracefulness of dance to habitual actions that develop increasing levels of generality through repetition. Bodily organization and character always have some form of external expression indicating life, underpinned by the individual will and the vital impetus, even if the individual's experience in all its haecceity is not retrievable.

What is highlighted here is a difference between a philosophy of *durée* in which life reveals itself in the particularity of intuition communicated through an artist's vision and a vitalist approach that concerns itself with expressions of life. Inasmuch as it highlights the vital processes underpinning the movement of organisms, Bergson's philosophy can be regarded as a form of vitalism, not in the strict biological sense in which a theory of entelechy or final causality is proposed to replace mechanical causes, but a general vitalism in which life is foregrounded in ethical and aesthetic judgements. Georges Canguilhem argues that the term 'vitalism' should not be reserved for a few self-nominated biological theories, for it also describes those theories in which there is a general awareness of life and sympathy for other living organisms.[105] Bergson can be nominated a vitalist insofar as an attention to life informs much of his work, in particular *Creative Evolution*, and it is this vitalism that drew many other thinkers to his philosophy. The art theorist Herbert Read states that Bergson's philosophy informed his own approach to vitalism in art: 'I must acknowledge the inspiration I continue to receive from the only metaphysics that is based on biological science – the metaphysics of Henri Bergson.'[106] This raises the question as to how vitalism should be used in the critique of art, and for Read it always concerns a balance between the beautiful – the 'serenity' found in good form and harmony – and the desire to live expressed as a vital energy,[107] a 'will to live' that is most thoroughly evinced in primitive art[108] with its external articulation of an internal living energy. With reference to cave art, Read states that

> [t]he running limbs are lengthened because in the act of running they *feel* long. In fact, the two main prehistoric styles are determined on the one hand by the outwardly realized *image*, on the other hand by the inwardly felt *sensation*, and 'imagist' and 'sensational' would do very well as descriptive labels.[109]

In this example, understanding the visual arts through vitalism requires some means of translating life and feeling into a visible form, and one could readily reimagine Bergson's own example of Achilles in terms of vitalist art, where his strides are lengthened or stretched to better indicate his intention to overtake the tortoise. In many respects, vitalism should describe an internal impetus that exceeds the body's own boundary, which is certainly the case in Boccioni's *Unique Forms of Continuity in Space*, discussed in the first chapter, or even in Art Nouveau, where the movement of vegetation as ornamentation operates at the limits of the spatial articulation of the living body. Unlike Bergson's discussion of the deep aesthetic feelings and the ipseity of personality, the concept of life is much more readily imagined in the physical and spatial organization of the work.

Unfortunately, Bergson does not develop a positive theory of life in art, for, as we have already noted, most of his work derives from a critique of the spatialization of time, including mechanistic explanations for evolution and life. It is therefore understandable that Bergson's most detailed examination of aesthetic activity is of the mechanistic tropes of comedy (which he describes as a peripheral art) in the short book *Laughter* – a collection of three articles that first appeared in the *Revue de Paris* in 1900. Comedy and laughter are more amenable to analysis because they operate on the threshold of lived and mechanical action. Bergson does not present a detailed study of drama, painting, sculpture or literature because great art in each of these fields should be underpinned by the particularity and specificity of life, and therefore remain resistant to any form of analytical generalization. The comic, however, operates on the other end of the spectrum where life tends towards the mechanical through its exploitation of character types and classes of behaviour. What distinguishes the comic is a form of aesthetic attention to human life that reveals patterns and repetition rather than an actual sympathy for the feelings of another. For Bergson, in a joke there is 'always [...] some resemblance to man' in such a way that the whole context is marked by an *'absence of feeling'*.[110] Conversely, it would be impossible to laugh in a world in which all things are imbued with 'sentiment' because such sentiment does not allow sufficient abstraction from an event. It is only by standing outside an event, by becoming a 'disinterested spectator', that laughter is possible, which is demonstrated in his example of watching a dance without music:

> Now step aside, look upon life as a disinterested spectator: many a drama will turn into a comedy. It is enough for us to stop our ears to the sound of music in a room, where dancing is going on, for the dancers at once to appear ridiculous. How many human actions would stand a similar test? Should we not see many of them suddenly pass from grave to gay, on isolating them from the accompanying music of sentiment? To produce the whole of its effect, then, the comic demands something like a momentary anesthesia of the heart. Its appeal is to intelligence, pure and simple.[111]

This does not constitute a total absence of feeling because laughter is still linked to a feeling of pleasure; however, what Bergson is trying to highlight here is a type of attitude that is characterized by a general disinterest in the interior life of the participants in the dance. Music is the vehicle of sympathy because it attributes to them a motivating force and, indeed, consciousness. Without the music, the spectator can only look at the dancers in terms of the external, instrumental and formal properties of movement, which appear absurd, leading to laughter. Moreover, due to this instrumentality the spectator can never penetrate beneath the surface of a movement to sympathetically connect with the life of another, which is the basis for true aesthetic feeling.

The separation of behaviour from a broader context of feeling is central to *Laughter* for the more behaviour is subject to an intellectually abstracted gaze, the more it operates as an object of humour. Abstracted behaviour not only eschews sentiment but also remains distant from the integration of past, present and future in the whole of personality and, consequently, the comic as a genre cannot attend fully to the seriousness and sincerity of life. Jankélévitch states in reference to *Laughter* that to take life seriously in its entirety is to be free, which can be contrasted with the comic in which life is treated partially as a mechanical or a social representation of the life of a person, in effect reducing life to how it is seen by others.[112] When Bergson refers to character, it is certainly an expression of life, but one that has two poles, one that is coincident with the sincerity of the whole personality – the immanence of intuition in the 'Introduction to Metaphysics' – and the other that discloses itself to the intellect as a partial view contracted in the direction of mechanical action. The intellect is able to reveal only those aspects of character that fuse into generality and, in doing so, ignores a character's relationship to an enduring past and the complexity of feeling. The intellectual gaze inherent to the comic divests any event of its particularity and appropriate sentiment but nevertheless retains something of the human – a mere trace whose resonance triggers laughter.[113] When the intellect is applied to life it creates an ambivalence between two types of movements: a true living movement and its material shadow. In this argument, the role of life in art, its vitalism, is revealed only in contradistinction to the intellectual characterization of life, and appears in the comic only at the point where the general description of character and material behaviours overcomes ipseity.

In *Laughter*, the fundamental source of the comic is the interplay of the movement of life with other behaviours and movements that are more readily associated with matter and machines. Comedy always holds onto the human life in the form of competing tendencies (i.e., the vital versus the material) where the non-human or mechanical appears, or reveals itself, within the context of human behaviour. From this perspective, the psychological theory of Behaviourism could be a great source of humour, for it suppresses life's intention and flexibility in favour of a series of learned responses. What distinguishes drama from comedy is the degree to which traits and behaviours are assimilated into a person's character. Drama demonstrates a greater attention to life because it is able to assimilate a whole range of feelings – the qualitative multiplicity of feeling is manifest in each action – whereas comedy creates characters whose actions are driven by a fixed principle. Their adherence to this principle forms the basis for their errors and humour, for example, a character might fall over because they are fixated on something or because their personality is characterized as absent-minded. Bergson states that the significance of the fixed principle or easily distinguished character trait is evinced in the titles of many theatrical comedies, such as Molière's L'Avare (*The Miser*) or Jean-François Regnard's *Le Joueur* (*The Gambler*).[114] He also speculates that we could easily imagine the comedy title, *le Jaloux*, but would not apply the same title to high drama, such as Shakespeare's *Othello*.[115] This argument still holds true for many contemporary film comedies, for example *An Idiot Abroad*, *Liar Liar* or *Dumb and Dumber*, in which the traits identified in the titles become the basis for most of the jokes. Bergson argues that we laugh at these comedies because the character's movements are 'involuntary' and underpinned by a kind of '*mechanical inelasticity*'. We are less likely to laugh at behaviours that express a willingness to adapt to 'accidental' changes in an environment and display self-awareness.[116] This behavioural inflexibility is 'visible' to an audience but not to the characters, who are unwittingly subject to the demands of the principle or trait, and the comic effect is derived from the audience's recognition of how the inflexible principle governs the characters' actions.[117] In most cases, the comic requires irony because the viewer knows something that a character does not, but unlike dramatic irony it derives from the character's lack of self-awareness, or lack of proper attention to what it means to live.

Bergson argues that laughter has a social function insofar as we laugh at those behaviours that we regard as inappropriate. This argument is not justified through reference to an analysis of a particular social system or a set of moral principles; rather, it is placed within the framework of evolutionary theory and phylogenesis and in many respects is a prelude to the grand genetic arguments in *Creative Evolution* and *The Two Sources of Morality and Religion*, where life is valued in the degree to which it resists habits or those social obligations acquired through habit and instinct.[118]

Laughter has an ethical function in highlighting those behaviours that run counter to the general progression of life and in so doing contributes to the preservation of the social body. In this vitalist ethics, inflexible behaviour is not suited to mutual adaptation because individuals who rigidly follow their own course fail to attend to the needs of the collective. Laughter corrects this 'inelasticity' and 'eccentricity' and, consequently, asks individuals to be more attentive to how they behave within a social context.[119] Laughter also has an aesthetic function because in order to serve the social order, we become more attentive to the types of behaviour we adopt. Laughter creates a space in which the individual is scrutinized and provides a moment of judgement on the individual who has set themselves apart.[120] This scrutiny shifts from attention to the behaviour of a singular individual to the general practices of art, 'since the comic comes into being just when society and the individual, freed from the worry of self-preservation, begin to regard themselves as works of art'.[121] The visible qualities of absent-mindedness and single-mindedness alert the viewer to a lack of flexibility in how the person operates within a social system and the lack of autonomy in their conduct. The individual is not receptive to the demands of others, the needs of the society or the vicissitudes of social and environmental change.[122] 'Elasticity' in behaviour is an outward expression of adaptability, where to live properly is to participate in a 'struggle for life' and to resist the pressure of 'acquired habits', as well as developing sufficient mental 'tension'[123] in which the mind is able to hold in suspension a range of different states across increasingly flexible durations. As previously stated, freedom and creativity are dependent on the individual's capacity to inflect the past in a present action, that is, for the past to be active in the constitution of a willed action. The most advanced species and the most aware individuals are able to draw upon more of their past in response to the present, and thus they are freer and more flexible in their actions. Automatic responses, by contrast, lack tension because the individual does not have to creatively rethink each moment due to a dependence on habits.

There are, of course, many problems with this argument – or any other quasi-biological explanation of social functioning, popular during the nineteenth century and the early part of the twentieth century – for it does not take into account ideology, cultural difference or even other genetic arguments. Moreover, there is no mention of Friedrich Nietzsche's claims that the will participates in an evolutionary overcoming of existing social and biological categories, and that cruelty might be central to the overcoming of habits.[124] Even if the general premise is accepted, one could argue conversely that laughter is a means of correcting those behaviours that are eccentric rather than merely rigid and, in doing so, could re-establish rigid social norms without cultivating an evolutionary flexibility. Canguilhem argues that normality is often only invoked to correct an infraction, in which case, the abnormal is prioritized and used to negatively determine what is normal.[125] So, is Bergson looking to negatively impose his own particular notion of social normality and the idea of a proper life in the shadow of habit, spatialization and mechanism? Interestingly, in focusing on the aesthetics of conduct, *Laughter* marks the beginning of an examination of the continuity of duration that does not require constant reference to the haecceity of consciousness. Social action can be evaluated according to the external traces of life and how they are integrated into social action. Certainly, Bergson always assumes the immanent movement of life but attends specifically to how it becomes visible through the difference between flexibility and inflexibility. In many ways it is *durée* becoming visible through the coordination and intersection of bodies and movements. Flexibility, tension, spontaneity, self-direction are all features of life but they are also features of a tangible body that endures. A superficial art, such as comedy, considers the body and its behaviours through the lens of intellectual disinterest but still reveals something about life, even if it is placed in direct confrontation with mechanical movement. Furthermore, it opens a space for the discussion of art in general and whether or not it should be judged as an index of life.

Focusing on life shifts Bergson's focus from freedom as inclination in *Time and Free Will* and freedom as virtual action in *Matter and Memory*, to freedom as autonomy and flexibility in *Laughter*, which presages the living creative freedom in *Creative Evolution*. The highlighting of the relationship between life and mechanism in *Laughter* was also one of the first responses by Bergson to an intellectual milieu in which there was a growing appetite for a full critique of Darwin and other mechanical approaches to the understanding of life and nature. Grogin argues that Bergson's work coincided with vitalism, popular during the nineteenth century, as one of a number of 'voluntaristic' theories that foregrounded principles of energy, impetus and life that could not be explained by mechanistic models.[126] In foregrounding mechanical behaviour, rather than scientific and philosophical approaches to the spatialization of time, *Laughter* commences a critique of mechanism on its own ground in the externally visible interaction between living and non-living bodies. Comic characters, who absent-mindedly follow a determinate path, are analogues for mechanism, which absent-mindedly applies principles such as efficient causality to explain everything including life.

In Bergson's theory of the comic, life's patterns compete on the same plane as mechanical patterns, and laughter arises when the audience recognizes that one supplants the other. Although Bergson argues that the role of such recognition is a social corrective, he gives it a much broader relevance later in *Creative Evolution*, when he examines the relationship between two orders, the physical and the vital. In this work, what is important is not the affirmation of the social body but the recognition of differences in kind and whether or not living bodies can be characterized according to their physical attributes – a practice that differs from modern science, in which many natural processes are reduced to the operation of general physical laws on material bodies, again due to the ostensible similarity between the living and the non-living.[127] Conversely, in ancient philosophy, for example, Aristotle's *Metaphysics*, the physical world is interpreted in terms of types of living movement, in which case the physical world acquires some of the general properties of life. In this case, Bergson argues that despite the visible reproduction of bodies, as well as cells and organs, this generalizable physical appearance should not serve as a basis for understanding life, because as a representation, it abstracts from, and obscures, the life's continuum.[128] John Dewey in his *Art as Experience* takes a slightly different approach in arguing that the main connection between the arts and sciences in early Greece derives from *techne*, and seeking to account for the regularity of visible movements, in other words, coming to terms with rhythms. Early philosophical treatises in Greece were written in verse and contained narrative rhythms that can be compared to the rhythms and cycles of the natural world.[129] He argues that natural rhythms still form the basis of physical and natural laws, especially when science seeks to produce increasingly accurate statements about periodical and regular changes, many of which are invisible.[130] The issue for Dewey is less one of representation, and more a question of understanding how movements are materially manifest. When it comes to the study of the arts, movements remain thoroughly tied to the material conditions as well as the natural rhythms of the maker, which can be contrasted with the codification of natural laws in the sciences.

Bergson does not develop a general theory of rhythm and focuses, instead, on the representation of living and non-living bodies. Both the vital and physical orders arise from attention to the movement of bodies, albeit according to different tendencies. The physical order requires a relaxation of *durée* in which matter devolves into separate parts, which are then organized according to principles such as efficient causality and 'automatism'. Moreover, it presupposes that the future reorganization of parts is foreseeable.[131] By contrast, the 'vital' order is underpinned by the will, freedom and voluntary action, which in a great artwork is 'unforeseeability itself'. We might choose to discuss the natural world in terms of individual organisms, principles of biological organization, the repetition of form, or even final causes, but if the point of view is sufficiently expanded to take into account evolution, life should be characterized by continuous variation and novelty.[132] When applied to visual culture, life is something that could be visible in material gestures and style, for they may indicate the voluntariness of the artist's actions, or in the depiction of a character's flexibility and adaptability – an argument that is developed in detail in *Laughter*. What could also be of interest is the way that living vital movements operate in tension with the physical order. Judging the work could be a matter of understanding the degree to which the vital order exceeds the automatism of the material or physical order. In comedy, the two are in balance, each playing off the other, but in great art the focus is firmly on the vital order and the way in which the work, and the actions of the artist, reveal a much more comprehensive living movement akin to evolution. The repetition of form and any other generic categories must give way to a broader understanding of life as a push from the past to an unforeseeable future.

In visual culture, the relationship between the vital and physical orders can be readily discerned in those works that accentuate and interrogate human movement. This is a key feature of slapstick comedies that foreground the structure and form of movement through the repetitious and somewhat predictable movements of the protagonists. When a character acts in a clearly distinguishable way, such as Monsieur Hulot serving in a game of tennis using a sequence of staccato movements in *Les Vacances de Monsieur Hulot* (1953), we know the sequence will be repeated. The mechanism and automatism of the movement has to be confirmed through repetition. When a body evinces automatism, it separates itself from the internal life and consciousness of the individual, thus setting up a dialogue between the two orders. This division plays a significant role in the films of Charlie Chaplin and Jacques Tati, whose protagonists often repeat behaviours that have proved unsuccessful, each time failing to recognize the specific demands of the circumstances in which they find themselves. Interestingly, both have satirized the mechanism and materialism of modern life, Chaplin in *Modern Times* (1936) and Tati in *Playtime* (1967). The film theorist Laura Mulvey states that film is ideally placed to theorize the mechanization of human movement and to mount a critique of modernity, because film can easily render the body still or moving in line with its own mechanism.[133] Chaplin regularly stages the difference between living movement and mechanistic abruptness: 'Chaplin's screen persona celebrates the cinema as an apotheosis of the human as machine and as a realization of the fascinating, ancient ambivalence between movement and stillness as ambivalence between the animate and the inanimate, from automata to the rhythmic movement and pose of dancers.'[134] Mulvey foregrounds the alternation between stillness and movement as a way of understanding the animate and inanimate – an alternation that is central to the comedy. However, it is not simply stillness or movement that is in question, but the type of movement and stillness. Stillness in the human body could be attributed to states of waiting and contemplation, but the movement or stillness of a machine indicates a state in which thought was never present or no longer intervenes.

When the audience watches a performance, they first expect to find bodies infused with life and responding appropriately to the situations they find themselves in; as soon as mechanical actions supplant the vital order, laughter ensues. One of the most famous examples is Chaplin's performance as a production line worker in *Modern Times*, where he is required to repetitively fix bolts onto objects that are passing along a rapidly moving production line. It soon becomes apparent that he does not have the requisite speed to properly complete the task, which soon undermines the whole production process. Much of the humour is derived from Chaplin's failed attempts to rectify these problems and to work according to the movements and time of the machine. He multiplies the number of his actions as he tries to adapt, when, in fact, he should be minimizing or reducing the number and be much more efficient in what he does. The humour derives from this tension between the unrelenting repetition of machine time and the variability of the human response. If he had been able to master the movement like his co-workers, in effect to become an appendage to the machine, the vital and physical orders would not be in competition – life would be subsumed in the mechanical. After disrupting the whole production line, Chaplin is drawn away from the machine but continues to embody its mechanical movements with the external physical order replacing intention. In addition to the competition between the two orders, this movement, due to its separation from the utility of both human and machinic action, also describes an aestheticization of the body. The audience scrutinizes each of Chaplin's movements, assessing the degree to which they reproduce the movements of the machine, and realizing that he fails in both responding to the machine in the production line and in shrugging off its mechanical movements when standing apart. Chaplin's maladroitness discloses life that operates at the periphery of these machinic movements – the human becoming machine becomes human again.

One of the features of mechanical movement is its repetition and predictability – in contrast to life's constant variability and openness to novelty – which differs from the rhythmic predictability of gracefulness in *Time and Free Will* that takes the form of a lulling rhythm guiding the spectator to the deep feelings. Bergson addresses this issue in *Laughter* by arguing that the comic asks us to forget the opposition between beauty and ugliness in art and, instead, attend to the distinction between 'gracefulness' and materiality.[135] Grace is an expression of the 'soul' (*âme*) underpinned by a tendency towards 'lightness' and 'immateriality', as well as a flexibility of attitude that corresponds to a 'living ideal', which can be contrasted with movements governed by the inertia of matter, the repeatability of movement and the stereotyping of action.[136] To regard movement as graceful is to 'disregard in it the elements of weight, of resistance, and, in a word, of matter; we forget its materiality and think only of its vitality which we regard as derived from the very principle of intellectual and moral life'.[137] In this argument, Bergson does not return to the predictability of grace and retains only the notion of lightness from *Time and Free Will*, albeit placed in a slightly different dyad that highlights the autonomy of life rather than the sympathy of feeling. Life is graceful because it overcomes matter from the perspective of the being who moves and not just from the perspective of the movement seen. It concerns the flexibility of movement underscored by conscious control. In contrast to the higher arts, the comic foregrounds the materiality of movement, the weight of the body and its resistance to life.[138] The body imbued with weight comes to resemble a thing and in this thingness becomes an object of comic ridicule.[139] The comic is not a property of matter itself, we cannot laugh at the repetition of a machine or the dull obstinacy of a rock, but only at life that conducts itself in a way that resembles matter. The comic describes a process of becoming material or becoming a thing, while always retaining an aspect of the living, whereas high art operates in an opposing direction, whereby matter is transformed by living movement into the immaterial.

This argument is appropriate when applied to the physical humour of performers like Chaplin and Tati, where the weight of the body seems to resist the will of the performer and the audience's expectations with regard to how a body should move. Unfortunately Bergson does not properly discuss types of graceful movement, or even how it should be distinguished from quotidian movement, as both are opposed to the mechanical. At what point does the mere act of walking, a definite expression of life, lose its materiality and acquire the gracefulness of the high arts? To explore this issue from another angle, should mechanical movement, as opposed to dumb resistant matter, always be associated with heaviness and a lack of life? Again, this is a question of speed and not just the difference in the orientation of the movement. If we look at one of the most repetitive movements in the visual arts, Marcel Duchamp's *Rotoreliefs* in which spiral designs rotate on a turntable, we have a clear example of mechanical movement that is imbued with jerkiness in addition to the repetition. Rosalind Krauss argues that this mechanical repetition actually undermines the stability of form central to Modernism in the visual arts, due to the imposition of a monotonous beat derived from reproductive technologies and popular media.[140] However, at certain speeds, especially those chosen by Duchamp in the Dadaist film *Anémic Cinéma* (1926), the spirals transform into organic shapes that expand and contract, or grow and shrink, and, as such, exhibit the qualities of life, albeit in a truncated and repetitive form. The emergence of these sinuous movements masks the underlying mechanism in what is a reversal of Bergson's comic – the living arises out of the mechanical. At a lower speed, the continuity of movement could devolve into staccato steps; at a higher speed, the line would disappear into a blur. The movements here are not necessarily human and are not easily incorporated into the theory of the comic, but they can nevertheless appear to be internally animated due to changes in speed, and therefore need to be considered in any comparison of the living and mechanical.

Even human movements can appear mechanical when undertaken at different speeds, whether fast or slow. Paul Souriau argues that the body operates best at moderate speeds according to his principle of the minimization of effort in the aesthetics of movement. Activities executed at too high a speed waste energy and lack the appropriate rhythm, whereas slow movements expend excess energy due to the fact that the muscles are held in positions of tension. He gives the example of slow walking, where the focus shifts from locomotion to balancing.[141] The actual form of the movement also changes, for example, the smooth arcs that we usually associate with graceful movements become 'rectilinear' (and therefore less graceful and more machine-like) when we rush to complete an action:

> when we move rapidly, we cannot pass from one movement to another with the roundness and sinuous, varied inflections that are characteristics of calm, leisurely movements. We observe, for example, that the more our movements are rectilinear, the more abrupt they are. A woman who is doing her hair puts her hand to her head leisurely; instinctively her hand will make a large rounded gesture. But if she is in a rush to remove a pin that is pricking her, her hand will rise quickly in a straight line.[142]

When we adopt a leisurely pace, the various muscles find the easiest line, usually in the form of an arc, in which the muscles are appropriately balanced, but when rushing, the limb moves straight to the object.[143] According to this argument, aesthetically pleasing movements operate within particular speeds, which accord with the natural articulations of the body. The movement of the rushed person would consequently appear jerkier than that of someone moving at a moderate pace and may even take on some of the features of the comic. What this means is that differences in speed have to be taken into account in any examination of living and non-living movements, for they can change the impression of life as opposed to the ontological state of a living being.

Although Bergson emphasizes the immateriality and immanent movement of life, Bergson's theory of comedy is mainly concerned with how behaviours appear to others and hence many examples are derived from the theatre, where the emergence of mechanical behaviours can be contrasted directly with normal conduct. In his discussion of verbal jokes, Bergson also focuses on the inflexibility of comic behaviour rather than the complexity of linguistic structure or wordplay. He cites jokes that refer to the rigidity of conduct associated with particular professions, for example, customs officials who ask the survivors of a shipwreck if they had 'anything to declare' upon disembarking from their lifeboats.[144]

Here comedy highlights automatic and unconscious 'gestures' that are partially disconnected from the action of the will, owing to their rigidity and inflexibility.[145] Conversely, tragedy and drama reveal those feelings and actions that give meaning to the whole of a person's life,[146] and cannot be reduced to a collection of traits. Gestures are external functions of the body and thus 'profoundly different from action', which is fully implicated in the interior life of the individual.[147] This distinction is similar in many respects to Jean-Paul Sartre's description of the bad faith of a waiter's gestures in *Being and Nothingness*, which appear mechanical because they mimic a model of the good waiter rather than articulate the waiter's freedom,[148] although, in contrast to Bergson, Sartre proposes that freedom issues from the autonomy of the *for-itself* rather than the impetus of a continuous past. In each case, determining the freedom, and, indeed, life of an act depends on separating the externally responsive false gesture from the internally motivated legitimate action.

How can this argument be applied to the visual arts which is largely gestural – unlike the constantly varying movements of drama and the performing arts in which the body is usually fixed in a particular stance and movement. Why should we not find humour in some of the great works of painting and sculpture, if the fixity of gesture is one of the key elements? Even in the most celebrated works, it is these fixed and external gestures that guide the viewer's attention. In Michelangelo's *Pietà* (1498–9), Mary immovably gazes down at her dead son with her left hand fixed in a position that invokes Christ's own sign of benediction. Indeed, gestures in many religious works are designed to be read, and can be exaggerated to increase this readability.[149] The more we attend to such gestures and their significance, the more our attention isolates them from the material form of the body and, most importantly, from the internal continuity of life. How should Bergson's theory of the comic evaluate the fixity and readability of the gesture in the visual arts? One way to adapt the argument is to understand that such gestures form a continuum with the body and contribute to its overall movement. They might be immovable but they are certainly not rigid if they visually extend the flow of the figures – in this case, Mary's left hand not only functions as a symbol of benediction but also draws attention to the sinuous and mobile line of Christ's body.

Bergson gives some indication of the functioning of the comic in visual culture when he refers to the role of caricature. The relationship between caricature and the visual arts is analogous to the relationship between comedy and tragedy. Caricature not only fixes the gesture, or, indeed, any other physical feature, but also renders it partially independent, such that it works in contradistinction with other components of the body. Laughter is provoked by the viewer's recognition of the relative independence of grotesque and comic features from the wholeness of the body or face. There must be a fixed or 'stereotypical' expression that overcomes or overrides the range of lived expressions that usually course through a face and immobilizes the personality of its subject.[150] This is why we do not automatically laugh at 'deformity' because it may be integral to the body, as in many congenital physical deformities, and can only laugh when it can be clearly mimicked, for example, in the stoop of the hunchback.[151] Deformity can only be subject to ridicule when associated with the automatism of movement and mechanical repeatability.[152] We can easily laugh at the stereotypical expressions and emotions depicted by Franz Xaver Messerschmidt in his sculptured heads, but not at Henry Tonks's depiction of soldiers wounded in the First World War, because in the former, the expressions only fleetingly pass through the body unlike the images of soldiers whose deformities cannot be separated from the materiality of the face.

Bergson's arguments about caricature can be applied inversely to interrogate the relationship between life and great art, an approach that is most easily adapted to figurative art which operates on the same plane as caricature, particularly naturalist and realist art that does not seek to isolate bodily features from the general visual environment. An individual line does not readily evince an ambivalence between the mechanical and the living; however, drawn caricature can often emphasize the living movement of the line in contrast with the compositional whole, and much of the inventiveness of drawing depends on the relative independence of the line. Leonardo da Vinci drew many 'grotesque' figures in his notebooks, which Adam Gopnik argues began as 'doodles' rather than studies of models.[153] Likewise, Picasso drew caricatures from an early age, many of which can be found in the margins of his school notebooks in which the aim was not to reproduce 'likeness' but, rather, to experiment with visual and pictorial forms: 'Picasso had an apparent compulsion not simply to record faces in a virtuoso shorthand but to reinvent faces, and to push caricature to new extremes of simplification.'[154] In these examples, each line suggests its own direction and therefore moves independently of a broader artistic vision (the compositional whole), and is living in a way that relates directly to the artist's material actions. Inventiveness and creativity derive from the fact that the lines are aleatory rather than contingent on the representation or expression of a character's life. Caricature might decompose the body into independent parts when examined on the level of character, but reveal the life of the artist at the level of the line. What is missing from Bergson's discussion of the comic is a full consideration of the different ways in which life is manifest as spontaneity and indeterminacy. Bergson argues for novelty and freedom based on the contraction of the past into a single action, but this does not properly attend to the novelty produced within the specious present of inscription, where movement may take an unexpected course (cf. Surrealist experimentation with the exquisite corpse collaborative drawing game). Bergson's focus on adaptation and flexibility in *Laughter* suits his overall belief in the normative function of life as part of a broader evolutionary movement, but the shorter duration of doodling shifts the emphasis to another aspect of evolution: divergence and contingency. Picasso's and Da Vinci's doodles become vehicles for invention because the artist allows the hand to follow divergent movements within a contracted present that are later incorporated into a broader artistic vision.

In arguing that great art requires the contraction of the past into free acts and an aesthetic unity, comedy and caricature come to be defined as impure composites where life competes with matter. However, the more one scrutinizes life, the more it differentiates into smaller movements operating at shorter intervals; differentiation is as much a feature of life as integration. This can be highlighted in the arts, for example in the cinema, life can be revealed in visible micromovements that are not constrained by the narrative or the organization of the mise en scène. Jean Epstein talks about the use of the close-up in early cinema that directs the viewer's attention away from the coherence of a character's willed movements to the variability of corporeal movement:

Muscular preambles ripple beneath the skin. Shadows shift, tremble, hesitate. Something is being decided. A breeze of emotion underlines the mouth with clouds. The orography of the face vacillates. Seismic shocks begin. Capillary wrinkles try to split the fault. A wave carries them away. Crescendo. A muscle bridles. The lip is laced with tics like a theater curtain. Everything is movement, imbalance, crisis. Crack. The mouth gives way, like a ripe fruit splitting open. As if slit by a scalpel, a keyboard-like smile cuts laterally into the corner of the lips.[155]

These micromovements are not just divisions within the body as a whole, but they also describe a type of incipient movement that is always ready to change – a type of movement that Epstein explains is always in preparation and unpredictable:

> I love the mouth which is about to speak and holds back, the gesture which hesitates between right and left, the recoil before the leap, and the moment before landing, the becoming, the hesitation, the taut spring, the prelude, and even more than all of these, the piano being tuned before the overture. The photogenic is conjugated in the future and in the imperative. It does not allow for stasis.[156]

In the attention to the minutiae of life, cinema reveals that movement 'is no longer the function of a variable but a variable itself'.[157] In Epstein's account, life operates within gestures, actions and the interstices of the body, which leads to a form of contingency that operates independently of the much more holistic will. If we translate this to the visual arts, life could also be regarded as an integrated bundle of micromovements, from the living variability of a drawn line to the vibrancy of small taches of colour describing the surface of a figure's skin. These infra-gestures and infra-actions might not be integrated into the singular tension of consciousness, but they nevertheless are integral to life and can be distinguished from rigid and repetitive movements that Bergson associates with mechanism. Life in this sense is invoked not only by the continuity of willed movement but also by the various infra-movements, or even micro-durations, that operate within it.

Creation as variation

One of the difficulties with using a common term such as life is that it can refer to a whole range of processes, and we have to ask each time that the term is invoked, which process is actually referred to. Moreover, its meaning is often derived through opposition to other general processes or concepts, such as automation, fixity, weight and matter. In most of the discussion so far, life has largely been associated with human action, where it subtends a body that is already individuated. For the most part of *Laughter*, life is something that is visible in macroscopic behaviours as a 'continual change of aspect, the irreversibility of the order of phenomena, the perfect individuality of a perfectly self-contained series'.[158] Here it is defined in direct opposition to macroscopic and visible aspects of mechanical movement: repetitiveness, the reversibility of a present cut off from the past and a lack of individuality due to the purely external operation of physical parts. However, if we look at just one of these features, the 'continual change in aspect', it is not entirely clear how this relates to the contraction of the artist's life as mentioned elsewhere in the text. In unifying the past into the ipseity of the work, the artistic vision does not necessarily become manifest as a change of aspect, in the sense of demonstrating an adaptability to new situations. This slippage in the use of the term life is somewhat acceptable because all can be integrated into a more far-reaching notion of life that allows for heterogeneity, but it is still important to outline the conditions in which each appears. Life makes itself visible in different ways and under different conditions, and therefore it is important to discuss such differences as the microscopic and the macroscopic, the long duration and short duration disclosure of life.

To truly think about life in aesthetic judgement and artistic practice, it is important to examine other aspects of *Creative Evolution* where life is much more differentiated and extends beyond the individual. As the title suggests, *Creative Evolution* conjoins creativity with life in a way that extends well beyond the actions of individuals to the very principles of ontogenesis and phylogenesis. The theory of evolution is conjoined with *durée* to create a far-reaching philosophy, which Moore notes could be criticized as a veiled attempt to posit a complete philosophy that unifies the sciences with metaphysics, even though Bergson has argued against any conceptual unification in articles such as 'Philosophical Intuition'.[159] Pilkington echoes this critique by stating that *Creative Evolution* marks a significant departure from Bergson's earlier works because life is overly used as an explanation and principle of evaluation. It becomes the linchpin of a theory of everything – such as the will, idea and so on – something that Bergson criticized in the work of many other philosophers.[160] However, John Mullarkey notes that although life acquires some generality in the book, and is often mistaken for a vitalist philosophy, in particular in the invocation of the *élan vital* (vital impulse), the work does not posit a general energetic theory. Life is not presented as a force that infuses matter but, rather, as an organizing process, with all the diversity this entails.[161] One of the key principles of evolution is 'dissociation', most clearly expressed in the splitting of cells, which underpins the diversification of living organisms. It is tempting to imagine this process through the metaphor of the tree of life, but Mullarkey notes that the changes are much more novel and abrupt, proceeding through 'explosions':[162]

> It follows that there is no 'life in general' marching inexorably towards some goal, but simply sporadic currents of life with real creation ongoing at all points along them. Evolution does not operate gradually by slowly accumulating minute changes mechanically until a new species is created. For Bergson, life is a continuum of heterogeneity, with each species representing a sudden emergence of novelty and invention.[163]

In any evolutionary movement, there is a balance between the 'sudden release' of energy, creating divisions and new organic forms, and the gradual 'accumulation' of characteristics along a single line of evolution.[164] Bergson rejects the mechanistic theory of evolution because it does not explain this diversity within continuity or life's indivisibility. He also rejects finalism's adoption of a telos, and even the theory of adaptation, because both attempt to shoehorn evolutionary change into 'pre-existing' moulds, and there is nothing to suggest such moulds exist.[165] Instead, he argues that the similarity between species and their diversity can be explained by an impetus, the *élan vital*, that remains connected to the past while requiring the organism to change.[166] From this perspective, life incorporates two seemingly incompatible processes into a single movement, so when discussing the continuity of the past in artistic practice, one must also be aware of an immanent divergence in the same act.

There are ways of thinking about this divergence in creative practice without turning directly to the question of cell division or the differentiation of species. In drawing and painting, this duality of life as a movement can be revealed in the projection of a unifying compositional whole that directs all creative acts and which is contingent upon the artist's past, but in the deviations created in the short duration of interacting with the material surface, as well. To give a brief example, Focillon argues that the spontaneity of movement, which we here characterize as deviation and division, is a function of the speed of the artistic gesture. He states that the Japanese artist Hokusai's movements display a capriciousness that contrasts directly with machinic approaches to the production of works:

He is a prestidigitator (I like this long, old word) who takes advantage of his own errors and of his faulty strokes to perform tricks with them; he never has more grace than when he makes a virtue out of his own clumsiness. This excess of ink flowing capriciously in thin black rivulets, this insect's promenade across a brand-new sketch, this line deflected by a sudden jar, this drop of water diluting a contour – all these are the sudden invasion of the unexpected in a world where it has a right to its proper place, and where everything seems to be busy welcoming it. For it must be captured on the fly if all its hidden power is to be extracted. Woe to the slow gesture, and to stiff fingers! The involuntary blot with its enigmatic grimace enters, however, into the world of free will. It is a meteor, a root twisted by time; its inhuman countenance fixes the decisive note where it had to be, and where it was not sought for.[167]

In some respects Hokusai's actions could be regarded as material accidents, produced externally as in the example of the 'insect's promenade' – an argument that conflicts with Bergson's rejection of genetic accidents in the emergence of new species. However, like the doodling of Picasso and Da Vinci, he is also referring to a type of novelty and invention that depends on the artist's will and their capacity to allow for deviation within the longer duration of compositional continuity. Prestidigitation refers here to the nimble fingers (of the hand) of a conjuror, which in this case is a capacity to bring life to a movement. The stiff fingers are somewhat weighed down by the past – they might be living, but they have begun to acquire mechanical weight – and it is only speed that can push the living action beyond the constraints of a comprehensive artistic vision. The marks are produced due to the liveness of action – the 'continual change in aspect' – but are only incorporated into the composition *post facto*. Earlier in this chapter, I noted a similar process in Barnett Newman's work, where he had to open up the body to the speed of invention in order to develop new works. In both examples, two types of movement and life combine in the creative process, one that responds spontaneously to what is present to the hand and the other that incorporates what has already occurred into the living whole of the work.

Understanding life as variation depends largely on understanding the relationship between life and matter, or how life works upon or through matter. This is not easily addressed if duration and life are constantly placed in opposition to matter; where matter is inviolable in its geometric certainty and directly opposes the natural flow of an artist's movements. Bergson does not address this issue in any detail in relation to creative practice; however, he does ponder a similar problem with respect to phylogenesis, by asking how it is possible to talk about creative variation, novelty and unforeseeability in evolution when there seems to be little variation in physical appearance. There is a genetic generation of similarity rather than the expression of creative difference. When we refer to life we usually do so in reference to physical bodies that are analysable using similar principles to those used to analyse solid bodies. Living bodies move in space, they are affected by gravity, they resemble each other and are reproduced as discrete entities. In describing life in terms of genera, there are many similarities between a living being and other types of physical organization: 'Thus the vital order, such as it is offered to us piecemeal in experience, presents the same character and performs the same function as the physical order: both cause experience to *repeat itself*, both enable our mind to *generalize*.'[168] The action of the genes in producing organisms that resemble their forebears is an example of repetition in nature that can be compared to the physical and geometrical repetition. If the same argument is applied to the visual arts, one could say that the capacity to organize works according to genres, styles and periods is a means of reducing them to a set of physical characteristics that can be repeated. It is a matter of organizing works in terms of classes that have much in common with logical classes or Plato's ideas engendering actual objects according to a principle of resemblance. Under this approach, styles such as Cubism or Futurism are a means of categorizing works, as if they were produced by a set of historical and formal principles or are driven by final or formal causes. They could be seen as a template that conditions artistic practice or as a means of imagining the finished work before the hand has touched the material. In either case, these arguments oppose Bergson's own claims about the haecceity and immanence of creativity.

In the discussion of both art and life, it can be difficult to distinguish between the discernment of conceptual differences and the natural formation of difference – a de facto difference produced by life itself. In the notion of individuation, Canguilhem states that there is an oscillation between the universal and the particular in developing a concept of life:[169] whether living organisms are separated in practice and constitute definable individuals, or whether universal categories should act as the basis for differentiating individuals, in which case it is 'the individual that lends its color, weight and flesh to that ghostly abstraction, the universal'. The issue is further complicated by the fact that individuals might not be easily separated, for example, a disease can be seen as a quality of the individual or as an organism in its own right. Bergson addresses the question of the individual by arguing that the vital order is distinguished by the fact that the 'living body has been separated and closed off by nature herself'.[170] In this focus on individuation, Bergson momentarily aligns with Vitalism in which, according to one of the most prominent biological Vitalists of the early twentieth century, Hans Driesch, 'wholeness' is the 'most essential character' of the organism, demonstrated in ontogenesis where the organism develops towards a given form, and in other processes such as bodily repair and 'adaptation'.[171] In contrast with the Vitalists, Bergson accentuates the difficulty in separating individuals in the natural world, especially in the plant kingdom, and consequently argues against a 'vital principle' or an 'entelechy' on the basis that the body of the organism is not 'sufficiently independent' to warrant an internal principle, and even proposes that in human beings, the individual is 'merely a bud that has sprouted on the combined body of both its parents'.[172] Bergson accepts a principle of individuation, for living organisms tend to form natural wholes that are self-generating and self-repairing unlike physical systems – something that is increasingly questioned in contemporary chemistry in the notion of autocatalytic systems – but does want to place too much emphasis on the discrete physical body as the basis for life, which in many respects is an abstraction like the separation of matter into discrete particles.

Although relatively stable bodies are prevalent in nature, Bergson argues that the examination of life should not begin with individuals but, rather, with qualitative movements or tendencies. A theory of individuality cannot account for the process of reproduction, such as in a unicellular organism, where a new individual splits off from the 'complete' organism.[173] In reference to 'a sea-urchin's egg whose fragments develop complete embryos' – an example that was also very important to the Vitalists – Bergson asks: Where is the 'individuality of the egg, the hydra, the worm?' The individual could be posited at any stage in the process characterized as much by division as unification. In such cases, the organized living body can be regarded as an individual only in opposition to the unorganized bodies studied in physics.[174] For Bergson, wholeness is not the sole determining force in life and should, instead, be regarded as a transitory state within a broader process of change.

Bergson states that in evolution the continuity of life is an 'impulse and impetus' that drives the organism to split into a range of directions when interacting with matter.[175] In focusing on differentiation, Bergson is able to remove life from a purely biological context, and address, instead, the metaphysical question of whether or not the human subject should be examined as a unity or a manifold. Consciousness comprises a unity of states but also a splitting of functions, forms of expression and feelings:

> Matter divides actually what was but potentially manifold; and, in this sense, individuation is in part the work of matter, in part the result of life's own inclination. Thus, a poetic sentiment, which bursts into distinct verses, lines and words, may be said to have already contained this multiplicity of individuated elements, and yet, in fact, it is the materiality of language that creates it.[176]

This marks a shift from the notion of artistic creativity as the expression of a particular sensibility or as an immaterial movement, because the division of the living into discrete parts is afforded by the material interaction. Dissociation is one of the key ideas in the development of an organism because it describes the splitting of cells to create new cells and the formation of new organisms and organs.[177] In this reformulation of the idea of creation, life coordinates a differentiating impetus with movement's capacity to maintain the continuity of form and direction.[178] Organisms might be closed off by nature but they are also unmade through the same process. In the common metaphor of a stream, it is not sufficient to follow the flow of one movement back to its source but to understand the many points of bifurcation, where the flow confronts the resistance of matter and matter changes in the process.

Bergson differs significantly from the Vitalists because he rethinks individuation through *durée*. Life can be understood in terms of the closing off of nature from within when addressed through the growth of a single organism, and also the integration of such differences into the much more expansive notion of life coincident with *durée*. In the creative action of evolution, life is an indivisible continuity in which the discrete divisions between organisms, species and even the internal differentiation of organs, are only traces of this continuous movement.[179] Each species might repeat itself through the reproduction of various physical characteristics but underlying this repetition is an impetus that continually varies.[180] The presence of an impetus means that the vital order is 'willed' unlike the physical order which is 'automatic',[181] although this should not be seen as an autonomous 'voluntary' will but, rather, one that is coextensive with the tension of life. It is a form of will that crosses the boundaries between species and describes a constant process of variation. This marks a shift from Bergson's examination of life in *Laughter*, for life here extends beyond the body, as both antecedent and precedent, in which case the body is no longer a container for life, but is itself contained by life.

This tension between the weight of the past, the maintenance of what already exists, and evolutionary novelty is central to *Creative Evolution*. Consciousness is always moving forward in alignment with a future that is continually 'being-made', which requires the coincidence of the will with perception in a way that is most fully realized in intuition. The past pushes the will forward to enact a type of freedom that through creation extracts the subject from the fixity of the present, which can be contrasted with the intellect that looks back to what is 'already-made' in order to reconstruct it:[182]

> Every human work in which there is invention, every voluntary act in which there is freedom, every movement of an organism that manifests spontaneity, brings something new into the world. True, these are only creations of form. How could they be anything else? We are not the vital current itself; we are this current already loaded with matter, that is, with congealed parts of its own substance which it carries along its course. In the composition of a work of genius, as in the simple free decision, we do, indeed, stretch the spring of our activity to the utmost and thus create what no mere assemblage of materials could have given (what assemblage of curves already known can ever be equivalent to the pencil-stroke of a great artist?).[183]

Invention, and this includes evolutionary invention, is produced continually due to the impetus of consciousness, movement and life, in which novel forms accrue. It concerns formal invention that works in concert with matter rather than the situation of creating something materially new. Bergson gives the example of a poet writing new poems, who does not add new letters to the alphabet, but nevertheless makes novel contributions through a type of formal invention characterized by creative movement rather than the mere rearrangement of parts.[184] The 'pencil stroke' for Bergson is always more than the material trace because it describes a movement that extends through the artist's consciousness across the work, in order to contribute to the continual process of becoming. To return to the example of Hokusai, we have to ask to what degree this formal invention remains tied to the continuity of a movement or to what degree it operates at the edge of consciousness and life in the aleatory and variable form of material engagement.

One of the distinguishing features of time in Bergson's philosophy, is its capacity to endure, but this endurance entails variation and invention. *Durée* can be contrasted with inert matter which perdures, demonstrated in such principles as the conservation of matter, rather than endures. This issue has been addressed by philosophers who have attempted to dispense with substantialist arguments to give time, and by extension life, concrete specificity. Deleuze argues that it is important to move away from questions organized around the primary question, '*What is this?*' and focus, instead, on the 'Idea as multiplicity' and its manifestation in space, time, movement and intensity – a method that seeks to understand how process and differentiation lead to 'specification', 'organization' and the distribution of parts.[185] Like Bergson and the Vitalists, Deleuze uses the example of the development of an egg and its immanent properties of division and individuation found in such processes as 'cellular migrations, foldings, invaginations, stretchings'. If we accept that any form of change is not enacted from outside then these 'sub-representational dynamisms' are a means for understanding all processes such that it can be argued that 'the whole world is an egg'.[186] This theoretical manoeuvre resembles the development of Bergson's argument in *Creative Evolution*, where continued examination of the interiority of life leads eventually to an argument that all is interiority, including the bodies that have been thought to house life.

Similarly, Gilbert Simondon argues that it is important to distinguish between the individuated and the pre-individual states. Individuation is understood in terms of the finished individual in both the substantialist and hylomorphic viewpoints, and can be characterized as 'ontogenesis "in reverse"'.[187] In other words, the individual is first posited and then the theory determines how ontogenesis contributes to the realization of that individual; for example, initial human cell differentiation is understood only in terms of the adult human being. Even though it is much more difficult to describe or analyse, Simondon argues that the focus should be on pre-individuation, in which case the adult being is regarded as a stage of the pre-individual, a stage that is passed through and cannot be used as a means of explaining individuation.[188] This leads to a greater emphasis on process and the moments of change and variation, or the capacity for change immanent to the system. Simondon characterizes metastability in terms of pre-individuation, arguing that it describes a system that has the potential to develop in any number of directions often provoked by a simple catalyst, as is the case with crystal formation in supersaturated systems. Individuation is not the imposition or realization of a form but *the conservation of being through becoming* where the metastable system falls 'out of step with itself' but retains continuity.[189] If we reflect on Bergson's early arguments about creativity, he largely focuses on the conversation of being in movement at the level of the artist – the creative act is a culmination of the whole of an artist's life. However, there is scope to examine this conversation at micro-levels, from the conservation of a movement in a pencil stroke, the division of a chisel, the flooding of a surface with paint, in which case, the medium can be foregrounded as a catalyst. The artist does not simply express their will when painting with watercolours; they allow the absorption of the paper and the dispersal of the paint to create stable taches of colour.

The idea of creation as differentiation is not directly applied by Bergson to a theory of art and, indeed, it is not examined much outside of *Creative Evolution*. In subsequent major works, Bergson shifts his attention to other fields of inquiry: the relationship between science and metaphysics; the occlusion of time in the special theory of relativity; and the role of belief and obligation in static and dynamic religions. Creative differentiation provides a much better platform for the analysis of art than the notion of a free, creative gesture because it allows for a dynamic relationship between materiality, central to the plastic arts, and the processes of individuation immanent to life and duration. Often, matter and life are strongly contrasted, for example, when Bergson argues in *Creative Evolution* that life is characterized as *a reality which is making itself in a reality which is unmaking itself*,[190] in which the theory of entropy is invoked to compare life's formal invention with matter's dissolution. Matter is also analysed in terms of its rigidity, conceptual clarity and geometry, in contrast to life's flexibility, multiplicity and dynamic organization. However, in later works Bergson softened some of these distinctions; for example, in the lecture 'Life and Consciousness', presented and published in 1911, he talks about living matter that can accommodate the actions of consciousness due to its 'elasticity'.[191] Thinking through how life intersects with matter should form part of a rethinking of Bergsonian ideas, and, in any theory of creativity, it is essential that matter is both malleable and resistant. One way of addressing the issue, which has been alluded to on a few occasions in this chapter, is to think of the temporal differences between life and matter. Various materials might be either resistant or malleable due to their duration – paint takes a particular time to dry, movement becomes mechanical at particular speeds and so on. In this context, figurative art could be distinguished by the relative stability of its figures – similar to the relative stability of organisms – that operate in a time that stands outside the plastic form of the work. Furthermore, it could also shift the focus from the work as artefact, to a notion of rethinking the work within the time of its generation – as a surface to be worked upon that continually provokes creative differentiation.

One artist who explicitly developed a theory of art driven by creative differentiation and the vital impetus is Paul Klee. Although he began his artistic career in the period following the enormous success of *Creative Evolution*, Klee does not directly draw upon Bergson's work. Nevertheless, his interest in the relationship between becoming in nature, *natura naturans*, and the becoming of the work invites investigation using Bergson's arguments on differentiation and the vital impetus. One of Klee's main contentions is that artistic creativity is aligned with the vital impetus and that the artist serves as a conduit between nature and the work, which he illustrates using the metaphor of a tree. The roots of the tree draw a vital force from the earth that flows through the trunk, which Klee identifies as the artist, into the branches. The branches and leaves are the points at which the energy terminates in material form, that is, the creative product or work: 'Moved and compelled by the power of those streaming juices, he conducts what he is looking at into the work.'[192] What is most notable about this image is that it combines three different aspects of creativity into a single organic body – the general impetus of nature, artistic activity and the material form – in order to accentuate the continuity between matter and life. The artist does not merely look upon nature, they are incorporated into it. The creative product is not shaped from outside, but concretizes an internal movement. The continuity and connectivity in this common metaphor of the tree is also underpinned by difference, for 'the below and the above cannot mirror one another perfectly'. The artist is instrumental in assisting the divergence of vital energy into novel creative forms,[193] as well as the transformation of this vital energy into matter. The lack of symmetry in the creative process also means that the natural world is not merely reproduced in material form by the artist. There is a transformation of the movement through the roots, into a new form, which bears some comparison to Bergson's argument that the whole of the past contributes to the free act, which only drops at a certain stage like a ripe fruit. The creative act does not repeat the past, for at the very moment the past is actualized, it is transformed into something that is qualitatively different.

In his writings on artistic practice, Klee often examines the formal aspects of image-making, from the creation of colour scales to the division of lines, in terms of the generation of form, in particular, the generation of natural forms. When Klee refers to pure forms he is not talking about ideal geometrical figures or colours placed on an immutable colour wheel, but, instead, primordial or elemental forms that constitute the living framework of the visible, in which the role of the artist is to understand how these primordial forms push up from underneath and lead to the generation of an image.[194] Studying nature involves isolating and understanding these 'formative forces', which is a type of practice that can in many ways be compared to philosophizing and the continual derivation of new ideas[195] – an argument that is akin in many respects to Deleuze and Guattari's claim that the main role of the philosopher is to 'cultivate' or create concepts within the lived time of philosophizing. Rather than aiming at metaphysical universality or the discovery of existing concepts, the philosopher is engaged in a limitless process of producing concepts.[196] This presupposes that nature is dynamic, creative and emergent. For Klee, the creation of natural forms must evince 'spontaneity' because it is embedded in becoming and 'the act of forming rather than the form itself, form in the process of growth, as genesis, rather than as the ultimate appearance'.[197] The artist certainly might arrive at this 'ultimate appearance' or resemblance but the external appearance should not drive artistic production.[198] Unlike the Vitalists and their emphasis on how the organism becomes whole, Klee does not propose that form should act as a telos or a final cause that stands before the work, because this does not sufficiently acknowledge movement in nature and unduly restricts creativity. Nature is always 'mobile' and the process of forming drives creativity forward and by doing so generates a range of new forms that are somewhat unforeseen.[199] Klee's interest in formative forces is similar in many respects to Bergson's *élan vital* or vital impetus where change is immanent to the creative process and form is a product of this change. To allow for the repetition that is inherent in nature, in reproduction and genera, Klee accentuates the primacy of movement over the relative stability of the individual body. Klee is not burdened by biology and the theory of evolution and only needs to find living principles that are operative in nature that can aid the artist in the discovery of new forms.

Throughout his work, Klee seeks to come to terms with the relationship between form and forming, particularly in his images of plants and in his experimentation with iteration and ramification. He also examines the relationship between the continuous movement of a line and how this culminates in a final form in a number of works including *Mother Dog with Three Litters* (1927) and *When I Rode on a Donkey* (1940). In one of his lesser known works, *Hardly Still Walking, Not Yet Flying* (1927), Klee uses an unbroken line of a pen to create an image of a figure walking (see Figure 3.2). When viewing the work, the viewer could respond to the represented figure or attend to the line, trying to follow and recreate its continuity and in doing so, re-experience the effort that Klee must have experienced in maintaining contact with the paper. Philip Rawson argues that drawing is one of the visual arts that remains close to the lived time of creative practice because the line invokes a form of touch that is

FIGURE 3.2 Paul Klee. *Hardly Still Walking, Not Yet Flying* (1927).

continuous with the hand of the artist.[200] Using very long lines without any breaks accentuates this touch and gives the viewer an indication of the actual time in which the mark was produced: the longer the line, the more this lived time is accessible to the viewer.

Directly invoking the time of drawing in the work creates a tension between the movement of the line and the coherence of the outline which is particularly accentuated in those aspects of the image where the line diverges from the outline. In *Hardly Still Walking, Not Yet Flying*, the figure's eye appears as little more than a kink in the movement of a line that passes from head to foot, and in *Mother Dog with Three Litters*, the back of the dog in the far left exists only in the intersection between two lines, one moving downwards and the other upwards. María López states that Klee explores the idea of making movement visible by highlighting the 'uninterrupted, unfinished, and never fulfilled process of its becoming'.[201] The uninterrupted line simulates the openness of becoming and for as long as it remains a line, its movement cannot be fully closed off as a form. In *Hardly Still Walking, Not Yet Flying*, the aleatory movement of the line describing the legs and feet does not have a clear outline. The lines articulate a general direction and create planes through looping back upon themselves, such that the final form is only an approximation derived from this movement. The aleatory movement of lines also creates the impression of movement that is conferred onto the representation: 'horizontal lines have been drawn across the figure's chest and upper body in order to visually underline the oscillation produced by walking.'[202] Lines unhinged from the outline of a figure invoke speed because they resemble in many aspects the act of scribbling, which is a feature of other works, such as *Violence* (1933) in which the scribbles themselves convey an intensity of movement. In all of these works, the movement of the line and the visibility of the artist's gestures stands before the articulation of a figure. In some, such as *When I Rode on a Donkey*, the movement of the painted line is stable and deliberate in its articulation of an outline, whereas in others the line is liberated from the task of representing due to the speed of the execution and the fact that the line extends through and beyond the figure.

Klee interrogates the process of individuation, in which lines oscillate between the individual form of an organism closed off by nature, and what Simondon refers to as the pre-individual states of becoming. In every change in direction, the line indicates that an organism could emerge but as the line continues, many of these forms remain virtual.

John Sallis argues that in Klee's work, and he here draws upon Merleau-Ponty, the line is not a property of the visible form of the object, but a type of movement that subtends the visible as one of the conditions for it becoming visible: 'the line renders visible the invisible of the visible, it offers a diagram of the genesis of things.'[203] The outline of an organism or body is the visible of the visible, whereas the underlying movement of life, the vital impetus, is something that is not directly visible in the same way that the *élan vital*, as the impetus underlying all formal innovation and variation, is not visible. In *Crystallisation* (1930), Klee demonstrates the importance of this principle even in the depiction of an inorganic object, in this case a crystal that is ostensibly defined by the rigidity of its surfaces and the straightness of the lines (see Figure 3.3). In a work that invokes Cubism's interleaving planes, Klee demonstrates more interest in understanding the internal movement of the crystal rather than its objective form. Most of the straight lines are oblique, or at least on a slight angle, and thus indicate a possible path of movement. Because the form is incomplete without the symmetrical organization that is typical of a crystal, it appears that the forms are unfolding to assume

FIGURE 3.3 Paul Klee. *Crystallisation* (1930).

this form. Looking into the work reveals an absent centre, a virtual centre of becoming, that is as elusive as the centre of an origami object in the process of being folded. Although the spatial centre is absent, interestingly, the act of artistic creation is still rendered visible by the concrete fullness of the line, in which we can easily imagine the artist working across the surface of the paper or canvas, and it is through the visibility of the artistic gesture that the process of genesis is also made visible. The line of genesis is something that is gestured towards in the work even if it is not realized materially.

Unlike Bergson, who takes a particular interest in the integration of all movements into *durée* or tendencies such as the *élan vital*, Klee directs most of his attention to the short durations of natural becoming that are more readily translated into artistic practice. He argues that these small movements describe principles of animation and change that are immanent throughout the life cycle. One does not have to look to clearly differentiated organisms to understand living movement, for even small particles are resonating with a principle of change.[204] In his theory of art, Klee talks about this approach as *ab ovo* (from the egg) in which he searches for visual principles for origin and growth, where often the least significant point can give birth to the larger forms. In drawing, the living form is invoked through the formal properties of the line but for Klee it is important to recognize that the point indicates latent energy, as each point can be considered a point of origin. Klee distinguishes between 'Tectonic forms' and 'Energetic forms' with the former describing the relationship between parts and the latter, forms of tension and movement in the work. The tectonic forms are associated with verticality and the organization of the plane, but it is the energetic or dynamic forms that are most important to understanding the work's organization.[205] To explain this, Klee refers to the latent energy within a seed that at first glance appears largely undifferentiated but, nevertheless, has the capacity to adopt a variety of forms due to its immanent primary impulse.[206] Klee discusses the principles of the seed in terms of drawing, arguing that it is a point of compressed energy and when provided with an external stimulus will unleash its 'logos', its formal principles, in becoming 'linear'. The line first pushes into the earth to secure its position and then moves upwards towards the light.[207] Irrespective of the external appearance of the work, energy inheres within it, which is why Klee argues that the 'interior is infinite' and the exterior form is a means of placing limits on these 'dynamic forces'.[208] The interior is infinite due to its endless capacity for modification and individuation, and, indeed, dividuation, and this contrasts with exterior form which places optical limits on life. The exterior form contracts into the outline whereas the interior divides, grows and reforms.

In his writings, Klee is seeking principles of individuation that can assist artists in rethinking the nature of nature and, because these principles are always mobile, genetic and formative, they easily translate into pedagogical statements on artistic practice. Klee's genetic principles have much in common with Bergson's theory of creative evolution because both address life through formal invention and creativity. Klee draws parallels between the material movements of creative activity, such as ramification and individuation, and the latent energies immanent with a seed. These living movements can be emulated in artistic practice, often through formal experimentation, for example in *Prehistoric Plants* (1920), new species of plants are imagined materially by varying the vertical forms of lines. The invention is possible due to the swiftness of line drawing, which can economically and rapidly contract the living principles of vegetal becoming into material traces and forms. By contrast, Bergson generally maps life over the *longue durée* of evolution where even the lifespan of a single organism is only a by-product of a greater process of change. It is not easy to visualize creative evolution in a way that directly informs artistic practice. However, the principle of pre-individuation – which is also post-individuation – does accommodate material variation due to its foregrounding of incompleteness. Bergson does not address this in most of his comments on art because he usually invokes art to describe the continuity of the artistic vision which is manifest in the finished work. It only requires a slight change of perspective in which the work, like evolution, remains in progress, to align Bergson's theory of creative evolution with Klee's philosophy of art.

Conclusion

Throughout his oeuvre, Bergson indicates that art can be understood through life, for both are linked to the continuity of consciousness and lived time and stand in contradistinction to the fragmentation of matter and the rigidity of mechanism. The relationship is never fully articulated because Bergson's aim is never to develop a theory of art but, rather, to refer to art as an example of the highest expression of life. The particular form of art and artistic practice changes depending on the particular aspect of life that Bergson is foregrounding. In a number of texts, art is associated with the continuity of life and the freedom of action in which the whole of the past, and in some respects an evolutionary past, gives impetus to meaning in artistic creation. The argument has value when contrasted with other types of mental activity and action that presuppose a clear division between the past and the present, but it leads Bergson to neglect reference to the concrete specificity of making a work, and, instead, invokes the idea of a singular artistic vision. The more the art work is linked to the ipseity of the artist's mind, the less the visible material processes can be invoked in the study of creation. Indeed, Bergson does not sufficiently distinguish the act of producing a literary work from that of painting or music as they all attest to the continuity of time and creative activity. In contrast to this unification of the past in the present, for many artists, including Barnett Newman and Paul Klee, the value of the work is often realized only after the process of material experimentation, as a *post facto* judgement. Nor does Bergson focus on the actual time of making a work, which is central to both the work's visibility and connecting the time of production to the time of reception. In many respects, the artist's gesture only becomes visible in the degree to which it reveals the actual time of engagement with the work – divulged in quick brushstrokes and lines while obscured in those surfaces that are continually worked upon.

In *Laughter*, life is examined from the position of the observer rather than the artist, in which actions are judged on whether they are living or mechanical. In Bergson's theory of the comic, life appears at the fringes of the mechanical as the assertion of ipseity, adaptability and flexibility. The idea that the organism can adapt to its environment is proof that it is free and this freedom is again associated with art. However, the relationship between the movement of an individual person and the movement inherent in creative practice are not easily reconcilable, for the body remains intact in any spontaneous or living action whereas in art, the body itself is produced through a living action that remains at the threshold of the foreseeable. The unforeseeability entails a material variability in which change and differentiation operate at the very point where the creative gesture engages with the material. Continuity and divergence can be somewhat joined in the organic metaphors of the ripe fruit falling from the tree and the image of individual buds separating themselves from the continuity of the tree branch. The free gesture might come through the maturation of the organism, where the past comes to bear on the present, but also through a process of internal differentiation and formal invention. Bergson usually talks of this differentiation in terms of evolution and species differentiation, but he also indicates that it can be found in individual creative acts when matter both resists and conforms to life's variability. The whole of the past could still be found in the gesture but rather than consolidating this past into a singular vision, it could provide the impetus for the line to take its own direction and provoke the unforeseeable.

4 PERCEPTION

For Bergson, the role of art is to cultivate a form of aesthetic attention underscored by intuition that allows the viewer to comprehend and experience the processual reality of *durée*. Over and above questions of aesthetic value and judgement, art serves as a prolegomena to metaphysics due to its restaging of the artist's aesthetic and metaphysical vision. This raises the question of why, when we are already embedded in this metaphysical reality, we require art and also philosophy to assist us in its disclosure, for our intuition should automatically provide us with an enduring vision of *durée*. Moreover, Bergson often argues that his theory of time is based on common-sense knowledge concerning our own movements and the manner in which time is disclosed in consciousness. The problem does not directly relate to intuition and its capacity to reveal the real, but, rather, with perception and its role in obscuring a proper processual understanding of what we perceive. Bergson states that normal perception actually restricts a processual understanding of the real and operates in a direction counterposed to intuition – focusing on externalities that mediate our perception of internal movement and time. Normal perception is driven by need and utility and is closely tied to the motor functions, insofar as it shapes the sensual environment in terms of the body's capacity to act on things. Rather than addressing the temporal differences inherent to matter, or those differences that extend well beyond any momentary instantiation of an object, normal perception divides the sensible into objects that appear to stand outside of qualitative change. In particular, visual perception configures the world according to a logic of solid bodies replete with stable objects and clearly articulated spatial divisions. As this substantive ontology is generated in the very moment of seeing as a contraction of qualitative differences into a stable hylomorphism, art has the difficult task of realigning perception with an enduring real, which involves expanding attention and perception to reveal variability, difference and flow. Some artists, such as Turner, are able to achieve this through the accentuation of painterly movements over and above the articulation of the outline, where the object is only a relatively stable moment in a compositional flux. Other artists, in particular the Futurists, attempt to recreate the movement inherent in matter and perception, and regardless of whether they achieve this, provoke the viewer to rethink the object itself in terms of the contraction of qualitative difference in perception. Although Bergson argues that all art is underpinned by an aesthetic vision shaped by an understanding of the processual real, only some art actively engages in an investigation of the difference between processual and substantive accounts of the real.

Utilitarian perception and the logic of solid bodies

For Bergson, the continuity of becoming is characterized both by the endurance of the past in a present that also stretches towards the future, and by a process of formal differentiation in which discrete organisms and material objects are only by-products. Movement is primarily qualitative change and not an accidental property of moving bodies, putting into question the idea that the body is a stable vehicle for movement, in the way we might refer to an object traversing space. In this heterogeneity of change, living or physical bodies only appear to be discrete because they are addressed through the limited time frame of human and animal perception. These bodies would lose their separateness when examined from the perspective of evolution as a whole, or, indeed, even at a microphysical level in which matter gives way to energy. In Bergson's philosophy, it would be more appropriate to say that the body is a 'relatively closed system', 'a snapshot view of a transition' or the '*mean* image' of a continual process of change.[1] In this context, Bergson proposes that art is distinguished by its capacity to present movement or mobile images as metonyms for the metaphysical truth of becoming, rather than to depict the external movement of living or physical bodies. This metaphysics of becoming can be revealed through the expansion of time beyond the present perception of a physical body, as in evolutionary movement, or through following an interior movement in which the rigidity of material form gives way to the qualitative multiplicity of consciousness. The former is the main focus of *Creative Evolution* and the latter, of *Time and Free Will*.

In *Time and Free Will*, Bergson argues that it is through grace and rhythmic sympathy that the audience of a work is able to access the consciousness of the artist. The role of art is to establish a sympathetic connection with an audience and, in doing so, cultivate an understanding of the deep feelings and the qualitative multiplicity of *durée*. However, this places art at one remove from the lived experience of the artist, and therefore we must ask what exactly art offers when *durée* can be accessed directly through internal contemplation. Why look outwards to art only to look inward again, when all can be revealed through introspection? Moreover, if art is simply a moment within the broader impetus of nature, then why not cut out the intermediary and simply speak of nature and its qualitative differences? In *Laughter*, after a long discourse on the importance of life in the understanding of comedy and art, Bergson raises a similar point by stating that if we were perfectly attuned to life, there would be no need for art and that we do not generally 'enter into an immediate communion with things and ourselves'.[2]

> Deep in our souls we should hear the strains of our inner life's unbroken melody, – a music that is ofttimes gay, but more frequently plaintive and always original. All this is around and within us, and yet no whit of it do we distinctly perceive. Between nature and ourselves, nay, between ourselves and our own consciousness a veil is interposed: a veil that is dense and opaque for the common herd, – thin, almost transparent, for the artist and the poet.[3]

From this perspective, we are aligned with life and the continuity and ipseity of our own duration; however, we cannot attend fully to the particularity of *durée* because we generally act according to our practical, often physical, needs that also render the world perceptually stable. In following these patterns of behaviour and acquiring perceptual habits, 'all other impressions must be dimmed or else reach us vague and blurred' and suppress a direct understanding of *durée*. We do not perceive the internal 'melody' of life because life is always mediated by a 'veil' of 'utilitarian' activity.[4] In this argument, life proceeds in two directions: one that is organized around appetition and the separation of objects according to need and the other that aligns itself with the continuity of becoming, evinced in the immanence of creative activity and aesthetic attention. Jae Emerling states that aesthetic attention aligns the perceiver with the material forces and becoming of the work as part of a general attentiveness to life, which contrasts with habit and utilitarian perception which impose a set of constraints on the perception of a work. This view of aesthetic attention can also be contrasted with art history's placement of artworks within a thoroughly overdetermined set of categories or more formalist approaches. This placement effectively extracts the artwork from the radicalness of *durée* and from a proper understanding of becoming in all its indefiniteness and uncertainty.[5] Although there is a particularly Bergsonian focus on *durée*, the separation of aesthetic attention from utilitarian perception also places his work within the context of post-Kantian continental aesthetics.

Bergson does not explicitly develop a theory of aesthetic attention or perception in *Laughter* or any of his other works, for it is developed, as are most of his ideas, through a critique of spatialization. In *Matter and Memory*, aesthetic perception is a necessary counterpoint to the theory of 'pure perception', according to which, perception, when examined outside of its relationship to memory, primarily redirects the movement of images and does not, as many scientists and philosophers would presume, create representations. The images refer to qualitative relationships between bodies that bear some relationship to Leibniz's monadology, which is no surprise as Bergson presented classes on Leibniz in his early years at Clermont-Ferrand and Lycée Henri IV. Like the monadology, Bergson's ontology emphasizes perspectival relationships in which bodies redirect, and are affected by, the movement of images. There is no need to reproduce here the many arguments that justify this position; suffice to say that Bergson believes it extends from the common-sense assumption that the world exists for the perceiver independently of consciousness: 'For common sense, then, the object exists in itself, and, on the other hand, the object is, in itself, pictorial, as we perceive it: image it is, but a self-existing image.'[6] This leads to the radical claim that matter is an 'aggregate of images' rather than a type of substance, which is equally real in its material or phenomenal aspects – images are as much in the world as available for perception. Although visual perception is the source of most of Bergson's examples, these images should not be likened to a photograph or drawing. They are extended, qualitatively differentiated, continuous movements that pass through the body longitudinally rather than static transverse snapshots of the real, as posited in cinematographic models of perception.

Accepting that the world is comprised of images existing independently of the body overcomes many of the problems of the dualism in *Time and Free Will*, but it also offers a means of bridging the trenchant split between realism and idealism. Removing representation from pure perception precludes explaining how these representations are derived from or translated into material form in a mind-body dualism, as well as presenting an alternative to realist approaches in which qualia are secondary phenomena derived from a purely physical reality. Without representation, Bergson argues that perception describes the body's capacity to receive material movements and redirect them into motor actions. Importantly, in this schema, cerebral activities are not fully distinguishable from material processes, as the neurological structure of the brain is also composed of vibrations, movements and images. Without the intermediary of representation, matter and the brain operate on the same plane, with the brain's role limited to 'the reaction of my body to the action of external objects'.[7] Instead of interpreting images in this circuit between perception and action, the brain operates like a 'telephonic exchange' in which perceptions are linked with appropriate actions. This may seem like a very peculiar argument in light of the complexity of cerebral activity but it presages some recent work in brain physiology where vibratory movements are privileged over the neural network. For example, neuropsychologist Karl Pribram argues that networks of brain cells are attuned to particular vibrations that pass through the receptors.[8] The brain develops a sympathetic relationship with specific bandwidths and this forms the ground for perception and action.

In many respects, Bergson is looking to place the brain within an ontology of perception rather than deriving a theory of perception from the operation of the brain, which is evident in his analysis of the role of the brain in neurological and perceptual evolution:

> For if we follow, step by step, the progress of external perception from the monera to the higher invertebrates, we find that living matter, even as a simple mass of protoplasm, is already irritable and contractile, that it is open to the influence of external stimulation, and answers to it by mechanical, physical and chemical reactions.[9]

The capacity to be moved or stimulated underpins all perception, from the sudden contraction of pseudopodia upon contact with objects in unicellular organisms to the redirection of images into action in the human brain. What changes in the progression from lower to higher species is the complexity of the circuit between perception and movement and the degree to which the response slows down as it passes through the body. There is greater delay in the higher organisms due to the increase in the array of possible actions and the consequent degree of uncertainty as to which response will be taken.[10] In general, the brain-body selects those images that directly translate into action, and thus operates like a 'compass' directing the body to the relevant objects.[11] Unlike phenomenological accounts of intentionality in perception, Bergson foregrounds utility in the selection of images in a deliberately restrictive analysis that separates the operation of perception from memory. He seeks to outline the key principles of perception before addressing how memory works upon those images that pass through the body.

In the background of the theory of pure perception in *Matter and Memory* is a processual ontology, in which matter is an effect of the complex interaction of vibratory movements, qualities and images rather than being comprised of objects, or particles, spread out in space. When applied to visual culture, a primitive or founding processual reality always precedes the description of objects in an artwork or visual environment. It is noteworthy that this processual ontology does not readily accord with the common-sense view of perception, in which the perceptual field is divided into objects that occupy relatively stable positions against a fixed ground. In visual perception, what is most noticeable is the stability of visual form, especially when considered in the context of material objects. Those features of the environment that are not easily reducible to objects, such as the shimmering of light on water, are often accorded a secondary status. This is evinced in the history of the visual arts, where there has been greater emphasis on resemblance than in coming to terms with process. Of course, there are numerous exceptions, from Da Vinci's studies of water to Turner's clouds, Futurist dynamic sensation and Impressionist divisionism, but the prominence of mimesis and the clear articulation of objects in the arts has much to say about everyday perception. We often admire that which conforms to our own perceptual prejudices.

The question that Bergson seeks to address in the theory of pure perception is why visual perception is often construed in terms of discrete physical objects when the reality of conscious experience, perception and the material world is processual. There are a number of ways to frame this issue depending on what is configured as the principle of stability, from Plato's Ideas to Kant's synthetic *a priori*. Edmund Husserl, writing in a similar period to Bergson, sought a principle of invariance that could explain the relationship between mental phenomena and the stability and depth of the visual field. He argues that perceptual invariance is a 'style' in which appearances are coordinated by the assumed invariability of certain objects in perception and the way in which they relate to a particular space.[12] For example, a key aspect of our perceptual style is a tacit understanding of how objects vary in relation to a horizon line, consistently disappearing into the zero point of the horizon or becoming increasingly differentiated as they move closer to us.[13] Following a similar line of inquiry, the environmental psychologist J. J. Gibson argues that the most significant aspect of embodied perception is the variability of the perceptual field, insofar as the eyes, head and body are always mobile, yet, despite this mobility, there is a tendency to see 'rigid things' and stable spatial relationships. This leads Gibson to argue that constancy and invariance in perception should be explained before other aspects of form and visual structure are analysed.[14] He proposes that we first learn to accept the variance of the body relative to the invariance of a spatial ground as an epistemological foundation for understanding the position and movement of other objects.[15] Like Husserl, Gibson argues that invariance is produced through situating the body in relation to a relatively stable background or horizon and, by doing so, the body develops its own way of seeing that appears to be stable. For both Husserl and Gibson, human perception requires the correlation of the body's movement with the most stable aspects of a visual world, and from this initial condition of stability developing general principles for all perception.

Bergson also sought to understand the nature of invariance in perception, but rather than attending to the particular affordances of human visual perception, he posited a biological argument derived from his belief that action and perception constitute a circuit. Unlike Husserl and Gibson, who accept a ground level of spatiality and solidity, Bergson argues, instead, that the body stabilizes the perceptual field through the projection of its biological needs and that the reiteration of these needs extracts, or selects, some images and disregards others.[16] Milič Čapek argues that this biological epistemology is probably derived from William James who argued that human knowledge is essentially selective and dependent on needs at all levels including that of sensory perception, although some aspects may have come from Leibniz or other theories of appetition.[17] This raises the question as to what actually constitutes a need.

In *Matter and Memory*, Bergson gives the example of the immediate need to flee a threat or avoid a danger, in which complex sensory systems allow for greater variance in the type of response. For example, animal visual perception is more complex than the tactile perception of single-celled organisms because it alerts the organism to threats at a distance. This depth perception provides more time to respond to a threat, increases the degree of choice in action, and provides greater perceptual control over the spatial field. Not only is there a greater indetermination in the organization of the brain of the higher organisms, but also an increased flexibility in responding to threats due to the perception of objects at a distance.[18] As this example demonstrates, Bergson sometimes moves too quickly from biological examples, and a biological epistemology, to ontological and physical arguments that do not necessarily have the same processual logic. In the context of process philosophy, Nicholas Rescher describes this as causal processism in which substance, thingness, subjectivity and causality are all founded in process, and which can be contrasted with the weaker form of conceptual processism that investigates those processes involved in our perception or understanding of particular objects or substances.[19] In obtaining the main principles from arguments about seeing objects at a distance, Bergson derives his causal processism from a conceptual processism in which objects are already constituted in space as possible threats. This lessens the impact of his general processual argument in which bodies are produced through a type of sensory discrimination, and where the recognition of threats must come after the discrimination of qualia, such as colour and line.

These shifts between a processual ontology and a biological epistemology raise many questions, but the main point is that the body's needs are central to the discrimination of perceptual features. In *Matter and Memory*, Bergson mainly uses examples derived from visual perception, where sight picks out those objects that can be moved, handled, eaten or avoided and the relative distance in the visual field describes the degree to which they can affect the body. What is seen and highlighted in vision are those objects that can touch or be touched by the body: '*The objects which surround my body reflect its possible action upon them.*'[20] Moreover, as Bergson argues later in *Creative Evolution*, the perception of visual properties is itself constituted through this possible action: 'It is the plan of our eventual actions that is sent back to our eyes, as though by a mirror, when we see the surfaces and edges of things.'[21] The world is not primarily comprised of solid objects with hard surfaces, for these spatial and tactile differences are derived through action or through the implication of action in perception. Bergson develops an ontology based on the separation of real and virtual action, with real action proximate to the body and defined by touch, and virtual action operating at a distance through vision – a difference that is also implicated in the separation of bodies from a background. The gradations in light, colour, form, texture, patterning might all be visible but the eye will give greater attention to the qualities that assist in the discrimination of physical bodies.

This idea of a virtual action is also the basis for Bergson's theory of consciousness, which he explains using the metaphor of optical refraction. In refraction, when light passes obliquely from one medium to another it changes its angle due to changes in the resistance of the materials it encounters. At particularly acute angles of incidence, the ray of light reflects off the surface of the medium rather than passing through it, creating a mirror image. Bergson maps this physical process onto the circuit of perception and action, arguing that an image that does not pass directly into action creates a '*virtual* image' describing our possible action on things: 'The objects merely abandon something of their real action in order to manifest their virtual influence of the living being upon them.' We have an image of how we could act in the space between virtual and real action that creates the 'mirage' of consciousness.[22] This optical metaphor is a little awkward because Bergson's notion of the passage of images can easily be confused with the passage of light, for images do not reflect off bodies but actually constitute them. However, it does highlight the temporality of perception, where the contents of vision must take some time to be received and translated into action. Consciousness is effectively produced through the slowing down of the movement between perception and action, which at its fastest is nothing more than a reflex action. In slowing down the perception–action circuit, the mind can contemplate a possible action on things and this is why Bergson argues that consciousness is a form of hesitation. One way of reworking this in the context of aesthetic perception could be to argue that aesthetic contemplation is a particularly strong case of hesitation because the viewer is not required to act, and, instead, responds with a multitude of virtual actions that cohere to form the aesthetic feelings. The slowing down of perception draws greater attention to the sensual aspects of seeing, which can be contrasted with the fast perception–action circuit of habit.

The theory of pure perception does not provide a fine-grained analysis of the differences between the senses, which is demonstrated in the broadness of the metaphors Bergson uses. He often argues that perception carves or cuts out (*découper*) those features of the sensual environment that respond to the body's needs and, in doing so, removes, or cuts away, what is not relevant. This metaphor is used throughout Bergson's work to explain a spatialization bias in perception. In *Creative Evolution* Bergson uses this metaphor to describe how scientific epistemology is derived from this perceptual tendency to cut out features of the real: 'The real whole might well be, we conceive, an indivisible continuity. The systems we cut out (*découper*) within it would, properly speaking, not then be *parts* at all; they would be *partial views* of the whole.'[23] Cutting out is a strongly visual metaphor that depends on the clear separation of a figure (the object or quality) from a stable background that does not sufficiently attend to the differences between taste, vision, touch, smell and audition, never mind those senses yet to be properly addressed in the nineteenth century, such as kinaesthesia, proprioception, thermal perception and nociception. This is important because, depending on which of the senses is used as a starting point, the ontology could change significantly. For example, it would be difficult to propose that perception concerns the clear isolation of parts or the presentation of solid bodies if kinaesthesia is the main object of analysis. As was mentioned in Chapter 2, kinaesthesia is the sense that most clearly reveals a processual account of time because the kinaesthetic feelings are not easily isolated and resist clear conceptualization in terms of external movement.[24] Bergson does refer to the processual aspects of hearing and touch in contrast to visual perception – that is, the value in attending to these senses with one's eyes closed – but not in relation to the theory of pure perception. Although he proposes an ontology of perception, what Bergson most effectively highlights is the importance of vision in substantialist theories, as well as the value in understanding action in any account of perception.

Another problem with the metaphor of cutting out is that it obscures the relationship between individual willed action in perception and the notion that the body serves as a precondition for such action: Does the will drive attention to particular objects, or are these objects already framed by the body as sites of possible attention? Mark Johnson criticizes William James's use of the terms 'selects' and 'cuts' to describe perception because they imply a centralized agency, when, instead, they could be seen, in line with cognitive psychology, as 'affordances' or forms of cognitive discrimination inherent in perception.[25] This provides a basis for discriminating between active and passive aspects of perception, for although the subject might be actively engaged in attending to aspects of the environment with the body, it also passively distinguishes between things and qualia.[26] Bergson's theory of pure perception can be subject to the same critique, insofar as it draws upon James's biological epistemology and often obscures the relationship between motivated and structural distinctions in perception. In reference to vision, does cutting out only concern those aspects of the visible field that the eyes are structurally able to see? For example, human vision is trichromatic and can only use three colour channels to discriminate between colour and form, whereas many birds have tetrachromatic vision, which allows them to see forms invisible in human perception. In this case, selection is hard-wired into the body and operates before any division of the visual field into objects – it is a condition upon which other types of selection can be made. Bergson does not make such a distinction when referring to the body's selection of images and mainly uses examples that operate in a semi-conscious or conscious present of individual need (appetition, identifying a threat, etc.). A problem with Bergson's theory of pure perception is that it does not sufficiently distinguish between perceptual affordances hypostatized over the long duration of phylogeny, perceptual habits developed within the much shorter duration of ontogeny, and consciously willed actions that operate within these corporeal constraints.

Although Bergson conflates different levels of perception, his general argument that perception isolates and creates stable forms in an otherwise mobile field remains important to the study of visual culture. It highlights how normal perception not only reveals the sensible world but also suppresses sensual differences. In *Laughter*, he argues that this suppression accompanies the accentuation of resemblances between qualities and objects and the classification of nature according to its usefulness – each event loses its 'individuality' and differences are only valued insofar as they help distinguish between objects.[27] In contrast to the presentness of pure perception, the theory of resemblance extends Bergson's argument beyond selection, to a form of temporality structured around repetition and comparison – unifying an action over time and acknowledging its repetition requires the retention of the past. The theory of pure perception is only a partial account of perception, used as a limit point to expose the misconceptions of realism and idealism, for in actual lived perception, memory and perception are 'always exchanging something of their substance as by a process of endosmosis'.[28] Perception involves the prolongation of events over a definite duration, such as the endurance of the material vibrations of a sound, which always presumes the operation of memory. This argument also applies to visual perception despite its apparent immediacy, for the vibrations of light also have to endure if we are to see colours or forms. Memory also operates at the higher levels of visual perception, for even an ostensibly static image, such as a painting or photograph, is not given all at once in perception and actually requires a time of perusal, where the eye traverses the visual field through a sequence of saccadic movements. Although memory is central to the endurance of the past and differentiation, when conjoined with utilitarian attention, it contributes to the stability, invariance and coherence of a visual field that would otherwise be characterized by constant movement.

One of the most striking arguments in *Matter and Memory* is Bergson's explanation of recognition based on the intertwining of memory and perception in action, which also serves as a counterpoint to disinterested aesthetic perception. His argument differs significantly from many other philosophers and psychologists writing at the end of the nineteenth century, in particular the Associationists, who saw memory as a collection of stored percepts linked to perception through resemblance, for whom recognition is based on the comparison of discrete memories with the present contents of perception. Reference to discrete memories raises an important question: At what point can a percept be separated from the continual passage of images, such that it forms the basis of an association? Rather than addressing this question directly, Bergson reframes the issue in terms of the circuit between perception and recognition, arguing that the most rudimentary form of recognition involves linking corporeal movements to objects through the nervous system, which over time become more firmly established.[29] This argument is similar in many respects to the contemporary notion of neural networks except that the Bergsonian images cannot be decomposed into discrete signals. Recognition here describes the acquisition of habitual behaviours that are thoroughly invested in the presentness of action without a representation acting as an intermediary. To explain this, Bergson uses the example of a dog recognizing its master, which could be explained by stating that the dog sees its master, creates a representation, compares this representation with past representations and then responds with the appropriate action. However, this introduces too much complexity, for Bergson argues that the perception can automatically trigger a type of behaviour, an incipient action that serves as the basis for recognition, without a representation – the past returns to the present in the form of a habit without conscious recollection or the deployment of a principle of resemblance.[30] Recognition is based on movement and utility where '[t]o recognize a common object is mainly to know how to use it'.[31] The perception provokes a response invested in the motor functioning of the body, and these motor schemas are types of memory that guide, organize and structure perception without necessarily representing it. The representation is derived from the repetitions that are already operative in the motor schema.

To justify this claim, Bergson refers to a number of empirical studies in the field of psychology in which there is a breakdown in recognition, such as aphasia, agnosia and apraxia. He argues that the failure to recognize something does not mean the memory image is lost, but, rather, that there is a breakdown in the capacity to respond appropriately to the perceptual object.[32] The pathway linking memory to perception is disrupted, which is supported by studies showing that the breakdown in recognition is also accompanied by a loss of the ability to navigate. The sufferer might be able to invoke individual images of a particular location but not use them to find their way.[33] Other authors since Bergson have also noted the importance of navigation and orientation in recognition. Paul Schilder notes that autotopagnosia, a condition where the subject has difficulty in recognizing their own body, is often accompanied by the inability to distinguish left from right and other directional parameters.[34] Merleau-Ponty in the *Phenomenology of Perception* argues that recognition is essentially 'physiognomic' insofar as it describes a particular way in which the body is orientated to its environment. Bodily movements are interconnected like a 'melody' in response to perceptual stimuli, and this can be contrasted with the agnosic, who has to consciously reconstruct the parts to make the whole. The agnosic can no longer recognize an object immediately but must proceed to understand the meaning of perceptual data through external inference.[35] For the agnosic, perception is caught in a contracted present without the coherence of overall bodily movement or the 'intentional arc' that extends from the past into the future.[36] This intentional arc underpinning recognition is a form of navigation inasmuch as it describes how the body is orientated towards objects, rather than a purely cerebral process in which percepts are juxtaposed against the contents of memory. For Bergson, navigation is fundamental to all forms of perception because bodies are orientated towards the images they refract. In *Matter and Memory*, using an analogy related to recognition, he notes a significant difference in perception between navigating an unfamiliar town, where each movement must be initiated by the walker, and walking through the streets of a town that is so familiar that each action is automatic and does not require attention to the specificity of the place. In the first, the perceiver must consider which movements are most appropriate to the environment, whereas in the second the relationship between percept and action is so firmly established that there is no cause for reflection. These two states constitute the extremes of how movement is constituted in perception, although, in reality, perception is 'mixed', combining automatic movements with 'discontinuous' movements that are created anew in response to an unfamiliar place.[37] The foregrounding of movement and navigation in recognition is evinced in the macroscopic level of overall bodily coordination but also, when talking about visual perception, in the smaller movements of the eye as it seeks to find patterns that accord with expectation.[38] Attention to the visual environment involves both a responsiveness to the particularity differences in the visual field and the deployment of habitual eye movements that render the visual data coherent.

Recognition is based on what is already known; however, the already known reveals itself in movements because perception is continuous, rather than discrete images. Perception draws together the past of the recently perceived with a near future of the yet to be perceived, which is also the basis for Merleau-Ponty's intentional arc, Husserl's primary memory and James's specious present. Although grounded in memory, recognition involves some degree of prediction as to what will be perceived, for at the very moment the perceiver comes into contact with an object, they have an incipient idea of its outline in the form of a movement that guides the perceptual process. The example that Bergson most often uses to explain this is the act of reading. When we read words as part of a sentence, we do not read each letter in turn and wait to the conclusion of each word to recognize it. Instead, our memory guides perception by providing a general outline of the word's form, which acts as a template through which the reader fills the gaps to create a cohesive whole. Memory projects itself across the written sequence, combining letters and words into meaningful sentences.[39] Bergson compares this action to a process of 'divination' because we see the word before we have completely scanned its detail.[40] The movements of recognition are nascent because they are initiated at the beginning of the perceptual process before the object has been perceived in its entirety. In a contemporary context, one could argue that memory operates in a similar way to predictive text, casting forward possibilities before the word is complete. However, there is a significant difference because predictive text is based on algorithmic possibility – words are presented in terms of their statistical probability – whereas Bergsonian recognition requires the continuation, or variation in continuity, of bodily movement – it is more a disposition than a prediction.

The analysis of recognition foregrounds memory as a means of orientating the body to a perceptual object – a departure from many theories of memory that focus on the recollection of discrete contents stored by the mind. However, it should be noted that Bergson does not limit the function of memory to motor responsiveness, for he also proposes a theory of recollection in which recollections are not housed by the brain. In his quite radical theory of pure memory, Bergson claims that recollections accumulate without loss; everything that we have seen, heard, tasted and so on remains tied to the particular time and context in which it first appeared in perception. Memories are continuously preserved in all their particularity; however, the retention of memory and the manner by which memories are recalled are two different things. When memory is recalled in the service of recognition, it is modified to suit the requirements of present action and perception. Automatic and habitual motor images are invoked to help complete a task, such as recognizing words or an object and only reveal as much of the past as is relevant to the task. When reading a single word, the reader does not need to remember every iteration of the word they have ever heard or read with the innumerable differences in font, style and sound, in order to make a judgement on what they perceive. Notably, not all memory is contracted into the service of recognition, for example dreams and spontaneous recollections are likely to appear only when the subject does not fully attend to the present and action.[41] For Bergson, dreams and reveries are the most likely states in which memories can be recalled in their historical and contextual specificity because this mode of imagining is not tethered to recognition and its idea–motor function. Specific recollections most readily appear in a relaxed mind that does not have to attend to the present. In this sense, dreams and reveries run counter to utilitarian perception and could play a role in understanding aesthetic attention by accentuating the continuity of memory and time, and by inhabiting the time of aesthetic contemplation.

Recognition is the very basis for treating the world in terms of utility, for it transforms the temporal continuity of perception into clear differences that eventually function as representations. This relationship is explored in the second introduction to *Creative Mind* where Bergson asks: '[h]ow should a cow that is being led stop before a meadow' unless some form of representation provokes this action?[42] Does the cow *read* the field in terms of key differences in types of vegetation and then choose to stop? Bergson argues that the cow does not require a sign system in order to know when to stop; all that matters is that the perceptual difference indicating the beginning of the meadow is linked to a particular action of stopping. The representation is first articulated as a habit or motor response, and through the repetition of such responses comes 'the automatic extraction of resemblances'.[43] Human action and perception extends well beyond biological necessity; however, the principle remains the same: resemblance is extracted from the plenitude of the sensible environment through the repetition of certain actions. Resemblance combines the perceptions and actions of the perceiving subject with the particular qualities of the sensual environment, which Bergson explains using the example of bell-ringing:

> Thus a bell, under the most varied form of impact – a blow with the knuckle, a breath of wind, an electric current – will give out a sound which is always the same, will in that way convert these forms of impact into bell-ringers, and thus will make them resemble one another, individuals constituting a genus simply because the bell remains the same: bell, and nothing but bell, it cannot do otherwise, if it reacts at all, than ring.[44]

Resemblance is partly determined by the object, for the bell will ring regardless of the type of movement or action to which it is subjected, which draws together a diverse set of actions under a common category, that of bell-ringing, and draws together the subjects who perform the action under a common genus of bell-ringers. Through the repetition of the actions resemblances are extracted – and here is the proper meaning of *découper* or cutting out – and many other perceptual differences are erased.

Bergson's processual account of resemblance is the basis for a theory of representation. The repetition of actions might be an unconscious act for the cow standing before the field, but in human perception, these behaviours are also consciously nominated through language, theories and ideas. In *Laughter*, Bergson argues that stable symbols, such as words, come to stand in for these generic actions and for the particular perceptual differences that provoke them: 'For words – with the exception of proper nouns – all denote genera.'[45] In addition to the reduction of difference in perception, the label or word reinforces those movements first initiated by corporeal utility and further limits access to the qualitative variation that is the basis of all experience. It is part of a utilitarian reorganization of perception in which 'we do not see the actual things themselves; in most cases we confine ourselves to reading the labels affixed to them.'[46] In visual perception, representations sketch out spaces and behaviours that can initiate recognition even before the spectator attends to specific differences in the visual field. Our eye is conditioned to seek out generic features and objects, a process that is redoubled in representation, which must reduce the haecceity of any perceptual event, temper aesthetic awareness and prevent access to the durational real.

Because they do not begin with a clearly defined referent or object, processual accounts of representation foreground the role of the sign in reducing sensible difference. Floyd Merrell argues that, in addition to separating an object from a continuum, words refigure the real in terms of a structured set of external and internal relationships. For example, understanding a tree in all its plenitude involves placing it within a whole range of biological, perceptual and material systems and recognizing that in the course of its development it is always becoming something other than itself – it grows and varies internally and in relation to its environment – such that it is difficult to know where the tree begins and ends. Upon the application of the word tree, however, the potentially infinite number of aspects contingent on the processual reality of a tree coalesce into a definite object and its associated concepts. Perception is the starting point for the unfolding of a system of ideas latent in the word 'tree.'[47] Depending upon what semiotic system the word is placed in, the tree becomes a source of carbon, a carbon sink, the tree of life, an example of plant life and so on. The concepts overlay the perception of a particular tree by reconfiguring it in terms of a genus, in other words, a set of pre-existing relations. Martin Heidegger sets out a similar process when he talks about how the language of mathematics informs perception. Mathematics provides a means of understanding things according to general categories, in which case there is reference to thingness before there is specific attention to what a thing is – knowing how to handle a thing or to be cognizant of it rather than deriving a specific knowledge from the thing itself.[48] In numeration, the application of a number reconfigures the thing in terms of the property of being counted. Number is not 'grasped' in the thing itself, for it describes a type of knowledge that 'we already have' and numerical understanding involves placing the thing within this way of knowing.[49] Number, like language, stands before and outside sensual and empirical experience as a guide to how we should use objects, in the same way that Bergson's bell can be reduced to its capacity to generate repetitive sounds. In Bergson's philosophy, semiotic and numeric categories are the final product of a genetic process that starts with biological utility, which is then stabilized in recognition and representation, and finally systematized in various languages. Once established, these languages preempt our engagement with the real, and mediate our understanding and apperception of time.

Up to this point, the focus has been on utilitarian perception, which casts a 'veil' over perception and precludes or limits aesthetic engagement with the sensual field as well as intuition's grasp of lived time. It is difficult to imagine how this can be incorporated into visual analysis when the idea of utilitarian perception is so broad that it applies to all levels of perception, from the biological selection of images to the role of signs in systemizing acts of recognition. To say, as Bergson does, that aesthetic perception lifts the veil of utility could involve resisting any form of signification, or even fundamental structures of resemblance and visual organization. Most importantly, all figurative artworks reduce, to some extent, the plenitude of the visual field by organizing difference in terms of genera and the logic of solid bodies, where colour, tonal variation and other plastic qualities are somewhat delimited by their relationship to the pictorial objects and representation. In Johannes Vermeer's *The Kitchen Maid* (1658), I can readily describe the scene of a young woman dressed in a yellow and blue dress pouring milk into a bowl that sits on a table with other foodstuffs. I can also refer to other objects in the scene including a foot warmer, a basket hanging from the wall, the window on the left-hand side casting light behind the woman while creating a shadow in the left-hand corner and so on. The scene is rendered salient because it is aligned with generic verbal description, which also has some value for the artist in their choice of theme, subject and visual organization. However, in tending such a description, other aspects of the work are occluded or suppressed – the mottling underneath the window, the fold in a tablecloth, the taches of light paint at the edge of the milk jug.

Indeed, how can the tonal variation in a fabric fold actually be described in any way that properly realizes its visual specificity? Bergson argues that we could multiply the words endlessly without ever recovering the immediacy of the perception. However, this still leaves the question of what role figuration plays in art, and whether or not all genera prevent an intuitive engagement with the real.

The facility of description is associated with both utility and the ease of recognition and operates in a way that does not support aesthetic engagement with the work. Bergson notes that philosophical intuition requires effort in order to break down the 'ready-made' (*déjà faites*) generalities that underpin most theorizing,[50] and there should be a similar effort in aesthetic appreciation in order to overcome the habits of perception. Due to the focus on the immediacy of the aesthetic vision, Bergson does not provide a proper discussion of the processes leading to aesthetic intuition, which could actually mirror the retroactivity of intuition in philosophy where differences between readily recognizable ideas and things are rethought in terms of enduring differences in kind. Other theorists have outlined the problem in more detail, including John Dewey, who states that in aesthetic judgement, the viewer needs to engage creatively with the artwork in order to understand its materiality and plasticity and counter the habits of recognition. The problem with recognition is that it engages pre-established schemas that actually limit the variety of perceptual experience:[51]

> The difference between the two is immense. Recognition is perception arrested before it has the chance to develop freely. In recognition there is a beginning of an act of perception. But this beginning is not allowed to serve the development of a full perception of the thing recognized. It is arrested at the point where it will serve some *other* purpose, as we recognize a man on the street in order to greet or avoid him, not so as to see him for the sake of seeing what is there.[52]

Recognition is utilitarian insofar as it extracts from perception only that which serves a particular purpose. As this purpose exists before the perception itself and cannot be eschewed, the only way to properly attend to the object is to maintain the perception to the point that it overcomes recognition, as in aesthetic contemplation. The recovery of the specificity of the real is a *post facto* process that recovers perceptual detail and undermines the facility of representation. In *Discourse, Figure*,

Jean-François Lyotard frames this in terms of writing, arguing that the main function of the various visual features of a printed letter is to aid recognition and comprehension rather than displaying any visual particularity. These features increase the legibility of the text such that the reader is able to read quickly and easily. The easily readable line is 'what does not impede the eye's racing' whereas, to attend to the plasticity of the line, it is necessary to halt the movement of recognition.[53] Lyotard argues that readability should not be confused with visibility for the eye that reads searches only for a very limited array of signals and consequently sweeps across the page with only scant attention to the visual details of the text.[54] When this is translated to visual culture, the image should cultivate a slowness in the process of seeing so that the eye can attend to the visibility of the 'figural' rather than the transparency of the legible.[55] For Dewey and Lyotard aesthetic engagement requires a slowing down of the time of spectatorship, in which the transparency and immediacy of recognition gives way to the specificity and opacity of the visible.

Many types of art place particular emphasis on language, recognition and transparency, in which the visual form mainly serves as a vehicle for meaning, and one could not imagine that they would meet Bergson's expectation that art must lift the veil on reality. Norman Bryson argues that early Christian art is based on the primacy of the word, where the role of the work is to relay a religious message and thereby instruct the congregation in the values of the church.[56] The works mainly serve as mnemonic aids, in which the visual properties of the image are 'self-effacing' in order to draw attention to the Word that lies beyond.[57] The importance of recognition in many forms of art leads Bryson to question the meaning of mimesis, which is often characterized in terms of the work's correspondence to the model, in which the judgement on correspondence can be regarded as a 'universal visual experience'.[58] However, this account of mimesis does not sufficiently take into consideration what is communicated in a work, which primarily concerns recognition.[59] Bryson argues that recognition expresses an 'attitude' towards the image, a way of responding appropriately to it, and recognizing what it refers to without fully engaging with its visual form.[60] It is not the accuracy of the correspondence between the visual form of the work and the represented object – which could operate on the level of visual detail – but the facility with which the object can be recognized in the image. In mimesis, the work does not simply imitate a perceptual given but cultivates a type of visual and semantic expectation grounded in recognition. This habitual attitude is mediated by a set of social values and codes invested in language. We take a stance before the image primarily in terms of what can be recognized – a mimetic realism that contrasts with Bergson's durational realism. Bryson asks the viewer to consider the plasticity of the visual image; however, this plasticity could be described spatially in terms of the organization of visual detail. Bergson has to go one step further in unveiling *durée* by revealing the plasticity of the work in a way that truly endures within the lived time of spectatorship.

From perceptual utility to the processual real

A question for aesthetics is what will remain if this layer of recognition were to be removed or, as Bergson characterizes it, the veil were to be lifted. From one perspective, an aesthetic approach to art should mainly be concerned with the plastic features of the work and its perceptual plenitude – an attitude that is more likely to be fostered in non-figurative works that hinder simple recognition and do not rely on mimesis. However, Bergson did not take much interest in non-figurative painting or drawing, possibly due to an aesthetic sensibility informed by a figurative nineteenth-century visual art tradition. Although his work was co-opted by many in the avant-garde, there is little to indicate that he appreciated the push towards abstraction immanent to these artistic movements. Bergson did not find much value in Cubism because it appeared to be driven by a set of principles rather than directly responding to the real,[61] and it is notable that he does not make reference to contemporary artists in his writings. Bergson took some interest in fin-de-siècle music, from Debussy to Franck, but again did not directly embrace the avant-garde. The idea that Bergson's philosophy could complement Modernism's turn towards non-representational art cannot be resolved through the philosopher's own writing; nonetheless, his philosophy offers a means of rethinking art and aesthetics from a processual standpoint. Rather than talking about the complete removal of a veil of utility, it is possible to talk about the degrees by which this veil (comprised of solid bodies, recognition, genera and resemblance) can be lowered. This would constitute a movement away from mimesis and structures of resemblance without a complete eschewal of art's role in depicting the contents of normal perception.

In the lecture 'The Perception of Change' delivered at Oxford in 1911, Bergson gave some indication of the conditions by which art can encourage non-utilitarian perception. Central to his argument is the claim that artists and metaphysicians share a common vision that reveals the metaphysical truth of *durée*. Artists achieve this through drawing on their own direct experience of a processual real in a way that can be communicated to others.[62] Despite the fact that an artist's vision is 'fixed' on the canvas, it still provokes the spectator to reimagine their own way of seeing the world: '[t]he great painters are men who possess a certain vision of things which has or will become the vision of all men. A Corot, a Turner – not to mention others – have seen in nature many an aspect that we did not notice.'[63] It is noteworthy that Bergson directly refers to the artists J. M. W. Turner and Camille Corot, both nineteenth-century figurative artists working in the landscape tradition, who do not directly undermine mimesis or recognition. They certainly experiment with aspects of perception, but not necessarily in a way that could be immediately associated with the complete upheaval of metaphysics that Bergson sought in his own work. Both artists seek to derive resemblances from the natural world, which, to a certain extent, aligns their work with quotidian perception. Bergson might argue that metaphysics is the '*science which claims to dispense with symbols*',[64] but it is difficult to imagine how visual art that addresses the natural world can fully dispense with resemblances. What is at issue here is not the complete removal of resemblance, but rather the removal of those resemblances that are disengaged from the sensual specificity of an object, most notably fixed concepts and abstractions. As long as the artworks guide attention to the concrete and lived time of perception, they can be aligned with metaphysics.

Resemblances can be regarded as abstractions when they separate discrete qualities from the overall play of appearance; however, they still remain grounded in perception. Understanding art in terms of a Bergsonian metaphysics requires some consideration of how resemblances are derived from concrete perception and under what conditions they can initiate intuition. Resemblances can gesture towards the endurance of time only as mobile concepts that recreate some aspects of the movement of the object to which they refer. A processual resemblance is always a little different from a static resemblance because it unmakes the object at the same time as provoking recognition. The manner in which Corot recreates the movement of leaves with thick highlights, or how Turner uses long brushstrokes to create atmospheric turbulence is of greater significance than a direct resemblance to leaves or clouds. The philosopher of art Meyer Schapiro argues that resemblance in art should not be limited to a principle of correspondence linking the image to an external visual object, for the image does not have to take on the exact form of what is seen. More important are the many techniques that can be used to create this resemblance and how the 'image-substance' relates to the image as a whole.[65] To explain this, he refers to the work of the Impressionists who were able to create likenesses by experimenting with the relationship between colours and brushstrokes, instead of constructing likeness through the use of outlines. This leads Schapiro to argue that abstract art does not necessarily use principles that are fundamentally different from those of mimetic art if the focus is on technique. What distinguishes the two is how the marks are organized in relation to the whole.[66] In many respects, there is greater similarity between the techniques used in Impressionism and Abstract Expressionism than between Impressionism and Classicism, despite the importance of mimesis for the latter two. The techniques of creating resemblances can encourage the viewer to see the world processually even if the canvas is populated with a number of recognizable objects.

In Bergson's philosophy, art and aesthetic perception cannot simply point to the real as something recognizable, because most recognition follows particular habitual modes of perceiving especially when mediated by representation. For the resemblance to be supple enough to reveal the fluidity immanent in all things it must be aligned with and incorporated into the artist's vision, which is itself embedded within *durée*. Of course, the artist is constrained by the medium, which is of particular relevance to literature where the author must use the generic signs of a natural language to create the semblance of the author's thought. Bergson acknowledges this in *Time and Free Will* and states that the way the work is written has the capacity to exceed individual categories in order to divulge the enduring present of consciousness:

> Now, if some bold novelist, tearing aside the cleverly woven curtain of our conventional ego, shows us under this appearance of logic a fundamental absurdity, under this juxtaposition of simple states an infinite permeation of a thousand different impressions which have

already ceased to exist the instant they are named, we commend him for having known us better than we knew ourselves. This is not the case, however, and the very fact that he spreads out our feeling in a homogeneous time, and expresses its elements by words, shows that he in his turn is only offering us its shadow: but he has arranged this shadow in such a way as to make us suspect the extraordinary and illogical nature of the object which projects it; he has made us reflect by giving outward expression to something of that contradiction, that interpenetration, which is the very essence of the elements expressed. Encouraged by him, we have put aside for an instant the veil which we interposed between our consciousness and ourselves. He has brought us back into our own presence.[67]

Here the novelist seeks to reveal the qualitative difference of their own feeling, but they can do so only through generic categories which, in themselves, cannot reveal the nuances of *durée*. However, the author can succeed in aligning the reader with a particular perspective that exceeds the representation and discloses the insufficiency of language as a means of positing resemblance. The ineffability of duration appears between the words in the impossibility of language representing the real. Words by their alterity bring into relief the continuity of the artistic vision, and any artistic project must be one that invokes an aesthetic vision that challenges direct correspondence between signs and the objects they represent.

Another way of lifting the veil is to investigate those aspects of utilitarian perception that can be dispensed with in order to better approach the real. It is about removing concepts that interfere with the direct intuition of the real as much as it is about a direct vision. In relation to metaphysics and science, Bergson rejects the application of ready-made concepts that overly prefigure any relationship with the real in proposing generic categories and identities. All resemblance presupposes prefiguration, because what has already been seen, experienced or comprehended shapes what is seen in the present moment or is about to appear. Bergson argues in 'Intellectual Effort' that we are always deploying schemes as a means of orientating perception. However, he distinguishes between mechanical schemas that limit experience to the operation of a category and 'elastic or mobile' schemas that provide some flexibility, allowing for a wider variety of images and memories to be interpolated into its concrete expression.[68] Bergson, in his 'Introduction to Metaphysics', states that there has been too much emphasis on rigid concepts in philosophy, and that philosophy should, instead, seek to discover 'flexible, mobile, almost fluid representations, always ready to mould themselves on the fleeting forms of intuition'.[69] These mobile representations are suppler because they are not reducible to the external logic of a philosophical system, such as the logic of non-contradiction, because they cleave to the objects they describe. Art produces such representations because, in most cases, it must adapt to the particularity of a sensual environment and the constraints of the medium, as well as, as Bergson often points out, the ipseity of the artistic vision.

Art certainly imposes concepts and resemblances but insofar as it deploys mobile schemas, it can maintain attention to its own materiality and temporality. Philip Rawson argues that art can never be truly abstract because abstractions are static and therefore divorced from the continuity of time; and art, in contrast to conceptual knowledge, is always thoroughly emplaced within this continuity.[70] Of course, art deals with forms, genera and objects that have a relative independence from the work but Rawson states, like Hegel, that they should not be considered abstractions so much as 'concrete universals':

> We really image mountains as much by their shape-shifting peaks and ridges, troughs and valleys, thrusting and collapsing, their differentially interacting sliding and eroding slopes, as by standard abstractly calculated – and hence fixed – contour lines. Such insights reveal another order of universals than the abstract. They are often called 'concrete universals', and are directly perceived through the senses.[71]

In this example, the formal differentiation remains continuous with the particular material conditions of the landscape, and to remove the lines from the mountains and valleys that sustain them is to deny the processual reality of matter. The concrete universal refers to a different type of generalization that coordinates the perceiver's relationship with a particular object or event by linking particulars together under a common form, for example the universal form of the human face that provides a condition for understanding a particular human face.[72] We can recognize a face or landscape only because we are attuned to a concrete universal, and from Bergson's perspective, such universals should always bring with them some understanding of how life or matter endures. In the example of a mountainous landscape, each feature of the work should gesture towards the process of becoming a mountain – a line can make visible the division of geological movements as much as the outer border of an object – or the mutability of all landscapes.

Lifting the utilitarian veil is never absolute, in which all representations, resemblances and concepts are removed, for it concerns developing more flexible concepts that act as signposts to the real. Mobile concepts operate in the interstices between Bergson's many dualisms – memory rather than matter, time rather than space – aligning themselves with the contours of duration. This is demonstrated in Bergson's account of aphasia in which he focuses on the aphasic's loss of ability to recognize common lexical classes. In the lecture 'The Soul and the Body', Bergson argues that this loss is progressive, in which the aphasic first suffers the loss of proper nouns, then common nouns, adjectives and finally verbs. The verbs are the last to disappear because they better approximate the movement of the real, and are less mediated than nouns and adjectives:[73]

> The verb is directly expressible in action, the adjective only by the mediation of the verb, the substantive by the double mediation of the adjective which expresses one of its attributes and the verb implied in the adjective, the proper name by the triple mediation of the common noun, the adjective and also the verb: therefore, according as we go from the verb to the proper noun, we get farther and farther away from directly imitable action, action the body can play, and a more and more complicated device becomes necessary in order to symbolize in movement the idea expressed by the required word.[74]

Although Bergson argues that all words are abstractions from the processual reality of thought, the level of abstraction differs depending on the word's relationship to lived duration and action. Nouns are at the furthest remove from the real, in particular proper nouns, because they divide process into discrete objects, whereas verbs are most closely aligned with corporeal movement. It is interesting that Bergson places adjectives between the two when an adjective is an attribute of the noun and therefore contingent on it. However, in Bergson's processual world view, qualities are primarily aspects of a qualitative multiplicity before they are hypostatized as objects. For example, colour is a property of the variability and movement of light, but we have come to regard it as a property of objects, or even a substance due to the isolation of materials for use in painting. In the context of visual culture, the aim would be to recover those signs that are most closely aligned with lived duration and qualitative variation, which continue to gesture towards process. A work could be described in terms of the moving lines of a pencil or strokes rather than in terms of outlines that subtend objects; as Klee's work demonstrates, the object could just be an effect of this movement.

The problem with deriving mobile concepts from the visual arts is that most of Bergson's arguments about the extraction and immobilization of qualities are derived from examples associated with the sense of sight. Hearing is much more closely linked to lived time because parts are not easily extracted and although notes may be separated in musical notation (a visual object), they are always implicated in a harmonic or melodic whole for the listener.[75] By contrast, sight spreads out into space in which recognizable objects are separated from the mobile perceptual field, to which movement is then added as an attribute:

> the sense 'par excellence' is the sense of sight, and because the eye has developed the habit of separating, in the visual field, the relatively invariable figures which are often supposed to change place without changing form, movement is taken as super-added to the mobile as an accident.[76]

In the differentiation of the visual object, the qualitatively changing visual field is rendered immobile such that it serves as a ground for potential movement of the object. This separation creates a conceptual gap between figure and ground that extends beyond the particular instantiation. In a primarily visual logic, a moving object requires homogenous space through which to move, which is central to Newtonian absolute space, the homogenous ground for all possible movement, or even Euclidean geometry, where movement is presented in terms of the translation of figures. Utilitarian perception creates not only relatively stable properties through the extraction of qualities but also conceptual distinctions that lead to a notion of homogeneous space. To foster aesthetic perception involves working in the opposite direction away from abstraction towards a qualitatively variable understanding of movement and change in all types of visual forms.

The relationship between homogeneous space and visuality is often overemphasized in the visual arts, which can lead to a suppression of the proper attention to qualitative differences in perception. Rudolf Arnheim, in 'A Stricture on Space and Time', argues that abstract notions of space and time are too often applied in visual descriptions of movement in a way that runs contrary to how we actually perceive. In normal perception, there is an integration of the visual field around the movement and 'any distinction between the shape of static bodies and the shape of motion is artificial'.[77] In actual visual perception, the movements of bodies form visual wholes which cannot be easily separated into discrete parts, and therefore we should resist trying to explain action in terms of spatial and temporal coordinates and, instead, examine its character or movement.[78] Based on this critique, Arnheim deploys a useful distinction in the analysis of art between two types of space: 'extrinsic space', in which the visual field and movement are defined in relation to clearly differentiated parts and their vectors; and 'intrinsic space', which is more closely aligned with actual visual perception, in which all movement is implicated in the unity of the whole:[79]

> Starting from a composition as a whole, we see a tissue of interwoven units and intervals, all fitting in one unbroken overall system and held together by intrinsic space. When, however, we start from the units, we see subsystems meeting, crossing, repelling, or paralleling one another, all this taking place in the arena of an extrinsic space system. The meaning of the work requires the apprehension of both structural versions: the nature of the whole and the behavior of its parts.[80]

Arnheim argues that intrinsic space is much more relevant to the analysis of modern art, and gives the example of Monet, whose visual objects cannot be easily isolated and whose backgrounds are active, dynamic and integrated into the whole movement of the work, thus undermining the distinction between foreground and background.[81] This is in marked contrast to 'traditional' figurative paintings, where figures are grouped separately from the background creating 'a clear distinction between the systems of vectorial forces issuing from the objects and the environment into which the forces flow'.[82] This notion of intrinsic space can be employed to understand many modern and contemporary artworks in which the picture plane is unified through movement, and where the vectors of movement are integrated in the formal structure of the work. In colour field painting, the emphasis is on the surface of the work without an identifiable object, in which artists such as Mark Rothko require the viewer to attend to space through colour modulations. The

Impressionists unify the picture plane in the play of light but also in the repetition of the divisionist brushstrokes, creating surface movement rather than perspectival depth. Bridget Riley's optical art demonstrates that even though the canvas may be rendered in terms of discrete lines, the intrinsic space immanent to our perception operates in the interstices between the lines to create flow and movement.

Arnheim emphasizes unity in visual perception, unlike Bergson who focuses on the capacity of the eye to separate objects, but in many respects they are in agreement, just working at different levels of analysis. Bergson describes a metaphysical tendency in visual perception, which in its fullest conceptual expression is characterized by homogeneous space, rather than arguing that homogenous space is immanent to all visuality. Despite his critique of spatialization, Bergson does discuss degrees of spatialization in his work, with preference given to those forms that cleave to the percept. In *Creative Evolution*, he refers to a 'natural geometry' in which individuals have an understanding of form, direction and magnitude without relying on concepts derived from a theory of homogenous space. This natural geometry operates according to the inclinations and affordances of the body and precedes any formal geometry, which has the tendency to 'degrade itself into logic'.[83] Even in the early work *Time and Free Will*, Bergson argues that animals have a direct understanding of space, demonstrated in their uncanny ability to find their way home over great distances without the mnemonic, geometrical or visual aids required in human navigation:

> Attempts have been made to explain this feeling of direction by sight or smell, and, more recently, by the perception of magnetic currents which would enable the animal to take its bearings like a living compass. This amounts to saying that space is not so homogeneous for the animal as for us, and that determinations of space, or directions, do not assume for it a purely geometrical form. Each of these directions might appear to it with its own shade, its peculiar quality.[84]

This also applies to a human understanding of space, where the differences between right and left are felt as qualitative differences or feelings, and invested in the body as extensity rather than the projection of geometrical space.[85] Edward Casey refers to concepts of space that cleave to the body as the 'concrete dimensions' of before, behind, left, right, above and below that are not structurally equal – for example, *left* has a different quality as well as direction to *above*. Importantly, these dimensions also change as the body moves through its environment and, therefore, cannot be reduced to fully external categories such as the Cartesian planes.[86] For Bergson, space should be understood in terms of the plenitude of lived experience which would include the temporality of moving through space and the feelings associated with orientation. The particular feelings of any organism are contracted into the concrete dimensions, which function here like concrete universals, providing a means of understanding the organization of the body and, significantly, a nascent spatial sensibility.

Bergson does not apply these arguments directly to visual culture, but they nevertheless complement some of the experiments with the integration of the picture plane in Modernism and attempts to understand perception in ways that are not reducible to the abstract and external of Cartesian space. For example, Mark Antliff argues that Henri Matisse employed a Bergsonian 'extensive' idea of colour, in which the gaze constantly shifts between depth and surface due to the variation in attention to the fields of colour, which also contributes to the rhythmic properties of the work as a whole.[87] Colours are arranged and spread out in space to cover a surface, but their spatiality is not reducible to the areas they occupy. Each colour brings with it a different qualitative tension that relates to the concreteness of human perception and the context in which the colour is revealed. Even in a non-figural or abstract work, the placement of light and dark colours can affect the viewer's orientation to the work. Large swathes of dark colours located at the top of a painting might make it appear top heavy even without representational content. This aligns the composition with the viewer's lived relation to particular places, where the difference between light and dark could be felt as directional markers such as high and low. In not corresponding with a common-sense and utilitarian conception of space, the organization of the work makes itself visible as a feeling, leading the viewer to attend more to its plastic qualities.

Understanding art through extensity and intrinsic space requires attention to the temporal conditions of seeing, in which aesthetic perception is not obscured by the ease of recognition and utilitarian perception. It concerns a form of perception that stands before any narrative structure or even the simplest forms of representation, which was explored in some of the Modernist movements, which sought a 'neo-primitive vision' complemented by careful studies of how people actually see.[88] For example, Wassily Kandinsky directly addresses the specificity of painting through the investigation of qualitative differences from tonal values to the arrangement of shapes on the picture plane, and argues that colours create primary impressions that also give rise to psychological states.[89] These primary impressions include the attraction or repulsion of the spectator to particular colours and the feeling that colours are warm or cold:

> If two circles are drawn and painted retrospectively yellow and blue, brief concentration will reveal in the yellow a spreading movement out from the centre, and a noticeable approach to the spectator. The blue, on the other hand, moves in upon itself, like a snail retreating into its shell, and draws away from the spectator.[90]

Kandinsky acknowledges that there is no scientific foundation for these responses because they are based on 'spiritual experience',[91] and this is precisely the point. What he is most interested in is the moment in art when we pass from the exteriority of the object to the interiority of the work as a living form: 'to experience its pulsation with all our senses'.[92] The analysis of the elements of pictorial art is undertaken only with the overall aim of achieving a synthesis in which the plasticity of the work is coincident with the spiritual or divine.[93] One way of interpreting this is to argue that Kandinsky was in search of mobile concepts that could lead to a synoptic understanding of the work, and his analysis was aimed at foregrounding the qualitative variation in aesthetic engagement. What is at stake here is the articulation of a middle ground between concrete ideas and principles integrated into the haecceity of *durée* and a spatial logic of representation.

The difference between a conceptual approach to perception and a direct aesthetic engagement is discussed by Maurice Merleau-Ponty in 'Eye and Mind', a text that also draws upon Bergson's critique of utilitarian perception. He argues that the scientist creates a distance between their own body and the object under investigation due to the development of models and the application of principles of measurement. It is about general categories rather than sensual data.[94] Similarly, in *Duration and Simultaneity*, Bergson states that the main problem with Einstein's theory is that his virtual observers are not embodied, and consequently divorced from lived time. In contrast with the model building of science, Merleau-Ponty argues that the painter attends to the sensual conditions of the lived world and is distinguished by their capacity to articulate the 'coming-to-itself of the visible'. The artist places their body within the process of figuration and uses colour, form, shape and other pictorial values to bring out the 'internal animation' of matter,[95] just as Kandinsky aims to do in both his painting and writings on art. This foregrounding of the body and mind within a process of autofiguration is similar in many respects to Bergson's processual vision, in which the artist does not so much create models of the perceptible world as communicate how he or she experiences its sensual variation. Therefore, it is not surprising that a few pages later, Merleau-Ponty claims that Bergson

> was on the threshold of . . . [a] . . . gripping discovery, already familiar to the painters, that there are no lines visible in themselves, that neither the contour of the apple nor the border between field and meadow is in *this* place or that, that they are always on the near or the far side of the point we look at. They are always between or behind whatever we fix our eyes upon; they are indicated, implicated, and even very imperiously demanded by the things, but they themselves are not things. They were supposed to circumscribe the apple or the meadow, but the apple and the meadow 'form themselves' from themselves, and come into the visible as if they had come from a prespatial world behind the scenes.[96]

This notion of a 'prespatial world' can be directly linked to Bergson's notion of extensity and natural geometry, in which spatiality is felt without the aid of contours or visible lines; it is just another expression of qualitative difference. For Merleau-Ponty, the line or contour is not of the world, but, rather, a means of conceiving the world in terms of a fixed notion of space, in which there is no overlapping of objects and where boundaries are readily discernible. In arguing that these lines are not truly 'things', he is downplaying the function of space in the constitution of the world. In many respects, the line is an afterthought that is applied to a world once constituted rather than an aspect of the world in the process of formation. Like the trajectory that subtends corporeal movement, it describes and contains what has already been seen.

Unlike Bergson, who only mentions artists such as Turner and Corot in passing, Merleau-Ponty has a much more definite idea as to what it means for a painter to engage with the becoming visible of the world. In his essay 'Cézanne's Doubt', he describes how Paul Cézanne sought to understand how objects reveal themselves through colour rather than line. This investigation of the nature of appearance differed from the Impressionist's examination of the play of light on the retina, because Cézanne still focused on the object and the retention of its 'sensuous surface'. Consequently, he was reluctant to draw the outlines of objects or to rigidly place objects in a 'perspectival or pictorial arrangement'.[97] Although Cézanne strove for compositional balance in many of his landscapes – he greatly admired the works of Poussin for their formal beauty and attention to the object – this balance had to be derived from nature rather than the artifice of the studio.[98] Merleau-Ponty states that Cézanne's aim was to reveal all the sensual plenitude of the object through a visual synthesis of colour, demonstrating how a shifting set of hues creates a 'lived perspective' in which form comes into being rather than being imposed through a rigidly constructed perspective. The paintings have a virtual centre that integrates the different senses such that the viewer also sees the 'depth, the smoothness, the softness, the hardness of objects' in addition to colour and light – a 'primordial perception' that precedes any formal or scientific breakdown of the visual field into discrete elements.[99] In Merleau-Ponty's characterization of Cézanne's painterly project, the integration of the senses and the sensual interconnection of qualities in intrinsic space forms the basis of perception.

This turn towards a 'primordial' and 'prespatial' condition of seeing relates to Bergson's claim that art sees beyond the veil of utilitarian perception and that we have a feeling for spatial difference before any mensural codification, for Cézanne is concerned with the particular sensual conditions of perception rather than the development of a set of principles by which to translate the visual object onto the canvas. However, Bergson does not address this notion of the primordial vision outside of extensity and the critique of spatialization, because he does not sufficiently attend to the unity of the senses. In *Matter and Memory*, touch is described in a Berkeleyan manner in terms of the body's capacity to act on objects, and operates in concert with vision to create a utilitarian and abstract notion of space. However, it is only through recombining the senses in a single intuition that perception can truly disclose the sensuality of a processual world. Of course, it is a question of *durée*, but *durée* that is disclosed through concrete qualitative differences that are not fully demarcated by the external operation of the senses. The novelist D. H. Lawrence recognized this when he argued that Cézanne sought a vision that was 'neither optical nor mechanical nor intellectual-psychological' insofar as it attended directly to the substance of things. The painter achieved this directness through a form of visuality underpinned by touch, what Lawrence refers to as 'intuitive touch'.[100] Cézanne does not simply paint the resemblance of an apple, he reveals through touch the concrete plenitude of the apple, its 'appleyness': 'For the intuitive apperception of the apple is so *tangibly* aware of the apple that it is aware of it *all round*, not only just at the front'.[101] This bears some relation to Bergson's belief in intuition's capacity to enter into the interiority of things thus bypassing the partiality of external perspectives; however, this only be achieved only through the mediation of the senses, in particular, those that maintain contact with the object, such as touch. Rather than merely describing the capacity to act on things, touch reveals a continual variation in tactility that undermines the distance and spatial separateness of vision.

The removal of distance and the qualitative variability most clearly evinced in touch could mark the beginning of an intuitive process that invests the object and painting with a durational reality as well as uniting the senses in a compositional whole. What this demonstrates is the value in understanding art through proximity, in which the artist's closeness to the object – regardless of whether this concerns its surface or interiority – is what leads to an awareness of *durée*. George Hamilton argues that although there is nothing to indicate that Cézanne had read Bergson or that Bergson had ever taken an interest in Cézanne's work, the two are connected by a 'parallelism' in the themes and ideas they worked on during a shared period in cultural history.[102] The most important connection can be found in Cézanne's interest in creating images of the real in the process of becoming through his own slow and thoughtful engagement with the pictorial subject. This interest in the shifting forms of visual objects matches Bergson's argument that sensation is always changing such that even a visual object is never entirely at rest.[103] Many of the visual objects that Cézanne examines are quite stable, such as the fruit in his still lives, and do not automatically suggest temporal change especially when observed over a short duration. Hamilton points out that, unlike the Impressionist *plein air* painters, Cézanne worked on a painting over a number of days and this required that he incorporate the visual changes he noticed over this period into a single painting.[104] The supposed 'distortions' of space that critics often refer to, are not truly distortions but, rather, an indication of how Cézanne worked through the images of a particular object across different temporal periods.[105] For the spectator, engaging with Cézanne's paintings demands a much slower time of viewing than does an Impressionist work, in order to occupy the different positions and angles in turn rather than taking the whole of an image in a single glance.[106] Hamilton draws the argument away from a Bergsonian perspective by overly accentuating spatial coherence rather than the slight sensual differences found in the movement of colour and paint across the surface of an apple, mountain or field. The argument, however, provides a basis for understanding how visual objects can acquire tactility, as Lawrence argues, for the tactile is revealed in the slight movement of a hand across a surface and diminishes when the hand is still. In asking the eye to attend to minor changes in colour, light and texture – to shift across the painted surface – Cézanne's painting can simulate this tactility in vision, and therefore unite the senses.

Reintegrating touch into the sensorium undermines the optical completeness of an artwork – the harmonious and autonomous whole isolated in aesthetic attention – by highlighting the artist's role in producing the work and the overall lived time that encompasses the work and its creation. Touch foregrounds movement in vision in a way that integrates seeing and making into a processual whole. Joyce Medina argues that Bergson privileges the tactility of movement in duration and intuition. In her extended study of Modernism, late-nineteenth-century psychological theories, and the work of Cézanne, Medina proposes that Bergson's approach can form the basis for rethinking Cézanne's painting.[107] Cézanne's work reveals 'abstract emotions' through the tactile combination of painterly elements, as well as the processual interplay between part and whole.[108] The part–whole relationship is a feature of the individual work but also of the life of the artist whose feelings and creative endeavour extend across a number of works. Consequently, Medina proposes that Cézanne sought to 'convey the harmonious oneness and creativity of being as operative in the craft of painting' in a way that can best be understood through Bergsonian intuition[109] and the integration of pictorial form and the creative impulse.[110] In intuition, Bergson proposes that reflection is tied directly to action rather than to disembodied conscious introspection, and 'can be defined only as the depth of attention, that is, as either projective or recollective duration'.[111] Cézanne's painting is guided by a type of attention that is indicative of his life as a whole, that is, as a 'montage' in which the past and the present gesture towards the future in the material form of the artwork.[112] Unlike many of his fellow artists, Cézanne did not seek to recreate the impression;

rather, he projected his painterly experience and 'temperament' into the work in a way that is revealed in the pictorial elements and themes.[113] In his late period from 1890 to 1906, Cézanne developed a way of working that brought together 'creative action' and contemplation, which is best exemplified in the Mont Sainte-Victoire series:

> the new sense of contemplation is totally congruous with the intensities of the multiple views of Monte Sainte-Victoire, with the implied effort spent in reaching every viewing point and the tranquillity achieved after arriving, with the viewer's involvement in the instantaneous temporality of a flashing partial perspective and in the interminable geological time that it took to form the whole.[114]

Here Cézanne's contemplation draws together a range of times, characterized as efforts, into a singular temperament or mood, which extends across a number of works. Contemplation as action is not restricted to the subject of the painting, for Cézanne also used a smaller range of colours combined in complementary pairings in his later works, which created an overall mood separated from local colour that is projected across the whole series as part of the unity of 'lived time'.[115] The brushstrokes also integrate various figures into the overall organization of the plane and, in doing so, display a type of 'facture' linked to both the making of the work and the human labour of the figures depicted in the landscape.[116] Here tactility underpins the pictorial style but is also continuous with the duration and lived time of the artist, an argument that could apply to many artists, but for Medina, it is most evident in the work of Cézanne.

In the reinvigoration of the work through the temporality of the viewing process, resemblance can still be discussed if it coincides with the time of production and the artist's engagement with the natural world. The philosopher Andrew Benjamin notes, like Merleau-Ponty, that Cézanne does not use outlines and that, instead, his objects are formed through different types of brushstrokes – horizontal, vertical and diagonal – that constitute a mode of 'landscaping'.[117] The use of the gerund is important here because painting, for Benjamin, is an ongoing process of cultivation that is linked to the perception of the natural world in which the artist continually confronts the incompleteness of nature and the image.[118] This image cannot be rigidly tied to a model through principles of verisimilitude, because perception is never complete or exhaustible and, therefore, the artist must seek, instead, to paint that which is 'suggested' by nature.[119] Consequently, resemblance cannot be found in the external relationship between two objects because the world is not comprised of bounded qualities that can be readily transcribed onto the canvas. Nature always has the capacity to reveal more aspects, even when painting the same scene. Cézanne, who regularly painted Mont Sainte-Victoire, continued to try out new methods in an attempt to engage with those elusive aspects of the visual world. Benjamin argues that the artist addresses and values reality in the degree to which it resists objecthood, or a fully determinable extra-sensible meaning, and there is freedom in this incompleteness because the artist can follow in any number of ways what is suggested by the model.[120] Notably, this '[b] reaking the hold of the model does not mean that painting then becomes abstract. Freedom occurs to the extent that the model and the response to it – these elements are the reconfiguration of nature – are rethought'.[121] This notion of thinking through the engagement with the real means that the image does not, necessarily, match the spatial structure of the visual field as in a photograph or topographical diagram. The present is incomplete in the sense that it can never be atomistically sealed off within a discrete time period, and certainly not an instant, for the artist works in a continuous present with a work that occupies its own continuous present. This principle applies as much to the philosopher's engagement with nature in Bergson's metaphysics as it does to the artist.

Regardless of whether the work is figurative, the style of painting could encourage a form of aesthetic engagement underscored by the unity of perception and the critique of the utilitarian construction of extrinsic space. Indeed, style could be indicative of a particular ontology that is not reliant on the theme of the work. Heinrich Wölfflin, in his *Principles of Art History*, outlines a number of principles for understanding variations in style, with specific reference to the transition from the Classical to the Baroque period, including the key distinction between the linear and painterly.[122] The linear accentuates the solidity and tangibility of objects – in which outlines contain objects and precisely articulate their limits – over transient qualities of light and movement.[123] Wölfflin contrasts this with the painterly, which places greater emphasis on the mass, texture, colour and tonality of the pictorial field. The division is not absolute, for linear art can also explore these visual qualities, for example shading and chiaroscuro, but they are usually subordinate to 'stressed' edges, whereas in the painterly style the edges are 'unstressed'.[124] When the edges are unstressed, aspects of the image, including light, depth, shadow and so on, can take on a form that is partially independent of the object. The painterly image is much more transitory, and consequently Wölfflin describes it in processual terms, as a whole which 'takes on the semblance of a movement ceaselessly emanating, never ending'.[125] The painterly approach allows light and tonal differences room to play across and against the form and surfaces of objects, such that there is a decrease in interest in the formal clarity and discreteness of visual elements.[126] The movement on the material surface in the painterly style is conferred on the work as a whole.

The linear style can be associated with a substantive ontology, where objects are delineated as stable entities, and qualia such as colour, texture and shading are attributes of the object. Wölfflin confirms this when he argues that in linear works, the object is tangible and something to be grasped and thus the representation coincides with the object,[127] which can be linked to Bergson's argument that pure perception describes the visual field in terms of how things can be acted upon. In stating that the visual object can be grasped, the eye finds correspondence between the two sensual modalities in the constitution of the object. However, it should be noted that Wölfflin has left out the directionality of the line in his discussion of linearity, which, as is demonstrated in the works of Klee, could indicate forms of processual movement, including growth. In contrast with the linear, the painterly style gestures towards a phenomenological or processual ontology, because it is driven by qualitative and temporal engagement, where the discrete object is secondary to its mode of appearing. Physicality is eschewed in the painterly due to the foregrounding of a purely optical relationship to the image as 'mere appearance'.[128] It should be noted that this emphasis on appearance is not part of a progression towards optical verisimilitude or the illusion of depth, in which the various incomplete forms coalesce into the figure at a certain distance. This may indeed occur, but the aim is to create greater vibrancy through the variation in the painterly style: 'What radically distinguishes Rembrandt from Dürer is the vibration of the picture as a whole, which persists even where the eye was not intended to perceive the individual form-signs.'[129] This vibrancy comes about due to the indeterminacy of the object and the lack of unequivocal structural and descriptive lines.[130] This shift towards the painterly undermines the substantive aspects of the work and in so doing foregrounds the immanent movement of the act of painting. Cézanne's apples might refer to the physical presence of an apple, Lawrence's appleyness, but due to the interpenetration of colour that overflows the outline, they also indicate living, optical indeterminacy.

The use of the outline in the visual arts doubly reduces the visual field. First, there is the containment of a section of the visual field within the outline, which once given can take on a single attribute, such as a colour – a feature of cell-based animation, comic books and even Pop Art. Second, it separates this set of visual properties from a background in a figure–ground relationship, in which movement is imagined in terms of the displacement of the figure against that background. In *Matter and Memory*, Bergson argues that if we engage with nature without the mediation of the outline, that is, 'we open our eyes', there is a 'whole field of vision' in which visual attributes, such as colour, continually vary. In contrast with the earlier statement that touch describes how an object can be acted upon in pure perception, Bergson also states that touch can reveal the continuity of matter, 'since solids are necessarily in contact with each other, our touch must follow the surface or the edges of objects without ever encountering a true interruption'.[131] This tactile continuity subtends the Bergsonian real in a way that the perception of solids in quotidian perception and linearity in art cannot, both of which impose artificial boundaries that give the false impression of substance. A processual ontology requires that the senses operate against the grain of quotidian perception, in which colour interacts with other colours without the mediation of the object, and in which tactility reveals continuity in a similar way to how the senses reveal the flesh of the world in Merleau-Ponty's philosophy. It is a pity that Bergson did not discuss tactility in greater detail, because it demonstrates his interest in a type of materiality that allows for sensual differentiation within the continuity of duration.

The visual arts can gesture towards qualitative variability and differentiation and thus invoke *durée*, but there is also a much more radical aspect to Bergson's process metaphysics. He argues in the latter part of *Matter and Memory* for a processual ontology that thoroughly departs from atomism, and the Newtonian notion of absolute space and time, which were adopted by most scientists in the late nineteenth century. The only reason there is a tendency to think of the atom as a hard object that bumps against other hard objects (the billiard ball model of efficient causality) is due to a projection of the logic of solid bodies onto microscopic entities. To support this rejection of simple causal interaction, Bergson refers to other physical theories including Clerk-

Maxwell's field theory which eschew contact in favour of action at a distance, and states that

> the materiality of the atom dissolves more and more under the eyes of the physicist. We have no reason, for instance, for representing the atom to ourselves as a solid, rather than as a liquid or gaseous, nor for picturing the reciprocal action of atoms by shocks rather than in any other way.[132]

For Bergson, if atomism is put to one side, physics actually reveals that the universe is composed of forces and movements, such as gravity, constantly interpenetrating across all spaces such that it is impossible to refer to any region as a void.[133] This interpenetration of forces also operates within the object, and in reference to the work of the British physicist Michael Faraday, Bergson states that the atom should not be seen as a solid body but, rather, as 'a center of force', which confirms Lord Kelvin's proposal that the atom maintains its form through activity, similar to a vortex or whirlpool.[134] Bergson acknowledges that although these processual models are only approximations or metaphors, nevertheless, they are valuable in indicating an appropriate 'direction' for an examination of the 'real': 'they show us, pervading concrete extensity, *modifications*, *perturbations*, changes of *tension* or of *energy* and nothing else.'[135] The idea of solid matter, and even the quantitative conceptions of force, is only a by-product of the interaction of qualitative movements within the limits of perception.

Bergson's processual reality presages many aspects of twentieth-century physics, where even the constituent units (atom, proton, electron, quark) are underpinned by processual and energetic states. In the second introduction to *Creative Mind*, Bergson states that when he 'began to write, physics had not yet made the decisive advances which were to bring a change in its ideas on the structure of matter'.[136] This changed with some of the discoveries in the early part of the twentieth century, which the theoretical physicist David Bohm argues required physical theories to recognize some principle of 'undivided wholeness'. For example, the older theory of atomism had to be reconfigured such that atomic units are regarded as relatively stable entities subject to processes of formation and held together by an 'inner' formative cause: any entity 'has been formed within the whole flowing movement and will ultimately dissolve back into this movement'.[137] Like Bergson, Bohm also argues that a theory that properly understands this processual reality, and the patterns underpinning the dissolution and formation of matter, should remain coincident with the object it describes.[138] The theory must be integrated into the very material reality it seeks to analyse and reveal. In many respects, the arts provide the means of disclosing this radical continuity and 'undivided wholeness', in particular the plastic arts, because the process of formation is often visible in the work itself. This is particularly true of the painterly style, where forms merge into each other due to the unstressed edges, and where brushstrokes can operate at a speed coincident with the processual reality they describe.

Bergson repeatedly states that artists lift the veil on *durée*, without providing a direct statement on how they do this, with only broad references to following the line of experience, attending to life, and contracting the real; the rest has to be inferred from his other writings. Nonetheless, his stated preference for the work of the painter J. M. W. Turner in 'The Perception of Change' provides some indication of how the artist's experience can be conjoined with painterly technique to embody this metaphysical reality. Turner placed great value on perceptual experience in his painting. He probably developed cataracts from looking too long into the sun which may have also contributed to his use of extremely bright yellows.[139] The artist also claimed to have been strapped to a mast in order to paint the elaborately titled, *Snow Storm – Steam-Boat off a Harbour's Mouth making Signals in Shallow Water, and going by the Lead. The Author was in this Storm on the Night the Ariel left Harwich* (1842) (see Figure 4.1). Even if the story is apocryphal, as many critics argue, the fact that Turner repeated the claim to Ruskin attests to the importance he placed on artistic experience. It is not simply a matter of painting the real, but painting the real under specific perceptual conditions. This is not to say that Turner necessarily sought *plein air* realism in the way that the Impressionists or even Corot did, as his paintings were largely studio constructions and many were imaginary landscapes drawn from classical and biblical narratives. Instead, he was interested in experimenting with some of the effects of light, colour and movement as they are disclosed in experience. From a Bergsonian perspective, the painting must bear a trace of the qualities and feelings implicated in a concrete visual experience. Does this mean that the painting should eschew all forms of representation only to present continuous variation in colour, tone and form, or should the artist seek to present directly the processual reality that underpins such continuity?

FIGURE 4.1 J. M. W. Turner. *Snow Storm – Steam-Boat off a Harbour's Mouth Making Signals in Shallow Water, and Going by the Lead. The Author was in this Storm on the Night the Ariel left Harwich* (1842).

Either approach cannot be readily aligned with most of Turner's work, or, indeed, Bergson's interest in landscape rather than abstract painting. However, the experimentation with light and other atmospheric effects in many of Turner's works foregrounds the transmission of light through the atmosphere and succeeds in highlighting a dynamic and qualitatively variable space between viewer and the subject of the painting.

In another Turner painting, *The Fighting Temeraire tugged to her last berth to be broken up* (1838–9), the large ship drawn by a tugboat is clearly shown on the left-hand side of the work, but what truly draws the attention of the viewer is the visual weight of the sun-streaked clouds on the right-hand side (see Figure 4.2). They are painted with such impasto thickness that they appear to congeal on the surface, and this foregrounding is further enhanced by the bright yellows and oranges. The more the gaze attends to this expansive field of colour, the more the main subject of the painting, the *Temeraire*, recedes into its perspectival depth. This brings into question the subject of the painting – whether it is the ostensible historical subject or the way that bright light overwhelms the visual field, for, in some respects, the former is just a means of revealing

FIGURE 4.2 J. M. W. Turner. *The Fighting Temeraire Tugged to Her Last Berth to be Broken Up* (1838–9).

the latter. In expanding the surface of the work, the clouds indicate the thickness of a space in which light is mediated by the atmosphere, similar to how light is mediated and separated by a prism. Light is not reflected off objects and limited to the articulation of solid surfaces. Its movement is retarded by the clouds to reveal the thickness of space and connect the viewer to the work in terms of a lived relationship to colour, as in Kandinsky's claim that colour can expand and contract to draw the viewer into the work. Turner demonstrated a practical and theoretical interest in how light and colour appear in the world as effects under a variety of conditions and argued that daylight 'is not a cause but an effect, since it is the reflection and diffusion of sunlight from cloud'.[140] In *The Fighting Temeraire*, light and colour overflow the form of the clouds and their outlines as an indication of their intensity but do not exist independently of these atmospheric conditions. The clouds become vehicles for light, holding as well as amplifying its qualitative intensity and variability in various effects, and this distinguishes Turner's work from that of other artists of the period, for example John Constable, whose clouds, despite their sculptural detail, are more obviously contained by the borders of trees and sky.

This lived relationship to the effects of light and atmosphere creates a felt relationship to space, and discloses a processual reality in which all aspects of the pictorial field combine in movement. What is incipient in *The Fighting Temeraire* becomes a full-blown feature of the late works painted between 1835 and 1850. These works were not received well by the public and critics, often decried as unintelligible because Turner began to experiment much more forcefully with intense colour, dynamism and the dissolution of form: 'in the sense of presenting the world as mutable, ever-changing, where solid forms become tremulous in light, water turns into vapour, diurnal and seasonal rhythms of light transmogrify the landscape they illuminate'.[141] The works are engulfed in a singular movement, which is certainly important in directing the viewer towards an understanding of processual indeterminacy. This is often closely tied to the pictorial subject, for example, the direct investigation of atmospheric turbulence in the famous *Rain, Steam, and Speed – the Great Western Railway* (1844), in which the train appears to form itself, sui generis, out of a rain-mottled background. It is also noteworthy that the title refers to atmospheric processes before the substantive subject of the work, the railway.

This interest in turbulent movement is particularly evident in the seascapes. *Snow Storm* not only depicts a storm at sea but the composition and brushwork operate in concert to display a movement that is akin to the interpenetrating atmospheric processes. The steamboat is a vague black mass in the centre of the canvas, distinguished mainly by the swirling plume of brown, red and orange smoke issuing from its smokestack. The smoke has its own internally generated movement but it is also buffeted by the forces of the wind to form a curve. This curve is crucial to the composition, a sinuous line that is indexically linked to all the other forces of the storm. The movement of the waves in the foreground of the painting mimics the line of the smoke, although transposed from the vertical into the horizontal. The fall of snow in the left-hand side also curves to match the smoke and, in doing so, joins the smoke and clouds to the sea. This coincidence of curving motion, complemented by the long brushstrokes, gives the impression that the whole work is a whirlpool with the ship at the centre. The ship dissolves into the maelstrom, as the clouds, smoke, sea and snow all combine to create a cycle of formation and dissolution. This idea of a broader processual reality is further indicated by the duplication of colours in the various moving forms. The dark blues and greens of the sky on the right-hand side merge into a sea of a similar colour, and, if we continue to follow this movement in a clockwise direction, the colour of the sea changes to reddish-brown and then a sky of similar colour, and eventually to an intensification of the colours in the smoke. The oscillation of colour indicates a greater processual reality that subtends each of the material processes. There are various levels of material dissolution in the work, from the uncertain boundaries of the boat, through the maelstrom of sea, sky and snow, to the transformation of colour.

This interest in qualitative variation reaches its apotheosis in the later work *Light and Colour (Goethe's Theory) – The Morning after the Deluge – Moses Writing the Book of Genesis* (1843), in which the viewer sees Moses sitting and writing calmly in a blue and yellow mist in the distant centre of the work. Below him is a dark mass of rocks emerging from the water accompanied by new life rising in the form of bubbles. As in *Snow Storm*, it is not the central figure that draws most of the attention but, rather, the cycle of colour that encircles the whole of the painting. Red, vermillion, blue and yellow all mingle with each other to create a colour wheel, which is Turner's pictorial response to Goethe's colour theory in the *Farbenlehre* – a colour wheel joining warm and cool colours.[142] The work, directly examines the 'sublimity of light', particularly when placed alongside the companion piece *Shade and Darkness: The Evening of the Deluge* (1843), which investigates the 'sublimity of darkness'.[143] Although, *Light and Colour* attends to the differentiation of colour, it is noteworthy that Turner does not present a static colour wheel in which the colours are discretely placed side by side and can easily be grouped into hues or even shades. The blurred lines and merging of colours create a sense of turbulence in which the living bubbles and all forms of life are drawn along into a process of continual admixture. In this creation scene, colour overcomes form, and, indeed, form seems to be the product of this chromatic turbulence.[144] In general, continuous qualitative variation, which Bergson argues is central to non-utilitarian vision, usurps a substantive ontology in which qualities are clearly differentiated in their relationship to the surfaces of objects.

It is unlikely that Bergson saw any of Turner's watercolours as they were rarely exhibited, nevertheless they exemplify the fluid intermixing of qualities and energetic forces central to his metaphysics. In many of the watercolours, Turner experimented with new techniques that contravened the late-eighteenth-century practice of beginning with pencil outlines before adding neutral washes and finally colour. Instead, he applied '[d]elicate washes of pure colour, applied unerringly to the blank page' in an attempt to invoke the 'directness of vision'[145] – a directness achieved because the colour is not reduced to its function as a modifier of an existing stable object or surface. Deleuze made a similar point about the use of colour in Francis Bacon's works, by arguing that it adds a presentness to painting which can directly invoke a response from the nervous system unlike other pictorial features such as line and form.[146] As in *Light and Colour*, colour motivates vision by exceeding the limits of a representational surface and by refusing to confirm the status of the object as a sign. Moreover, watercolour reveals the fluid movement of the paint as it soaks into the paper, which is enhanced by the fact that Turner chose to paint onto wet paper, the wet on wet process allowing the washes of colour to bleed into each other. One of the most remarkable watercolour paintings is *Ship on Fire*, painted around 1830, in which the ship is a watery blotch of dark paint, the fire an expanding star of red and orange, and the sea and smoke little more than grey-green washes. Despite the title, the ship is not given any greater pictorial stability than the more ephemeral movements of sea, fire and smoke. There are no outlines and nothing to indicate truly the boundaries between smoke, sea and fire, inducing the colours to intermingle and create a continuity of expressive force and ceaseless perturbation.

In the watercolours and *Light and Colour*, Turner demonstrates an interest in investigating the movement of colour without reference to a set of clearly differentiated boundaries. Form develops through the expansion and interpenetration of colours rather than by conforming to a set of pre-existing categories (genera, objects, outlines, etc.) or ready-made concepts. In calling attention to the process of formation in the very material of the work, there is also an indication of a processual theory of movement that is aligned directly with Bergson's thesis in 'The Perception of Change', in which all change is based on the variation of qualities rather than on the movement of solid objects in space: '*There are changes, but there are underneath the change no things which change: change has no need of a support. There are movements, but there is no inert or invariable object which moves: movement does not imply a mobile*'.[147] Particularly in Turner's late work, this principle is either directly addressed or implied. In the depiction of storms, fires, rain and snow, form is a by-product of immanent movement and turbulence: fire becomes a star, waves create a vortex, and snow becomes water – something that is akin to Bohm's description of subatomic processes and their formative causes. The greater the turbulence in a body of water, the less it can serve as the ground upon which ships move, for in its movement it creates a plethora of transient forms that visually compete with the image of a ship. This is also manifest in the movement of paint in the brushstroke, or the absorption of paint by the paper. The more the brushstrokes indicate their own fluid movement, the more the paint congeals on the surface of the work or finds its own patterns of absorption, the less the artistic gestures are contained by spatially discrete forms or representations. Like Wölfflin's painterly image, movement is always present in the stroke and is not dependent on the status of the object. This also applies to the transmission of light through a medium, which makes the flow of light visible in its own right as a change without support, because it is no longer tethered to a determinate space. Light forms its own shapes in contact with a material, or in Turner's depictions of sunlight, in the way that it advances towards the eye.

The perception of difference and the contraction of quality

Bergson promotes an idea of aesthetic attention and artistic production that are invested in the particularity and presentness of appearance. Although art often deploys general symbols, they are always being placed within a singular concrete perspective and 'individualized': 'Hence it follows that art always aims at what is *individual*. What the artist fixes on his canvas is something he has seen at a certain spot, on a certain day, at a certain hour, with a colouring that will never be seen again.'[148] In focusing on what the artist 'has seen', Bergson accentuates the temporal particularity of a sensory given, which resembles the particularity of recollection in the theory of pure memory. However, this does not necessarily mean that the artist is rigidly tied to reproducing a singular appearance, for attending to the particular also signals a certain awareness to changes in appearance. To say that an appearance is tied to a very particular time is also to argue that it must vary over the course of time, an idea that is fundamental to understanding aesthetic perception.

In the *Aesthetics of Appearing*, Martin Seel argues that what distinguishes aesthetic perception is attention to sensual appearing, which involves 'apprehend[ing] something in the process of its appearing for the sake of its appearing'.[149] Fundamental to this type of attention is a form of sensuousness not contained by a *conceptually determinable* exterior image, sound, or feel'.[150] The question then is: In what way does sensuousness resist or undermine the determinable? It could be realized through unstressed edges, intrinsic space or the suppression of spatial boundaries, particularly contours in painting and drawing. It also concerns a temporal process that refers as much to how we view a work as to what is fixed on the canvas or the represented objects. Seel focuses on the latter, stating that presence in aesthetic attention concerns how the concrete objects of perception present different perceptual aspects within a particular time and place.[151] In short, aesthetic perception requires variability. An aspect, nuance or shade is not a fixed property or clearly delimited quality of what is perceived, and cannot be simply combined to constitute the object, because these aspects appear only under certain perceptual conditions that are transitory and inexhaustible:

> Not only the conceptual inaccessibility of the *nuances* of the sensuous phenomenon is responsible for this inexhaustibility, nor only the impossibility of the *complete* characterization of all of its sensuously discernible features. Over and above these there is a conceptual incommensurability that follows, first, from a *simultaneous* reception of various aspects of the object and, second, from a consideration of their *momentary* appearance.[152]

In this characterization of aesthetic perception, there has to be some consideration of the duration of perception because it is only over time that aspects can vary: 'Beholding the play of appearances on an object is possible only if we *linger* in its presence and encounter it with an *end-in-itself* attentiveness.'[153] The notion of lingering before an image testifies to the continued presence of the perceiver in the act of attending to perceptual nuances and variations, a process that forms the basis of aesthetic contemplation. Consequently, aesthetic attention is 'an attentiveness to ourselves',[154] for the perceiver becomes self-aware through the process of testifying to the variation in the appearance of the object – an indirect way of invoking the deep feelings in consciousness. The variation in appearance is an aesthetic fact that is contingent on a viewer's attentiveness over time, which presents a challenge to utilitarian perception which seeks to fix objects in perception.

Bergson does not discuss aesthetic attention in terms of a process of becoming perceptually aware as Seel does, although it is implied in the theory of *durée*. The concrete reality of the art object must always stand alongside the variability of the artist's or viewer's perception within the context of their own *durée*. Raymond Bayer states the Bergson's metaphysics is founded upon a particular notion of aesthetic attention and to explain this, he refers to Bergson's penchant in his later years to listening to classical music on record. As a recording, the materiality of the sound does not greatly change but, nevertheless, with each iteration the listener hears 'les *différences*', due to both attentiveness and the fact that over the time of listening, the listener changes and ages. Most importantly, it is the attentiveness to these differences that leads Bergson, as a listener, closer to the core of the artistic work.[155] Repetition as variation drives aesthetic engagement. How can this be reconciled with Bergson's argument that intuition provides a direct apprehension of the real, unlike the intellect, which produces multiple viewpoints without ever arriving at a true understanding of a phenomenon? The problem hinges on two types of awareness: a unifying awareness of a temporal whole, and an aesthetic awareness of phenomenal variation in perception. The two can be reconciled if we focus on how intuition varies with its object, which involves the awareness of temporal variation at the same time as the integration of these differences in the continuity of *durée*. Intuition might directly apprehend objects but only in the context of a temporality in which differentiation and integration are always in a state of variable tension. Even if it does not directly reveal a metaphysical real as Bergson suggests, aesthetic perception does provide an understanding of phenomenal variability and, consequently, an incipient awareness of an enduring self.

Bergson is certainly interested in the relationship between material difference and perceptual variability, which is often characterized in terms of disinterest rather than perceptual attentiveness in his discussions of art. In raising the question of disinterest, Bergson clearly draws upon Kant's *Critique of Judgement*, in which judgements of taste are distinguished by a lack of interest in the utility, purpose or the conceptual description of an object: 'The judgment is called aesthetical just because its determining ground is not a concept, but the feeling (of internal sense) of that harmony in the play of the mental powers, so far as it can be felt in sensation.'[156] The problem with concepts is that they limit the free play of the imagination in the appreciation of beauty, in particular, in what Kant refs to as 'free beauty'.[157] We might find some pleasure in conceptually determined objects such as geometrical figures, but they cannot sustain the imagination in a way that a fire or 'rippling brook' can, even if the latter are not intrinsically beautiful.[158] For Bergson, aesthetic perception also eschews utility in terms of the capacity of an object to be acted upon, and in doing so, opens up the imagination to an aesthetic way of engaging with the object as phenomenon. However, Bergson's idea of disinterest also invokes the metaphysics of *durée* because when removed from a conceptual yoke, temporal differences become more apparent and we become attentive to the notion of continuous qualitative change. Bergson argues that disinterest is a function of the 'absent-minded' artist, who is 'less adherent to life',[159] which appears at first to contradict his argument in *Laughter*, in which art is distinguished by the way that it cleaves to life. However, the apparent contradiction arises from the fact that Bergson uses life in a dualism with mechanism in *Laughter*, whereas in 'The Perception of Change', from which the above quotation was taken, it is placed in contradistinction to normal perception and quotidian action. In this case, the artist is less adherent to a perceptual environment configured in terms of need but that could still be attentive to the movement of life:

> When they look at a thing, they see it for itself, and not for themselves. They do not perceive simply with a view to action; they perceive in order to perceive, – for nothing, for the pleasure of doing so. In regard to a certain aspect of their nature, whether it be their consciousness or one of their senses, they are born *detached*; and according to whether this detachment is that of a certain particular sense, or of consciousness, they are painters or sculptors, musicians or poets. It is therefore a much more direct vision of reality that we find in the different arts; and it is because the artist is less intent on utilizing his perception that he perceives a greater number of things.[160]

It is noteworthy that, for Bergson, philosophers also attain a 'direct vision of reality' by reducing the 'practical purpose' of perceptual attention rather than due to being born with an absent-minded disposition.[161] The philosopher must work towards a particular attitude through the cultivation of an intuitive approach whereas the artist is detached from practical necessity from the outset. This distinction may be due to Bergson's nineteenth-century romanticism and the celebration of the singularity of the artist's vision and artistic genius. However, the artist's approach to the real should also be considered a form of labour or, as Benjamin states, a way of rethinking, because the artist does not simply see, but sees through the medium they work in.

In contrast to the direct apprehension of the real, disinterest describes a broadening of the qualitative variability of the present that is directly associated with the 'number of things' that are perceived within a particular duration. There is still undivided continuity in lived time – often explained by reference to the indivisibility of gesture – but the emphasis has shifted to conditions of discernment within this indivisibility. Disinterestedness is a state in which '[a]rt enables us, no doubt, to discover in things more qualities and more shades than we naturally perceive'.[162] It is the condition for the qualitative differentiation of the visual field rather than the contraction of sensible differences into temporal unities. Intuition is a form of direct understanding or sympathy by which the object is known from inside as an internal movement that generates the whole, whereas disinterestedness describes a relaxing of perception's grip on the present that allows for greater phenomenal and temporal variability. On the one hand, it is about adumbrating more nuances in perception, being more attentive to a particular moment, and on the other, it is about expanding the duration of the present such that more differences endure in a single moment. This balance between the recognition of difference and the increase in the range of differences is central to Bergson's aesthetics. Aesthetics requires an intuition of the real that is thoroughly invested in the apprehension of life, but life can be disclosed in different ways depending on the duration of the present moment and the variety of differences that pertain to it.

This aesthetic approach requires the examination of the relationship between material differences and the perception of differences. Is the role of the artist simply to rearticulate the qualitative differences present in the particularity of the present moment? This is certainly not a straightforward process because the real is never entirely given in intuition if it depends on the viewer's level of discernment, the degree of disinterestedness, and the viewing duration. How the particular moment endures in perception has the capacity to change the very nature of what is viewed. In *Matter and Memory*, Bergson addresses the relationship between material differences and qualitative differences in perception through reference to the temporal restrictions governing perception, for in a 'given interval' there are only 'a limited number of phenomena of which we are aware'.[163]

This reference to an interval and its contents invokes a quantitative multiplicity, and seemingly steers Bergson away from his broader claims that duration can only be understood in terms of non-measurable qualitative change. However, this notion of the interval should not be regarded as an abstraction, for it is contingent on apperception and the range of material and qualitative differences distinguished and brought to awareness in a concrete present. It describes the quality of attention rather than the measurement of events in an interval. To explain this, Bergson distinguishes between the materiality of red light, with its '400 billion vibrations' per second, and the time that would be required to notice them as individual vibrations. With reference to a psychological study, he argues that the shortest interval in which a person can distinguish between events is 0.002 of a second and, therefore, it would take 25,000 years to attend to each of the vibrations in a single second of red light.[164] The concrete time of perception is not infinitely divisible, unlike Zeno's trajectory, because it is always restricted by apperception – what it means to be aware of an event over a particular duration. Interestingly, recent work by Benjamin Libet (2004) suggests that we do not become aware of a new signal until approximately half a second after it begins, which would greatly alter Bergson's calculations and also imply that continuity is constructed post facto.[165] At the basis of his account of perception is a form of aesthetic attention that remains attentive to changes in appearance, in which a truly disinterested perception is part of the broader process of becoming aware, as Seel argues, through attention to variations in the sensorium and the sensuousness of objects.

Despite referring in the above example to countable divisions between vibrations, Bergson does not propose a quantitative approach to aesthetic attention or perception. The viewer does not simply notice some vibrations and dismiss billions of others. What the example suggests is that our incapacity to notice differences forms the basis for the differentiation of qualities in perception, a form of differentiation that is always moderated by time. There is alternation between qualitative differences and vibrations depending on the duration of perception:

May we not conceive, for instance, that the irreducibility of two perceived colors is due mainly to the narrow duration into which are contracted the billions of vibrations which they execute in one of our moments? If we could stretch out this duration, that is to say, live it at a slower rhythm, should we not, as the rhythm slowed down, see these colors pale and lengthen into successive impressions, still colored, no doubt, but nearer and nearer to coincidence with pure vibrations? In cases where the rhythm of the movement is slow enough to tally with the habits of our consciousness – as in the case of the deep notes of the musical scale, for instance – do we not feel that the quality perceived analyzes itself into repeated and successive vibrations, bound together by an inner continuity?[166]

The viewer or listener is able to notice vibrational differences in sensory events according to a type of aesthetic attentiveness to the momentary aspects of appearing, but is unable to note these differences in those durations that are 'too narrow to permit the separation of its moments',[167] in which case other qualities emerge. There is an oscillation between two states of perception depending on the overall duration of the present and the rhythmic properties of seeing and listening. When the rhythm is sufficiently slow, the colours 'pale' until the point at which they are no longer colours, but when the rhythm is sufficiently fast, the colours contract into solid, extensive fields of colour. Continuity is a condition of both states – time still subsists in the vibrations and the colours – but what has changed is the viewer's capacity to discern these differences. The more the field is contracted into a particular duration, the greater the range of differences that are subsumed within a single quality. The more the tension in perception is relaxed, the greater the number of differences that can be interpolated by the perceiver.

The idea that perception has an immanent tension that modulates between identity and difference can be mapped onto some optical principles incorporated into the practice and study of art. Ptolemy proposed in his study of optics that multiple colours combine to create single colours when the observer is at a sufficient distance, or when the multicoloured object, such as a spinning disc, moves at a sufficient speed.[168] Artists working with mosaics cultivated this 'optical fusion' by varying the size of the tesserae, such as using smaller tesserae for the face to give the impression of softness. Much later, Seurat also created different levels and types of optical fusion by altering the size and direction of his brushstrokes, for example, when he used smaller dots to create clearer contrasts and contours.[169] John Gage argues that the variation in the size of the brushstrokes in a number of his works meant that Seurat had not yet chosen an optimal viewing distance, for the colours could fuse at different distances depending on the brushstroke and colour combination.[170] In general, the Neo-Impressionists investigated and deployed many optical effects and were guided by the principle that colours should be mixed perceptually rather than on the palette because this creates a much more vibrant effect.[171] Optical fusion ostensibly describes a spatial principle in which the differences between colour fields disappear and contract to form new colours when the observer stands at an appropriate distance. Conversely, when the observer walks towards the mosaic or painting, they can notice the differences again and consequently the mixed colour disappears. This process differs from the fusion of vibrations into a colour or sound because the vibrations are necessarily temporal, whereas tesserae and taches of paint have a spatial configuration. However, the two can be linked if we accept that perception is always in movement and that consciousness cannot easily attend to both the parts and the whole at the same time. Optical fusion at a distance relates directly to the fusion of colours in spinning discs on which are painted multiple colours – a process used by Helmholtz and Newton, in addition to Ptolemy[172] – because the eye does not have time to attend to individual colours when the disc reaches a sufficient speed. In optical fusion at a distance, the further the viewer stands from the work, the broader the sweep of the eye across the canvas and the greater the speed with which the eye will cross the various colour fields and patches. Distance certainly makes it more difficult to discern colour differences, but the movement of the eye within the time of attention also contributes to optical fusion.

The importance Bergson places on the variable relationship between the enumeration of differences and the unification of qualities could be drawn from Leibniz's distinction between confused and clear perception, which also plays an important role in aesthetics. Alexander Baumgarten thought that insufficient attention was given to confused (sensory) perception, and that the field of aesthetics was needed to address this, although he also noted that sensation might only appear to be confused as it is comprised of many 'imperceptible' forms that have their own clarity.[173] What aesthetics offers is an examination of confused perception in a way that attends to the specific qualitative differences operating at different levels, rather than assuming hylomorphism in which clear ideas are merely projected onto inchoate sensation or matter. This idea was discussed by Bergson in a number of his lectures at Clermont-Ferrand and Lycée Henri IV, where he highlighted, in particular, the variability in perception with respect to consciousness. Confused and clear perception are infinitely variable in consciousness – for example, confused perception operates at the lowest level of consciousness in which there is little self-awareness or mental unity – but the two are always entwined. To illustrate this, Bergson uses Leibniz's example of the sound of waves crashing on a beach, where the listener can hear 'distinctement' the sound of the waves but not the sound of each droplet, even though the latter is a sonic component of the former.[174] These 'petites perceptions' are found in all perception even though they often go unacknowledged, and what drives the progression from confused to clear perceptions is the internal effort, or appetition, of the monad.[175] This type of clear perception is valuable from a Bergsonian perspective, because it describes a perceptual process underpinned by intellectual effort and continued action of the will rather than the application of logically determined concepts. It requires the activity of the mind unlike Descartes's spatial notion of clear ideas, for without the effort of an observer, the sensible world will just disaggregate into 'petites perceptions'. Bergson does not completely follow this line of thought in his own account of perception, although he retains a principle of contraction – which is often linked to the will – by which confused perceptions, the simple aggregate of images or vibrations, become qualities that are grasped in apperception. Moreover, in intuition, confused perceptions cannot be fully reduced to clear perceptions, for the observer must be able to distinguish differences while still contracting them in a single intuition. The 'petites perceptions' are always making themselves present even though the perceiver cannot fully attend to them within the broader unity of attention in a particular present. This is quite different to utilitarian perception, where these micro differences are effectively erased in the perception of a quality.

The relationship between the will, unity and uncountable differences can play a role in aesthetic judgement, as can be inferred from a presentation given by Bergson in New York in 1913 on the state of French–American relations.[176] As is typical of a speech forging amity between two nations, Bergson made reference to what pleased him about the visit, and referred specifically to his positive impression of the New York skyscrapers. Based on what he had read about New York, he was predisposed to think that they might be ugly, and was therefore pleasantly surprised to find that many of them were quite beautiful.[177] Bergson qualifies this judgement by stating that they might not suit a French urban environment but when placed in the more modern context of the American city they can be 'saisissant' (*striking*).[178] He states, however, that he was a little surprised by this impression because it seems to contradict an unattributed aesthetic principle, in which houses of more than two stories are regarded as visually displeasing. The taller the building, the less attractive it is, which led Bergson to explain the principle of internal organization underlying his judgement. He states that houses of two stories or less can be understood in terms of the lived experience of a single family, whereas houses with a greater number of floors extend beyond this lived experience and therefore appear composite. This judgement is based on a simple act of seeing the building as an organic unity, whereas, in contrast, when addressing the taller building, attention is distracted due to the building's lack of 'the unity, without which there is no work of art' (*l'unité, sans laquelle il n'y a pas d'oeuvre d'art*).[179] There is no unity because each additional floor appears as a countable supplement to the original unity, which leads Bergson to speculate on why he finds skyscrapers aesthetically pleasing. He solves the dilemma by stating that beyond a certain level, unity is reconstituted because the viewer can no longer count the individual levels.[180] If the observer is unable to enumerate or count the individual levels, then the building takes on the quality of an 'indivisée' (*undivided*) unity in the same way that the smaller house does. Unlike the house of three, four or five stories, the skyscraper is no longer perceived in terms of the original unity of the house, no longer an aggregate of parts or a composite, but a building with its own distinct aesthetic unity.[181] Bergson rarely talks about the value of a particular visual object and this is, in many respects, only a passing judgement; however, it highlights the importance of organic unity in Bergson's aesthetics. It also indicates a temporal dimension, in which the house is unified by the lived time of the family, whereas the skyscraper is unified by the impossibility of enumerating individual differences in the *durée* of the gaze.[182] Unlike the organic unity of life which is derived internally, in this case from the house, the time of perception confers a principle of aesthetic unity onto the object because it delimits perception, while also indicating a possible differentiation of the parts. The movement between the different states of unity is a key factor in developing a Bergsonian aesthetic.

Bergson does not fully distinguish between conscious and unconscious states when referring to contraction and relaxation in perception. In seeing colour, the perceiver is not aware of the individual vibrations; however, in seeing the skyscraper the individual floors retain their individuality within the contraction, such that the viewer has some control over what they will attend to – the whole building or individual floors. In *Difference and Repetition*, Gilles Deleuze draws upon the phenomenological tradition in arguing that the 'passive synthesis' or contraction of micromovements and vibrations should be distinguished from other types and levels of synthesis insofar as it serves as the basis for lived time. As with Husserl's theory of primary memory, the retention of sensual givens or vibrations constitutes the perception and also confirms the continuity of time. For Deleuze, the quality of the series changes over time depending on the number of past iterations that 'contract' into this moment, or what can be referred to as the 'contractile power' of the present perception.[183] This passive synthesis, with a contractile power that stretches towards the future in anticipation, is 'constitutive' of all other types of lived time in memory and perception, and can be contrasted with the 'active synthesis' of recollection. Recollection accords each present moment its place within the primary temporal continuity of passive synthesis and creates an image of the future derived from reflecting upon the past.[184] Deleuze also distinguishes other levels of synthesis including the 'primal vital sensibility' of the biological body, in which biological needs and cellular memory are contracted as 'organic syntheses', which in turn form the basis of habits.[185] The difference between the levels of synthesis provides a means of making ontological distinctions while maintaining an overall processualism, and could be useful in distinguishing between gesture, perception, matter and biology in Bergson's philosophy. With regard to art, the passive synthesis of colour could operate within the contraction of an artist's past, which in turn could be divided into two movements, recollection and the organic synthesis of movement in habit. However, Bergson does not develop a full ontology of syntheses because, in most cases, he wants to demonstrate the unity of *durée* and consciousness and, therefore, different synthetic processes disappear into the increases and decreases of the contractile tension of consciousness. For example, rather than talking about a separate evolutionary contraction, he speculates on a consciousness that could contract the whole of human evolution into a single moment,[186] while at another level contracting the vibrations of matter into a single colour. Perception as passive synthesis, which does not involve the will, and the conscious acts of creating unities and distinguishing differences central to aesthetic analysis are all confounded in the general logic of temporal contraction.

This notion of contraction is important in a discussion of aesthetic perception because it refers to the interplay between movement and immobility in attention, which is central to both a processual ontology and utilitarian perception. Contraction describes a process by which qualitative and material differences are produced and reduced, as well as a form of reduction that leads to the perception of movement. When material vibrations combine to form a single colour or sound, they are also extracted from the qualitative variability of becoming – they become qualia or qualities attendant on objects. Following this line of reasoning, contraction in perception could be considered utilitarian, whereas relaxation in the tension of perception would be more clearly aligned with aesthetic attention and the disclosure of qualitative differences. This argument has some validity; however, Bergson argues that, in the case of colour and sound perception, the greater the relaxation of attention, the more perception resolves itself into the loose continuous vibrations that compose the universe.[187] Here consciousness relinquishes its capacity to act on matter because it has become coincident with the dissolute movements of matter. We could speculate that the relaxation in attention would still yield noticeable differences, but they would not necessarily demonstrate the freedom implied in the aesthetic attentiveness to the play of difference. In this tensional scale between contracted qualities and material vibrations, the extremes do not support the intuitive revelation of a truly processual real. When Bergson theorizes the role of contraction as an attribute of intuition, it comes to describe the conscious control over material necessity and an awareness of difference: 'By allowing us to grasp in a single intuition multiple moments of duration, it frees us from the movement of the flow of things, that is to say, from the rhythm of necessity.'[188] Intuition could here be regarded as an active synthesis associated with freedom because it extends beyond the necessity of material movement and the passive synthesis of qualities – in which qualities are fixed in a particular state. Bergson often talks of both types of contraction as if they are both part of the same scale, but it is important to distinguish between them. The contraction in intuition is much more readily aligned with aesthetic perception because it reveals the momentariness and variability of appearance as well as the disinterested disclosure of difference, whereas passive synthesis could be more readily tied to the needs and affordances of the body in utilitarian perception.

Perceptual contraction explains how qualities are derived in an ontology in which the universe is a pulsating collection of interpenetrating movements, and where even objects that appear to move in space can actually be decomposed into colours, and into qualitatively distinct vibrations. Bergson strongly argues against the notion of objects that move independently in space because the 'alleged movement of a thing is in reality only a movement of movements.[189] What we regard as independent objects is the product of a synthesis whereby material vibrations, or other types of movement, are rendered relatively stable in utilitarian perception – although, of course, this is also a feature of aesthetic perception. In *Matter and Memory*, Bergson argues that rendering movement in the visual arts, which is usually discussed in terms of the haecceity of vision, can be compared to the contraction of the elementary vibrations of colour: 'the multitudinous successive positions of a runner are contracted into a single symbolic attitude, which our eyes perceive, which art reproduces, and which becomes for us all the image of a man running.'[190] This differs fundamentally from a cinematographic snapshot or Zeno's imagined positions, for it contracts a range of virtual positions and movements integral to the act of running into a single symbolic attitude. This argument is similar to Auguste Rodin's belief, expressed in his interviews with Paul Gsell, that good sculpture should give the impression of life in movement by incorporating *'the transition from one attitude to another'* in the time of viewing, which he explains using Ovid's account of Daphne changing into a bay tree.[191] The corporeal attitude of the sculpture does not need to indicate two precise moments of a movement, but, rather, the general tendency or inclination to move. For example, in Rodin's *Nijinsky* (1912), the sculpture does not have a definite telos but every part of the body indicates transition: the head twisted to the right could turn back to the left; the bent left leg could be extended or returned to the ground; and the slightly bent arms could be flattened or extended outwards.

It is not surprising that Rodin is also critical of 'instantaneous photography', which produces images in which figures are fixed in a single motionless position. They lack the impression of life because the body is 'reproduced' according to a very precise and indifferent 'twentieth or fortieth of a second', without a 'progressive development of movement as there is in art'.[192] In the photograph, the figures are understood only in terms of what A. N. Whitehead refers to as simple location, where all that is given is the placement of a body in a particular time and place, without reference to a broader temporal or processual reality.[193] The photograph isolates the body from the continuity of time in a number of ways. With regard to the photographs of horses in motion by Eadweard Muybridge, Thierry de Duve states that the photograph either creates singular events by freezing the movement of the horse in a particular pose and thus separating it from future and preceding events, or the image creates a gestalt that operates according to its own spatial logic rather than that of the represented object.[194] In the first, time contracts around a very truncated gesture in which there is little progression or transition between states, and in the second, compositional logic of the image draws attention away from the very conditions of movement – we appreciate the horse's position with respect to the frame, the organization of geometric patterns and so on. In highlighting the symbolic attitude or progressive development in the visual arts, Rodin and Bergson suggest that art can recreate life by engaging virtual movements that extend well beyond the immediacy of either the pose or the compositional whole – the horse must be seen in a transition between states. It is not only a matter of contracting time in the visual arts but also one of extending the range of the contraction.

Before Rodin contrasted the contraction of movement in the visual arts with photography, Bergson proposed a similar comparison in *Creative Evolution* between ancient art and the new technologies of instantaneous photography and the cinematograph, as part of a broader argument on the differences between ancient and modern science. He argued that modern science and photography – and he was probably thinking of Eadweard Muybridge and Étienne-Jules Marey – decompose movement into instants without an indication of its underlying form, direction and intention, whereas the ancients used their senses to create a single attitude that could summarize the whole path of a movement:[195]

> Of the gallop of a horse our eye perceives chiefly a characteristic, essential or rather schematic attitude, a form that appears to radiate over a whole period and so fill up a time of gallop. It is this attitude that sculpture has fixed on the frieze of the Parthenon. But instantaneous photography isolates any moment; it puts them all in the same rank, and thus the gallop of a horse spreads out for it into as many successive attitudes as it wishes, instead of massing itself into a single attitude, which is supposed to flash out in a privileged moment and to illuminate a whole period.[196]

In this example, Bergson distinguishes between the fusion of movement in human perception and the technological isolation of instants. In this perceptual fusion or contraction, the movement 'radiates over a whole period' and is strongly linked to the actual duration of the viewer's lived time. Unlike the contraction of vibrations in a fixed colour, each movement of the legs, torso, mane and so on of the horse does not disappear into a single quality. The viewer still notices the disaggregated movements even though they dissolve into the continuity of the overall movement, and in doing so, creating a tension between appearance and disappearance. For example, in the Mannerist sculpture of Giambologna (Giovanni da Bologna), dynamism is often created through the use of different planes of action, which are revealed as the viewer circumnavigates the work.[197] As the viewer's movement reveals new planes, they are immediately reintegrated into a whole to create the impression of movement. By contrast, for Bergson, the instantaneity of the photograph reveals only one perspective and therefore does not lead to contraction or what he refers to as a schematic attitude.

What Bergson does not acknowledge in his critique of photography is that the rendering of an image is certainly not instantaneous. There is actually duration in the photographic process, the twentieth or fortieth of a second mentioned by Rodin, which is determined by the amount of light required to expose the film stock and render clarity to objects. Unlike the perception of the artist, this machinic contraction operates over very short durations and without reference to human lived time, which Bergson does not investigate due to his tendency to contrast matter with life when referring to art. In many respects, this is a missed opportunity because it could contribute to a fully developed processual ontology or aesthetics in terms of living, machinic and material syntheses. Does the duration of a material make itself visible in the artwork? For example, do the weight of the material – bronze, plaster, stone and so on – and the time of hardening, casting and manufacture contribute to the impression of movement in a sculpture? The different durations by which paint is absorbed, dried and dispersed could also be considered forms of material synthesis underpinning the gestural and compositional contractions of painting. It is worth addressing this issue by returning to the Futurists, who attempted to come to terms with some of Bergson's ideas by linking them to technological advances. They referred to the processual interconnectedness of things revealed by the x-ray, the impression of movement brought about by the increasing speed of transportation and, most importantly, the disclosure of duration in photographic after-images. Paul Crowther states that the Futurists believed that the after-image presents a concrete representation of the interpenetration of past, present and future that is grounded in a spectator's relationship to the depicted event and to the work. The after-image was a visual means of working through the idea of *durée*, and the persistence of the past, which was not available to Bergson due to the self-imposed limits of his philosophy.[198] Crowther does not explicitly state what these limits are, but it is implied that Bergson's claims about art's capacity to lift the veil on the real do not provide a sufficient ground by which to understand the aesthetic properties of movement, and how it can be imagined through the materiality and plasticity of the work.

There were many attempts by the Futurists to visually incorporate Bergson's ideas into their works, notably Umberto Boccioni's notion of dynamic force lines that describe the internal living impetus of a sculpture, and the more far-reaching ideas of dynamic sensation and *compenetrazione*.[199] The ontological principle of *compenetrazione* refers to the interconnectedness of the universe in the form of a vibratory processual whole without empty space, in which matter is constituted through the movement of dynamic forces[200] – a notion of the universe that is likely to have drawn some inspiration from the processual philosophy outlined in the final section of *Matter and Memory*. Despite the use of a mechanical apparatus, the investigation of after-images in photography by the brothers Anton Giulio and Arturo Bragaglia draws closest to Bergson's notion of qualitative contraction and the schematic attitude. The brothers used long-exposure photographs to render visible the whole path of a movement rather than individual segments or the fixed outline of a moving body, and found that when a body moves at speed its surfaces cannot be captured in a single period of exposure, leading to a loss of solidity and coherence. The discrete body dissolves into a blur of movement, which is further highlighted when juxtaposed against the stability of a non-moving background with its legible surfaces. They used a variety of techniques over a period spanning from 1911 to 1913, but most were designed to show movement as a continuum. Unlike Étienne-Jules Marey and the scientific analysis of movement, the Bragaglia brothers sought to understand movement's living impetus in sudden gestures and the deformation of the figure, which Anton Giulio considered to be a vitalist aesthetic in which movement 'transcends matter' and rejects verisimilitude.[201] The vital movement arises from within the body but, nevertheless, effaces it through willed exertion and the endurance of gesture.

Of the brothers, it was Anton Giulio who most directly responded to Bergson's ideas in his book *Fotodinamismo futurista*, in particular the notion of the 'becoming of form' and the critique of the cinematograph in *Creative Evolution*. He was also aware of Rodin's published discussion of his own sculpture *L'Homme qui marche* in his interviews with Paul Gsell, which was widely discussed in Rome when the work was exhibited there in 1910.[202] Despite the interest in the impression of movement through transition, Bragaglia disagreed with Rodin's foregrounding of the two states of the transition, claiming, instead, that art must depict all the states in between.[203] It is about revealing the fullness of motion liberated from the solidity of visual objects or particular stable features of those objects. In 'Futurist Photodynamism', Anton Giulio Bragaglia argues that the image of a movement cannot be represented with a single line for this does not fully indicate the internal vibratory divisions and infinite number of submovements.[204] He ascribes wholeheartedly to a processual ontology in which the real is comprised of a series of nested rhythms and vibrations that stretch out to infinity. Consequently, photodynamism reveals relationships in which there is no separation of the subject from rhythmic movement and its 'infinite quantity of vibrations'.[205] Bragaglia argues that the problem with the representation of movement in cinematography and chronophotography is that both take an analytical approach in which the reproduction of the figure is given greater prominence than the reality of movement. Photography is overly concerned with the 'perfect anatomical reproduction of reality', where the figure is clearly distinguished from the act of moving, which chronophotography extends to the sequential depiction of movement in terms of instantaneous cross-sections, each of which has lost the capacity to depict movement. Bragaglia argues that Marey's chronophotography is more useful as a means of describing the steps of an action rather than revealing the quality and flow of motion. Cinematography performs a similar subdivision in which the flow of movement is reconfigured as a collection of parts which eschew the 'aesthetic' properties of rhythm, for 'cinematography never synthesizes movement' in terms of its full qualitative variability.[206] These criticisms drawn upon many of the themes that have already been discussed with regard to the limits of photography, as the articulation of a singular event or an isolated image, as well as the importance of understanding movement through difference and qualitative change.

Bragaglia is clearly indebted to Bergson in his critique of the photographic and cinematographic representation of movement in terms of fixed parts and the ontology of solid bodies traversing a neutral and homogeneous space. Bergson criticized any method that sought to characterize movement in terms of a fixed trajectory or its subsections without properly recovering its vital impetus. Based on the ongoing discussion in this chapter, it is evident that synthesis is also important in offering a means of understanding the qualitative multiplicity of movement in addition to describing a relationship between immanent movement and the trajectory. Photodynamism certainly produces images that have definite spatial forms with lines that resemble trajectories; however, these lines are highly variable with tiny variations in the degree of exposure, and therefore cannot be decomposed into discrete parts. Anton Giulio Bragaglia's 1911 photograph *Change of Position* depicts the movement of a figure from an upright position sitting in a chair with hands crossed to a position in which head and body are brought forward with hands raised to the face (see Figure 4.3). These two visible positions are in themselves unremarkable and are clearly recognizable despite some blurring, and it is likely that the figure stayed still in the initial and end positions in order to allow for the body to be sufficiently exposed. These two positions can be likened in some respects to Rodin's aspects of movement that provide the foundation for creating the virtual image of transition in sculpture, but what definitely distinguishes the photograph is the nature of the transition between the positions. Insofar as the body

FIGURE 4.3 Anton Giulio Bragaglia. *Change of Position* (1911). © Anton Giulio Bragaglia/SIAE. Copyright Agency, 2020.

is thrown forward – or possibly thrown back – at high speed, the surfaces of the body dissolve into the speed of the gesture without completely disappearing. The face intermittently appears through tonal variation in the trajectory: the whole face remains distinguishable by the movement lines that pass through it; the line joining the lips extends across the full trajectory while varying in width and form; the cheekbone is a flash of brightness, and the eye socket a dark canal that carves its way through the blur of movement. Every line and contour operates on a variety of levels: as a trajectory, as a marker of dissolution and reformation, as a corporeal surface, as a veil, and as a forward gestural movement. The lines and contours describe the interpenetration of form in movement through the revelation of what Bragaglia calls 'intermovemental fractions',[207] which are not usually consciously acknowledged despite inhering in the perception of all movement. From Bergson's perspective, this is because the perceiver focuses on the solid body cut out from a homogeneous background rather than the concrete form of the movement and its endurance. Bragaglia's photodynamic images might commence with a notion of extrinsic space in which the body traces a definite trajectory, but the trajectory is merely the trace of a broader qualitative variation.

The qualitative variability of concrete movement is revealed only in photodynamism because the movement of light is contracted or synthesized by the camera and the film stock within a particular duration. Within any particular time of exposure, Bragaglia points out that the nature of the movement changes, with faster movements distorting the body and slower movements maintaining its integrity. If the exposure time is much shorter, many of these effects would disappear and the discrete body would stand out from a background, which means that it is the slowness of exposure that allows *durée* to become visible in intrinsic space. By contrast, the faster movement of the body undermines the 'real', by which he means the real of clearly definable bodies, and can be characterized, instead, as a striving towards the 'ideal'.[208] It could also be considered a dematerialization of movement that operates in inverse proportion to the tangibility of the discrete body. The slowing down of the time or registration, or conversely the speeding up of motion, is aesthetically productive because it provides the basis for a transition between two states of a body but also between two ontologies – a process ontology and one based on the logic of solid bodies. The slowing down marks a transition from a utilitarian epistemology to an aesthetics of movement, because the viewer is made aware of the variations in appearance usually elided at normal speeds of viewing. The greater the number of qualitative differences that are revealed in the particular duration of a movement, the more that movement operates outside of a logic of utility. What this demonstrates is that visual difference is dependent on the degree of contraction of the apparatus, in this case the camera, in relation to the synthesis of differences in human perception.

Photodynamism posits a type of unity in movement that coincides with Bergson's notion of aesthetic unity, in which new qualities emerge because the perceiver is unable to enumerate material differences. The complex trace rendered on the photographic plate is unified due to the failure of the camera, in particular the lens and film stock, to render the movement of the body in an instant. The particular quality of the image is firmly linked to a limitation. Mary Anne Doane notes that a central argument in much of the nineteenth-century discussion about the relationship between perception and motion concerned the fallibility of the eye. The production of the after-image on the retina comes about because the eye is not capable of keeping up with the changes in the visual field, in which case, instantaneous photography was, to some degree, an attempt to address this insufficiency.[209] In the early discussions of apparent motion in cinema, this was discussed in terms of the persistence of vision in which images are retained due to the relative slowness of the retina. However, more recent discussion has referred to the 'phi-phenomenon' in which the spectator fills in gaps between events to establish continuity: 'the spectator has mentally established a continuity and movement where there was technically only discontinuity and stasis.'[210] In many ways, Bergson's idea of contraction fits between these two modes – the viewer is certainly incapable of attending to the differences implicit to all moving and changing phenomena within any definite duration, and therefore posits unity. He also argues that all time endures, which could be materially explained through the persistence of images in the retina – there are no instants. However, for Bergson, this is not strictly a material insufficiency, for the endurance of all sensual phenomena is an ontological condition which pre-exists any division.

This argument about insufficiency could also be applied to the camera. Should the revelation of intermovemental fractions in photodynamism be regarded merely as effects of the camera and its film stock, a chemical and mechanical insufficiency rather than a true indication of what it means to move? One way of addressing this issue is to question the capacity of photography and film to depict movement, as Bergson, Bragaglia, Rodin and so on have done. The photograph that accentuates the clean lines of the solid body, and devolves all movement into properly delineated surfaces, does so due to a structural deficiency. This deficiency is accepted as best approximating the real because it more closely approximates utilitarian perception, at least in the depiction of non-moving bodies. In both the unity of aesthetic appreciation and utilitarian perception, the principle of contraction leads to the formation of emergent qualities. The contractions of colours or sounds or windows in a skyscraper are the result of a perceptual process that seeks to reduce difference, and this raises the question: Should this process be thoroughly distinguished from the cutting out (*decouper*) of solid bodies in utilitarian perception? Bergson states that in the contraction of material differences '[t]o perceive means to immobilize'[211] and, in this sense, contraction resembles the extraction of qualities based on need. However, it is worthwhile noting that despite both positing a gestalt, to cut out and contract have different connotations, and in a philosophy that depends heavily on mobile images and metaphors, it is important to attend to these differences. The notion of cutting out was a provisional metaphor used in the description of one aspect of pure perception, a spatial ontology in which the body is orientated according to utility. The objects are defined spatially in a figure–ground relationship without consideration of the time in which they appear or the role of memory in unifying qualitative difference – they are demarcated more than contracted. By contrast, the synthetic immobilization or contraction refers to a process in which there is no complete erasure of the movement inherent in perception. The extracted qualities continue to invoke the temporal processes of which they are comprised. Like a concertina which expands and contracts, regardless of the level of immobilization, there is always the implication of a remobilization, where the movements that are contracted expand again. Immobility is just a temporary state of a broader processual mobility.

In his essay on Félix Ravaisson reproduced in *Creative Mind*, Bergson provides a foundation for a more thorough explanation of the differing roles of contraction in terms of two main unifying tendencies in philosophy. He argues that Ravaisson produced a novel interpretation of Aristotle's philosophy, by focusing less on the consistency of his ideas and more on the unity of his thought. The first process of unification involves the intuition of clearly definable properties, which serve as a foundation for increasing levels of abstraction. Of greater value to Bergson, Ravaisson also refers to a second type of unification in which intuition conjoins a series of 'sensible intuition[s]' without recourse to abstraction.[212] To illustrate the first of these types, abstract unification, Bergson again uses the example of colour, where specific qualities are abstracted from the context in which they appear and their general properties are organized in a system underpinned by negation.[213] Similar to a structuralist language, each colour is defined by differential relationships with other colours – blue is not red, black not white and so on – and in this type of unification, the quality is defined relative to its place within the system. By contrast, unification derived through intuition, which is exemplified in Ravaisson's metaphysics,

> consists in taking the thousand and one different shades of blue, violet, green, yellow and red, and, by having them pass through a convergent lens, bringing them to a single point. Then appears in all its radiance the pure white light which, perceived here below in the shades which disperse it, enclosed above, in its undivided unity, the indefinite variety of multi-colored rays.[214]

Here, the role of the metaphysician is to retrace the colours and the rays back to their source,[215] which is a temporal process where the tendencies are unmixed in perception in order to demonstrate how they recombine in duration. The various colours of light subsist in the unified whole of white light, but each colour is independent insofar as it describes a material process that is subject to its own process of contraction. From an aesthetics standpoint, perceptual contraction does not necessarily lead to the isolation of qualia to be organized in a logical system, as long as the contraction retains the trace of the material and perceptual movement of each of the colours. The aesthetic lens not only contracts the sensible but also refracts it.

As Bergson states in 'The Perception of Change', philosophy expands our attention outside the bounds of the immediate present such that we are able to comprehend the real in terms of general tendencies, and to think and live 'sub specie durationis'[216] – in which case, each unity should be understood as a moment or period within a particular tendency. Art is aligned with metaphysics insofar as it is derived from the same type of perception of the real, in which qualitative differences are foregrounded over quantitative distinctions, leading to the veil being raised on a durational ontology. However, Bergson also argues that art differs from metaphysics because this disclosure of difference is 'on the surface rather than in depth. It enriches our present, but it scarcely enables us to go beyond it.[217] This depth is ontological and relates to the different levels of contraction between philosophy and the arts. Philosophy discloses broad unifying tendencies – unified at the source but differentiated as they progress – that operate over a *longue durée* and include everything from scientific spatialization to intuition. Imagining the movement of matter and thought in terms of these tendencies is an intuitive contraction of difference that is central to Bergson's metaphysics. In referring to how art 'enriches our present', Bergson notes that it does not have the same depth as philosophy because contraction is largely limited to sensual qualities. Art contracts and unifies over shorter durations, from the contraction of the movement lines in a photograph to the transitions in sculpture, but nevertheless still has the capacity to reveal metaphysical depth. To return to the metaphor of the prism, the differences in colour are still unified but there is no requirement to disentangle the colours by tracing them back to a source. Instead, they are allowed to co-exist in a single present in such a way that they are both available to the perceiver. Art's capacity to stage this co-existence is one means by which it is linked to metaphysics.

Conclusion

Bergson's critique of utilitarian perception underpins both his aesthetic ideas and his claims about the relationship between art and metaphysics. Aesthetics is primarily concerned with sensual difference and the play of appearances but can also serve as an incipient metaphysics that orients the perceiver towards a particular ontology. The problem with utilitarian perception is that sensual variation cleaves to objects, in which case the object precedes any process of qualitative differentiation – an approach that is grounded in a metaphysics of solid bodies and the theory of recognition. Bergson approaches the aesthetics of appearances from a different perspective, arguing that the solid bodies are actually products of a particular way of engaging with the real through action. Pure perception isolates aspects of the perceptual field as sites of possible action, which are rendered stable in the form of objects in recognition. We perceive what we expect to perceive and this is determined by both the need and the affordances of the body. In critiquing utilitarian perception, Bergson prepares the ground for a processual aesthetics in which appearances are not contingent on objects. The role of art, in this context, is to disabuse the perceiver of a false metaphysics of solid bodies founded on utilitarian perception, as well as gesturing towards the reality of *durée*. Bergson does not provide any extended analyses of how art can achieve this besides referring to art's vitalism, the singular aesthetic vision of artists and the role of sympathy in communicating this vision.

In 'The Perception of Change', Bergson explicitly refers to the artists Corot and Turner in terms of art's relationship to a durational metaphysics. Corot has not been properly discussed in this book, but the interest could relate to his depiction of forest scenes in which individual leaves become little more than the play of light and colour. The reference to Turner is important because he was an artist who progressively experimented with atmospheric effects to such a degree that, in his later works, the boundaries of objects began to dissolve. Turner's brushstrokes, scratches, dabs, coruscations of colour, and application of the wet on wet technique suggest that the real is always in movement or characterized by the ephemerality of atmospheric events. This real is found in the presentness of the marks in addition to the presentness of the painting's subject. For Bergson, the singularity of artistic creativity operates in concert with the singularity of a processual real in which turbulence and lines of force are key features. In some respects, the real can only be represented through indicating qualitative variation over time, such as the variation in colour and tone in Cézanne's paintings that can be linked to the time he took to work on the paintings. The aesthetic vision is drawn from the real over a definite duration, and can only be relived by the spectator if this duration becomes a plastic property of the work.

Art defamiliarizes perception by suggesting that the spectator work backwards from the perception of fixed qualities to the movements that generated those qualities, and create perceptual events in which movement and stable qualities co-exist in a metastable state. In the idea of perceptual contraction, qualitative variation and difference are unified as fixed qualities, which explains how processual movements are transmuted into bodies moving in space, as well as providing a ground for a processual aesthetic. Perceptual contraction can operate on the level of an aesthetic and a metaphysic, for it describes the production of difference in a processual reality but also a particular way of depicting this processual real. The contraction can produce relatively stable qualities but still give some indication of the underlying processual movement, which is a feature of Rodin's sculpture or any artwork that seeks to represent the successive phases of movement in a single body. There is an oscillation between the sensual and the material that constantly undermines a representational, conceptual and substantive conception of the real. Art movements such as Futurist photodynamism extend Bergson's theory of *durée* by experimenting with levels of temporal contraction in the photographic apparatus and finding the living and vital within the immateriality of the gesture. Contraction is only briefly alluded to by Bergson in terms of aesthetics or the philosophy of art, but it provides a uniting principle for many of his other aesthetic distinctions. The mechanical movements of the comic could be seen as a contraction of the living, the notion of the continuous corporeal gesture could be regarded as an active synthesis of the ipseity of consciousness into habit, and the aesthetic vision a contraction of a series of perceptual states. In each case, the role of aesthetics is to disclose the moment when one state shifts to another, that is when the contraction in utilitarian perception yields a little to aesthetic attention.

NOTES

Introduction

1 Charlotte de Mille and John Mullarkey state that Bergson's philosophy of immanence, which is primarily concerned with aisthesis and the novelty of perception, cannot be easily adapted into the study of the arts and art history's investigation of the 'finished' or complete work. Instead, from a Bergsonian perspective, art can be approached through its immateriality and the processes of making and unmaking that extend before and beyond the work. Charlotte de Mille and John Mullarkey, 'Introduction: Art's Philosophy – Bergson and Immanence', in *Bergson and the Art of Immanence: Painting, Photography, Film*, ed. Charlotte de Mille and John Mullarkey (Edinburgh: Edinburgh University Press, 2013), 3, 8.

2 Henri Bergson, *Creative Evolution*, trans. Arthur Mitchell (New York: Random House, [1907] 1944), 295.

3 Henri Gouhier, introduction to *Oeuvres*, by Henri Bergson (Paris: Presses Universitaires de France, 1959), ix.

4 Vladimir Jankélévitch, *Henri Bergson* (Paris: Presses Universitaires de France, 1999), 2.

5 Gabriel Marcel, 'Bergsonism and Music', trans. C. K. Scott Moncrieff, in *Reflections on Art: A Source Book of Writings by Artists, Critics, and Philosophers*, ed. Susanne K. Langer (London, Oxford and New York: Oxford University Press, 1961), 142–3.

6 Vladimir Jankélévitch, 'With the Whole Soul', in *The Bergsonian Heritage*, ed. Thomas Hanna (New York and London: Columbia University Press, 1962), 156.

Chapter 1

1 Philippe Soulez and Frédéric Worms, *Bergson: Biographie* (Paris: Presses Universitaires de France, 2002), 64–5.

2 Sanford Schwartz, 'Bergson and the Politics of Vitalism', in *The Crisis in Modernism: Bergson and the Vitalist Controversy*, ed. Frederick Burwick and Paul Douglass (Cambridge: Cambridge University Press, 1992), 280.

3   Soulez and Worms, *Bergson*, 35.

4   Marcel Bataillon, 'A Tribute to Bergson on the Occasion of the Bergson Centennial in Paris, 1959', in *The Bergsonian Heritage*, ed. Thomas Hanna (New York and London: Columbia University Press, 1962), 114–16.

5   Schwartz, 'Bergson and the Politics of Vitalism', 288.

6   Enid Starkie, 'Bergson and Literature', in *The Bergsonian Heritage*, ed. Thomas Hanna (New York and London: Columbia University Press, 1962), 79.

7   Schwartz, 'Bergson and the Politics of Vitalism', 288.

8   Starkie, 'Bergson and Literature', 82.

9   R. C. Grogin, *The Bergsonian Controversy in France: 1900-1914* (Calgary: University of Calgary Press, 1988), 81.

10 Grogin, *Bergsonian Controversy*, 82.

11 Bertrand Russell, 'Philosophy in the Twentieth Century', in *Essays in Language, Mind and Matter*, ed. John G. Slater and Bernd Frohmann (London: Unwin Hyman, [1924] 1988), 458.

12 Schwartz, 'Bergson and the Politics of Vitalism', 289.

13 Henri Bergson, *Œuvres*, ed. André Robinet (Paris: Presses Universitaires de France, 1959), 1392 fn1.

14 Jacques Chevalier, *Bergson* (Paris: Librairie Plon, 1926), ix.

15 Henri Bergson, *The Creative Mind*, trans. M. L. Andison (New York: Philosophical Library, [1934] 1946), 225.

16 Jacques Chevalier, *Entretiens avec Bergson* (Paris: Librairie Plon, 1959), 28.

17 Giuseppe Bianco, 'Experience vs. Concept? The Role of Bergson in Twentieth-Century French Philosophy', *The European Legacy* 16, no. 7 (2011): 860.

18 Gilles Deleuze, *Bergsonism*, trans. Hugh Tomlinson and Barbara Habberjam (New York: Zone, 1991), 14.

19 Deleuze, *Bergsonism*, 14.

20 Bergson, *Creative Mind*, 126.

21 Gabriel Marcel, 'At the Sorbonne', *The Bergsonian Heritage*, ed. Thomas Hanna (New York and London: Columbia University Press, 1962), 125–6.

22 Marcel, 'Sorbonne', 125.

23 Henri Bergson, 'La Politesse', *Mélanges*, ed. André Robinet (Paris: Presses Universitaires de France, 1972), 330–1.

24 Chevalier, *Entretiens*, 63.

25 Bertrand Russell, *A History of Western Philosophy*, 2nd edn (London: Counterpoint, 1984), 764.

26 Russell, *History*, 763–4.

27 Bergson, *Mélanges*, 285. Author's translation.

28 William James, 'W. James à Bergson', 13 juin 1907, in Bergson, *Mélanges*, 724. My translation.

29 Bergson, *Mélanges*, 960.

30 Bergson, *Creative Mind*, 128.

31 John Mullarkey, '"For We Will Have Shown it Nothing": Bergson as Non-Philosopher (of) Art', in *Bergson and the Art of Immanence: Painting, Photography, Film*, ed. Charlotte de Mille and John Mullarkey (Edinburgh: Edinburgh University Press, 2013), 211–12.

32 Paul Valéry, *Henri Bergson: Allocution prononcée à la séance de l'académie du jeudi 9 janvier 1941* (Paris: Domat-Montchrestien, 1945), 4–6.

33 Valéry, *Bergson*, 7.

34 Valéry, *Bergson*, 7–8.

35 Vladimir Jankélévitch, *Music and the Ineffable*, trans. Carolyn Abbate (Princeton, NJ: Princeton University Press, [1961] 2003), 32.

36 Gilles Deleuze, 'Bergson 1859-1941', in *Les philosophes célèbres*, ed. Maurice Merleau-Ponty (Paris: Editions d'Art Lucien Mazenod, 1956), 292–3. My translation.

37 Deleuze, 'Bergson 1859-1941', 293.

38 Bergson, *Creative Evolution*, 132.

39 Algot Ruhe and Nancy Margaret Paul, *Henri Bergson: An Account of His Life and Philosophy* (London: Macmillan, 1914), 17.

40 Henri Bergson, *Duration and Simultaneity*, trans. Leon Jacobson, intro. Herbert Dingle (Indianapolis, IN: The Bobbs-Merrill, [1922] 1965), 44.

41 F. C. T. Moore, *Bergson: Thinking Backwards* (Cambridge: Cambridge University Press, 1996), 58–9.

42 Bergson, *Duration and Simultaneity*, 44–5.

43 Jankélévitch, *Bergson*, 27.

44 Deleuze, 'Bergson 1859-1941', 295.

45 Deleuze, 'Bergson 1859-1941', 295. My translation.

46 A. E. Pilkington, *Bergson and His Influence: A Reassessment* (Cambridge: Cambridge University Press, 1976), 14.

47 Pilkington, *Bergson and His Influence*, 14.

48 Henri Bergson, *Laughter: An Essay on the Meaning of the Comic*, trans. Cloudesley Brereton and Fred Rothwell (Kobenhavn and Los Angeles: Green Integer, 1911), 140.

49 'L'objet de la philosophie, telle que je l'entends, est simplement de nous permettre à tous de voir, et de voir de plus en plus profondément, comme un peintre paysagiste nous apprend à voir de mieux en mieux un paysage. C'est pourquoi, si nous arrivons à l'intuition, il ne peut être question de créer avec elle de nouveaux concepts, à moins que ces ne soient de ces 'concepts mobiles' destinés à guider les autres hommes à travers cette même intuition ou à les mettre sur la voie'. Henri Bergson, Letter to W. R. Boyce Gibson, 9 February 1911, Box 2, folio 41, Gibson Papers, University of Melbourne Archives. My translation.

50 Art and philosophy are inextricably linked, for metaphysics is a multiplicity of attitudes, rhythms and movements in which 'there are only directions, orientations, or vectors' and philosophy acquires the form of a 'general art' attending to the aisthesis of movements, rhythms and attitudes. Mullarkey, 'Bergson as Non-Philosopher', 224.

51 Georges Aimel, 'Une heure chez Henri Bergson', *Paris-Journal*, 11 December 1910, in Bergson, *Mélanges*, 843. My translation.

52 Aimel, 'Une heure', 844.

53 Aimel, 'Une heure', 844.

54 Aimel, 'Une heure', 844. My translation.

55 Henri Bergson, *Matter and Memory*, trans. W. S. Palmer and N. M. Paul (New York: Zone Books, [1908] 1991), 15.

56 Henri Bergson, *The Two Sources of Morality and Religion*, trans. R. Ashley Audra and Cloudesley Brereton (Westport, CT: Greenwood Press, [1932] 1963), 44–5.

57 Bergson, *Two Sources*, 46.

58 Bergson, *Laughter*, 150.

59 Bergson, *Laughter*, 150.

60 Shiv K. Kumar, *Bergson and the Stream of Consciousness Novel* (London and Glasgow: Blackie and Son Ltd., 1962), 20.

61 Kumar, *Bergson*, 31.

62 Ruth Lorand, *Aesthetic Order: A Philosophy of Order, Beauty and Art* (London: Routledge, 2000), 93.

63 T. E. Hulme, 'Bergson's Theory of Art', in *The Collected Writings of T. E. Hulme*, ed. Karen Csengeri (Oxford: Clarendon Press, [1922] 1994), 191–2.

64 Hulme, 'Bergson's Theory of Art', 192.

65 Arthur Szathmary, *The Aesthetic Theory of Bergson* (Cambridge, MA: Harvard University Press, 1937), 73–4.

66 Szathmary, *Aesthetic Theory*, 74.

67 Bergson, *Mélanges*, 1146–50.

68 Bergson, *Mélanges*, 1148.

69 Paul Atkinson, 'The Movement of Dissolution: Bergson and the Aesthetics of Durational Difference', in *Sensorium*, ed. Barbara Bolt et al. (Newcastle: Cambridge Scholars Press, 2007), 52–62.

70 Andrey Tarkovsky, *Sculpting in Time: Reflections on the Cinema*, trans. Kitty Hunter-Blair (London: Faber and Faber, 1989), 63.

71 Tarkovsky, *Sculpting*, 68.

72 Paul Atkinson, 'Turning Away: Embodied Movement in the Perception of Shot Duration', *Image [&] Narrative* 15, no. 1 (2014): 89–101.

73 Gilles Deleuze, *Cinema 1: The Movement Image*, trans. Hugh Tomlinson and Barbara Habberjam (Minneapolis, MN: University of Minnesota Press, 1986), 59.

74 Deleuze, *Cinema 1*, 60.

75 Deleuze, *Cinema 1*, 58.

76 Deleuze, *Cinema 1*, 66.

77 Mark Hansen, *New Philosophy for New Media* (Cambridge, MA, and London: MIT Press, 2004), 7. Although he argues for a return to Bergson, Hansen does not place the theory of images in the philosophical context of *Matter and Memory*, where it forms part of an investigation of pure perception and a critique of utilitarian perception. This will be discussed further in Chapter 4.

78 Hansen, *New Philosophy*, 7–8.

79 Hansen, *New Philosophy*, 8.

80 Hansen, *New Philosophy*, 210–11.

81 Hansen, *New Philosophy*, 11. Hansen does not make a clear distinction here between the artist's and viewer's role in creating images from information.

82 de Mille and Mullarkey, 'Introduction: Art's Philosophy', 3.

83 Samuel Dresden, 'Les Idées Esthétiques de Bergson', in *Les Études Bergsoniennes*, vol. 4 (Paris: Presses Universitaires de Paris, 1956), 67.

84 Dresden, 'Idées', 71–2.

85 Dresden, 'Idées', 67.

86 Dresden, 'Idées', 69.

87 Maurice Merleau-Ponty, *Phenomenology of Perception,* trans. Colin Smith (London: Routledge & Kegan Paul, 1962), 415 n.1.

88 Susanne K. Langer, *Feeling and Form* (London: Routledge & Kegan Paul, 1953), 114.

89 Langer, *Feeling*, 114.

90 Langer, *Feeling*, 113.

91 Langer, *Feeling*, 116.

92 Langer, *Feeling*, 113.

93 Langer, *Feeling*, 76.

94 Langer, *Feeling*, 76.

95 Langer, *Feeling*, 49–50.

96 Langer, *Feeling*, 76.

97 Étienne Souriau, *La Correspondance des arts: Éléments d'esthétique comparée* (Paris: Flammarian, 1969), 74.

98 Souriau, *Correspondance*, 75–6.

99 Langer, *Feeling*, 111.

100 Dresden, 'Idées', 56.

101 Jacques-Émile Blanche, *Portraits of a Lifetime: The Late Victorian Era, The Edwardian Pageant, 1870-1914*, trans. Walter Clement (London: J. M. Dent & Sons, 1937), 245.

102 Langer, *Feeling*, 114–15.

103 Paul Crowther, *The Language of Twentieth-Century Art: A Conceptual History* (New Haven and London: Yale University Press, 1997), 56.

104 Crowther, *Language*, 57.

105 Giovanni Lista, *Futurism and Photography* (London: Merrell Publishers, 2001), 22.

106 Ardengo Soffici, 'The Subject in Futurist Painting', trans. Robert Brain, in *Futurist Manifestos*, ed. Umbro Apollonio (London: Thames and Hudson, [1914] 1973), 134–5.

107 Henri Bergson, 'Life and Matter at War', *Hibbert Journal* 13, no. 3 (1914): 466.

108 Mark Antliff, 'The Fourth Dimension and Futurism: A Politicized Space', *Art Bulletin* 82, no. 4 (2000): 727.

109 Antliff, 'Fourth Dimension', 728.

110 Mark Antliff, *Inventing Bergson: Cultural Politics and the Parisian Avant-Garde* (Princeton, NJ: Princeton University Press, 1993), 53.

111 Bergson, *Creative Mind*, 189.

112 Gino Severini, 'The Plastic Analogies of Dynamism – Futurist Manifesto', trans. J. C. Higgitt, in *Futurist Manifestos*, ed. Umbro Apollonio (London: Thames and Hudson, [1913] 1973), 121.

113 Brian Petrie, 'Boccioni and Bergson', *The Burlington Magazine* 116, no. 852 (1974): 142.

114 Petrie, 'Boccioni', 142–3.

115 Crowther, *Language*, 65.

116 Umberto Boccioni, 'The Plastic Foundations of Futurist Sculpture and Painting', trans. Robert Brain, in *Futurist Manifestos*, ed. Umbro Apollonio (London: Thames and Hudson, [1913] 1973), 89.

117 Boccioni, 'Plastic', 89.

118 Boccioni, 'Plastic', 89.

119 Crowther, *Language*, 67.

120 Umberto Boccioni, 'Absolute Motion + Relative Motion = Dynamism', trans. Robert Brain, in *Futurist Manifestos*, ed. Umbro Apollonio (London: Thames and Hudson, [1913] 1973), 152.

121 Stephen Kern, *The Culture of Time and Space 1880-1918* (Cambridge, MA: Harvard University Press, 2003), 122.

122 Paul Atkinson, 'Dynamic Sensation: Bergson, Futurism and the Exteriorisation of Time in the Plastic Arts', in *Art and Time*, ed. Jan Lloyd-Jones, Paul Campbell and Peter Wylie (n.p: Australian Scholarly Publishing, 2007), 72.

123 Antliff, *Inventing*, 39.

124 Antliff, *Inventing*, 3.

125 It is noteworthy that Jean Metzinger painted some works in the Impressionist style with broad taches of colour, in particular his *Coucher de soleil no. 1 (Landscape)* (1906). John Gage argues that Metzinger, unlike the Impressionists, did not seek to resolve the colours in the impression of light in these works and, instead, retained the vibrancy of the original colours in the broad brushstrokes. John Gage, *Colour and Meaning: Art, Science and Symbolism* (London: Thames and Hudson, 1999), 254.

126 Antliff, *Inventing*, 13.

127 Mark Antliff, 'Bergson and Cubism: A Reassessment', *Art Journal* 47, no. 4 (Winter 1988): 343.

128 Antliff, *Inventing*, 43.

129 Albert Gleizes and Jean Metzinger, *Du 'cubisme'* (Sisteron: Editions Présence, 1980), 49. My translation.

130 Gleizes and Metzinger, *Du 'cubisme'*, 44.

131 Antliff, 'Cubism', 343.

132 Antliff, 'Cubism', 342.

133 Gleizes and Metzinger, *Du 'cubisme'*, 52.

134 Timothy Mitchell, 'Bergson, Le Bon, and Hermetic Cubism', *Journal of Aesthetics and Art Criticism* 34 (Winter 1977): 181.

135 Mitchell, 'Bergson', 180.

136 Mitchell, 'Bergson', 181.

137 Norman Bryson, *Looking at the Overlooked: Four Essays on Still Life Painting* (London: Reaktion Books, 1990), 84–5.

138 Paul Edwards, 'Wyndham Lewis's Vorticism: A Strange Synthesis', in *The Vorticists: Manifesto for a Modern World*, ed. Mark Antliff and Vivien Greene (London: Tate Publishing, 2010), 39.

139 Mary Ann Gillies, *Henri Bergson and British Modernism* (Montreal: McGill-Queen's University Press, 1996), 50.

140 Charlotte de Mille states that Lewis's antipathy to Bergson was mainly driven by a fear of appearing to be influenced by the philosopher and a resentment of his popularity. To escape this appearance of influence, Lewis often inverted Bergson's ideas, including the theory of the comic and the relationship between human and vegetative states in *Creative Evolution*. Charlotte de Mille, '"Blast ... Bergson?" Wyndham Lewis's "Guilty Fire of Friction"', in *Understanding Bergson, Understanding Modernism*, ed. Paul Ardoin, S. E. Gontarski and Laci Mattison (New York and London: Bloomsbury, 2013), 141–3.

141 Gillies, *Bergson*, 51.

142 Wyndham Lewis, 'Our Vortex', in *Blast No. 1: Review of the Great English Vortex*, ed. Wyndham Lewis (London: J. Lane, 1914), 147–9.

143 Sigmund Freud, 'Negation', in *On Metapsychology*, vol. 11, Pelican Freud Library, ed. Angela Richards and Albert Dickson (London: Penguin, 1991), 437–42.

144 Philip Rylands, 'Introduction', in *The Vorticists: Manifesto for a Modern World*, ed. Mark Antliff and Vivien Greene (London: Tate Publishing, 2010), 24.

145 Geoffrey Wagner, 'Wyndham Lewis and the Vorticist Aesthetic', *The Journal of Aesthetics and Art Criticism* 13, no. 1 (September 1954): 11.

146 Wagner, 'Wyndham Lewis', 1.

147 Wagner, 'Wyndham Lewis', 1–2.

148 Wyndham Lewis, 'Futurism, Magic and Life', in *Blast No. 1: Review of the Great English Vortex*, ed. Wyndham Lewis (London: J. Lane, 1914), 132.

149 Gleizes and Metzinger, *Du "cubisme"*, 40.

150 Hilary L. Fink, *Bergson and Russian Modernism, 1900-1930* (Evanston, IL: Northwestern University Press, 1999), 26.

151 Fink, *Bergson*, 113.

152 Fink, *Bergson*, 42.

153 Fink, *Bergson*, 43.

154 Fink, *Bergson*, 85.

155 Fink, *Bergson*, 82.

156 Wassily Kandinsky, *Concerning the Spiritual in Art*, trans. M. T. H. Sadler (New York: Dover Publications, 1977), 11–12.

157 Isabel Wünsche, 'Life into Art: Natural Philosophy, the Life Sciences, and Abstract Art', in *Meanings of Abstract Art: Between Nature and Theory*, ed. Paul Crowther and Isabel Wünsche (New York and London: Routledge, 2012), 14.

Chapter 2

1 Grogin, *Bergsonian Controversy*, 114–15.

2 Hippolyte Taine, *Philosophie de l'art* (Paris: Fayard, 1985), 16–17.

3 Schwartz, 'Bergson and the Politics of Vitalism', 281.

4 Bergson, *Mélanges*, 1170–1.

5 Bergson, *Mélanges*, 1171.

6 Bergson, *Mélanges*, 1171. My translation.

7 Pierre Maine de Biran, *De l'aperception immédiate: mémoire de Berlin, 1807*, ed. Anne Devarieux (Paris: Librairie générale française, 2005), 62.

8 Biran, 'l'aperception', 84–5.

9 Henri Bergson, *Time and Free Will: An Essay on the Immediate Data of Consciousness*, trans. F. L. Pogson (London: George Allen and Unwin, [1889] 1910), 10–11.

10 Bergson, *Time and Free Will*, 3–4.

11   Bergson, *Time and Free Will*, 4–5.

12   Bergson, *Time and Free Will*, 4.

13   Bergson, *Time and Free Will*, 4.

14   Bergson, *Time and Free Will*, 7.

15   Bergson, *Time and Free Will*, 8.

16   Bergson, *Time and Free Will*, 11–12.

17   Bergson, *Time and Free Will*, 8.

18   James, 'W. James à Bergson', 725.

19   Bergson, *Mélanges*, 727.

20   Bergson, *Time and Free Will*, 22 fn. 1.

21   William James, *The Principles of Psychology*, vol. 2 (New York: Dover Publications, [1890] 1950), 448–9.

22   James, *Principles of Psychology*, 449. Capitalization and italics are in the original.

23   James, *Principles of Psychology*, 450.

24   Bergson, *Time and Free Will*, 29.

25   Bergson, *Time and Free Will*, 30.

26   Bergson, *Matter and Memory*, 194.

27   Jonathon Crary, *Techniques of the Observer: On Vision and Modernity in the Nineteenth Century* (Cambridge, MA: MIT Press, 1990), 72.

28   Crary, *Techniques*, 72.

29   Henri Bergson, *Mind-Energy: Lectures and Essays*, trans. H. Wildon Carr (London: Macmillan, [1919] 1920), 173.

30   Bergson, *Mind-Energy*, 177–8.

31   Bergson, *Time and Free Will*, 21.

32   Bergson, *Time and Free Will*, 23–4.

33   Bergson, *Time and Free Will*, 24–5.

34   Bergson, *Time and Free Will*, 26.

35   Soulez and Worms, *Bergson*, 58.

36   Bergson, *Creative Mind*, 109.

37   Herbert Spencer, *Literary Style and Music: Including Two Short Essays on Gracefulness and Beauty* (London: Watts, 1950), 46.

38   Spencer, *Literary Style*, 46.

39 Spencer, *Literary Style*, 47.

40 Spencer, *Literary Style*, 48.

41 Bergson, *Time and Free Will*, 48.

42 Spencer, *Literary Style*, 49–50.

43 Spencer, *Literary Style*, 52.

44 Bergson, *Time and Free Will*, 28.

45 Bergson, *Time and Free Will*, 44–5.

46 Bergson, *Time and Free Will*, 45.

47 Jankélévitch, *Music*, 90–1.

48 Jankélévitch, *Music*, 90.

49 Mark Johnson, *The Meaning of the Body: Aesthetics of Human Understanding* (Chicago and London: University of Chicago Press, 2007), 239.

50 Johnson, *Meaning*, 249.

51 Johnson, *Meaning*, 254.

52 Bergson, *Time and Free Will*, 31.

53 Francis Sparshott, foreword to *The Aesthetics of Movement*, by Paul Souriau, trans. and ed. Manon Souriau (Amherst, MA: The University of Massachusetts Press, 1983), viii.

54 Sparshott, foreword, ix.

55 Sparshott, foreword, vii.

56 Spencer, *Literary Style*, 107.

57 Spencer, *Literary Style*, 112.

58 Spencer, *Literary Style*, 108.

59 Spencer, *Literary Style*, 110.

60 Spencer, *Literary Style*, 111.

61 Spencer, *Literary Style*, 109.

62 Paul Souriau, *The Aesthetics of Movement*, trans. and ed. Manon Souriau (Amherst, MA: The University of Massachusetts Press, 1983), 9–10.

63 Bergson, *Time and Free Will*, 13.

64 Bergson, *Time and Free Will*, 12.

65 Bergson, *Time and Free Will*, 12.

66 A. T. Poffenberger and B. E. Barrows, 'The Feeling Value of Lines', *Journal of Applied Psychology* 8, no. 2 (1924): 189.

67 Bergson, *Time and Free Will*, 12.

68 Bergson, *Time and Free Will*, 12–13.

69 Spencer, *Literary Style*, 112–13.

70 Susan Leigh Foster, *Choreographing Empathy* (London and New York: Routledge, 2011), 127–8.

71 Foster, *Choreographing*, 155.

72 Foster, *Choreographing*, 156–7.

73 Bergson, *Time and Free Will*, 14.

74 Bergson, *Time and Free Will*, 14–15.

75 Bergson, *Two Sources*, 40.

76 Bergson, *Two Sources*, 40.

77 Bergson, *Two Sources*, 41–2.

78 Susanne K. Langer, *Problems of Art: Ten Philosophical Lectures* (New York: Charles Scribner's Sons, 1957), 5.

79 Langer, *Problems*, 6.

80 Langer, *Problems*, 10.

81 Langer, *Problems*, 7.

82 Langer, *Problems*, 8.

83 Brian Massumi, *Semblance and Event: Activist Philosophy and the Occurrent Arts* (Cambridge, MA: The MIT Press, 2011), 24.

84 Massumi, *Semblance*, 17–18.

85 Massumi, *Semblance*, 6.

86 Victor Zuckerkandl, *Sound and Symbol: Music and the External World*, trans. Willard R. Trask (Princeton, NJ: Princeton University Press, 1969), 245–6.

87 Zuckerkandl, *Sound*, 60.

88 Zuckerkandl, *Sound*, 67.

89 Zuckerkandl, *Sound*, 68.

90 Zuckerkandl, *Sound*, 68–9.

91 Zuckerkandl, *Sound*, 61.

92 Bergson, *Time and Free Will*, 16.

93 Bergson, *Time and Free Will*, 15.

94 Bergson, *Time and Free Will*, 16–17.

95 Bergson, *Mélanges*, 1250. My translation.

96 Sarah Posman argues that Bergson's approach to language is an extension of the classical rhetorical notion of energeia that emphasizes the rhythm and energy of speech, and which later informed Romanticism's valorization of the figurative and affective aspects of poetic language (217). Sarah Posman, 'Modernist Energeia: Henri Bergson and the Romantic Idea of Language', in *Understanding Bergson, Understanding Modernism*, ed. Paul Ardoin, S. E. Gontarski and Laci Mattison (New York and London: Bloomsbury, 2013), 213–27.

97 Bergson, *Mélanges*, 322.

98 Bergson, *Mélanges*, 323.

99 Bergson, *Mélanges*, 323. My translation: 'sympathie pour la légèreté de l'artiste, l'idée que nous nous dépouillons nous-mêmes de notre pesanteur et de notre matérialité. Enveloppés dans le rythme de sa danse, nous adoptons la subtilité de son mouvement sans prendre notre part de son effort, et nous retrouvons ainsi l'exquise sensation de ces rêves où notre corps nous semble avoir abandonné son poids, l'étendue sa résistance, et la forme sa matière'.

100 Bergson, *Time and Free Will*, 13.

101 Bergson, *Time and Free Will*, 17.

102 Bergson, *Time and Free Will*, 17.

103 Bergson, *Time and Free Will*, 18.

104 Bergson, *Time and Free Will*, 18.

105 Bergson, *Mind-Energy*, 173–4.

106 Bergson, *Mind-Energy*, 175.

107 Mark Antliff, 'The Rhythms of Duration: Bergson and the Art of Matisse', in *The New Bergson*, ed. John Mullarkey (Manchester: Manchester University Press, 1999), 185.

108 Alastair Wright, *Matisse and the Subject of Modernism* (Princeton, NJ and Oxford: Princeton University Press, 2004), 137.

109 Wright, *Matisse*, 157.

110 Wright, *Matisse*, 155–6.

111 Wright, *Matisse*, 159.

112 Albert Kostenevich, '*La Danse* and *La Musique* by Henri Matisse: A New Interpretation', *Apollo*, 100 (1974): 511.

113 This type of transversal movement is common in caricature and comics, where the figure is clearly differentiated from the background. See Paul Atkinson, 'Between Movement and Reading: Reconceptualizing the

Dynamic Picture Plane in Modernist Comics and Painting', *ImageTexT* 9, no. 3 (2018): n.pag.

114 Hal Foster, Rosalind Krauss, Yve-Alain Bois and Benjamin H. D. Buchloh, *Art Since 1900* (New York: Thames & Hudson, 2004), 101.

115 Foster et al., *Art*, 101.

116 Foster et al., *Art*, 102.

117 Eric Alliez, 'Matisse, Bergson, Oiticica, etc', in *Bergson and the Art of Immanence: Painting, Photography, Film*, ed. Charlotte de Mille and John Mullarkey (Edinburgh: Edinburgh University Press, 2013), 67. Matisse still operates within the general Fauvist project and the recognition that colour has a vital energy which undermines form through becoming. This is evident in his *Interior with Aubergines* (1911), where the interconnection between patterns and planes disrupts the division between inside and outside, creates an unresolvable tension, and centrifugally disrupts the function of the image as a window onto an architectural scene. Alliez, 'Matisse', 66-68. Similarly, Antliff states that, in this work, the frames do not enclose or present objects to the gaze; instead, the decorative elements segue into each other to blur the distinction between picture and frame. Antliff, 'Rhythms', 195. In each of these accounts, the plenitude of space operates as a multiplicity of immanent forces that are always in a state of tension.

118 Alliez, 'Matisse', 69.

119 Antliff, 'Rhythms', 189.

120 Matisse discussed these aspects of his method in an interview with Estienne. Henri Matisse, *Écrits et propos sur l'art*, ed. Dominique Fourcade (Paris: Hermann, 2009), 60.

121 Matisse, *Écrits*, 62.

122 Georges Mourélos, *Bergson et Les Niveaux de Réalité* (Paris: Presses Universitaires de France, 1964), 61.

123 Félix Ravaisson, *De l'habitude Métaphysique et morale*, intro. Jacques Billard (Paris: Presses Universitaires de France, 1999), 151.

124 John Dewey, *The Early Works, 1882-1898: Vol. 2: 1887 Psychology*, ed. Ann Boydston (Carbondale and Edwardsville, IL: Southern Illinois University Press, 1967), 220.

125 Dewey, *Psychology*, 220.

126 Dewey, *Psychology*, 225.

127 Mikel Dufrenne, *The Phenomenology of Aesthetic Experience*, trans. Edward S. Casey et al. (Evanston, IL: Northwestern University Press, [1953] 1973), 262.

128 Dufrenne, *Phenomenology*, 263.

129 Dufrenne, *Phenomenology*, 263.

130 Dufrenne, *Phenomenology*, 264.

131 Dufrenne, *Phenomenology* 71.

132 Jankélévitch, *Music*, 63.

133 Jankélévitch, *Music*, 68.

134 Jankélévitch, *Music*, 70.

135 Jankélévitch, *Music*, 70

136 Jankélévitch, *Music*, 69.

137 Jankélévitch, *Bergson*, 41.

138 Jankélévitch, *Bergson*, 42.

139 Bergson, *Laughter*, 140–1.

140 Langer, *Feeling*, 184.

141 Langer, *Feeling*, 184.

142 Langer, *Feeling*, 185.

143 Bergson, *Creative Mind*, 272–3.

144 Bergson, *Creative Mind*, 273.

145 Félix Ravaisson, *L'Enseignement du Dessin dans les Lycées* (Paris: Ministère de l'instruction publique et des cultes, 1854), 5–6.

146 Ravaisson, *Dessin*, 13–14.

147 Bergson, *Laughter*, 141.

148 Jean-François Lyotard, 'The Pictorial Event Today', in *Miscellaneous Texts 1: Aesthetics and Theory of Art*, trans. Vlad Ionescu (Leuven: Leuven University Press, 2012), 235.

149 Lyotard, 'Pictorial', 231.

150 Lyotard, 'Pictorial', 237.

151 Lyotard, 'Pictorial', 229.

152 Frederick Copleston, *A History of Philosophy: Greece and Rome*, vol. 1, part 1 (Garden City, KS: Image, 1962), 74.

153 Copleston, *History*, 74.

154 Bergson, *Creative Evolution*, 337.

155 Bergson, *Creative Evolution*, 337–8.

156 Paul Valéry, 'Seeing and Drawing', in *Degas Manet Morisot*, trans. David Paul (New York: Pantheon Books, 1960), 36.

157 Valéry, 'Seeing and Drawing', 36.

158 Valéry, 'Seeing and Drawing', 37.

159 David Freedberg and Vittorio Gallese, 'Motion, Emotion and Empathy in Esthetic Experience', *Trends in Cognitive Sciences* 11, no. 5 (2007): 197.

160 Freedberg and Gallese, 'Motion', 197.

161 Freedberg and Gallese, 'Motion', 198.

162 Paul Atkinson, 'Invisible Rhythms: Tracking Aesthetic Perception in Film and the Visual Arts', in *Seeing into Screens: Eye Tracking the Moving Image*, ed. Tessa Dwyer, Claire Perkins, Sean Redmond and Jodi Sita (London: Bloomsbury, 2018), 42.

163 Drew Leder, *The Absent Body* (Chicago: University of Chicago Press, 1990), 14.

164 Leder, *Absent*, 14.

165 Bergson, *Duration and Simultaneity*, 50.

166 Jean-Marie Guyau, 'La genèse de l'idée de temps', in *Guyau and the Idea of Time*, ed. John A. Michon et al. (Amsterdam: North-Holland Publishing Company, 1988), 55.

167 Guyau, *Idea of Time*, 56.

168 Maxine Sheets-Johnstone, *The Primacy of Movement*, 2nd edn (Amsterdam and Philadelphia, PA: John Benjamins, 2011), 120.

169 Sheets-Johnstone, *Movement*, 117.

170 Sheets-Johnstone, *Movement*, 131.

171 Sheets-Johnstone, *Movement*, 131.

172 Sheets-Johnstone, *Movement*, 132.

173 Sheets-Johnstone, *Movement*, 122.

174 Sheets-Johnstone, *Movement*, 123.

175 Sheets-Johnstone, *Movement*, 123–4.

176 Sheets-Johnstone, *Movement*, 124.

177 Louis Horst and Carroll Russell, *Modern Dance Forms in Relation to the Other Modern Arts* (San Francisco, CA: Impulse, 1961), 17.

178 Horst and Russell, *Modern Dance*, 18.

179 Massumi, *Semblance*, 140.

180 Massumi, *Semblance,* 138.

181 Massumi, *Semblance*, 141.

182 Mark Antliff, 'Shaping Duration: Bergson and Modern Sculpture', *The European Legacy* 16, no. 7 (2011): 916 fn. 1.

183 Antliff, 'Shaping', 909–10.

184 Rudolf Arnheim, *Art and Visual Perception: A Psychology of the Creative Eye* (London: Faber and Faber, 1954), 406.

185 Arnheim, *Art*, 407.

186 Antliff, 'Shaping', 908.

187 Antliff, 'Shaping', 913–14.

188 Stanley W. Hayter, 'Orientation, Direction, Cheirality, Velocity and Rhythm', in *The Nature of Art and Motion*, ed. Gyorgy Kepes (New York: George Brazillier, 1965), 74.

189 Hayter, 'Orientation', 74.

190 Nicholas Cullinan and Nicholas Serota, '"Ecstatic impulses": Cy Twombly's "Untitled (Bacchus)", 2006–08', *The Burlington Magazine* 152, no. 1290 (September 2010): 613.

191 Cullinan and Serota, '"Ecstatic impulses"', 613.

192 Starkie, 'Bergson and Literature', 82.

193 Henri Focillon, *The Life of Forms in Art*, trans. Charles B. Hogan and George Kubler (New York: Zone Books, [1934] 1992), 141.

194 Focillon, *Life*, 85.

195 Focillon, *Life*, 96.

196 Focillon, *Life*, 109.

197 Focillon, *Life*, 97.

198 Focillon, *Life*, 110.

199 Focillon, *Life*, 173–4.

200 Focillon, *Life*, 122–3.

201 Focillon, *Life*, 162–3.

202 Focillon, *Life*, 167.

203 Bergson, *Creative Mind*, 101.

204 Bergson, *Creative Mind*, 100. Touch also describes an orientation towards the future that is thoroughly grounded in a material present, and as such aligns with a pragmatic notion of orientation in which paths are constantly being formed within a processual real. Paul Atkinson, 'The Inclination of Philosophy: *The Creative Mind* and the Articulation of a Bergsonian Method', in *Understanding Bergson, Understanding Modernism*, ed. Paul Ardoin, S. E. Gontarski and Laci Mattison (New York and London: Bloomsbury, 2013), 89–104.

205 Bergson, *Creative Mind*, 102.

206 Bergson, *Creative Mind*, 102.

Chapter 3

1   Bergson, *Matter and Memory*, 184–5.

2   Bergson, *Matter and Memory*, 186.

3   Bergson, *Creative Evolution*, 11.

4   Bergson, *Creative Evolution*, 12–13.

5   Bergson, *Creative Evolution*, 13.

6   Bergson, *Creative Evolution*, 14.

7   Michael Polanyi, 'Life's Irreducible Structure', in *Topics in the Philosophy of Biology*, ed. Marjorie Grene and Everett Mendelsohn (Dordrecht: Reidel, 1976), 129.

8   Polanyi, 'Life's Irreducible Structure', 130.

9   Polanyi, 'Life's Irreducible Structure', 136–8.

10 William James, 'The Sense of Time', in *Psychology, Briefer Course* (Cambridge, MA: Harvard University Press, 1984), 246.

11 James, 'The Sense of Time', 246.

12 Edmund Husserl, *On the Phenomenology of the Consciousness of Internal Time (1893-1917)*, trans. John Barnett Brough, ed. Rudolf Bernet (Dordrecht: Kluwer Academic Publishers, 1991), 37.

13 Husserl, *Phenomenology*, 37.

14 Husserl, *Phenomenology*, 38.

15 David Carr, *Time, Narrative, and History* (Bloomington, IN: Indiana University Press, 1986), 41.

16 Keith Ansell-Pearson, *Bergson: Thinking Beyond the Human Condition* (London and New York: Bloomsbury 2018), 155–6.

17 Bergson, *Matter and Memory*, 153.

18 Bergson, *Mind-Energy*, 56.

19 Bergson, *Mind-Energy*, 56.

20 Bergson, *Mind-Energy*, 30.

21 Bergson, *Time and Free Will*, 165.

22 Leszek Kolakowski, *Bergson* (Oxford: Oxford University Press, 1985), 6.

23 Bergson, *Time and Free Will*, 174.

24 Bergson, *Time and Free Will*, 175.

25 Bergson, *Time and Free Will*, 72.

26 Bergson, *Time and Free Will*, 176.

27 Bergson, *Time and Free Will*, 167.

28 Bergson, *Time and Free Will*, 172.

29 Bergson, *Creative Evolution*, 9.

30 Bergson, *Creative Evolution*, 9.

31 Bergson, *Creative Evolution*, 9.

32 Bergson, *Creative Evolution*, 100–1.

33 Bergson, *Creative Evolution*, 102.

34 Bergson, *Creative Mind*, 187.

35 Bergson, *Creative Mind*, 190.

36 Bergson, *Creative Mind*, 188.

37 Martin Heidegger, 'The Question Concerning Technology', trans. William Lovitt, in *Basic Writings: From Being and Time (1927) to The Task of Thinking (1964)*, ed. David Farrell Krell, 2nd edn (New York: HarperCollins, 1993), 326.

38 Bergson, *Creative Evolution*, 194.

39 Bergson, *Creative Evolution*, 172.

40 Bergson, *Creative Evolution*, 172.

41 Bergson, *Creative Evolution*, 194.

42 Bergson, *Creative Evolution*, 194–5.

43 Maurice Merleau-Ponty, *In Praise of Philosophy*, trans. John Wild and James M. Edie (Evanston, IL: Northwestern University Press, 1963), 15.

44 Friedrich Wilhelm Joseph Schelling, *Ideas on the Philosophy of Nature as an Introduction to the Study of This Science*, trans. Errol E. Harris and Peter Heath, 2nd edn (Cambridge: Cambridge University Press, [1803] 1988), 12.

45 Schelling, *Philosophy of Nature*, 11.

46 Souriau, *Correspondance*, 59.

47 Souriau, *Correspondance*, 61.

48 C. H. Waddington, *The Nature of Life* (London: George Allen & Unwin, 1961), 27.

49 Bergson, *Creative Evolution*, 330.

50 Bergson, *Creative Evolution*, 330.

51 Olivier Messiaen, *Traité de Rythme, de Couleur, et d'Ornithologie: (1949-1992)*, Tome 1 (Paris: Alphonse Leduc, 1994), 55–8.

52 Messiaen, *Traité*, 55.

53 Bergson, *Creative Mind*, 122.

54 Bergson, *Creative Mind*, 121.

55 Dresden, 'Idées', 65.

56 Bergson, *Creative Mind*, 110.

57 Bergson, *Creative Mind*, 110–11.

58 Deleuze, *Bergsonism*, 92.

59 Deleuze, *Bergsonism*, 93.

60 Deleuze, *Bergsonism*, 95.

61 Deleuze, *Bergsonism*, 96.

62 Bergson, *Mind-Energy*, 45.

63 Bergson, *Mind-Energy*, 46.

64 Norman Bryson, *Vision and Painting: The Logic of the Gaze* (Houndmills and London: Palgrave, 1983), 7.

65 Bryson, *Vision*, 11.

66 Bryson, *Vision*, 92.

67 Bryson, *Vision*, 94.

68 Bryson, *Vision*, 92.

69 Bryson, *Vision*, 120.

70 Bryson, *Vision*, 122.

71 Bergson, *Creative Evolution*, 100.

72 Micheline Sauvage, 'Notes on the Superposition of Temporal Modes in the Works of Art', in *Reflections on Art: A Source Book of Writings by Artists, Critics, and Philosophers*, ed. Susanne K. Langer (London, Oxford and New York: Oxford University Press. 1961), 161–3.

73 Barnett Newman, *Selected Writings and Interviews*, ed. John P. O'Neill (New York: Alfred A. Knopf, 1990), 257.

74 Newman, *Selected*, 257.

75 Newman, *Selected*, 173.

76 Newman, *Selected*, 253.

77 Foster et al., *Art*, 365.

78 Newman, *Selected*, 256.

79 Harold Rosenberg, *Barnett Newman* (New York: Harry N. Abrahams, 1978), 32.

80 Jean-François Lyotard, *The Inhuman: Reflections on Time*, trans. Geoffrey Bennington and Rachel Bowlby (Stanford, CA: Stanford University Press, 1991), 78–9.

81 Lyotard, *Inhuman*, 79.

82 Lyotard, *Inhuman*, 82.

83 Lyotard, *Inhuman*, 88.

84 Newman, *Selected*, 190.

85 Newman, *Selected*, 253.

86 The relationship between the various layers of a painting over the long period of its production can be discussed in terms of the layering of memory in Bergson's famous cone diagram, for the productive past is always preserved somewhere with the material constitution of the work. Memory is both the reconstitution of the present in terms of action and the preservation of a past within its own present. Sarah Wilson, in an examination of *informel* painting, argues that Jean Fautrier's works exemplify some of these Bergsonian themes, for the material layering constitutes a form of memory that is material and geological while remaining strongly inflected with the artist's emotional engagement with the work. Sarah Wilson, 'Bergson before Deleuze: How to Read Informel Painting', in *Bergson and the Art of Immanence: Painting, Photography, Film*, ed. Charlotte de Mille and John Mullarkey (Edinburgh: Edinburgh University Press, 2013), 86.

87 Edward S. Casey, *The World at a Glance* (Bloomington and Indianapolis, IN: Indiana University Press, 2007), 289.

88 Casey, *Glance,* 290.

89 Casey, *Glance*, 291.

90 Casey, *Glance*, 293.

91 Casey, *Glance*, 297.

92 Newman, *Selected*, 189.

93 Newman, *Selected*, 189.

94 Ibid Newman, *Selected*, 90.

95 Newman, *Selected*, 255.

96 Newman, *Selected*, 282.

97 Deleuze, *Bergsonism*, 1.

98 Bergson, *Creative Evolution*, 8.

99 Bergson, *Creative Evolution*, 8.

100 Bergson, *Mind-Energy*, 13.

101 Bergson, *Mind-Energy*, 6.

102 Bergson, *Mind-Energy*, 13.

103 Henri Bergson, *Correspondances*, ed. André Robinet (Paris: Presses Universitaires de France, 2002), 910. My translation.

104 Bergson, *Time and Free Will*, 161.

105 Georges Canguilhem, 'Knowledge and the Living', in *A Vital Rationalist: Selected Writings*, ed. François Delaporte, trans. Arthur Goldhammer (New York: Zone, 1994), 287–8.

106 Herbert Read, *Icon and Idea: The Function of Art in the Development of Human Consciousness* (London: Faber and Faber, 1955), 19.

107 Read, *Icon*, 32.

108 Read, *Icon*, 21–2.

109 Read, *Icon*, 25.

110 Bergson, *Laughter*, 9.

111 Bergson, *Laughter*, 10–11.

112 Jankélévitch, *Bergson*, 78.

113 John Mullarkey makes an interesting observation about the similarity between comedy and horror, arguing that both concern the subjection of the living to the non-living. However, the comic always retains some aspects of the living, for a subject only momentarily and willingly adopts mechanical attitudes, whereas horror describes the forced infliction of the mechanical on the living. Horror can reflexively lead to humour when the viewer laughs at their own automatic (intellectually unmediated) responses to the genre. John Mullarkey, 'Bergson and the Comedy of Horrors', in *Understanding Bergson, Understanding Modernism*, ed. Paul Ardoin, S. E. Gontarski and Laci Mattison (New York and London: Bloomsbury, 2013), 248–50.

114 Bergson, *Laughter*, 19.

115 Bergson, *Laughter*, 19.

116 Bergson, *Laughter*, 14–15.

117 Bergson, *Laughter*, 20.

118 Bergson, *Two Sources*, 25–6.

119 Bergson, *Laughter*, 23.

120 Bergson, *Laughter*, 23.

121 Bergson, *Laughter*, 24.

122 Bergson, *Laughter*, 22.

123 Bergson, *Laughter*, 22.

124 Friedrich Nietzsche, *Daybreak: Thoughts on the Prejudices of Morality*, ed. Maudemarie Clark and Brian Leiter, trans. R. J. Hollingdale (Cambridge: Cambridge University Press, 1997), 23.

125 Georges Canguilhem, *The Normal and the Pathological*, trans. Carolyn R. Fawcett and Robert S. Cohen (New York: Zone Books, 1989), 241–2.

126 Grogin, *Bergsonian Controversy*, 75.

127 Bergson, *Creative Evolution*, 249.

128 Bergson, *Creative Evolution*, 247.

129 John Dewey, *Art as Experience* (New York: Perigee, [1934] 2005), 155.

130 Dewey, *Experience*, 155–6.

131 Bergson, *Creative Evolution*, 244.

132 Bergson, *Creative Evolution*, 245.

133 Laura Mulvey, *Death 24x a Second: Stillness and the Moving Image* (London: Reaktion Books, 2006), 177.

134 Mulvey, *Death*, 178.

135 Bergson, *Laughter*, 31.

136 Bergson, *Laughter*, 30–1.

137 Bergson, *Laughter*, 49.

138 Bergson, *Laughter*, 49.

139 Bergson, *Laughter*, 56.

140 Rosalind Krauss, *The Optical Unconscious* (Cambridge, MA: MIT Press, 1993), 205.

141 Souriau, *Aesthetics*, 36.

142 Souriau, *Aesthetics*, 37.

143 Souriau, *Aesthetics*, 37.

144 Bergson, *Laughter*, 46.

145 Bergson, *Laughter*, 127.

146 Bergson, *Laughter*, 128.

147 Bergson, *Laughter*, 129.

148 Jean-Paul Sartre, *Being and Nothingness*, trans. Hazel E. Barnes (London: Methuen, 1969), 59.

149 Philip Rawson, *Art and Time*, ed. Piers Rawson (Madison, WI: Farleigh Dickinson University Press, 2005), 95.

150 Bergson, *Laughter*, 28.

151 Bergson, *Laughter*, 26.

152 Bergson, *Laughter*, 34.

153 Kirk Varnedoe and Adam Gopnik, *High & Low: Modern Art and Popular Culture* (New York: The Museum of Modern Art, 1991), 104.

154 Varnedoe and Gopnik, *High & Low*, 123.

155 Jean Epstein, 'Magnification and Other Writings', trans. Stuart Liebman, *October* 3 (Spring 1977): 9.

156 Epstein, 'Magnification', 9.

157 Epstein, 'Magnification', 10.

158 Bergson, *Laughter*, 83.

159 Moore, *Bergson: Thinking Backwards*, 10.

160 Pilkington, *Bergson and His Influence*, 17–18.

161 John Mullarkey, *Bergson and Philosophy* (Edinburgh: Edinburgh University Press, 1999), 62–3.

162 Mullarkey, *Bergson*, 64–5.

163 Mullarkey, *Bergson*, 65.

164 Mullarkey, *Bergson*, 66.

165 Bergson, *Creative Evolution*, 65.

166 Bergson, *Creative Evolution*, 62.

167 Focillon, *Life*, 176.

168 Bergson, *Creative Evolution*, 246.

169 Canguilhem, 'Knowledge', 306.

170 Bergson, *Creative Evolution*, 15.

171 Hans Driesch, *The Problem of Individuality* (London: Macmillan, 1914), 3.

172 Bergson, *Creative Evolution*, 49.

173 Bergson, *Creative Evolution*, 16.

174 Bergson, *Creative Evolution*, 17.

175 Bergson, *Creative Evolution*, 281.

176 Bergson, *Creative Evolution*, 282.

177 Bergson, *Creative Evolution*, 282–3.

178 Bergson, *Creative Evolution*, 284.

179 Bergson, *Creative Evolution*, 247.

180   Bergson, *Creative Evolution*, 252.

181   Bergson, *Creative Evolution*, 253.

182   Bergson, *Creative Evolution*, 259.

183   Bergson, *Creative Evolution*, 261.

184   Bergson, *Creative Evolution*, 261.

185   Gilles Deleuze, 'The Method of Dramatization', in *Desert Islands and Other Texts 1953-1974*, ed. David Lapoujade, trans. Michael Taormina (Los Angeles, CA: Semiotext(e), 2004), 96.

186   Deleuze, 'Dramatization', 96.

187   Gilbert Simondon, 'The Genesis of the Individual', trans. Mark Cohen and Sanford Kwinter, in *Incorporations*, ed. Jonathon Crary and Sanford Kwinter (New York: Zone, 1992), 298.

188   Simondon, 'Genesis', 301.

189   Simondon, 'Genesis', 301.

190   Bergson, *Creative Evolution*, 270.

191   Bergson, *Mind-Energy*, 13.

192   Paul Klee, 'On Modern Art', trans. David Farrell Krell, in *Paul Klee: Philosophical Vision: From Nature to Art*, ed. John Sallis (Chestnut Hill, MA: McMullen Museum of Art, 2012), 10.

193   Klee, 'Modern', 10.

194   Klee, 'Modern', 14.

195   Klee, 'Modern', 13.

196   Gilles Deleuze and Félix Guattari, *What Is Philosophy?*, trans. Hugh Tomlinson and Graham Burchill (London: Verso, 1994), 7.

197   Paul Klee, *Notebooks Vol. 2: The Nature of Nature*, trans. Heinz Horden, ed. Jürg Spiller (London: Lund Humphries, 1973), 43.

198   Klee, 'Modern', 12.

199   Klee, 'Modern', 14.

200   Rawson, *Art and Time*, 52.

201   María Del Rosario Acosta López, 'Tragic Representation: Paul Klee on Tragedy and Art', *Research in Phenomenology* 43, no. 3 (2013): 458.

202   López, 'Tragic', 458.

203   John Sallis, 'Klee's Philosophical Vision', in *Paul Klee: Philosophical Vision: From Nature to Art*, ed. John Sallis (Chestnut Hill, MA: McMullen Museum of Art, 2012), 22.

204   Klee, *Nature*, 66.

205   Eliane Escoubas, 'A Polyphonic Painting: Paul Klee and Rhythm', trans. Hakhamanesh Zangeneh, in *Paul Klee: Philosophical Vision: From Nature to Art*, ed. John Sallis (Chestnut Hill, MA: McMullen Museum of Art, 2012), 136–8.

206   Klee, *Nature*, 25.

207   Klee, *Nature*, 29.

208   Klee, *Nature*, 149.

Chapter 4

1   Bergson, *Creative Evolution*, 328.

2   Bergson, *Laughter*, 135.

3   Bergson, *Laughter*, 136.

4   Bergson, *Laughter*, 136.

5   Jae Emerling, 'Afterword: An Art Historical Return to Bergson', in *Bergson and the Art of Immanence: Painting, Photography, Film*, ed. Charlotte de Mille and John Mullarkey (Edinburgh: Edinburgh University Press, 2013), 264–5.

6   Bergson, *Matter and Memory*, 10.

7   Bergson, *Matter and Memory*, 23.

8   Karl H. Pribram, 'Bergson and the Brain: A Bio-logical Analysis of Certain Intuitions', in *Bergson and Modern Thought: Towards a Unified Science*, ed. Andrew C. Papanicolaou and Pete A. Y. Gunter (Chur: Harwood, 1987), 167.

9   Bergson, *Matter and Memory*, 28.

10   Bergson, *Matter and Memory*, 29.

11   Bergson, *Matter and Memory*, 23.

12   Edmund Husserl, 'The World of the Living Present and the Constitution of the Surrounding World External to the Organism', trans. Frederick A. Elliston and Lenore Langsdorf, in *Husserl: Shorter Works*, ed. Peter McCormick and Frederick A. Elliston (Notre Dame and Brighton: University of Notre Dame and Harvester Press, 1981), 239.

13   Husserl, 'Living Present', 240.

14   J. J. Gibson, 'Constancy and Invariance in Perception', in *The Nature of Art and Motion*, ed. Gyorgy Kepes (New York: George Brazillier, 1965), 61.

15 Gibson, 'Constancy', 63.

16 Bergson, *Matter and Memory*, 20.

17 Milič Čapek, *Bergson and Modern Physics: A Reinterpretation and Re-evaluation* (Holland: Reidel, 1971), 32.

18 Bergson, *Matter and Memory*, 32.

19 Nicholas Rescher, *Process Metaphysics: An Introduction to Process Philosophy* (New York: SUNY, 1996), 57–8.

20 Bergson, *Matter and Memory*, 21.

21 Bergson, *Creative Evolution*, 14.

22 Bergson, *Matter and Memory*, 37.

23 Bergson, *Creative Evolution*, 36; Bergson, *Oeuvres*, 520.

24 Sheets-Johnstone, *Movement*, 131.

25 Johnson, *Meaning*, 89.

26 Johnson, *Meaning*, 90.

27 Bergson, *Laughter*, 137.

28 Bergson, *Matter and Memory*, 67.

29 Bergson, *Matter and Memory*, 94.

30 Bergson, *Matter and Memory*, 82.

31 Bergson, *Matter and Memory*, 93.

32 Bergson, *Matter and Memory*, 93.

33 Bergson, *Matter and Memory*, 92.

34 Paul Schilder, *The Image and Appearance of the Human Body: Studies in the Constructive Energies of the Psyche* (New York: International Universities Press, 1950), 40–2.

35 Merleau-Ponty, *Phenomenology*, 132.

36 Merleau-Ponty, *Phenomenology*, 136.

37 Bergson, *Matter and Memory*, 93.

38 Paul Atkinson, 'Picturing Movement and Moving Pictures: Towards a Pragmatics of Pictorial Perception', *Southern Review: Communication, Politics & Culture* 33, no. 3 (2000): 308–22.

39 Bergson, *Mind-Energy*, 97.

40 Bergson, *Mind-Energy*, 98.

41 Bergson, *Matter and Memory*, 96.

42 Bergson, *Creative Mind*, 62.

43 Bergson, *Creative Mind*, 63.

44 Bergson, *Creative Mind*, 64.

45 Bergson, *Laughter*, 138.

46 Bergson, *Laughter*, 138.

47 Floyd Merrell, *Signs Becoming Signs: Our Perfusive, Pervasive Universe* (Bloomington, IN: Indiana University Press, 1991), 197–8.

48 Martin Heidegger, *What Is a Thing?* trans. W. B. Barton Jr. and Vera Deutsch (Lanham, MD: University Press of America, 1967), 71–3.

49 Heidegger, *Thing*, 74.

50 Bergson, *Creative Mind*, 40–1.

51 Dewey, *Experience*, 54.

52 Dewey, *Experience*, 54.

53 Jean-François Lyotard, *Discourse, Figure*, trans. Antony Hudek and Mary Lydon (Minneapolis, MN: University of Minnesota Press, 2010), 210.

54 Lyotard, *Discourse*, 211.

55 Lyotard, *Discourse*, 21.

56 Norman Bryson, *Word and Image: French Painting of the Ancien Régime* (Cambridge: Cambridge University Press, 1981), 1.

57 Bryson, *French*, 3.

58 Bryson, *French*, 43.

59 Bryson, *French*, 38.

60 Bryson, *French*, 41.

61 Antliff, 'Inventing', 3.

62 Bergson, *Creative Mind*, 159.

63 Bergson, *Creative Mind*, 159–60.

64 Bergson, *Creative Mind*, 191.

65 Meyer Schapiro, 'On Some Problems in the Semiotics of Visual Art: Field and Vehicle in Image-Signs', *Simiolus: Netherlands Quarterly for the History of Art* 6, no. 1 (1972–3): 17.

66 Schapiro, 'On Some Problems', 18.

67 Bergson, *Time and Free Will*, 133–4.

68 Bergson, *Mind-Energy*, 175.

69 Bergson, *Creative Mind*, 198.

70 Rawson, *Art and Time*, 36.

71 Rawson, *Art and Time*, 37.

72 Rawson, *Art and Time*, 37.

73 Bergson, *Mind-Energy*, 54.

74 Bergson, *Mind-Energy*, 54.

75 Bergson, *Creative Mind*, 174.

76 Bergson, *Creative Mind*, 173.

77 Rudolf Arnheim, 'A Stricture on Space and Time', in *New Essays on the Psychology of Art* (Berkeley, CA: University of California Press, 1986), 81.

78 Arnheim, 'Stricture', 81.

79 Arnheim, 'Stricture', 82–4.

80 Arnheim, 'Stricture', 84.

81 Arnheim, 'Stricture', 84.

82 Arnheim, 'Stricture', 85.

83 Bergson, *Creative Evolution*, 231–2.

84 Bergson, *Time and Free Will*, 96.

85 Bergson, *Time and Free Will*, 97.

86 Edward S. Casey, *Getting Back into Place: Toward a Renewed Understanding of the Place-World* (Bloomington and Indianapolis, IN: Indiana University Press, 1993), 73.

87 Mark Antliff, 'Creative Time: Bergson and European Modernism', in *Tempus Fugit: Time Flies*, ed. Jan Schall (Kansas City, MO: The Nelson-Atkins Museum of Art, 2000), 42–3.

88 T. H. Sadler, 'Translator's Introduction', in *Concerning the Spiritual in Art*, by Wassily Kandinsky (New York: Dover Publications, 1977), xv.

89 Kandinsky, *Spiritual*, 24.

90 Kandinsky, *Spiritual*, 36–7.

91 Kandinsky, *Spiritual*, 37.

92 Wassily Kandinsky, *Point and Line to Plane*, trans. Howard Dearstyne and Hilla Rebay (New York: Dover, 1979), 17.

93 Kandinsky, *Point*, 21.

94 Maurice Merleau-Ponty, 'Eye and Mind', trans. Carleton Dallery, in *The Primacy of Perception*, ed. James Edie (Evanston, IL: Northwestern University Press, 1964), 181.

95 Merleau-Ponty, 'Eye', 181–2.

96 Merleau-Ponty, 'Eye', 183.

97 Maurice Merleau-Ponty, 'Cézanne's Doubt', in *Sense and Non-Sense* (Evanston, IL: Northwestern University Press, 1964), 12.

98 Richard Verdi, *Cézanne* (London: Thames and Hudson, 1992), 120.

99 Merleau-Ponty, 'Cézanne's Doubt', 14–15.

100 D. H. Lawrence, *À Propos of Lady Chatterley's Lover and Other Essays* (Harmondsworth: Penguin, 1961), 50.

101 Lawrence, *À Propos*, 51.

102 George Heard Hamilton, 'Cézanne, Bergson and the Image of Time', *Art Journal* 16 (Fall 1956): 10.

103 Hamilton, 'Cézanne', 10–11.

104 Hamilton, 'Cézanne', 6.

105 Hamilton, 'Cézanne', 7.

106 Hamilton, 'Cézanne', 9.

107 Interestingly, Medina discusses tactile action in the artwork in terms of a 'metonymic axis' or 'axis of combination'. Although this rightly highlights how the artist's embodied movement appears across and through a work, it does not directly align with Bergson's notion of a simple gesture, in which any linguistic characterization is derived only retrospectively. Joyce Medina, *Cézanne and Modernism: The Poetics of Painting* (New York: State University of New York Press, 1995), 39.

108 Medina, *Cézanne*, 52.

109 Medina does not argue for a direct causal relationship between Bergson's philosophy and Modernist art, arguing, instead, that Bergson shares a 'historical present' with the artists. Bergson integrated a range of psychological theories and ideas on perceptual synthesis into a coherent theory that ran parallel with artistic modernism. Medina, *Cézanne*, 53.

110 Medina, *Cézanne*, 7.

111 Medina, *Cézanne*, 34.

112 Medina, *Cézanne*, 133.

113 Medina, *Cézanne*, 92.

114 Medina, *Cézanne*, 116.

115 Medina, *Cézanne*, 119.

116 Medina, *Cézanne*, 120.

117 Andrew Benjamin, *Disclosing Spaces: On Painting* (Manchester: Clinamen Press, 2004), 76.

118 Benjamin, *Spaces*, 74.

119   Benjamin, *Spaces*, 75.

120   Benjamin, *Spaces*, 75.

121   Benjamin, *Spaces*, 75.

122   Heinrich Wölfflin, *Principles of Art History: The Problem of the Development of Style in Later Art*, trans. M. D. Hottinger (New York: Dover, 1950), 30.

123   Wölfflin, *Principles*, 18.

124   Wölfflin, *Principles*, 19.

125   Wölfflin, *Principles*, 19.

126   Wölfflin, *Principles*, 20

127   Wölfflin, *Principles*, 21

128   Wölfflin, *Principles*, 21.

129   Wölfflin, *Principles*, 28.

130   Wölfflin, *Principles*, 29

131   Bergson, *Matter and Memory*, 197.

132   Bergson, *Matter and Memory*, 199.

133   Bergson, *Matter and Memory*, 200.

134   Bergson, *Matter and Memory*, 201.

135   Bergson, *Matter and Memory*, 201.

136   Bergson, *Creative Mind*, 84.

137   David Bohm, *Wholeness and the Implicate Order* (London: Routledge, 1980), 14.

138   Bohm, *Wholeness*, 18.

139   Brian Livesley, 'The Later Life of Turner: Body and Mind', in *The EY Exhibition: Late Turner – Painting Set Free*, ed. David Blayney Brown et al. (Millbank: Tate Publishing, 2014), 26.

140   In his lectures and courses, Turner explores how light and colour are refracted and reflected under different atmospheric and local conditions, for example, the refraction of light in rain or the reflection of the sun on water. John Gage, *Colour in Turner: Poetry and Truth* (London: Studio Vista, 1969), 113.

141   Sam Smiles, 'Turner In and Out of Time', in *The EY Exhibition: Late Turner – Painting Set Free*, ed. David Blayney Brown et al. (Millbank: Tate Publishing, 2014), 22.

142   David Blayney Brown, 'Squaring the Circle: New Formats from 1840', in *The EY Exhibition: Late Turner – Painting Set Free*, ed. David Blayney Brown et al. (Millbank: Tate Publishing, 2014), 177.

143 Turner was not overly interested in the more abstract aspects of Goethe's theory, and, instead, sought to examine the proper painterly and empirical implications. He noted Goethe's introduction of darkness into the colour spectrum, while arguing that he did not attend enough to darkness in art and nature. Gage, *Colour in Turner*, 186–7.

144 Turner's late works demonstrate processual features of hue and shade; however, this does not mean that the painter necessarily ascribed to a processual metaphysics. In many respects, and probably due to painterly practice, he thought that colours could have an elemental value. He stated 'in a lecture of 1818, yellow represented the medium (i.e., light), red the material objects, and blue, distance (i.e., air) in landscape, and in terms of natural time, morning, evening, and dawn'. Turner was like many other artists who found in colour a foundation for all forms that could be compared to primary geometrical objects. Gage, *Colour and Meaning*, 165.

145 Martin Butlin, *Watercolours from the Turner Bequest 1819-1845* (London: The Tate Gallery, 1968), 3.

146 Gilles Deleuze, *Francis Bacon: The Logic of Sensation*, trans. Daniel W. Smith (London: Continuum, 2004), 52.

147 Bergson, *Creative Mind*, 173. Italics in original.

148 Bergson, *Laughter*, 144–5.

149 Martin Seel, *Aesthetics of Appearing*, trans. John Farrell (Stanford, CA: Stanford University Press, 2005), 15.

150 Seel, *Aesthetics*, 22.

151 Seel, *Aesthetics*, 32.

152 Seel, *Aesthetics*, 27.

153 Seel, *Aesthetics*, 28.

154 Seel, *Aesthetics*, 16.

155 Raymond Bayer, 'L'Esthétique de Bergson', *Revue Philosophique de la France et de l'Étranger* 131, no. 3/8 (1941): 244.

156 Immanuel Kant, *Critique of Judgement*, trans. and intro. J. H. Bernard. Mineola (New York: Dover, [1914] 2005), 48.

157 Kant, *Critique*, 49.

158 Kant, *Critique*, 59–60.

159 Bergson, *Creative Mind*, 161–2.

160 Bergson, *Creative Mind*, 162–3.

161 Bergson, *Creative Mind*, 163.

162   Bergson, *Creative Mind*, 185.

163   Bergson, *Matter and Memory*, 206.

164   Bergson, *Matter and Memory*, 206.

165   Benjamin Libet, *Mind Time: The Temporal Factor in Consciousness* (Cambridge, MA: Harvard University Press, 2004).

166   Bergson, *Matter and Memory*, 203.

167   Bergson, *Matter and Memory*, 205.

168   Gage, *Colour and Meaning*, 78–9.

169   Gage, *Colour and Meaning*, 82.

170   Gage, *Colour and Meaning*, 215.

171   Gage, *Colour and Meaning*, 78.

172   Gage, *Colour and Meaning*, 220.

173   Ian Hunter, 'Aesthetics and the Arts of Life', in *Aesthesia and the Economy of the Senses*, ed. Helen Grace (Kingswood: University of Western Sydney, 1996), 29.

174   Henri Bergson, *Cours III: Leçons d'histoire de la philosophie moderne: Théories de l'âme*, ed. Henri Hude (Paris: Presses Universitaires de France, 1995), 28–9.

175   Bergson, *Cours III*, 111–12.

176   Bergson, *Mélanges*, 990–1001.

177   Bergson, *Mélanges*, 992.

178   Bergson, *Mélanges*, 993.

179   Bergson, *Mélanges*, 993. My translation.

180   Bergson, *Mélanges*, 993.

181   Bergson, *Mélanges*, 993.

182   Atkinson, 'Dissolution', 58–9.

183   Gilles Deleuze, *Difference and Repetition*, trans. Paul Patton (New York: Columbia University Press, 1994), 70.

184   Deleuze, *Difference*, 71.

185   Deleuze, *Difference*, 73.

186   Bergson, *Matter and Memory*, 207.

187   Bergson, *Matter and Memory*, 208.

188   Bergson, *Matter and Memory*, 228.

189 Bergson, *Creative Mind*, 175.

190 Bergson, *Matter and Memory*, 209.

191 Auguste Rodin, *Art*, interviews with Paul Gsell, trans. Romilly Fedden (Boston, MA: Small Maynard Company, 1912), 68–9.

192 Rodin, *Art*, 75.

193 A. N. Whitehead, *Science and the Modern World* (Harmondsworth: Penguin, 1938), 64.

194 Thierry de Duve, 'Time Exposure and Snapshot: The Photograph as Paradox', *October* 5 (Summer 1978): 115–16.

195 Bergson, *Creative Evolution*, 361.

196 Bergson, *Creative Evolution*, 361.

197 Tom Flynn, *The Body in Three Dimensions* (New York: Harry N. Abrams, 1998), 76.

198 Crowther, *Language*, 69–70.

199 Umberto Boccioni, 'Technical Manifesto of Futurist Sculpture', trans. Robert Brain, in *Futurist Manifestos*, ed. Umbro Apollonio (London: Thames and Hudson, [1913] 1973), 64.

200 Atkinson, 'Dynamic', 70.

201 Lista, *Futurism*, 22–3.

202 Lista, *Futurism*, 21.

203 Lista, *Futurism*, 26.

204 Anton Giulio Bragaglia, 'Futurist Photodynamism', trans. Caroline Tisdall, in *Futurist Manifestos*, ed. Umbro Apollonio (London: Thames and Hudson, [1912] 1973), 42.

205 Bragaglia, 'Photodynamism', 41.

206 Bragaglia, 'Photodynamism', 39.

207 Bragaglia, 'Photodynamism', 40.

208 Bragaglia, 'Photodynamism', 40.

209 Mary Ann Doane, *The Emergence of Cinematic Time: Modernity, Contingency, the Archive* (Cambridge, MA and London: Harvard University Press, 2002), 77–8.

210 Jacques Aumont, Alain Bergala, Michel Marie and Marc Vernet, *Aesthetics of Film* (Austin, TX: University of Texas Press, 1999), 122.

211 Bergson, *Matter and Memory*, 208.

212 Bergson, *Creative Mind*, 265.

213 Bergson, *Creative Mind*, 267.

214 Bergson, *Creative Mind*, 267.

215 Bergson, *Creative Mind*, 268.

216 Bergson, *Creative Mind*, 186.

217 Bergson, *Creative Mind*, 185.

BIBLIOGRAPHY

Alliez, Eric. 'Matisse, Bergson, Oiticica, etc.'. Translated by Hager Weslati. In *Bergson and the Art of Immanence: Painting, Photography, Film*, edited by Charlotte de Mille and John Mullarkey, 63–79. Edinburgh: Edinburgh University Press, 2013.

Ansell-Pearson, Keith. *Bergson: Thinking Beyond the Human Condition*. London and New York: Bloomsbury, 2018.

Antliff, Mark. 'Bergson and Cubism: A Reassessment'. *Art Journal* 47, no. 4 (Winter 1988): 341–9.

Antliff, Mark. 'Creative Time: Bergson and European Modernism'. In *Tempus Fugit: Time Flies*, edited by Jan Schall, 36–66. Kansas City: The Nelson-Atkins Museum of Art, 2000.

Antliff, Mark. 'The Fourth Dimension and Futurism: A Politicized Space'. *Art Bulletin* 82, no. 4 (December 2000): 720–33.

Antliff, Mark. *Inventing Bergson: Cultural Politics and the Parisian Avant-Garde*. Princeton: Princeton University Press, 1993.

Antliff, Mark. 'The Rhythms of Duration: Bergson and the Art of Matisse'. In *The New Bergson*, edited by John Mullarkey, 184–208. Manchester: Manchester University Press, 1999.

Antliff, Mark. 'Shaping Duration: Bergson and Modern Sculpture'. *The European Legacy* 16, no. 7 (2011): 899–918.

Arnheim, Rudolf. *Art and Visual Perception: A Psychology of the Creative Eye*. London: Faber and Faber, 1954.

Arnheim, Rudolf. *New Essays on the Psychology of Art*. Berkeley: University of California Press, 1986.

Atkinson, Paul. 'Between Movement and Reading: Reconceptualizing the Dynamic Picture Plane in Modernist Comics and Painting'. *ImageTexT* 9, no. 3 (2018): n.p.

Atkinson, Paul. 'Dynamic Sensation: Bergson, Futurism and the Exteriorisation of Time in the Plastic Arts'. In *Art and Time*, edited by Jan Lloyd-Jones, Paul Campbell and Peter Wylie, 57–74. North Melbourne: Australian Scholarly Publishing, 2007.

Atkinson, Paul. 'The Inclination of Philosophy: *The Creative Mind* and the Articulation of a Bergsonian Method'. In *Understanding Bergson, Understanding Modernism*, edited by Paul Ardoin, S. E. Gontarski and Laci Mattison, 89–104. New York and London: Bloomsbury, 2013.

Atkinson, Paul. 'Invisible Rhythms: Tracking Aesthetic Perception in Film and the Visual Arts'. In *Seeing into Screens: Eye Tracking the Moving Image*, edited by Tessa Dwyer, Claire Perkins, Sean Redmond and Jodi Sita, 28–45. London: Bloomsbury, 2018.

Atkinson, Paul. 'The Movement of Dissolution: Bergson and the Aesthetics of Durational Difference'. In *Sensorium: Aesthetics, Art, Life*, edited by Barbara Bolt, Felicity Colman, Graham Jones and Ashley Woodward, 52–62. Newcastle: Cambridge Scholars Press, 2007.

Atkinson, Paul. 'Picturing Movement and Moving Pictures: Towards a Pragmatics of Pictorial Perception'. *Southern Review: Communication, Politics & Culture* 33, no. 3 (2000): 308–22.

Atkinson, Paul. 'Turning Away: Embodied Movement in the Perception of Shot Duration'. *Image [&] Narrative* 15, no. 1 (2014): 89–101.

Aumont, Jacques, Alain Bergala, Michel Marie and Marc Vernet. *Aesthetics of Film*. Austin: University of Texas Press, 1999.

Bataillon, Marcel. 'A Tribute to Bergson on the Occasion of the Bergson Centennial in Paris, 1959'. In *The Bergsonian Heritage*, edited by Thomas Hanna, 105–18. New York and London: Columbia University Press, 1962.

Bayer, Raymond. 'L'Esthétique de Bergson'. *Revue Philosophique de la France et de l'Étranger* 131, no. 3/8 (1941): 244–318.

Benjamin, Andrew. *Disclosing Spaces: On Painting*. Manchester: Clinamen Press, 2004.

Bergson, Henri. *Correspondances*. Edited by André Robinet. Paris: Presses Universitaires de France, 2002.

Bergson, Henri. *Cours III: Leçons d'histoire de la philosophie moderne: Théories de l'âme*. Edited by Henri Hude. Paris: Presses Universitaires de France, 1995.

Bergson, Henri. *Creative Evolution*. Translated by Arthur Mitchell. New York: Random House, [1911] 1944.

Bergson, Henri. *The Creative Mind*. Translated by M. L. Andison. New York: Philosophical Library, [1934] 1946.

Bergson, Henri. *Duration and Simultaneity: With Reference to Einstein's Theory*. Translated by Leon Jacobson. Indianapolis: Bobbs-Merrill, 1965.

Bergson, Henri. *Laughter: An Essay on the Meaning of the Comic*. Translated by Cloudesley Brereton and Fred Rothwell. Copenhagen and Los Angeles: Green Integer, 1911.

Bergson, Henri. Letter to W. R. Boyce Gibson, 9 February 1911. Box 2, folio 41, Gibson Papers. University of Melbourne Archives.

Bergson, Henri. 'Life and Matter at War'. *Hibbert Journal* 13, no. 3 (1914): 465–75.

Bergson, Henri. *Matter and Memory*. Translated by W. S. Palmer and N. M. Paul. New York: Zone Books, [1908] 1991.

Bergson, Henri. *Mélanges*. Edited by André Robinet. Paris: Presses Universitaires de France, 1972.

Bergson, Henri. *Mind-Energy: Lectures and Essays*. Translated by H. Wildon Carr. London: Macmillan, [1919] 1920.

Bergson, Henri. *Oeuvres*. Edited by André Robinet. Paris: Presses Universitaires de France, 1959.

Bergson, Henri. *Time and Free Will: An Essay on the Immediate Data of Consciousness.* Translated by F. L. Pogson. London: George Allen and Unwin, 1910.

Bergson, Henri. *The Two Sources of Morality and Religion.* Translated by R. Ashley Audra and Cloudesley Brereton. Westport: Greenwood Press, [1932] 1963.

Bianco, Giuseppe. 'Experience vs. Concept? The Role of Bergson in Twentieth-Century French Philosophy'. *The European Legacy* 16, no. 7 (2011): 855–72.

Biran, Pierre Maine de. *De l'aperception immédiate: mémoire de Berlin, 1807.* Edited by Anne Devarieux. Paris: Librairie générale française, 2005.

Blanche, Jacques-Émile. *Portraits of a Lifetime: The Late Victorian Era, The Edwardian Pageant, 1870–1914.* Translated by Walter Clement. London: J. M. Dent & Sons, 1937.

Blayney Brown, David. 'Squaring the Circle: New Formats from 1840'. In *The EY Exhibition: Late Turner – Painting Set Free*, edited by David Blayney Brown, Amy Concannon and Sam Smiles, 176–91. Millbank: Tate Publishing, 2014.

Boccioni, Umberto. 'Absolute Motion + Relative Motion = Dynamism'. Translated by Robert Brain. In *Futurist Manifestos*, edited by Umbro Apollonio, 150–4. London: Thames and Hudson, [1914] 1973.

Boccioni, Umberto. 'The Plastic Foundations of Futurist Sculpture and Painting'. Translated by Robert Brain. In *Futurist Manifestos*, edited by Umbro Apollonio, 88–90. London: Thames and Hudson, [1913] 1973.

Boccioni, Umberto. 'Technical Manifesto of Futurist Sculpture'. Translated by Robert Brain. In *Futurist Manifestos*, edited by Umbro Apollonio, 51–65. London: Thames and Hudson, [1913] 1973.

Bohm, David. *Wholeness and the Implicate Order.* London: Routledge, 1980.

Bragaglia, Anton Giulio. 'Futurist Photodynamism'. Translated by Caroline Tisdall. In *Futurist Manifestos*, edited by Umbro Apollonio, 38–45. London: Thames and Hudson, [1912] 1973.

Bryson, Norman. *Looking at the Overlooked: Four Essays on Still Life Painting.* London: Reaktion Books, 1990.

Bryson, Norman. *Vision and Painting: The Logic of the Gaze.* Houndmills and London: Palgrave, 1983.

Bryson, Norman. *Word and Image: French Painting of the Ancien Régime.* Cambridge: Cambridge University Press, 1981.

Butlin, Martin. *Watercolours from the Turner Bequest 1819–1845.* London: The Tate Gallery, 1968.

Canguilhem, Georges. *A Vital Rationalist: Selected Writings.* Edited by François Delaporte. Translated by Arthur Goldhammer. New York: Zone, 1994.

Canguilhem, Georges. *The Normal and the Pathological.* Translated by Carolyn R. Fawcett and Robert S. Cohen. New York: Zone Books, 1989.

Čapek, Milič. *Bergson and Modern Physics: A Reinterpretation and Re-evaluation.* Holland: Reidel, 1971.

Carr, David. *Time, Narrative, and History.* Bloomington: Indiana University Press, 1986.

Casey, Edward S. *Getting Back into Place: Toward a Renewed Understanding of the Place-World*. Bloomington and Indianapolis: Indiana University Press, 1993.

Casey, Edward S. *The World at a Glance*. Bloomington and Indianapolis: Indiana University Press, 2007.

Chevalier, Jacques. *Bergson*. Paris: Librairie Plon, 1926.

Chevalier, Jacques. *Entretiens avec Bergson*. Paris: Librairie Plon, 1959.

Copleston, Frederick. *A History of Philosophy: Greece and Rome*. Vol. 1, part 1. Garden City: Image, 1962.

Crary, Jonathan. *Techniques of the Observer: On Vision and Modernity in the Nineteenth Century*. Cambridge, MA: MIT Press, 1990.

Crowther, Paul. *The Language of Twentieth-Century Art: A Conceptual History*. New Haven and London: Yale University Press, 1997.

Cullinan, Nicholas and Nicholas Serota. '"Ecstatic impulses": Cy Twombly's "Untitled (Bacchus)", 2006–08'. *The Burlington Magazine* 152, no. 1290 (September 2010): 613–16.

Deleuze, Gilles. 'Bergson 1859–1941'. In *Les philosophes célèbres*, edited by Maurice Merleau-Ponty, 292–9. Paris: Editions d'Art Lucien Mazenod, 1956.

Deleuze, Gilles. *Bergsonism*. Translated by Hugh Tomlinson and Barbara Habberjam. New York: Zone, 1991.

Deleuze, Gilles. *Cinema 1: The Movement Image*. Translated by Hugh Tomlinson and Barbara Habberjam. Minneapolis: University of Minnesota Press, 1986.

Deleuze, Gilles. *Desert Islands and Other Texts 1953–1974*. Edited by David Lapoujade. Translated by Michael Taormina. Los Angeles: Semiotext(e), 2004.

Deleuze, Gilles. *Difference and Repetition*. Translated by Paul Patton. New York: Columbia University Press, 1994.

Deleuze, Gilles. *Francis Bacon: The Logic of Sensation*. Translated by Daniel W. Smith. London: Continuum, 2004.

Deleuze, Gilles and Félix Guattari. *What Is Philosophy?* Translated by Hugh Tomlinson and Graham Burchill. London: Verso, 1994.

Dewey, John. *Art as Experience*. New York: Perigee, [1934] 2005.

Dewey, John. *The Early Works, 1882–1898*. Edited by Ann Boydston. Vol. 2. Carbondale and Edwardsville: Southern Illinois University Press, 1967.

Doane, Mary Ann. *The Emergence of Cinematic Time: Modernity, Contingency, the Archive*. Cambridge, MA and London: Harvard University Press, 2002.

Dresden, Samuel. 'Les Idées Esthétiques de Bergson'. In *Les Etudes Bergsoniennes*, 55–75. Vol. 4. Paris: Presses Universitaires de Paris, 1968.

Driesch, Hans. *The Problem of Individuality*. London: Macmillan, 1914.

Dufrenne, Mikel. *The Phenomenology of Aesthetic Experience*. Translated by Edward S. Casey, Albert A. Anderson, Willis Domingo and Leon Jacobson. Evanston: Northwestern University Press, [1953] 1973.

de Duve, Thierry. 'Time Exposure and Snapshot: The Photograph as Paradox'. *October* 5 (Summer 1978): 113–25.

Edwards, Paul. 'Wyndham Lewis's Vorticism: A Strange Synthesis'. In *The Vorticists: Manifesto for a Modern World*, edited by Mark Antliff and Vivien Greene, 34–45. London: Tate Publishing, 2010.

Emerling, Jae. 'Afterword: An Art Historical Return to Bergson'. In *Bergson and the Art of Immanence: Painting, Photography, Film*, edited by Charlotte de Mille and John Mullarkey, 260–71. Edinburgh: Edinburgh University Press, 2013.

Epstein, Jean. 'Magnification and Other Writings'. Translated by Stuart Liebman. *October* 3 (Spring 1977): 9–25.

Escoubas, Eliane. 'A Polyphonic Painting: Paul Klee and Rhythm'. Translated by Hakhamanesh Zangeneh. In *Paul Klee: Philosophical Vision: From Nature to Art*, edited by John Sallis, 135–47. Chestnut Hill: McMullen Museum of Art, 2012.

Fink, Hilary L. *Bergson and Russian Modernism, 1900–1930*. Evanston: Northwestern University Press, 1999.

Flynn, Tom. *The Body in Three Dimensions*. New York: Harry N. Abrams, 1998.

Focillon, Henri. *The Life of Forms in Art*. Translated by Charles B. Hogan and George Kubler. New York: Zone Books, [1934] 1992.

Foster, Hal, Rosalind Krauss, Yve-Alain Bois and Benjamin H. D. Buchloh. *Art since 1900*. New York: Thames & Hudson, 2004.

Foster, Susan Leigh. *Choreographing Empathy*. London and New York: Routledge, 2011.

Freedberg, David and Vittorio Gallese. 'Motion, Emotion and Empathy in Esthetic Experience'. *Trends in Cognitive Sciences* 11, no. 5 (2007): 197–203.

Freud, Sigmund. 'Negation'. Translated by Joan Riviere and James Strachey. In *On Metapsychology*, edited by Angela Richards and Albert Dickson. Vol. 11. Penguin Freud Library, 437–42. London: Penguin, 1991.

Gage, John. *Colour and Meaning: Art, Science and Symbolism*. London: Thames and Hudson, 1999.

Gage, John. *Colour in Turner: Poetry and Truth*. London: Studio Vista, 1969.

Gibson, James J. 'Constancy and Invariance in Perception'. In *The Nature of Art and Motion*, edited by Gyorgy Kepes, 60–70. New York: George Brazillier, 1965.

Gillies, Mary Ann. *Henri Bergson and British Modernism*. Montréal: McGill-Queen's University Press, 1996.

Gleizes, Albert and Jean Metzinger. *Du 'cubisme'*. Sisteron: Editions Présence, 1980.

Gouhier, Henri. Introduction to *Oeuvres*, by Henri Bergson, vii–xxx. Paris: Presses Universitaires de France, 1959.

Grogin, Robert C. *The Bergsonian Controversy in France: 1900–1914*. Calgary: University of Calgary Press, 1988.

Guyau, Jean-Marie. 'La genèse de l'idée de temps'. In *Guyau and the Idea of Time*, edited by John A. Michon with Viviane Pouthas and Janet L. Jackson, 39–92. Amsterdam: North-Holland Publishing Company, 1988.

Hamilton, George Heard. 'Cézanne, Bergson and the Image of Time'. *Art Journal* 16 (Fall 1956): 2–12.

Hansen, Mark B. N. *New Philosophy for New Media*. Cambridge, MA and London: MIT Press, 2004.

Hayter, Stanley W. 'Orientation, Direction, Cheirality, Velocity and Rhythm'. In *The Nature of Art and Motion*, edited by Gyorgy Kepes, 71–80. New York: George Brazillier, 1965.

Heidegger, Martin. 'The Question Concerning Technology'. Translated by William Lovitt. In *Basic Writings: From Being and Time (1927) to The Task of Thinking (1964)*, edited by David Farrell Krell, 311–41. 2nd edn. New York: HarperCollins, 1993.

Heidegger, Martin. *What Is a Thing?* Translated by W. B. Barton, Jr. and Vera Deutsch. Lanham: University Press of America, 1967.

Horst, Louis and Carroll Russell. *Modern Dance Forms in Relation to the Other Modern Arts*. San Francisco: Impulse, 1961.

Hulme, Thomas Ernest. 'Bergson's Theory of Art'. 1922. In *The Collected Writings of T. E. Hulme*, edited by Karen Csengeri, 191–204. Oxford: Clarendon Press, 1994.

Hunter, Ian. 'Aesthetics and the Arts of Life'. In *Aesthesia and the Economy of the Senses*, edited by Helen Grace, 19–54. Kingswood: University of Western Sydney, 1996.

Husserl, Edmund. *On the Phenomenology of the Consciousness of Internal Time (1893–1917)*. Edited by Rudolf Bernet. Translated by John Barnett Brough. Dordrecht: Kluwer Academic Publishers, 1991.

Husserl, Edmund. 'The World of the Living Present and the Constitution of the Surrounding World External to the Organism'. Translated by Frederick A. Elliston and Lenore Langsdorf. In *Husserl: Shorter Works*, edited by Peter McCormick and Frederick A. Elliston, 238–54. Notre Dame and Brighton: University of Notre Dame and Harvester Press, 1981.

James, William. *The Principles of Psychology*. Vol 2. New York: Dover Publications, [1890] 1950.

James, William. *Psychology: Briefer Course*. Cambridge, MA: Harvard University Press, 1984.

Jankélévitch, Vladimir. *Henri Bergson*. Paris: Presses Universitaires de France, 1999.

Jankélévitch, Vladimir. *Music and the Ineffable*. Translated by Carolyn Abbate. Princeton: Princeton University Press, 2003.

Jankélévitch, Vladimir. 'With the Whole Soul'. In *The Bergsonian Heritage*, edited by Thomas Hanna, 155–66. New York and London: Columbia University Press, 1962.

Johnson, Mark. *The Meaning of the Body: Aesthetics of Human Understanding*. Chicago and London: University of Chicago Press, 2007.

Kandinsky, Wassily. *Concerning the Spiritual in Art*. Translated by M. T. H. Sadler. New York: Dover, 1977.

Kandinsky, Wassily. *Point and Line to Plane*. Translated by Howard Dearstyne and Hilla Rebay. New York: Dover, 1979.

Kant, Immanuel. *Critique of Judgement*. Translated and Introduced by J. H. Bernard. Mineola: Dover, [1914] 2005.

Kern, Stephen. *The Culture of Time and Space 1880–1918*. With a New Preface. Cambridge, MA: Harvard University Press, 2003.

Klee, Paul. *Notebooks Vol. 2: The Nature of Nature*. Edited by Jürg Spiller. Translated by Heinz Horden. London: Lund Humphries, 1973.

Klee, Paul. 'On Modern Art'. Translated by David Farrell Krell. In *Paul Klee: Philosophical Vision: From Nature to Art*, edited by John Sallis, 9–14. Chestnut Hill: McMullen Museum of Art, 2012.

Kolakowski, Leszek. *Bergson*. Oxford: Oxford University Press, 1985.

Kostenevich, Albert. 'La Danse and La Musique by Henri Matisse: A New Interpretation'. *Apollo* 100 (1974): 504–13.

Krauss, Rosalind. *The Optical Unconscious*. Cambridge, MA: MIT Press, 1993.

Kumar, Shiv K. *Bergson and the Stream of Consciousness Novel*. London and Glasgow: Blackie and Son, 1962.

Langer, Susanne K. *Feeling and Form*. London: Routledge & Kegan Paul, 1953.

Langer, Susanne K. *Problems of Art: Ten Philosophical Lectures*. New York: Charles Scribner's Sons, 1957.

Lawrence, David H. *A Propos of Lady Chatterley's Lover and Other Essays*. Harmondsworth: Penguin, 1961.

Leder, Drew. *The Absent Body*. Chicago: University of Chicago Press, 1990.

Lewis, Wyndham. 'Futurism, Magic and Life'. In *Blast No. 1: Review of the Great English Vortex*, edited by Wyndham Lewis, 132–5. London: J. Lane, 1914.

Lewis, Wyndham. 'Our Vortex'. In *Blast No. 1: Review of the Great English Vortex*, edited by Wyndham Lewis, 147–9. London: J. Lane, 1914.

Libet, Benjamin. *Mind Time: The Temporal Factor in Consciousness*. Cambridge, MA: Harvard University Press, 2004.

Lista, Giovanni. *Futurism and Photography*. London: Merrell Publishers, 2001.

Livesley, Brian. 'The Later Life of Turner: Body and Mind'. In *The EY Exhibition: Late Turner – Painting Set Free*, edited by David Blayney Brown, Amy Concannon and Sam Smiles, 25–31. Millbank: Tate Publishing, 2014.

López, María Del Rosario Acosta. 'Tragic Representation: Paul Klee on Tragedy and Art'. *Research in Phenomenology* 43, no. 3 (2013): 443–61.

Lorand, Ruth. *Aesthetic Order: A Philosophy of Order, Beauty and Art*. London: Routledge, 2000.

Lyotard, Jean-François. *Discourse, Figure*. Translated by Antony Hudek and Mary Lydon. Minneapolis: University of Minnesota Press, 2010.

Lyotard, Jean-François. *The Inhuman: Reflections on Time*. Translated by Geoffrey Bennington and Rachel Bowlby. Stanford: Stanford University Press, 1991.

Lyotard, Jean-François. *Miscellaneous Texts 1: Aesthetics and Theory of Art*. Translated by Vlad Ionescu. Leuven: Leuven University Press, 2012.

Marcel, Gabriel. 'At the Sorbonne'. In *The Bergsonian Heritage*, edited and introduced by Thomas Hanna, 124–32. New York and London: Columbia University Press, 1962.

Marcel, Gabriel. 'Bergsonism and Music'. 1925. Translated by C. K. Scott Moncrieff. In *Reflections on Art: A Source Book of Writings by Artists, Critics, and Philosophers*, edited by Susanne K. Langer, 142–51. London, Oxford and New York: Oxford University Press, 1961.

Massumi, Brian. *Semblance and Event: Activist Philosophy and the Occurrent Arts*. Cambridge, MA: MIT Press, 2011.

Matisse, Henri. *Écrits et propos sur l'art*. Edited by Dominique Fourcade. Paris: Hermann, 2009.

Medina, Joyce. *Cézanne and Modernism: The Poetics of Painting*. New York: State University of New York Press, 1995.

Merleau-Ponty, Maurice. 'Eye and Mind'. Translated by Carleton Dallery. In *The Primacy of Perception*, edited by James Edie, 159–90. Evanston: Northwestern University Press, 1964.

Merleau-Ponty, Maurice. *Phenomenology of Perception*. Translated by Colin Smith. London: Routledge & Kegan Paul, 1962.

Merleau-Ponty, Maurice. *In Praise of Philosophy*. Translated by John Wild and James M. Edie. Evanston: Northwestern University Press, 1963.

Merleau-Ponty, Maurice. *Sense and Non-sense*. Translated by Patricia Allen Dreyfus and Hubert L. Dreyfus. Evanston: Northwestern University Press, 1964.

Merrell, Floyd. *Signs Becoming Signs: Our Perfusive, Pervasive Universe*. Bloomington: Indiana University Press, 1991.

Messiaen, Olivier. *Traité de Rythme, de Couleur, et d'Ornithologie (1949-1992)*. Tome 1. Paris: Alphonse Leduc, 1994.

de Mille, Charlotte. '"Blast ... Bergson?" Wyndham Lewis's "Guilty Fire of Friction"'. In *Understanding Bergson, Understanding Modernism*, edited by Paul Ardoin, S. E. Gontarski and Laci Mattison, 141–56. New York and London: Bloomsbury, 2013.

de Mille, Charlotte and John Mullarkey. 'Introduction: Art's Philosophy – Bergson and Immanence'. In *Bergson and the Art of Immanence: Painting, Photography, Film*, edited by Charlotte de Mille and John Mullarkey, 1–13. Edinburgh: Edinburgh University Press, 2013.

Mitchell, Timothy. 'Bergson, Le Bon, and Hermetic Cubism'. *Journal of Aesthetics and Art Criticism* 34 (Winter 1977): 175–84.

Moore, Francis C. T. *Bergson: Thinking Backwards*. Cambridge: Cambridge University Press, 1996.

Mourélos, Georges. *Bergson et Les Niveaux de Réalité*. Paris: Presses Universitaires de France, 1964.

Mullarkey, John. 'Bergson and the Comedy of Horrors'. In *Understanding Bergson, Understanding Modernism*, edited by Paul Ardoin, S. E. Gontarski and Laci Mattison, 243–55. New York and London: Bloomsbury, 2013.

Mullarkey, John. *Bergson and Philosophy*. Edinburgh: Edinburgh University Press, 1999.

Mullarkey, John. '"For We Will Have Shown it Nothing": Bergson as Non-Philosopher (of) Art'. In *Bergson and the Art of Immanence: Painting, Photography, Film*, edited by Charlotte de Mille and John Mullarkey, 206–31. Edinburgh: Edinburgh University Press, 2013.

Mulvey, Laura. *Death 24x a Second: Stillness and the Moving Image*. London: Reaktion Books, 2006.

Newman, Barnett. *Selected Writings and Interviews*. Edited by John P. O'Neill. New York: Alfred A. Knopf, 1990.

Nietzsche, Friedrich. *Daybreak: Thoughts on the Prejudices of Morality*. Edited by Maudemarie Clark and Brian Leiter. Translated by R. J. Hollingdale. Cambridge: Cambridge University Press, 1997.

Petrie, Brian. 'Boccioni and Bergson'. *The Burlington Magazine* 116, no. 852 (1974): 140–7.

Pilkington, Anthony E. *Bergson and His Influence: A Reassessment*. Cambridge: Cambridge University Press, 1976.

Poffenberger, Albert T. and B. E. Barrows. 'The Feeling Value of Lines'. *Journal of Applied Psychology* 8, no. 2 (1924): 187–205.

Polanyi, Michael. 'Life's Irreducible Structure'. In *Topics in the Philosophy of Biology*, edited by Marjorie Grene and Everett Mendelsohn, 128–42. Dordrecht: Reidel, 1976.

Posman, Sarah. 'Modernist Energeia: Henri Bergson and the Romantic Idea of Language'. In *Understanding Bergson, Understanding Modernism*, edited by Paul Ardoin, S. E. Gontarski and Laci Mattison, 213–27. New York and London: Bloomsbury, 2013.

Pribram, Karl H. 'Bergson and the Brain: A Bio-logical Analysis of Certain Intuitions'. In *Bergson and Modern Thought: Towards a Unified Science*, edited by Andrew C. Papanicolaou and Pete A. Y. Gunter, 149–74. Chur: Harwood, 1987.

Ravaisson, Félix. *De l'habitude: Métaphysique et morale*. Paris: Presses Universitaires de France, 1999.

Ravaisson, Félix. *L'Enseignement du dessin dans les lycées*. Paris: Ministère de l'instruction publique et des cultes, 1854.

Rawson, Philip. *Art and Time*. Edited by Piers Rawson. Madison: Farleigh Dickinson University Press, 2005.

Read, Herbert. *Icon and Idea: The Function of Art in the Development of Human Consciousness*. London: Faber and Faber, 1955.

Rescher, Nicholas. *Process Metaphysics: An Introduction to Process Philosophy*. New York: SUNY, 1996.

Rodin, Auguste. *Art: Interviews with Paul Gsell*. Translated by Romilly Fedden. Boston: Small Maynard Company, 1912.

Rosenberg, Harold. *Barnett Newman*. New York: Harry N. Abrahams, 1978.

Ruhe, Algot and Nancy Margaret Paul. *Henri Bergson: An Account of His Life and Philosophy*. London: Macmillan, 1914.

Russell, Bertrand. *A History of Western Philosophy*. 2nd edn. London: Counterpoint, 1984.

Russell, Bertrand. *Essays in Language, Mind and Matter*. London: Unwin Hyman, 1988.

Rylands, Philip. Introduction to *The Vorticists: Manifesto for a Modern World*, edited by Mark Antliff and Vivien Greene, 14–25. London: Tate Publishing, 2010.

Sadler, T. H. Translator's Introduction to *Concerning the Spiritual in Art* by Wassily Kandinsky, xiii–xxi. New York: Dover Publications, 1977.

Sallis, John. 'Klee's Philosophical Vision'. In *Paul Klee: Philosophical Vision: From Nature to Art*, edited by John Sallis, 15–24. Chestnut Hill: McMullen Museum of Art, 2012.

Sartre, Jean-Paul. *Being and Nothingness*. Translated by Hazel E. Barnes. London: Methuen, 1969.

Sauvage, Micheline. 'Notes on the Superposition of Temporal Modes in the Works of Art'. In *Reflections on Art: A Source Book of Writings by Artists, Critics, and Philosophers*, edited by Susanne K. Langer, 161–73. London, Oxford and New York: Oxford University Press, 1961.

Schapiro, Meyer. 'On Some Problems in the Semiotics of Visual Art: Field and Vehicle in Image-Signs'. *Simiolus: Netherlands Quarterly for the History of Art* 6, no. 1 (1972–1973): 9–19.

Schelling, Friedrich Wilhelm Joseph. *Ideas on the Philosophy of Nature as an Introduction to the Study of This Science*. 2nd edn. Translated by Errol E. Harris and Peter Heath. Cambridge: Cambridge University Press, [1803] 1988.

Schilder, Paul. *The Image and Appearance of the Human Body: Studies in the Constructive Energies of the Psyche*. New York: International Universities Press. 1950.

Schwartz, Sanford. 'Bergson and the Politics of Vitalism'. In *The Crisis in Modernism: Bergson and the Vitalist Controversy*, edited by Frederick Burwick and Paul Douglass, 277–305. Cambridge: Cambridge University Press, 1992.

Seel, Martin. *Aesthetics of Appearing*. Translated by John Farrell. Stanford: Stanford University Press, 2005.

Severini, Gino. 'The Plastic Analogies of Dynamism – Futurist Manifesto'. 1913. Translated by J. C. Higgitt. In *Futurist Manifestos*, edited by Umbro Apollonio, 118–25. London: Thames and Hudson, 1973.

Sheets-Johnstone, Maxine. *The Primacy of Movement*. 2nd edn. Amsterdam and Philadelphia: John Benjamins, 2011.

Simondon, Gilbert. 'The Genesis of the Individual'. Translated by Mark Cohen and Sanford Kwinter. In *Incorporations*, edited by Jonathan Crary and Sanford Kwinter, 297–319. New York: Zone, 1992.

Smiles, Sam. 'Turner In and Out of Time'. In *The EY Exhibition: Late Turner – Painting Set Free*, edited by David Blayney Brown, Amy Concannon and Sam Smiles, 14–23. Millbank: Tate Publishing, 2014.

Soffici, Ardengo. 'The Subject in Futurist Painting'. 1914. Translated by Robert Brain. In *Futurist Manifestos*, edited by Umbro Apollonio, 134–5. London: Thames and Hudson, 1973.

Soulez, Philippe and Frédéric Worms. *Bergson: Biographie*. Paris: Presses Universitaires de France, 2002.

Souriau, Étienne. *La Correspondance des arts: Éléments d'esthétique comparée*. Paris: Flammarian, 1969.

Souriau, Paul. *The Aesthetics of Movement*. Translated and Edited by Manon Souriau. Amherst: The University of Massachusetts Press, 1983.

Sparshott, Francis. Foreword to *The Aesthetics of Movement* by Paul Souriau, vii–xiv. Translated and Edited by Manon Souriau. Amherst: The University of Massachusetts Press, 1983.

Spencer, Herbert. *Literary Style and Music: Including Two Short Essays on Gracefulness and Beauty*. London: Watts, 1950.

Starkie, Enid. 'Bergson and Literature'. In *The Bergsonian Heritage*, edited and introduced by Thomas Hanna, 74–99. New York and London: Columbia University Press, 1962.

Szathmary, Arthur. *The Aesthetic Theory of Bergson*. Cambridge, MA: Harvard University Press, 1937.

Taine, Hippolyte. *Philosophie de l'art*. Paris: Fayard, 1985.

Tarkovsky, Andrey. *Sculpting in Time: Reflections on the Cinema*. Translated by Kitty Hunter-Blair. London: Faber and Faber, 1989.

Valéry, Paul. *Degas Manet Morisot*. Vol. 12 of *Collected Works of Paul Valéry*. Translated by David Paul. New York: Pantheon Books, 1960.

Valéry, Paul. *Henri Bergson: Allocution prononcée à la séance de l'académie du jeudi 9 janvier 1941*. Paris: Domat-Montchrestien, 1945.

Varnedoe, Kirk and Adam Gopnik. *High & Low: Modern Art and Popular Culture*. New York: The Museum of Modern Art, 1991.

Verdi, Richard. *Cézanne*. London: Thames and Hudson, 1992.

Waddington, Conrad H. *The Nature of Life*. London: George Allen & Unwin, 1961.

Wagner, Geoffrey. 'Wyndham Lewis and the Vorticist Aesthetic'. *The Journal of Aesthetics and Art Criticism* 13, no. 1 (September 1954): 1–17.

Whitehead, Alfred N. *Science and the Modern World*. Harmondsworth: Penguin, 1938.

Wilson, Sarah. 'Bergson Before Deleuze: How to Read Informel Painting'. In *Bergson and the Art of Immanence: Painting, Photography, Film*, edited by Charlotte de Mille and John Mullarkey, 80–93. Edinburgh: Edinburgh University Press, 2013.

Wölfflin, Heinrich. *Principles of Art History: The Problem of the Development of Style in Later Art*. 1932. Translated by M. D. Hottinger. New York: Dover, 1950.

Wright, Alastair. *Matisse and the Subject of Modernism*. Princeton and Oxford: Princeton University Press, 2004.

Wünsche, Isabel. 'Life into Art: Natural Philosophy, the Life Sciences, and Abstract Art'. In *Meanings of Abstract Art: Between Nature and Theory*, edited by Paul Crowther and Isabel Wünsche, 9–29. New York and London: Routledge, 2012.

Zuckerkandl, Victor. *Sound and Symbol: Music and the External World*. Translated by Willard R. Trask. Princeton: Princeton University Press, 1969.

INDEX